The Political Economy of South Africa's Post-apartheid Transition

Critical Reconstructions of Political Economy, Volume 7

Studies in Critical Social Sciences Book Series

Haymarket Books is proud to be working with Brill Academic Publishers (www.brill.nl) to republish the *Studies in Critical Social Sciences* book series in paperback editions. This peer-reviewed book series offers insights into our current reality by exploring the content and consequences of power relationships under capitalism, and by considering the spaces of opposition and resistance to these changes that have been defining our new age. Our full catalog of *SCSS* volumes can be viewed at https://www.haymarketbooks.org/series_collections/4-studies-in-critical-social-sciences.

The Political Economy of South Africa's Post-apartheid Transition

The Rejection of Alternatives to Neoliberalism

Critical Reconstructions of Political Economy
Volume 7

Ben Fine

Haymarket Books
Chicago, IL

First published in 2025 by Brill Academic Publishers, The Netherlands

Published in paperback in 2026 by
Haymarket Books
P.O. Box 180165
Chicago, IL 60618
773-583-7884
www.haymarketbooks.org

ISBN: 979-8-88890-798-6

Distributed to the trade in the US through Consortium Book Sales and Distribution (www.cbsd.com) and internationally through Ingram Publisher Services International (www.ingramcontent.com).

This book was published with the generous support of Lannan Foundation, Wallace Action Fund, and the Marguerite Casey Foundation.

Cover design by Jamie Kerry and Ragina Johnson.

Printed in the United States.

Library of Congress Cataloging-in-Publication data is available.

Contents

Preface

With this seventh Volume in the Series, I am running out of new things to say in the Preface, or new ways of saying the same things. For this Volume, I am the sole author of all of the pieces published, the bulk of which (three-quarters in chapters and far more in words) appear formally in print for the first time. Working on South Africa over what is now forty years has been a rewarding experience with amazing collaborations and engagements in training and research, and in activism and policymaking. But it has also been extremely disappointing and frustrating (as is apparent from within this Volume, even more so for the others to come). As always, thanks are due to all those who have contributed, directly or indirectly, wittingly or unwittingly, willingly or unwillingly, to making this Volume possible. Fuller acknowledgements along these lines and the rationale for this series is to be found in the Prefaces to previous Volumes.

CHAPTER 1

How South Africa Rejected Political Economy and Progressive Policy: A Personal Journey

1 Introduction

This Chapter consists of three main sections describing the contributions contained within the Volume. They were drafted in roughly three phases during the mid-1990s: around MERG; around the Presidential Labour Market Commission; and the immediate aftermath for COSATU. The last section, though, offers some personal observations on what was involved, and with what effects, in light of this being the immediate period of transition from apartheid.

2 From MERG …

This is the seventh Volume in the series of collections of articles designed to push for the reconstruction of political economy through highlighting and contextualising past contributions and adding some new. It is also the first of what is intended to be three on South Africa's political economy, something on which I have now worked for forty years. I had intended for the South African Volume(s) to be last, primarily because I considered the task to be the most difficult across the remaining themes for the other Volumes (for reasons to be explained in the later Volumes but mainly due to the complexities of the evolving literature and of South Africa itself). But, at some later point for varieties of reasons, I felt the challenge should be met earlier rather than later.

As things stand – they may change as I proceed after this Volume – this first Volume is organised around a single theme, soon to be elaborated. Generally, and increasingly, the post-apartheid economy has been conceived to be disastrous. One explanation for this is that neoliberal policy was adopted by the incoming Government of National Unity.[1] This itself has to be explained for which the best overview is Padayachee and van Niekerk (2019). One element amongst many in this explanation is that there were not alternatives available in the sense of policies on the table to be considered let alone rejected

1 That, thirty years later, a GNU is once more in place is indicative of the (lack of) progress that has been made.

(although the latter has also been used as a commonplace explanation in light of something between active coercion by capital and its representatives, dull necessity arising out of global forces and institutions, and judicious compromise with these factors, a 'Faustian pact', Kasrils, 2013).

Much of the literature on the earliest years of transition now focuses on the fate of the MERG (1993) Report in which I was heavily involved (Fine, 2022, for a personal account). Its rejection upon publication has been seen as a symbolic marker of the sharp turn towards neoliberalism even before the ANC had become a party of government. MERG provided a comprehensive set of policies for the post-apartheid economy. The argument that there were not alternatives is simply wrong as demonstrated by MERG and also by the much slower rejection (symbolic acceptance alone) and death of the RDP (Reconstruction and Development Programme). The point of this Volume is to extend the account beyond the MERG moment to show through my own contributions, over the short period both before and after MERG, how much alternative policy was available. This is not to exaggerate my own role, indeed it was ineffectual, but to raise the issue of why alternative policies were rejected and the capacity for alternative policymaking not adopted. As a result, what has to be explained is why the resistance against the neoliberal turn was so weak, not to dismiss the question on grounds of absence of alternatives.

My own engagement with alternative policymaking began with the formation of the EROSA group at the request of the ANC in the mid-1980s (Fine, 2022, for an account). As a small group, we prepared policy alternatives for post-apartheid South Africa, and participated in discussions and training in and around South Africa, mindful of apartheid 'restrictions'.[2] But in the early 1990s, EROSA morphed, with considerable expansion of personnel, into MERG which was itself hijacked in part to prepare the Report that bears its name (at the expense of attention to other training and research that both preceded

2 EROSA Working Papers included: "South Africa's International Trade and Trade Policy", no 1; "South Africa's Transport Industry and Transport Policy", no 2; "South Africa's Electricity Industry and Policy", no 3; "South Africa's Coal Industry and Policy", no 4; "South Africa's Manufacturing Industry: Chemicals", no 5; "South Africa's Internal Finance and Financial Policy", no 6; "South Africa's Agriculture", no 7; "South Africa's Gold Industry: Assessments and Prospects", no 8; and the unnumbered "Employee Share Ownership Plans"; "Employee Share Ownership: an Update"; "Privatisation and the South African Economy"; Defence Expenditure and the Post-Apartheid Economy: A Briefing Paper for the ANC; and "The Mixed Economy". I authored nos 3, 4, 8 and the unnumbered with the exception of the last. Other authors, and members of EROSA, included Helena Dolny, Laurence Harris, Maureen Mackintosh and Dave Wield. It was a Birkbeck (later SOAS)/Open University axis.

and followed the Report, with NIEP, the National Institute for Economic Policy, as MERG's successor).

The Volume does not include much by way of these earlier contributions. The MERG Report itself is readily available and has been widely discussed, ironically much more in retrospect to understand the neoliberal turn in policy than at the time as a policy alternative, simply being sidelined. Most of the EROSA Reports are of academic interest and, to be blunt, I could not be bothered to seek to convert their electronic versions on first generation floppies and software to render them usable. There are exceptions, though, from what were unnumbered EROSA papers of mine that were later and so on hard drive albeit in Wordperfect (and readily converted into Word with a glitch or two). These are included as Chapters 2 and 3, also in part to illustrate the spread of policy perspectives being addressed, employee share ownership plans and 'conversion' (or what to do about the economics of the apartheid military machine in a post-apartheid dispensation). Chapter 4 covers the issues of privatisation, as the newly, elected ANC-led Government of National Unity, began its warm overtures towards privatisation, a sharp index of its attachment to both neoliberalism and continuity of perspectives with the apartheid government (and World Bank and IMF advisors) that it was succeeding.

3 … through Labour Market Commission …

By 1994, with the Government of National Unity in place, increasingly embracing what for convenience will be designated as neoliberalism (with abandonment even of commitment in practice to the COSATU-inspired Reconstruction and Development Programme, RDP, and with the adoption of Growth, Employment and Redistribution, GEAR, on the horizon), my personal boat of engagement with economic analysis and policymaking for the ANC had not only sailed but sank with all hands, most notably with the precipitous rejection of the MERG (1993) Report. Although not yet fully understanding what had happened, I certainly experienced a profound sense of defeat across personal, political, analytical and policy dimensions. I know this in one small but symbolic respect, because it came as a complete surprise that I should be invited in 1995 by Tito Mboweni (then Minister of Labour) to be one of four international experts to serve on a newly formed Presidential Labour Market Commission (LMC). I have no idea why I was invited. I knew Tito from having worked with him on occasion in the Department of Economic Policy of the ANC (which he ran alongside Trevor Manuel once Max Sisulu had been sidelined). He was a close friend of Maria Ramos (who was on the rise) who was a close friend to me at that time and may have put in a word for me, plus Tito could also be a maverick and might have felt some guilt, or wish to provoke, in the wake of my own MERG-related fall from grace.[3] Perhaps it was simply a consequence of being thought of as honest, conscientious and delivering what has been asked for on time. Who knows?

So, whilst the first Chapters represent a phase of optimistic activity immediately around MERG although if, primarily, without inclusion of MERG material itself,[4] the single, fifth, Chapter arises out of my membership of, and work for, the Presidential Labour Market Commission (LMC) which lasted for about a year, spanning 1995/96. I was much more on the defensive and pessimistic but determined to put the case for progressive policies in ways that could be found acceptable. That there is only a single Chapter, however, is misrepresentative of my level of activity and engagement, in part because of my having drafted what could have included two further substantial Chapters that were drafted for the LMC, one on comparable worth (equal pay) and one on minimum wages. These, however, were updated and published in a later book on labour markets (Fine, 1998a), and can be consulted there. Only summaries and other odds and sods (on public works and income support) are included in Chapter 5.[5]

The other international experts on the LMC were Derek Robinson (well-established UK applied labour economist and policy advisor with labourist sympathies), Richard Freeman (prestigious US labour economist and historian, with tendency to rely upon mainstream framings but not in a headbanging way) and Sam Bowles (US radical political economist). To my surprise, my relations with Robinson and Freeman turned out extremely positively and, generally, we found ourselves on the same page. By contrast, Bowles seemed determined to teach the Commission and the Commissioners the simplest basics of mainstream economics and policymaking – to increase employment you need to make it cheaper and more flexible (exactly what progressives were fighting against). He even insisted upon presenting to the Commissioners a one-sector model of the economy in which higher wages meant higher capital-intensity and lower employment. My impatience at this lesson in

3 Sadly, Tito died too young whilst this was being drafted.

4 I would also point to Fine (1996a), something drafted for MERG but not included and offering a more general take on the provision of social and economic infrastructure in support of policymaking. Emphasis was placed on the heterogeneity by sector of the challenges posed (not just reducing inequalities and raising provision) and the need to develop the institutional capacity to deliver public services and policies for the majority.

5 I also found a briefing on Contract Compliance (to enhance labour conditions) but this was incorporated and marginally updated in Chapter 6.

elementary mainstream economics, tediously delivered to the Commissioners, made by blood boil, if not over. After all, many of the Commissioners had no idea of economic theory at all and were liable to be impressionable and intimidated. As a result, a key characteristic of my contributions to the Commission, verbally and in writing, were characterised by very patient elaboration of the 'best' of mainstream economics (of which its empirical results are of significance) and both drawing upon it and tearing it apart.[6] My files indicate drafts going through numbers of versions, and providing simplified summaries (some appearing in this Volume) in the attempt to get Commissioners on board.

The LMC also benefitted from support and a study from the ILO, led by Guy Standing and also engaging major contributions from John Sender and John Weeks (colleagues of mine from SOAS, with the former also a leading MERG participant as co-editor, managing much alongside Vella Pillay). Indeed, the MERG/SOAS axes did seem to have some continuing purchase as far as labour is concerned. And, in general, the composition of the Commissioners, and its advisers, was highly favourable to labour – surely politically essential as GEAR was about to be launched as a way of tempering union dissent and its influence upon policy – let them eat the cake of Commission talk shop.[7]

Although the LMC had status and powers equivalent to a UK Royal Commission, it was generally informal in its proceedings. I was even allowed to examine witnesses (which I should not have been, as not a Commissioner myself). Having studied South African mining in great detail, and its labour migration system, I was keen to tease out how numbers of problems were going to be handled going forward. One prominent issue was payment of remittances to those working on the mines from neighbouring countries (and appropriation of corresponding wages by intermediaries, including sending governments themselves). I was allowed to examine Bobby Godsell on this and requested that he release the minutes on the matter from the Committee of the Chamber of Mines meetings on its recruitment and payment practices.[8] Despite a massive and continuing reputation as a 'liberal', his response is best described as "expletives deleted" with accusations of being unduly harassed by communists

6 Although I was generally concerned that critique of the mainstream, or taking it as critical point of departure, should not be how the Commission presented itself as opposed to putting its own reasoning and policies, in favour of labour, positively and to the fore (most notably, raising black employment and reducing labour market inequalities more generally). See below, point 13.

7 A way in retrospect of perceiving NEDLAC (the tripartite forum for state, unions and business) as increasingly accepted by Eddie Webster et al. (2013), if far from explicitly.

8 In the late 1980s, as a white researcher, I had managed to infiltrate the Chamber of Mines Library and consult all sorts of revealing documents but not all that I wanted to.

(he got that right). Unfortunately, the Commissioners recoiled in embarrassment rather than using their powers to insist upon a view of Chamber minutes and policies.[9]

In the event, the LMC (1996) produced its own report together with that of the ILO (1996).[10] In retrospect, its main achievement was to formulate a system of industrial relations both legally and institutionally (there were top progressive labour lawyers appointed as Commissioners). However, like the very best of constitutions, there is no guarantee that getting the framing right and the substance will follow. I have long been particularly mindful that the LMC was extraordinarily weak in formulating policy to deal with each of the two main issues for South African labour markets – the levels of unemployment and the structures, processes, relations and agencies underpinning vast labour market inequalities.

However, in searching my electronic files to discover what texts I had drafted for the LMC, I found that I had commented in detail on the draft of the Report (including thirteen pages of minor changes) to Dave Lewis, joint Chair with Moss Ngoasheng, both of whom were friends. Dave had responded to my concerns in writing, and accepted many, but not all of my suggestions/criticisms and I responded to him in turn. What follows is taken from the drafts to Dave,

---

9 Interestingly, Godsell's position was that there should be free labour migration across southern Africa as a whole (as opposed to a rapidly forming stance across the Commissioners of reserving mining jobs for South Africans, and even discussion of the border technologies for keeping migrants out. So much for continuing post-apartheid solidarity across the region). I also like to repeat on every available occasion, I was able to question Chris Stals, continuing post-apartheid as Governor of the Reserve Bank. I asked the reason for high levels of unemployment in South Africa, he responded that the South African Reserve Bank's model indicated that real wages were too high. This led me to ask at what level of real wages would the Bank's model give rise to full employment, to which there was no answer, twtwna. I asked if there was a case for housing finance to be subsidised to generate employment and provide cheap homes. He responded that this was a microeconomic question but that he would have to advise government of the negative macroeconomic implications. Asked for his response to the idea of a subsidy to keep gold mines open, he replied this was a microeconomic question but that he would have to advise government of the negative macroeconomic implications. I pointed out that gold at that time contributed 40% of foreign exchange and this was surely a macroeconomic question, twtwna. None of these points were pursued further by the Commissioners. Stals continued in post until 1999 when he was succeeded by Tito Mboweni.

10 The Report was presented in person to President Mandela in Cape Town in the presence of all available Commissioners and International Experts. I was not there and appear in inset in the official photo. I was offered funding to fly to South Africa for the ceremony. But, because of teaching commitments, this would have meant flying there overnight, attending the ceremony and then flying back again overnight on the same day as arrival. I decided not to.

revealing an account of the major issues I raised, the point being to indicate what policies might have been considered and how they might be framed and justified.[11]

A recurring theme is to reject an approach to South Africa in general, and to its labour markets in particular, in terms of dualisms. Here is my opening comment on the draft:[12]

> Analytically, a dualism is set up between black and white labour markets and it is far from clear that this is appropriate … It might be more appropriate to see the development in labour markets as the consequence of the contradictions between separate development, on the one hand, and extreme dependence upon black labour, on the other hand. This has the advantages of incorporating other factors than the labour market itself as well as the capacity to address the uneven development of labour markets over time and across sectors, locations and gender and ethnic composition. Historically, the propositions are all put forward timelessly, as though the apartheid labour markets, strategies, outcomes, etc had not experienced considerable change. By the same token, there is limited empirical support given for the propositions put forward, and it is fairly clear that they are too blunt to deal with the extremely varied experiences across labour markets. It almost seems as if mining labour has been taken as the norm! This all seems a little unhelpful but there is now a sufficiently reasonable literature on the history and structure of South African labour markets that I think a decent piece can be done along the lines of bringing out adequate analytical principles, historical account, and empirical description of the status quo. How this actually looks depends very much upon the way in which you pick up on the themes in the body of the report.

---

11 I reproduce texts here, even if drafted by me alone, with slight hesitation as they were written for another individual. I have no reason to believe there is any reason for them not being made public, especially with some editing. But be mindful of the informality, the association of the individual with the Commission (although there may have been differences between them) and how the final Report may differ from the draft being commented upon.

12 These considerations led me to undertake, for other reasons too, considerable research on the history, trajectory and structures, etc, of South African labour markets, work which has never been published. Subject to review, this will be remedied in a future Volume, with the Minerals-Energy Complex (MEC) as theme.

And it is followed by much more of the same later on:

> There is a need to avoid a false and crude dualism between modern and the rest. I would like to see the schisms developed not only in terms of socioeconomic characteristics but also processes and more general provision such as housing, transport, education, etc. This para also is essentially self-contradictory by positing a dualism but also pointing to a multiplicity of factors that fragment the labour market into many different overlapping segments. The notion of unifying deeply segmented labour markets (deracialise, everybody paid the same over a life-cycle, or what?) is extremely misleading and misguided. All labour markets are segmented – the question is how and to what extent. Indeed, this whole paragraph could have been lifted out of a UK pamphlet on racism and employment in the UK. This might indicate that we need to probe deeper to get to the nature of segmentation in South Africa which is more than discrimination and modern and non-modern economic sectors. The word that does the work is systemic and the system needs to be specified.

I will pick up yet again on dualism below in my response to Dave's replies to me. But some of the other issues not covered later but raised in my initial comments are as follows:

> There is an argument ... that there is a serious trade-off between employment conditions and levels of employment. I thought we had moved substantially beyond this approach. I do believe that there is a serious issue about whether the Report be organised around a dialogue against this position or not – this is the orthodoxy, this is why we disagree and what we are going to do about it – but the position seems to be accepted here. On balance, I would prefer that the orthodox view be marginalised in order to present an alternative positively and with confidence. In particular, there are many ways in which employment can be generated both in the short term and, especially, in the long term. Particularly important is the level and composition of investment, the degree of infrastructural provision, the levels and composition of government expenditure, industrial policy, etc before we even begin to think about trade-offs between wages and employment. What I had thought we had agreed to go for, and I remember you formulating it yourself, is to highlight the policies and mechanisms through which employment and wages, etc can grow together. So I would reformulate the closing sentence to this section by

emphasising that the role of the Commission is to find policies that allow labour market objectives to be mutually reinforcing and to reject the false trade-offs that are often damagingly imposed upon policy design … it might be better to have a strong statement in support of the role of the labour movement historically, politically and as a continuing force for progressive change.

The notion of discrimination is not strong enough – the Commission needs to consider every aspect of pre- and post-entry labour market (dis)advantage even if they do not directly fall under its auspices.

Does the Commission have to take a view about whether the high profile SME strategy will deliver much in the way of good employment creation, and whether what I take to be its limited promise should be allowed to take precedence over other policies that might generate more employment themselves directly as well as indirectly through the SME itself? Do we not need to quantify some of these issues and take account of international experience?

There seems to be a wish to tie our policies in knots by finding the slightest objection and not emphasising the positive effects and mechanisms. What is the evidence for minimum standards impeding new technology and for collective bargaining powerfully undermining other interests (which are undermined because they are weak and unrepresentative, not because they are damaged by labour – and consumers is a tricky interest group, as it is everybody!).

You seem to have accepted the very narrow definition of flexibility and to be focusing exclusively on the (false) wage-employment trade-off.

It occurs to me that you may be using a model in which there is a core short-run trade-off between employment and wages but that the trade-off shifts up over time (ie at higher levels of employment) as we get rid of apartheid heritage, increase productivity (maybe), educate, develop SMEs, etc. This is certainly consistent with the text. But the point is to reject the necessity of the short-run trade-off, however much it shifts over time. Employment and wages etc can both be enhanced in the short run as evidenced by Keynesianism, for example, (your text is very pre-Keynesian) and by arguing that what are taken to be the slower longer-term factors can change faster than the putative wage-employment trade-off in any economy and especially that in South Africa where so much change enhancing output, employment and productivity can be released through a wide range of institutional and other reforms.

Why introduce income support programmes rather than public works?; towards end, how are you going to "regulate" migration in the light of historical experience and current conditions?; why are non-nationals unskilled – this is not the same as being poorly paid?

Those outside the market economy and engaged (exclusively) in subsistence agriculture is a myth, and land reform is not going to help many for a long time if at all – is the Commission going to say this?[13]

What is the evidence that training the unemployed either increases their employability or the overall level of employment (rather than playing musical chairs); is this a mechanism of social control or one of employment creation? would it not be better to spend the money training those who are already in employment or on job creation schemes rather than training youth without providing them with jobs (and probably lousy training as well).

This is again very blinkered. Let us put aside all the factors that determine the levels of investment and then all we are left with is the way in which wage bargaining is done, etc (with "flexibility" thrown in). The evidence for what you are arguing is very weak in the absence of a whole range of other factors of which high levels of wages in the first place is one. Lowering barriers is liable to allow the "informal" sector to persist in the worst possible forms rather than to graduate!

Flexibility-type arguments again – all hostages to fortune unless you specify the many different meanings of flexibility, how they affect the workings of the economy, and how they can be supported, not impeded by labour market regulation.

This is all Hamlet without the Prince; there has to be a discussion of the overall level and composition of investment as the single most important potential determinant of employment and productivity growth. Why is there no discussion of the role of the DTI and the IDC?

This is all written against, and in conciliation with, an imaginary orthodox neoclassical opponent; again, whatever they may be, why not put forward the arguments positively on their own merits.

I would place considerable emphasis on a sequenced and targeted job evaluation exercise, as argued in my paper on comparable worth.[14]

The rest is all a bit sketchy but I am disturbed by the absence of any serious consideration of public works and job creation schemes and the general lack of reference in this context and elsewhere to international

13 John Sender, SOAS and MERG colleague, and co-author of ILO (1996), has been unstinting over decades in promoting decent wages and working conditions in agriculture as opposed to small-scale, subsistence agriculture.

14 See Chapter 5.

> experience and lessons to be learned. It is important to quantify exactly what different programmes are expected to achieve eg employment subsidies and training of the unemployed, as against spending the money on job creation. I would also like the tone to be much more upbeat and pro-labour.

As mentioned, Dave responded to my comments and, rather than reproduce these, it suffices to provide a selection from my rejoinder to him in turn.

> One general comment is that there seems to be much of too strong a commitment to conforming to what the politicians wish to hear even where it is wrong. I cannot see the point of this. The Commission should address the issues and not pander to prejudices. I also remain profoundly disturbed by the continuing commitment to dualism. Am I right in suspecting that this has something to do with the previous point? If there is postulated a division between those in formal work and those out of formal work, for example, then this serves as the basis for arguing that those who are in work are better off and must not be advantaged at the expense of those who are out of work. It then is a small step to saying those in work must be subject to and accept worsened conditions in order to benefit those out of work. This is profoundly anti-labour and is fallacious at every step, even if it may have some validity for some sections of the workforce which would have to be identified. Otherwise:
>
> 1. My objection is to dualism but not to segmentation although how segmentation is understood is at issue. First, it cannot be done on a dualistic basis ... Second, segmentation is tricky because it is attached to multiple and overlapping criteria and causes whose effects shift over time – gender, race, sector, occupation, region, public vs private, unionised, degree of concentration, level of capital-intensity, etc. Third, the way in which segments are formed and function is different from segment to segment. It is not a matter simply of a complex, overlapping common structure but of structures and structuring of different types.
> 2. Flexibility (of labour markets) can be interpreted in the narrow terms of no downward rigidities in wage and conditions, but it needs to be emphasised and acted upon in the text that flexibility is a complex and slippery concept which needs to be married much more to the capacity to adjust positively towards creating more employment with favourable wages and working conditions. It is important to emphasise how the nature of flexibility and the extent

to which it is positively achieved is dependent upon how regulations and the labour markets interact with one another, not how they conflict with one another. This is most apparent, for example, in the formation of industrial relations.

3. It is not clear that the macro/micro distinction is always particularly helpful – where do industrial relations, technological change, etc, fit in. But there is a substantive point that needs to be addressed. If the macro is taken to be the determinants of the level and composition of investment and this lies beyond the scope of the LMC, then it remains imperative to say so, to assess the levels of employment, etc that are liable to be generated across various scenarios and how limited is the scope of the LMC in doing much more than adjusting around the edges of these core processes and determinants. I suspect that the LMC should not want to say that this is all that we can do because the rest lies outside of its scope of action or terms of reference. To the extent that you do, a case could be made for quantifying the room for (lack of) manoeuvre. It might be worth having a three-way categorisation – those things that the LMC cannot, or explicitly chooses not to, affect or address, those that it can and does and fall centrally within its remit, and those that fall somewhere in-between. My own inclination is to argue that the last two categories should be pushed to the limits not because of some labour ministry imperialism but because that is the way that labour markets work and which policy discussion must take into account, with coordination with other ministries around policy needs.
4. I do think that demand-induced expansion of employment is a legitimate measure, especially through public works programmes. But this Keynesian impetus is by no means the only nor the most important rationale for, or means to, it. There are issues such as crowding-in private through public sector investment which does not just come through effective demand mechanisms. The crucial point is that the Keynesian story totally neglects the supply-side. Demand is sufficient to call forth supply in a neat inversion of Say's Law. But the high returns from public provision and the need to guarantee effective delivery are well-documented.
5. I agree that the historical analysis is not an object in its own right. But the purpose is to present an account of the labour markets as they are and current problems. The problem with a stark account is that it is wrong and/or misleading. What we have to agree about is what are the features that need to be got across and what is the best

way to do this (appeal to the past or not, for example). The points that need to be got across are:

a) South African labour markets are segmented in highly complex ways both in terms of effects and underlying causes.

b) There are severe problems in employment creation at decent wages and conditions.

c) There are severe inequalities which are deeply rooted in non-labour market institutions.

d) TUs have played and are playing a positive role.

e) Whilst some policy responses can be general, many will have to be segment-specific.

...

9. My point is simply that discrimination and inequality are just not strong enough nor appropriate in capturing all the labour market and non-labour market factors that have created the labour market as it is. I would even say this for the 'discrimination' and 'inequality' by race and gender in UK labour markets so it applies even more so to South Africa. The problem is that discrimination and inequality tend to be thought of as (minor) distortions that can be corrected by policies rather than as socially systemic outcomes.

...

12. The important point here is that the relationship between employment and wages is not a simple trade-off if a trade-off at all. Both wages and employment levels in a sector are the product of other factors and these are liable to dominate causal relations between the two. Even at a macro-level consider, for example, the massive growth in both women's employment and wages in advanced countries over the post-war period.

13. I do think it is crucial to address and rebut the orthodoxy but that it should not be the central or organising form of exposition.

14. ...

c) otherwise I am appealing for a recognition for where the South African situation requires special measures and analysis; what distinguishes the extent and depth of segmentation and how does it differ, by race and gender, for example, from the situation in the UK. Part of the point of such comparisons is that if measures have not worked in the UK where conditions for success are greater and extent of inherited problems is so much less, why should they work in South Africa. More generally, as in comments elsewhere, experience elsewhere on race and gender, segmentation, etc can be used to assess the likely impact of policies given that they are liable to be less effective in many instances in South African conditions.

...

15. John Weeks' research across a range of countries for the ILO (1996), including South Africa, has shown that SMEs perform badly both over the cycle and along the trend and reasons that this is because they depend upon backward technology and low wages and conditions to survive. Rather than emphasising the potential of small black businesses, why not ask why small white businesses have failed to flourish despite their not suffering disadvantage and even being highly favoured?
16. There is a very large literature on public works in developing countries with which I am not particularly familiar. I suggest that ILO could look at this fairly easily.[15] A view has to be taken, however, about how much finance is available and how it will be spent. There is also the issue of whether it is better to support those in jobs already rather than the unemployed (as in NUM-type schemes, although I am not convinced of their special case other than to keep mines open). I would be extremely wary of the macro-models[16] since it is the capacity to deliver public works programmes with effective outcomes and knock-on effects that is important. Also, it is necessary to look at impact on labour markets. I did do a little piece on this for a previous meeting.

...

18. But there has to be a programme of action, with institutional mechanisms to deliver and a set of priorities.

From this extended commentary on the first draft of the LMC Report, I would draw the following conclusions. First, any number of policy issues were up for discussion for which I was pressing against what was some uneven levels of resistance. Analytically, I was looking for a much wider take on the complexity and heterogeneity of labour markets, and how they are structured and function (no simple dualisms). Second, I was concerned that such heterogeneity should be located within a framing that located labour markets within all major economic and social determinants, even those not immediately under the formal purview of the Department of Labour – levels and composition of investment

15 But see Chapter 5.

16 See also earlier footnote on Stals on "twtwna".

for example. Third, related if distinct, was an uneasy disquiet that the LMC would confine itself to issues, and their corresponding policy implications, that were acceptable to political taskmasters possibly doing so to push out the boat of impact whilst it remained tightly moored to the neoliberal bank. For, fourth, I was keenly aware of a sort of neoliberal parrot sitting on the shoulders of the Commissioners, endlessly reminding it of the arguments against supporting labour in case of negative effects on employment. Accordingly, fifth, I was keen to reduce the status of the mainstream within the presentation, as something to be argued against whenever proposing something, as opposed to putting the case positively for measures to support and appreciate the role of the labour movement in bringing about economic and social transformation including, but not confined to, the reconstruction of labour market functioning. Last, and by no means least, a source of bitter disappointment to me after a year's participation in the process, and as simply stated in the final point (18) above, the LMC offered very little that would have any impact whatsoever on levels of (un)employment. It did not, at least in draft, even propose a job summit to address the issue to put together a programme of action (something it should have done itself) even though these have been put together time and time again subsequently, with little impact beyond a talk shop.

4 … to NIEP/COSATU and Beyond

Following the LMC (although I must have written them at least in part during the LMC period given they run to over 75,000 words), I prepared three working papers for COSATU, on industrial policy (appearing here as Chapter 6), the steel industry (Chapter 7) and privatisation (Chapter 8). Formally, the papers were published under the auspices of the National Institute for Economic Policy (NIEP), the successor body to MERG that continued with considerable vigour if entirely undermined by at most token support from the ANC. It is significant that COSATU took this work under its umbrella as it sought to mount opposition to the ANC's neoliberal turn and pose alternatives. But this opposition was fading as symbolised for example by continuing references to the RDP as the policy framing through which to legitimise the posing of alternatives whereas, at the time if not long before, it was transparent that the RDP had been marginalised if not derailed. The consequences of the containment of COSATU, its subordination to the ANC in the Tripartite Alliance (and much the same can be said of the CPSA), and the subordination of the ANC to its (shifting) leadership have proven to be part and parcel of the increasingly disastrous post-apartheid trajectory – an exercise in going from bad to worse and beyond. Significantly, each of these Chapters not only puts forward alternative policies and policy approaches to those increasingly being adopted but also, subject to lack of Cassandra-like powers, points to the disastrous consequences of those increasingly being adopted. This is especially so of the closing Chapter of this Volume even though its main topic is privatisation. For, from before MERG, I judiciously pointed to two key issues to be addressed – finance for industry (and economic and social infrastructure more generally) and the need to build the institutional capacity to formulate, deliver and monitor policy. Whilst there is, understandably, no discussion as such of the prospective notions of financialisation and state capture that have become key aspects of the post-apartheid political economy, they are more than implicit. I have spent thirty years resisting the temptation to say I told you so – it wins no friends nor support – but let me indulge myself just this once.

But such considerations go far beyond the intentions of this Volume – simply to demonstrate that there were alternatives, they were not taken and were not even sought let alone built upon (in sharp contrast to the deliberate commissioning and dumping of the MERG Report which marks the beginnings of most of the Chapters). I do not want to exaggerate my role but it is the one I know best and it can be taken as symbolic of the rejection, not the absence, of the efforts made by others who were ignored if not shunned once the ANC assumed some formal degree of political power. In closing this Chapter, though, I will indulge myself further by reflecting upon my own personal trajectory over the period during which the contributions in this Volume were drafted.

It was a very short period, less than five years. I was, however, extremely active at that time on matters South African and otherwise. Over and above the Chapters in this book, there was the drafting of the MERG Report itself. Fine and Rustomjee (1996) was also being drafted (with much other material that did not make its way into the book). It was supported by a major research grant. This I had taken from Birkbeck to SOAS, alongside two other grants – one to finish work on the history of the British Coal industry (whilst also serving as an advisor to the UK's NUM), and the other a detailed empirical study, as part of a major ESRC research programme, of the UK's (unhealthy) diet. Having moved to SOAS, I had taken on the teaching of half of its MSc in Development Economics (the two theory papers of four in total) and the research student training programme (with as many as six or more research students of my own at any one time).

Although this work focused on different topics, often unrelated directly to South Africa, at the time and even more so subsequently and in preparing this Volume, I have realised that there are more connections across it than at first sight because of the methods, conceptualisations and theories being developed and deployed – around the MEC,[17] the system of provision approach to consumption (and public services), and building upon labour market analyses. This also enabled what is a common characteristic of nearly all of the contributions to this Volume. They offer swingeing and comprehensive criticisms of mainstream approaches, even if drawing freely on the empirical work on offer, as well as alternatives derived from political economy and social science more generally.[18] If I have erred in these contributions in terms of the goal of levering policy traction, it has been through being too academic (although many of the Chapters include summaries that were prepared at the time). On the other hand, I hope to have left a legacy of material that can be drawn upon by other scholars whether engaged in research, policy or advocacy with lessons to be drawn on how to be effective within and across them – possibly the best we can do when the politics turns against us.

And now for the sad, again symbolic, epilogue to this Volume. My work on South Africa, particularly in this period, has always been primarily what I have termed demand-driven (or, if more generally, what I have perceived to be in demand). I have done what I have done in response to requests or in order to be able to support them, possibly in anticipation. This has led to all sorts of academic publications, not as goals in themselves, but in order that others can engage and contribute, and to keep political economy traditions alive in South Africa and elsewhere, not least as they have been sorely constrained by the intolerances of mainstream economics. To put it personally and bluntly, quite apart from the MEC book, Fine and Rustomjee (1996), I published eleven journal articles on South Africa in the five-year period around the contributions reproduced in this Volume. I did not, though, publish a single other journal article on South Africa at all for the next ten years at which point some

17 In passing, it is worth observing how little the contributions in this Volume explicitly make reference to the MEC, even though it was at the fore of my thinking and approach at the time – ironically, the MEC explicitly and substantively appears as much as elsewhere in Chapter 2, drafted in 1992. There were two reasons for this: first, Fine and Rustomjee (1996) was only just about to be published; second, despite corresponding lack of familiarity with the notion, there was also considerable and concerted (informal) opposition to it from other perspectives whether because of its intrinsic content as such or because of its (MERG-related) origins and association with more progressive and interventionist policies – so better to argue for these directly without muddying the waters over for or against MEC. Subsequently, of course, the MEC has gained traction, especially with NUMSA, precisely for the reasons why it was initially opposed.

18 As is apparent from the individual chapters, there are considerable literature reviews underpinning the contributions, often in areas in which I had not previously had anything more than passing acquaintance. This is particularly so of the review of the literature on (international trade) dumping in Chapter 7.

(lesser) demand arose again in light of the growing opposition to the Mbeki Presidency,[19] see next two Volumes.

Not that I was inactive academically, including for South Africa where my energies went into helping to meet the demand that barely survived for heterodox teaching and training (especially through APORDE and support to heterodox economics at Wits).[20] Otherwise, with the 'loss' of South Africa, the late 1990s saw the launch of what continues to be a major research programme on economics imperialism as covered in the first three Volumes of this series (Fine 2024a–c) alongside a continuing and obsessive critique of social capital (Fine, 2025d, most recently), the Fessud research programme on financialisation (Fine, 2025a), and contributions to development economics and critique of the World Bank (Fine, 2025b and c) whilst work has continued on the system of provision (SoP) approach (Bayliss and Fine, 2021). My commitment and contributions to Marxist, heterodox and pluralist economics have remained strong, alongside uncompromising critical exposition and exposure of the mainstream (Fine, 2016a; and Fine and Dimakou, 2016, for example). I also played a leading role in establishing, and chaired, the International Initiative for Promoting Political Economy (https://iippe.org). In retrospect, this may have dulled, and partially compensated for, the loss of South Africa which has always proven the most challenging and rewarding of my intellectual endeavours, if not in outcomes.

19 The record for publications in edited volumes is similar if not so extreme, possibly because the demand is academic (editor) driven as opposed to activist/policy. See later Volumes.

20 https://www.aporde.co.za and through Corporate Strategy and Industrial Development (CSID) at Wits.

CHAPTER 2

ESOP's Fable: Golden Egg or Sour Grapes?

Postscript as Personal Preamble[1]

As observed at the outset of the Chapter that follows, my engagement with ESOPs in South Africa seems to have begun in the late 1980s,[2] almost certainly in critical response to one of the many alternative ways forward being proposed by corporate capital and its representatives on how it could negotiate a post-apartheid (economic) settlement. I do not recall being commissioned in some sense to address the issue but it is unlikely I would have done it simply on my own initiative. I subsequently revisited my earlier contributions and the later literature for a workshop organised by COSATU in mid-1997 for which I also prepared three other papers (Fine, 1997a–c).

Subsequently, ESOPs do not seem to have played a prominent role in post-apartheid discourses and practices although in a personal meeting with Julius Malema in London around 2018, I did warn him against them for the sorts of reasons covered in the Chapter. He immediately announced it as a policy measure upon his return to South Africa. In a word or, more exactly an acronym, ESOPs, as a means of sharing ownership with workers, have in South Africa been trumped by BEE (Black Economic Empowerment) in its various versions, with not a few individual workers and their representatives finding themselves the major beneficiaries with current President Cyril Ramaphosa to the fore. Who needs ESOPs when you have BEE? Well, obviously not the workers, the unemployed and those dependent upon economic and social provision other than through the wage (whether in part as nominal share in profit/loss) such as pensioners, children, and dependents, the sick and youth in vast numbers.

---

1 Thanks for comments on a first draft from participants at the COSATU workshop where it was first presented. It is, at least so far, the only piece to appear across this series of volumes that is a chapter in an edited volume, with Copyright from 2000 and reproduced by permission of Taylor and Francis Group, LLC, a division of Informa plc. This version draws upon Fine (2000). It was previously unpublished, even as a working paper, before being updated for a volume in honour of Sam Aaronovitch.

2 Unsurprisingly, I had some casual knowledge (of postures) on ESOPs in light of debates over market socialism. Such schemes, though, are based on workers common ownership without its being shared with capitalists.

I have not reviewed the subsequent literature, policies and empirical developments around ESOPs since this Chapter was first completed.[3] It would be a worthwhile exercise but suspect different conclusions would not emerge as opposed to being strengthened. In practice, ESOPs at their worst represent a way of imposing the costs of restructuring failing enterprises (and economies) on workers through restraining wages and employment and drawing upon their pension entitlements to keep businesses going, something that might be harder to achieve in the absence of workers' shared ownership and complicity in the pain involved. At their, extremely rare, best they allow for workers participation in decision making, take the form of collective not individual participation in ownership but still serve as an ideological bulwark against public ownership. By their very nature, as is so often overlooked by those who ought to know better, they are liable to be a source of consolidating inequalities within the working classes – since, as already highlighted, they tend to be confined to benefitting those who are already better placed in labour markets. Necessarily excluded are all the workers in the public sector, all of those in casual employment and all of those out of employment (but not those very few super-wealthy who graciously share their wealth for whatever purposes, explicit or otherwise). With apologies, my cynicism is running away with it.

1 ESOPs and Apartheid

Employee Stock Ownership Plans, ESOPs, now no longer appear to be novel, not even in South Africa. They first emerged to prominence in South Africa in 1987 (as covered in EROSA, 1989 and 1990).[4] After a blaze of publicity and debate, the matter fell quiet again. A decade later, ESOPs or similar schemes have come to the fore once more. It is not difficult to see why. Whenever a capitalist economy, even an individual firm, is going through a major period of change, it necessarily faces challenges from the labour movement and possibly other sectional interests. These have to be accommodated both materially and ideologically. How this is done depends upon the strengths and strategies of the contending parties. The situation can also prompt idiosyncratic thinking

---

3 As informed by Arabo Ewinyu, ESOPs are being tagged to approvals for mergers and acquisitions in terms of meeting the public interest as defined by the Competition Commission in terms of the goal of spreading ownership, in helping to transform BEE to Broad-Based BEE (BBBEE). See Smit (2024) with consultancies getting in on the act. Nobody ever refers to the previous BEE as NBBEE (Narrow-Based …) nor currently to NSNBBE (Not So Narrow …).

4 These were authored by me. Most of their texts have been incorporated into this much later piece. Summaries that were drafted for them are reproduced as appendices.

either to accommodate or to thwart change, frequently with the effect of obscuring and/or even deliberately concealing it.

In the late 1980s, it was the coming demise of the apartheid political system that had provided the stimulus to ESOPs. It was felt necessary for capitalism to be disassociated from apartheid. As one academic commentator suggested:[5]

> The mining industry forms part and parcel of the capitalist system. If this system is to survive in South Africa more strenuous efforts must be to explain the benefits of such a system to employees. The NUM's Fifth Congress noted that "Apartheid and capitalism are two inseparable evils that must be smashed." Capitalism has been equated with apartheid in the minds of many black employees; strenuous efforts must be made to negate this idea.

Not surprisingly, as part of its strategy to incorporate workers, Anglo-American was at the forefront in promoting ESOPs. In August 1987, Anglo and de Beers announced a scheme of offering shares free to employees. It was to begin with 2,600 employees at Head Office, with five shares per person, each worth R60. This was to be extended to all 250,000 employees with five shares each for Anglo workers and ten for those of de Beers. The scheme involved a total of 1.45 million shares which would be fully owned (and hence potentially resold) after four years. Meanwhile more shares would be made available, making up a total of 8.5 million after five years, worth R480 million in total.

This has, however, to be set against the total number of shares in the region of 220 million, so that the workers' portion was being limited to around a mere four percent. Whilst involving a significant sum in aggregate the price was being paid for favourable publicity. A year late Anglo was advertising in newspapers around the world that 114,485 workers had joined the scheme:

> Our objective is not only to broaden ownership of Anglo American, it is to enable people who mostly have not had the opportunity to accumulate even modest wealth in the past, to obtain a tangible stake in the free enterprise system, and through that in the prosperity and progress of the country.

This claim has to be set against a situation in which no more than 300,000 people in South Africa were shareholders at all (some 7% of the white population

5 I have no source for this quote, nor for others that follow unless given.

and 1% of the total population), not least because Anglo itself directly owned more than fifty percent of all shares! As Cyril Ramaphosa commented at the time:[6]

> The Anglo American Employee Share Ownership scheme stinks ... If every worker does actually take up the shares offered, this would amount to 0.6 percent of the total AAC share portfolio ... This is the most degenerated tokenism ... The workers' demand for a living wage remains. Workers demand that a bigger share of the profits should go towards wages and not to share ownership schemes ... This scheme is a ploy to undermine unions.

Anglo's interest in advertising its ESOP scheme on an international stage reflected two factors. First, was the wish to present itself, and South African corporations more generally, to the eyes of the international community, in a favourable light in view of the universal condemnation of apartheid and the prominence of sanctions against South Africa. Second, ESOPs were themselves particularly popular at that time, especially in the USA and the UK. Here, the rationale was obviously not one of brokering the transition from apartheid but more one of downsizing corporations with workers' acquiescence, as well as to ease the privatisation and deregulation of utilities against the potential opposition of the workforce.

Other ESOP schemes often emerged during divestment. Ford, for example, at the end of 1987, donated a 24% (R100 million) equity to a workers' trust fund plus $2 million for a community trust. It was, however, committed to continuing to supply components to Samcor which was effectively controlled by Anglo through its taking a 42% stake in the equity. The deal as a whole must be seen as a way of smoothing over the process of Ford's limited withdrawal from South Africa.[7] As Jack (1991, p. 8) commented at the time:

> It is hoped that by giving black workers a stake in the free enterprise system, however small, their ideological allegiance will shift toward support for this system ... Ford saw its step as introducing an "economic

6 Quoted in Nicol (1989, p. 94). The irony of this stance, from someone who is now not only President but also one of the wealthiest individuals in South Africa, should not be lost on the reader.

7 As argued by Adler (1989), an ESOP can serve to resolve problems – in this case of a global manufacturer such as Ford, suffering a squeeze on markets and the stigma attached to its collaboration with apartheid – by allowing it to continue to supply components after disinvestment. See also Matiko (1988).

> citizenship" for workers, but that certainly did not meet the demands for "political citizenship" for workers. The company also hoped that by donating shares to workers it could maintain a profitable relationship with SA in the future.

Even less generosity was evident in other cases associated with divestment. When Coca-Cola withdrew its 30% stake in its South African bottler, Amalgamated Beverages Industries, ABI offered 11% of its shares to 7,000 independent retailers and to 3,500 employees. The scheme, closed in October 1987, was to offer shares at R1 with guaranteed repurchase at R1.60 in July 1989. This is not so generous as it first appears, given a high interest rate and inflation running at that time at around 20% per annum. Neither the retailers, nor subsequently the Greater Soweto Chamber of Commerce and the Food and Allied Workers Union, took up the offer on the grounds that they were being offered only 11% of the shares whilst blacks made up 80–90% of the customers.

Similar discrimination occurred as the Standard Chartered Bank divested its subsidiary Standard Bank Investment Corp (Stanbic). Black customers were offered one million shares at R18.75 each. But another one million shares each were reserved for staff and selected customers. In each case, there was the motive both to raise money from as many sources as possible whilst retaining control over the business.

More generally, the *Financial Mail* in October 1987 explicitly linked ESOP schemes to the dual objectives of undermining trade union power and promoting people's capitalism along the lines of Mrs. Thatcher's Britain. It reported that eighteen newly listed companies had offered ESOP schemes and 150 companies already had them in place. These included Pick and Pay, the retail chain, with an 11% employee stake in the business expected to rise to 50% in the next two or three years and Basil Read, a construction company employing many black workers.

There were, however, many notable absences which indicates how ESOPs were not aimed at creating any degree of black control even over parts of the economy that predominantly served black consumers. In August 1987, SABTA, the black taxi drivers association, was set to take over Putco, a major bus company. The deal was eventually called off because of the unwillingness of the government to guarantee continuing subsidies to a SABTA-owned Putco.

In short, the first major ESOP venture in South Africa was marked by the following features. First, it remained almost entirely aloof from the literature and experience to be gained from ESOPs in other countries. This is reviewed below. Second, this is hardly surprising, since the sudden popularity of ESOPs amongst big business was primarily ideological. It was accompanied by a massive campaign to convince workers that a favourably caricatured capitalism is better than an unfavourably caricatured socialism – with nothing, such as the mixed economy, either chronologically or organisationally between the two extremes. And, on the international arena, South African corporations pictured themselves as empowering and incorporating the interests of its black employees. Anglo American, for example, apart from taking out one-page adverts in the foreign press in which its ESOP figured prominently, also funded its anti-nationalisation campaign to the tune of a R21 million budget.

Third, as a consequence of its ideological role, the criterion of success for ESOPs in the South African context moved away from any focus on economic performance and concentrated almost exclusively on the index of whether workers would continue to hold onto their shares or not once they had the opportunity to sell them. As Project Free Enterprise (1989, p. 50) suggested:

> It is probably too early to assess the success of this (Anglo) scheme. The acid test will be after five years when employees decide to either purchase additional shares or sell their options.

Otherwise, it concludes not that ESOPs be used to convert workers from socialism to capitalism but rather to persuade workers to convert their socialism into support for ESOPs, with their ultimately gaining more say in decision-making and even collectively buying out a major gold mine. Accordingly, priority is given to educating the workforce in the workings of the stock market – an extremely novel response to South Africa's desperate shortage and imbalance of skills!

Finally, the sudden emergence of ESOPs presented the labour movement with difficult problems both in principle and practice. From the outset, COSATU and its constituent unions attempted to hold to a principled position of recognising ESOPs as of limited significance with suspect motives, and pressed for as collective a form for their implementation as possible, rather than favouring schemes that targeted individual workers. But the unions were not always able to command the unified support of their membership which understandably sought more immediate and individualistically based payments. Thus, as particularly brought out in the disinvestment from SAMCOR by Ford, ESOPs can prove extremely divisive.[8]

8 For debate over ESOPs at the time, see Nicol (1989) and Maller (1987, 1988 and 1989a and b), for example.

2 Conceptual Issues

ESOPs, then, raise strategic issues for the labour movement as well as problems of detail. How are they to be understood? At one extreme, there are those who argue that they are simply a different form in which wages are paid, obscuring the fundamental conflict between capital and labour by misleading the latter into believing it has a stake in the firm or economy, other than as a wage-labourer. At the other extreme, ESOPs are considered to have turned workers into capitalists, to have given them a genuine stake in the system, and to have created a share-owning democracy or people's capitalism.

The truth is undoubtedly closer to the first version. There are many different ways of remunerating workers, and the difference in these methods should not lead us to consider that something fundamental has changed. Consider, for example, the British coal industry at the end of the nineteenth century. Then wages were on a 'sliding scale', going up and down on the basis of a pre-determined formula with the price of coal. Accordingly, the wages were higher in periods of prosperity (when the price of coal tended to rise) and lower in depressions. Sharecropping involves the division of output between the producer and the non-producer according to pre-determined proportions and the same is often true even of feudal society. The church used to receive a tithe, for example, the old English word for a tenth. Similarly, payments by piece-rates means that wages vary with performance, Consequently, this has similar characteristics to an ESOP or Profit Related Pay (PRP) in so far as extra work leads to extra pay and to extra profit, and much the same is true of the premium paid for overtime.

Yet, these different ways of paying wages are not particularly associated with a favourable or novel development for working people. Formally, much the same is true of the ESOP and PRP schemes. For the worker remains tied to employment irrespective of the forms in which wages are paid. At various times, for reasons of incentives and of control as much as for ideological reasons, capitalists find it convenient to vary the way in which wages are assessed and paid. Significantly, employee profit-sharing logically entails a profit share to non-employees, the preservation of the underlying capitalist motivation. As such there is no qualitative transformation in the relations between employer and employee.

And whether there is a quantitative change or not is not predetermined. Afterwards, it will appear as though wages are supplemented by the added element listed as profit share. But it may well be that the pre-profit wage will be driven down to compensate for the other elements making up wages. This is well understood in other circumstances. Increases in wage taxes, for example, may lead to compensating claims for higher negotiated settlements as take-home pay levels are restored. More dramatically, for piece rates, short run increases in overall wages may well be adjusted back to previous levels through increases in the piece rate norm or reduction in the payment per piece. The net result is harder work for the same or even less pay – speed-up at no extra cost to the capitalist.

More generally, ESOPs, etc, are aimed at leading employees to identify with their company and to have an added incentive to provide for its success. The idea is to work harder for some but not for all of the profits, to moderate conflict between "them" and "us", and to pose ESOPs and PRPs as alternatives to trade unionism and conflict and, as a longer-term objective, as an alternative to the social ownership of the means of production. As President Reagan crudely put it, "Could there be a better answer to the stupidity of Karl Marx than millions of workers individually sharing in the means of production?" This comment has to be set against the distribution of share ownership in the United States where the top one percent own fifty per cent of shares and the top six per cent own 80 per cent. Even so, worker share ownership can induce a feeling of corporate loyalty. One study even showed that this was true of workers *not* included in the ESOP scheme (Tucker, 1989).

As a form of paying wages and of commanding workforce loyalty and cooperation, it is hardly surprising that ESOPs are far from new. It is worth emphasising that profit-sharing, etc, has been around for a long time, going back 150 years or more in the UK, so that its apparent recent discovery and promotion as a form of people's capitalism, able to solve economic problems, has been tried, tested and has failed many times in the past. Matthews, D. (1989) reviews the British evidence and concludes, p. 461:[9]

> To sum up then, although some historians have viewed profit-sharing as the work of philanthropic employers, the historical experience suggests that it was usually a management strategy of labour discipline by profit maximizing companies. It is evident that interest in profit-sharing has fluctuated with the problems in labour relations; in the long run the bonus was set by management as a relatively fixed proportion of wages, not profits, while even the most outwardly altruistic employers refused to cede significant control of their companies.

9 See also Church (1971) and Hatton (1988).

Realistically, like many others, he suggests that the frequent reappearance of the idea through history is probably a consequence of the sporadic, altruistic impulses of the occasional employer (or the egalitarian champion of the free market and capitalism). Its reappearance may also be due to the difficulty of isolating its exact effects from other more important factors in explaining economic performance so, "the fact that the effects of profit-sharing are so difficult to quantify may have been a factor in preserving its credibility for so long", p. 462.

In modern times, the philanthropic or calculating sponsors of such schemes are no longer confined to the ranks of the idiosyncratic entrepreneur. In addition, governments have been prepared to offer tax relief or other subsidies to convince employees of their commitment to, and stake in, some form of people's capitalism. This means that ESOPs have flourished over the past two decades. It also means that there is a much sounder basis on which to judge their impact.

3 The Record of ESOP Performance

The recent literature on ESOPs has gone through a number of stages. Initially, there was a theoretical literature, less interested in the details of the schemes involved. These could vary according to the degree of share ownership or not, the freedom of workers to sell their shares or not, who takes control of them, whether it be the individual workers or a collective agency on their behalf, the use to which the dividends may be used, to supplement money wages or to promote worker or community welfare, and whether the ownership is offered free, at a price or as a reward for long service, skill or seniority and whether the state is supporting the scheme through offering tax relief on it, etc.

From the point of view of orthodox economics, these different schemes have small but significant differences. They lie along a continuum between a worker cooperative and a firm purely owned and controlled by an individual capitalist. According to the way and the extent to which workers share in profits or the equity of the firm, they are presumed to vary the way in which they supply labour – whether in total amount or in terms of the intensity with which they work. For example, if workers share in profits, they may wish to see fewer workers offered jobs so that their share is not diluted across too large a workforce. On the other hand, as they are perceived to have an interest in the performance of the firm, they have an added incentive to work harder to increase the profits from which they take a share.

As suggested, these motivations and the variations in how they can be realised have been the focus of the orthodoxy. The London School of Economics' Centre for Labour Economics alone, for example, produced at least eight discussion papers on the issue over a two-year period at the end of the eighties, as well as a number of published contributions across a range of journals in economics and industrial relations. This, usually abstract, theoretical analysis has also been accompanied by some assessment of the empirical results obtained and this is considered later.

Interest in ESOPs also inspired analysis at the macroeconomic as well as at the microeconomic level. Would an economy function more favourably if every worker was involved in an ESOP? One of the leading exponents in favour of ESOPs has been the US economics professor, Martin Weitzman, whose 1984 book was judged by the *New York Times* as the most important contribution to economic thought since Keynes's *General Theory*.[10] His argument is that, at the macroeconomic level, profit-sharing will lead to lower levels of unemployment. This is because it will handle supposed downward rigidities in the level of real wages, since labour's pay will fall in a recession along with profitability and make higher levels of employment than otherwise attractive to the firm paying profit related pay. This notion of dealing with inflexibility in the labour market is repeated again and again throughout the UK's Green Paper discussion document on PRP (HMSO, 1986). It should be emphasised that the Weitzman effect comes from the gaining of more jobs through the indirect acceptance of lower pay.[11]

This was also the motivation of James Meade, the Nobel Prize winner for economics. He favoured profit-sharing because, "many of the main conflicts of interest between capital and labour could be removed" (Meade, 1986, p. 140). Preferred is a scheme in which *new* employees do not share in profits, for otherwise, "there would be a conflict between 'insiders' and 'outsiders'.

10 Weitzman engaged in his own version of sharing. Accused of multiple manure thefts from a 98-year old farmer, he agreed to pay the farmer $600 and to make an additional $300 charitable donation in lieu of performing community service, see his Wikipedia entry.

11 For a discussion of Weitzman in historical perspective, see Outram (1985). Mitchell (1995) sees wage flexibility as just one of only three factors in favour of ESOPs, the other two being either to internalise transaction costs between owners and workers or to reduce informational costs in the valuation of a firm's assets. Note that Benner and Jun (1996, p. 502) use the latter as a device to explain ESOPs in terms of worker and entrepreneur strategies, "Owners of relatively unprofitable firms will tend to sell out for low prices instead of paying high wages, whereas owners of profitable firms will prefer pay high wages over receiving low firm prices; the buy-out serves as a screening mechanism. The probability of an employee buy-out decreases with the employees' outside options and increases with owners' outside options." See also Outram (1987).

Those already in employment in any successful partnership would be required to face a reduction in pay as a necessary condition for allowing unemployed outsiders to join in the concern's useful activities". This would impede the employment creation effects so that, for Meade, it is better to put forward a proposal that is essentially the same as taking on new workers at lower wages than those already employed and is an implicit attack on the basic principle of trade unionism – the same pay for the same job. In this context, Meade had been notable in the past for proposing taxes on wage increases as a means of controlling inflation. Keeping wages down has remained the aim, only the methods of doing so have changed.

This can be seen in another way, for one of the assumptions of the Weitzman-type analysis is the absence of trade unions. This ought, perhaps, to be seen the other way around, in that PRP is designed to nullify the effects of the presence of trade unions by making wages more flexible (downwards in recession as profits fall) and, with Meade, allowing new workers to be hired at lower wages than incumbents. All of this is a far cry from the ideology of higher pay (in the form of higher profit) and participation through share ownership that is the image offered by proponents of people's capitalism! Despite all of this grand theory, PRP in the UK was inspired by the government of Mrs. Thatcher with a deeply embedded hostility to trade unions and, in the event, her period of office over the 1980s witnessed a dramatic worsening of income distribution. In the UK, PRP and ESOPs were encouraged by various tax incentives. Assets involved increased from £1.5 to £2 billion between 1978 and 1985/86, covering 1.5 million workers.[12]

The second phase of literature concerned with ESOPs has addressed the issue of the impact upon performance, especially productivity. This poses certain problems of method since it is necessary to make a judgement about what would have happened in the absence of a scheme. Should ESOP firms be compared with non-ESOP? Or firms be examined for comparative performance before and after an ESOP? Even if all the necessary information is available, determining the effects is, in any case extremely difficult, since what differences there are may be the result of other factors unrelated to the ESOP, such as a boom or recession in market conditions. ICI, for example, has had a scheme in place in the UK since 1954. But to measure the impact of this scheme would require the existence of an equivalent ICI without the scheme and, as it is the overwhelmingly dominant chemicals company in the UK economy, this

12 For discussion of the details for the UK both here and below, see Smith (1986) Bradley and Gelb (1986), Estrin and Wadhwani (1986), Blanchflower and Oswald (1987), Poole (1988) and Pryce and Nicholson (1988). See also Estrin et al. (eds) (1988).

is impossible. Nor can comparisons be made with similar companies deriving from other countries, since national differences are liable to swamp any of the effects arising out of the presence of such schemes or not.

It could even be that any differences in economic and other characteristics across companies are the cause rather than the consequence an ESOP. If a firm is failing, it might launch an ESOP to persuade workers to take lower wages in return for shares. In doing so, it would hardly be fair to compare such a firm with one without an ESOP that is not in trouble. Similarly, it is known that large-scale companies are more likely to have ESOP schemes than small-scale. They are also more likely to be unionised and have a developed system of industrial relations. This may lead to bargaining for higher wages in the form of profit-sharing whilst productivity increase may arise independently out of the economies of scale enjoyed by the large company. Interestingly, however, the evidence appears to suggest that, where there is a strong union, PRP is less likely than for when there is a weaker union present (although the absence of unionisation makes PRP least likely). This is because the stronger union is able to prevent the company from setting workers' profits against wages. But this is just to confirm that wages tend to be higher where unions are stronger, irrespective of the form in which they are paid. A final point concerns the survival of firms with ESOPs which will be the only ones left to be recorded. This may bias assessment in ESOP's favour, although the same is true of non-ESOP firms. In effect, all firms have to meet commercial criteria to survive so that they will tend to have a degree of uniform performance, with presence or not of an ESOP being compensated by other non-observed factors.[13]

Putting these considerations aside, the evidence on ESOPs is conclusive in denying any significant effect. In the case of the UK, in an early study, Blanchflower and Oswald (1988) report that the impact of ESOPs is unproven. This is confirmed by Duncan (1988). Wadhwani and Wall (1990, p. 16) conclude after looking at micro-data:

> Nevertheless, if our results were correct, they would suggest that much of the recent debate on profit-sharing has been "much ado about nothing"!

Similarly, Aitken and Wood (1989, p. 166) conclude that:

> There is limited evidence that such plans will produce improvements in the employee motivational states and organizational performance.

13 McElrath and Rowan (1992) report that of fifty buy-outs by US workers since 1975, only 32 were still operating.

Two studies that do find a relationship between profit-sharing and productivity are those of Cable and Wilson (1989 and 1990). The first is for the UK and they conclude that, "estimates of productivity differentials between firms practising profit-sharing in the UK engineering industry and those without profit-sharing indicate overall gains of between 3 and 8%" (Cable and Wilson, 1989, p. 372). But they explain that this is not a simple relation, p. 373:

> more is involved than a simple shift ... due to increased work effort or 'cooperation' in some broader sense. Rather the effect is entwined with the firm's choice of technology, internal organisation and labour force characteristics. It follows that, contrary to what might be inferred from previous work ... the introduction of profit-sharing *ceteris paribus* will not necessarily have productivity enhancing effects; accompanying changes in other dimensions of organisational design are likely to be required.

Thus, the productivity effect is dependent upon the presence of other factors which are generally in themselves associated with better performance and in which a strong component of workers participation in decision-making is liable to be important.

For, in the later study for West Germany, they find a much more significant impact, p. 554:

> New estimates for West Germany indicate overall productivity differentials of 20–30% in favour of firms practising profit-sharing. These compare with estimates of 3–8% for comparable British firms ... Like the UK results, they reveal evidence of important interactions between profit-sharing and other aspects of the firms' organisation and operation. However, it appears that in Germany profit-sharing is being used in a different way, by different kinds of firms, than in the United Kingdom. Our previous general conclusion – that the effect of profit-sharing is intimately related to firms' choices of technology, internal organisation and labour-force characteristics, and that profit-sharing is to this extent an integral element of overall organisational design – is therefore reinforced by the new results, but with an important additional insight: that there is evidently no uniquely appropriate context and role for profit-sharing.

In short, where profit-sharing has succeeded, it requires particular types of firms, typical of the more progressive West German engineering firms in terms of technology, organisation and skill composition of the labour force. In addition, such schemes must not be simply tacked onto the existing wage-payment systems but must be an integral part of the management and industrial relations system. A similar conclusion can be drawn from the work of Jones and Kato (1993a and b) for Japan. They observe that the Japanese angle has been undeservedly ignored. For, by 1984, 90% of firms quoted on the Japanese stock exchanges were running ESOPs, applicable to over 50% of their workforce. The Japanese schemes have certain notable features which reinforce the workers' legendary loyalty to their employers – they are not granted tax relief, they are subsidised by the firms themselves, they are skewed towards benefitting the lower ranks in the workforce, there is limited opportunity for workers to sell their shares, and the workers have directors to represent their interests. The net impact appears to be a small improvement in productivity in such firms. As Jones and Kato (1993a, p. 366) conclude:

> Our finding of the largely favorable effects on company productivity of Japanese ESOPs points to the potentially important role played by specific institutional features in accounting for the observed variation in economic effects of ESOPs. Specifically, given the presence in most Japanese firms of mechanisms designed to encourage employee participation, our findings support the conclusion of ... others that both decision and financial participation are needed in order for improvements in business performance to be realized.

A much more extensive literature on productivity and ESOPs is to be found for the USA, not least because the ESOP movement has continued to prosper there longer. ESOPs flourished in the 1920s, with three hundred in place at the beginning of the century, with one of the first originating with the retailer Sears Roebuck in 1916. But 90% of these ESOPs were wiped out by the crash of 1929 and the Great Depression. In the 1950s, Louis Kelso, a US lawyer wrote a book entitled, *The Capitalist Manifesto: How to Turn Eighty Million Workers into Capitalists on Borrowed Money*. He claims in 1956 to have invented ESOPs in a preface to a publication from the right-wing *laissez-faire* Adam Smith Institute (Taylor, 1988). His history is as poor as his logic for he claims to be able to, "broaden the ownership of capital without invading the private property of anyone". This reflects the desire to avoid any fundamental shift in economic power or the redistribution of wealth; this being freely admitted in the form of seeking a "populism without Robin Hood"! From 1975 to 1992, the number of plans rose from 1,601 to 9,764 with the number of employees involved growing from 248,000 to over eleven million (Gianaris, 1996, p. 134).

The study of Blinder (ed.) (1990) was a relatively early confirmation of the positive impact of profit-related pay on productivity when it is combined with workforce participation in decision-making. More recently, Doucouliagos (1995) has undertaken a meta-analysis (or compilation) of forty-three studies, mainly for US firms, of the relationship between worker participation and productivity. He finds the productivity effects overall are positive but small, and dependent upon worker participation in decision-making in firms not wholly owned by the workers themselves. As confirmed by Kaufman and Russell (1995, p. 46):

> Insufficient attention has been given to coupling worker participation with ESOPs. The best research on ESOPs repeatedly has found that greater worker participation in decisionmaking is an indispensable ingredient in the design of successful ESOPs.

The most sophisticated study of the impact of ESOPs, in the US context, is provided by Kruse (1996), drawing upon a sample of 275 US firms (with a response rate of 61.6%). Unlike other studies, he employs panel data (observations on the different firms over time) so that the evolution and performance of firm behaviour can be charted chronologically. He finds that profit-sharing may have been adopted to raise productivity, with the older companies having higher R&D expenditure (suggesting collaboration between workforce and management), more job-enrichment and worker participation programmes, and higher capital-labour ratios.

A weakness in Kruse's interpretation of his results is that he takes outcomes, such as those reported in the previous paragraph, as indicative of motives. This reflects the passage to a new phase in the academic literature. It has become less concerned with the results of ESOPs and more concerned with why they are adopted. In this, the literature on the USA has been particularly prominent. This is because the productivity motive for ESOPs has become overtaken by others unrelated to worker participation as such.

Consider the dramatic increase in ESOPs in the late 1980s. Scholes and Wolfson (1989, p. 25) find that there were 4,028 plans in 1978; this had risen to 8,046 in 1986 and 9,500 in 1988. Corresponding numbers of employees covered were 2.8, 7.8 and 9.5 million, respectively, the latter making up more than 10% of the workforce. The answer to why this has happened is to be found in the company legislation for the state of Delaware! 179,000 companies are incorporated there, including 56% of the *Fortune* top 500 companies and 45% of those quoted on the New York Stock Exchange. According to Delaware state law, it has now been found that ESOPs legally expand the category of shareholders to include employees, all of whom have to be taken into account in voting for approval to change control (a wait of three years for a takeover unless 85% of shareholders vote in favour). Polaroid, for example, in early 1989 took out 14% of its shares for an ESOP in order to obstruct a hostile merger, and were backed by the courts in their strategy.

So Scholes and Wolfson (1989, p. 26) view, "The creation of impediments to changes in corporate control as the prime motivation for ESOPs". Nor is this all. In the first six months of 1989, US corporations acquired over $19 billion of their own stock for ESOPs compared with $5.6 billion for the whole of 1988 and less than $1.5 billion per annum from 1974 to 1987. This is partly for favourable tax reasons but equally it was used to raise capital through leveraged loans out of the implied future earnings on the employee-owned stock, $9 billion being borrowed in this way in 1989 up to May 10th. As it were, the company is borrowing against the future dividends of its employees – similar to the use of pension funds for speculative purposes. This all serves to confirm the point that ESOPs, far from shifting control to workers, may even act as a way of consolidating and redistributing corporate control amongst and between managerial elites.

So important has become the tax motive for engaging in ESOPs that the issue has now become the regular subject of academic journals such as *Journal of Financial Economics*, *Journal of Corporate Taxation*, *Banking Law Journal*, *Journal of Banking and Finance*, *Financial Management*, *Journal of Accountancy*, *Journal of Taxation*, *Securities Regulation Law Journal*, and *Journal of Accounting and Economics*. These journals, in the context of ESOPs, are primarily concerned with examining tax law and how it can be turned to the advantage of corporate managers. Even so, Dhillon and Ramirez (1994) find, following the Polaroid ruling, that ESOPs have primarily been adopted for yet another motive unconnected to workers' interests, that is as a defensive measure against hostile takeover.

Apart from tax and anti-merger strategy, perhaps the most significant aspect of the more recent wave of ESOPs is that they have involved companies under threat of bankruptcy, the Chrysler motor company, for example, and airlines that suffered under deregulation such as Eastern, Pan Am, and Republic. In negotiating employee share ownership, the *quid pro quo* has been wage cuts or restraint. At Chrysler, the US Government guaranteed a loan of $1.5 billion dollars to support an ESOP. But employees had to give up $585 million dollars in pay increases over the next three years in return for equity valued at $165 million. For $35 million in shares, 23,000 unionised employees at Pan Am had to suffer a ten per cent wage cut and a fifteen month pay freeze. Under such conditions, the granting of union representation on the Board could only be of limited, more accurately limiting, significance to the workforce. At Eastern, salary cuts of between 18% and 22% were the cost of a 25% employee share ownership. Put together a loss of $290 million in wages, and a subsequent net profit of $190 million, of which workers' pro rata share would be less than $50 million. It would not need worker managers to calculate a net loss to employees of over $240 million!

The introduction of an ESOP for a company in trouble is designed to allow for labour market flexibility under the guise of share ownership. It can involve redundancies and loss of wages but also other forms of flexibility. It is possible that the workers pension funds become dedicated to speculation in the corporation's prospects. Even more disturbing is the willing erosion of working conditions on the part of employees whose remunerations depends upon it. Grunberg et al. (1996, p. 235) draw the following conclusion from their study of the safety records in timber mills:

> Our findings are very disappointing for those who see employee ownership as a way to improve the quality of work life. The producer cooperatives had similar accident and injury experiences to the conventional mills but a worse days missed record. The ESOP did worse on all measures of safety. It is also clear that employee ownership does not necessarily translate into changes in the work process to make it less hazardous or into greater worker participation over shopfloor safety and working conditions. The picture is not improved when we look at levels of worker satisfaction and morale. Workers perceive working in these types of mills as particularly distressful.

In short, not surprisingly in his study of ESOPs, Kruse (1996) finds that the motives for adopting ESOPs have been mixed, across the search for productivity, flexibility, anti-merger strategy, and tax benefits.[14] For him, p. 518:

> In sum, profit-sharing or employee ownership may be implemented in order to: (1) enhance workplace cooperation and productivity … (2) increase compensation flexibility … (3) discourage unionization, or gain concessions from unions; and/or (4) gain tax incentives, have easy access to capital, or avoid takeovers in the USA.

Whatever the historical and specific motives that informed the formation of ESOPs, they have become more and more heavily embroiled in the general

---

14 Kruse, however, employs the notion of flexibility in a slightly different way, as the sharing of risk with employees over fluctuating corporate fortunes.

process of corporate strategy, with limited actual and potential deference to the interests of employees. The broader context within which schemes have operated in the USA has been one of widening pay differentials between the rich and poor, with high levels of unemployment and otherwise casualised service sector employment for the poor. A weak position in the more general labour market has encouraged a threatened workforce to accept wage cuts rather than redundancies, taking government tax hand-outs to smooth the process.

4 Trade Union Responses

Not surprisingly, in view of the history and underlying principles of ESOPs, trade unions have generally been hostile to these initiatives. As the British TUC reported in 1974, quoted in Baddon et al. (1989, p. 43):

> First, such schemes do not in reality provide for any real control over the managerial decisions … Second, there is no advantage to workpeople tying up their savings in the firm since this doubles the insecurity … (third) they do little or nothing to reduce the inequality of wealth.

And, the UK's TUC observed, such schemes exclude those who do not create commodities, thereby leaving out the majority of those who work in the public sector and also those in smaller scale and casualised or disadvantaged employment in the private sector. In Britain, for example, one way in which equal pay legislation has been avoided is through tying bonus payments predominantly to those jobs occupied by male employees, and much the same applies to the greater use of profit-sharing and discounted share offers to those who are placed higher up in the job hierarchy. Workers may also rarely be able to afford to keep the shares that they receive, rather selling them for cash when allowed to do so to supplement wages and buy essentials or tide over emergencies. Matthews, D. (1989, p. 461) points to:

> unpopularity of shares as opposed to cash. Until recently, most workers were not sufficiently well off to afford to save, especially in the form of shares. Indeed, holding shares of one company, particularly one's own employer, is simply unwise speculation. Therefore, for good reason, given the choice, workers would take a cash bonus, but given shares these would usually be sold immediately. If this were forbidden the shares were

> looked upon as 'dead money' … 80 per cent of employees free to choose between shares or cash took the money.

In the USA, trade union opposition to ESOPs and other forms of share ownership has mellowed. In part, this is a matter of economic necessity – trade unions are faced with negotiating with employers who only offer continuing employment on the basis of an ESOP. On the other hand, whether through pensions or other sources of funds, trade unions appear to have the potential to influence the level and composition of investment. Gianaris (1996, p. 143) estimates that ESOPs had accumulated $150 billion in stock by the 1990s, but this is totally dominated by the further $4.8 trillion which is held in workers pension funds. These are, however, managed as financial assets with little attention paid to using the ownership power that this might allow, with as much as $140 billion being held in foreign equities (Gianaris, 1996, p. 155).

Like ESOPs, pensions have been used to argue that workers have become shareowners and are a factor in the creation of a people's capitalism. This is incorrect for similar reasons as for ESOPs. For pensions do not turn workers into rentier capitalists; they merely pay back to the working class, in a particular form, a portion of the revenue that it has itself produced. In other words, pensions are a form of wages, paid, with delay, to workers for their subsistence during retirement.

Moreover, pension funds are generally administered by, and on behalf of, the banking system that controls them, whether directly or indirectly. They have given workers little control over the economy. According to the estimate by Minns (1982), well over 75% of pension fund investments in the UK are looked after by banks, insurance companies and stockbrokers. For this reason, socialist literature is occasionally awash with schemes to employ pension funds to regenerate British industry and for more modest schemes that put planning and need before profitability. But such are the legal and financial powers of the City's financial institutions that progress has been limited. Even attempts to withdraw investments from South Africa as a protest against apartheid proved difficult against the legal requirements that pension funds should maximise financial returns.[15]

The difficulties of taking control over the economy through worker ownership is best illustrated by the Swedish experience, where the strongest attempt has been made although, within Sweden itself, the strength of the labour movement was declining as attempts were made to push forward redistribution.[16]

---

15 See also Minns (1996).

16 See Standing (1988, Chapter 6).

Otherwise, the conditions for success could not have been more favourable for the following reasons. First, Sweden has had a strong trade union movement with high density of membership, customary rights to participate in policy formation, and intimate links with the Social Democratic Party.

Second, the latter has formed the Government in power in all but six years over the period from 1932 until the 1990s. It is perceived to have introduced the most enlightened form of the welfare state and has enjoyed rapid economic growth. Employers have also been highly unified in policy, partly reflecting the high degree of concentration of ownership, and the economy's success has depended upon competitiveness in international markets, given the small scale of the domestic market.

During the early seventies, support in the labour movement was won for a proposal that twenty percent of the annual profits of large firms should be owned by trusts representing the interests of wage earners as a whole. The reforms were proposed by the Meidner Committee in 1976 and were specifically linked to a fundamental shift in the balance of economic power, as quoted in Pontusson (1987, p. 32):

> We want to deprive the capitalists of the power that they exercise by virtue of ownership. All experience shows that it is not enough to have influence and control. Ownership plays a decisive role … we cannot fundamentally change society without changing its ownership structure.

Through a remarkable set of economic and political circumstances, the Meidner Plan gained widespread support and was adopted as policy. Ultimately, however, legislation to bring the workers' fund into being was only introduced in 1983. It was on a much smaller scale than originally planned and geared towards sustaining investment and subsidising pensions as part and parcel of an austerity programme. With the absolute opposition from employers, redistribution was at most confined to newly created wealth. No attempt was made to extend the democratic rights of workers in economic decision-making.

The reasons for this failure in terms of the original conception and in shifting the balance of economic power in favour of working people is not of direct concern here, although worsening economic conditions and unified opposition from capital were clearly of enormous importance, along with export of capital.[17] Rather the example of Sweden serves to illustrate what limited change

17 See also Meidner (1993), Pontusson (1994) and Minns (1996).

has been achieved even in the society which is arguably conceived to have travelled furthest and most successfully along the road of welfare capitalism.

5 Current Implications for South Africa

In short, the historical and comparative evidence on ESOPs and similar schemes points to the following conclusions.

(1) Such schemes are liable to come to prominence at times of major economic and/or political change or within a particular company or sector when it is subject to major restructuring.

(2) They are best understood as a different form in which wages are paid rather than as workers' participation in ownership or control, let alone as a source of some form of people's capitalism.

(3) At times, ESOPs have been motivated by hostility to trade unions or as a strategy to moderate their militancy and goals. They have also been seen as a way of inducing downward flexibility in real wages and conditions when profitability is under pressure.

(4) The benefits of such schemes are usually uneven within a company, often favouring those who are already better off in terms of wages, salaries or other parts of the remuneration package. This can be a source of division amongst the workforce. On an economy-wide level, ESOPs can only benefit those directly who are in the appropriate forms of employment, primarily with secure jobs in large (private) corporations, tending to reinforce existing economic inequalities by race, gender and location.

(5) ESOPs have been closely associated with corporate restructuring so that they have become heavily embroiled in corporate strategic behaviour, leading to the erosion of any genuine initial commitment to workers' advantage. This has been reflected in three different ways – workers accepting reductions in wages and working conditions in return for shares, corporations offering ESOPs as a way of enhancing tax status, and as part of anti-merger strategy by existing management.

(6) There is little or no general evidence of ESOPs or similar schemes enhancing economic performance except where it is accompanied by genuine participation of workers in management and decision-making, a factor that can be introduced independently of ESOPs. Significantly, ESOPs have been particularly successful in Japan and Germany where, for different reasons in each case, industrial policymaking and worker participation are more secure for reasons unrelated to ESOPs.

(7) The most fundamental attempt at increasing workers' control through share ownership was made in Sweden where conditions could not have been more favourable. It ultimately failed against the opposition of big business.

(8) Trade unions are faced with very serious challenges by ESOPs and similar schemes. As a form of wages offered by employers, as a tactic in economic restructuring, and as a potential object of favourable government policy, they cannot simply be set aside. On the other hand, they can be both divisive, according to differential benefits to the different sections of the workforce, and diversionary in drawing attention away from basic wages and conditions and the more general issues of economic and social transition.

It is against this background that the re-emergence of ESOPs in South Africa should be judged. The context has changed from that of the struggle against, and the demise of, the apartheid system, in which South African capitalism seemed to be under threat. Rather, it is the restructuring of that capitalism that is now at issue. ESOPs have become embroiled in four separate but related issues. These are, first, the government's privatisation programme where shares are liable to be offered to workers and others during the restructuring of state assets. Second, trade unions have built up formal ownership of assets in the form of pension and other funds. Third, large-scale corporate capital is going through a process of restructuring, with some pressure towards conglomerate unbundling.

Fourth, and most important, however, is the process of so-called black empowerment. It is crucial to recognise that the term embodies a variety of different aspects and is subject to shifting meaning over time. Departing from the original goals of the Freedom Charter, it has become increasingly associated with the promotion of small black businesses. Most recently, this has been complemented by the emergence of an elite of big black business groups which seek to advance their position through the use of privatisation, corporate restructuring and unbundling, ESOPs and other trade union assets. Those who have gained prestige and position through the trade union and liberation movements have inevitably been prominent in the promotion of big black business.[18] Such connections in the past should not be taken as indicative of future roles, and the trade union movement must secure sound commercial and principled decisions in its investments.

18 See SALB (1996 and 1997).

Because of these four factors, trade union strategic involvement in bargaining cannot be pre-determined, as it cannot simply be a matter of accepting an ESOP or not. However, certain guiding principles can be suggested.

(1) Black empowerment should be clearly understood at the plant, enterprise, sector or economy level as, first and foremost, the negotiation through centralised bargaining, for as broad a section of the workforce as possible, of secure employment, with decent wages and conditions.

(2) ESOPs and PRP have the potential to undermine this priority. The profit-share scheme introduced into the gold mining industry in 1993 had the effect of creating wage disparities and effectively undermines centralised collective bargaining for common wages and conditions. Where such schemes are negotiated, they should be pegged as far as possible to as broad a collective participation in the bonuses shared. More important than devising schemes of remuneration through ESOPs and PRP is the regular review of job evaluation and grading systems.

(3) More generally, priority in economic policy must be directed towards the meeting of basic needs. Far from supporting a review of tax policy by the Katz Commission to favour ESOPs or other forms of worker investment, the trade union movement should be pressing the Commission to review the financial systems and its inadequate role in raising and allocating finance for industrial and infrastructural investment. Much more important than the weight of shares owned by workers in the form of pensions, etc is the economic and financial system in which they are owned.

(4) The labour movement needs to set up a Portfolio Committee. Its main purpose would not be to provide advice on individual investments, etc, although it could accrue such expertise and monitor and register potential consultants to serve the trade union movement. Rather, the Portfolio Committee should review in detail and in principle the issues that are raised by ESOPs and pension funds. No member of the Committee should have any direct interest in corporate ownership or dealing.

In some respects, the availability of ESOPs and pension funds, etc poses challenges to the labour movement that are similar to those attached to health care. Should a union, promoting its members' own individual interests, buy into a private health scheme even though this consolidates expensive, inefficient and inequitable provision more generally? Or should such opportunities be sacrificed in favour of more principled, but nebulous and uncertain, campaigns for a genuinely universal health care system, free of the distortions associated with the interventions of the private health insurance industry? By analogy, should workers participate in ESOPs or pension plans which benefit some within the given functioning, ownership and control of the given financial system, or should they reject participation in the bargaining over and management of such schemes?

Whilst not dismissing the presence of trade-offs between the principles involved in these strategies, they can both be pursued together as they are not completely mutually exclusive. How individual workers, workforces and trade unions respond to offers around ESOPs, etc depends upon the scope of opportunities open to them. In the absence of more collective forms of participation, as in the case of illness, the only option would appear to opt for the best deal for oneself irrespective of broader implications. Consequently, the labour movement can adopt a dualistic strategy. On the one hand, it can set up a progressive mutual investment fund through which employees' ownership of shares and pension funds can be held and managed through a variety of participatory schemes. In this way, employees' interests could be pursued, as collectively as possible, through the existing financial system, even if with a continuing dependence upon the predominant position held by the financial conglomerates. Such a holding company would also be able to serve as a mutual fund for other collective forms of ownership, apart from employees' shares, such as cooperative saving schemes. In other words, it need not be exclusive to trade unions. In addition, a major role could be played in bidding for participation in the government's proposed National Empowerment Fund (earmarked for 10% of shares of restructured state assets). This participation would otherwise be fragmented and open to effective capture by the relatively few establishing control over the newly formed black business conglomerates. The progressive mutual fund would be able to call upon considerable international goodwill, experience and support from those who have pioneered and been concerned with ethical investment campaigns.

Whatever the immediate successes of the mutual investment fund in advancing workers living standards, redistributing wealth and redirecting and raising investment, they are liable to be undermined and negated by the weight of influence and mode of operation of the continuing financial system. Consequently, whether from the institutional base provided by the mutual investment fund, from the proposed Portfolio Committee, or otherwise, it is essential that a campaign be launched to reform the South African financial system in order to provide for more responsibility and accountability in the levels and composition of investment, the financing of the public debt, and the formulation, implementation and monitoring of investment, as argued in the companion paper on industrial strategy (Fine, 1997a).

Appendix 1: Summary from EROSA (1989)

1. Employee Stock Ownership Plans (ESOP) have emerged in South Africa during 1987. There are other schemes similar to these, which tie workers' remuneration to profitability, such as Profit Related Pay (PRP) but these have not as yet been prominent.
2. Such schemes have recently emerged in many western countries as part of an ideological campaign to seek support for 'people's capitalism', to moderate trade union conflict and to undermine its influence and to incorporate employees' interests into those of management. However, these schemes are not historically novel, having existed previously in different forms and even outside the capitalist system as in sharecropping. Analytically, under capitalism, such schemes should be viewed as a veiled way of paying wages rather than as a sharing of profits.
3. Both theoretical and empirical evidence suggests little impact of such schemes on company performance and on extension of workers' control. At an economy-wide level, PRP is designed to make wages more 'flexible' and, in particular, to reduce them during recession or whenever a company is in difficulty. In addition, it is associated with the idea that newly hired workers should be paid a lower rate of wages than incumbents.
4. In Sweden, where economic and social conditions have been most favourable to the adoption and progressive implementation of ESOPs, developments in practice have been both limited and more linked to winning support for an economic austerity programme than to an extension of economic democracy and greater equity in the distribution of income and wealth.
5. In South Africa, ESOPs are intimately linked to the campaign to convince non-whites that apartheid and capitalism are not inter-related. Anglo American has been at the forefront with the offer of free shares to its employees, although these are of an insufficient amount to affect company control in any way. More generally, ESOP schemes have often been proposed in the context of divestment and are not particularly favourable given the need of the purchasing company to raise credit quickly in these circumstances. Black people have been offered deals which reflect rather than challenge the existing structures of racial oppression.
6. Negotiation around share ownership should reflect two guiding principles; that any profit share should be prevented from being set against wages, and to prevent incorporation of workers' interests into those of

management. As collective a form of ownership for shares as possible should be arranged with the income accruing being set aside for purposes as far removed as possible from the immediate interests of the individual worker.

7. A trust, with aims as close as possible to those of the liberation movement, could be set up and act as a depository for all shares taken up, whether these be made available on an individual or a collective basis.

Appendix 2: Summary from EROSA (1990)

In a separate EROSA (1989) paper, an analysis has been made of the role of employee share ownership plans, ESOPs, and other schemes such as profit-related pay, PRP. Briefly, the conclusions are that such schemes are essentially a form of making wage payments – they aim at pre-empting or weakening trade union organisation and militancy, they offer no shift of management control to the workforce, they are often introduced to pass the costs onto employees of rescuing or restructuring the company or plant, and there seems to be no systematic relation between such schemes and economic performance *unless* worker participation in management is incorporated. In South Africa, ESOPs, etc seem to be a minimalist economic response by management to the crisis of apartheid, are often imposed without the consultation or approval of organised labour, and they have been associated with the restructuring of ownership following upon privatisation or disinvestment.

The purpose here is to reinforce these conclusions. This update is divided into three parts. The first reviews much of the recent literature on ESOPs that has appeared in response to its being widely mooted as a policy measure around the world. The basic conclusion remains how limited is the impact of ESOPs, especially in the absence of other changes or conditions that enhance broader worker participation in decision-making.

The second part argues that this literature has been predominantly ignored in the debate on ESOPs in South Africa, where such schemes continue to play an ideological role which remains the basis on which their success is judged. Nonetheless, ESOPs have also proved important in material struggles around privatisation, sanctions and disinvestment and are a potential mechanism for dividing the workforce.

The brief third part suggests that ESOPs might play a role if radically transformed. A post-apartheid wage policy might include a social fund for enterprise and community development and a bonus scheme divided between these two areas as well as money wages and taxation as required, with certain strategic objectives attracting subsidy from local or national government.[19]

19 More broadly, I have argued, irrespective of how they are financed, that (central) state policy on lower levels of provision should fall into the following categories: those that are mandatory; those that are discretionary but subsidised; those that are discretionary and not subsidised; and those that are forbidden without permission. For the latter, I was motivated by what I termed "the casino syndrome".

CHAPTER 3

Defence Expenditure and the Post-apartheid Economy: A Briefing Paper for the ANC

Postscript as Personal Preamble

The source of this chapter is simple. I was asked, indirectly, in late 1992, just as MERG (1993) was being commissioned, to draft material for a speech for Kader Asmal, a leading political figure in the ANC as it was preparing for government.[1] In anticipation, he had major responsibility for defence. From 1995 to 2004 he headed the National Conventional Arms Control Committee (what should South Africa produce and sell?). But he also served as Minister of Water Affairs and Forestry from 1994 and Minister of Education from 1999 until 2004. I never met him, do not know if and how he used my text, nor received any acknowledgment nor thanks for my efforts. I suspect this is not even oversight, just the busyness of the times.

The most obvious source for my efforts came from the Greater London Council (GLC). It had heavily promoted conversion, not least through GLEB (Greater London Enterprise Board),[2] so both literature and policy were familiar to me (as co-editor of GLC, 1995a, and a research editor for the Industry and Employment Branch of the GLC). No doubt South Africa had much conversion to do, given that it had in some senses been militarised to serve apartheid. This went extremely far especially if defence (of the regime) is extended beyond armaments (production and trading) as such (and apartheid South Africa had at least the beginnings of a nuclear weapon programme) to include domestic manufacture of oil from coal to beat sanctions (SASOL as a major part of the MEC) and varieties of facilities, skilled staff and technologies that could be converted to post-apartheid purposes. In retrospect, without going into details,

1 As the piece was for another to use as a speech, from a scholarly point of view, it might be considered a little rough around the edges. It has never been subsequently prepared for publication. A draft chapter for Fine and Rustomjee (1996) on what I dubbed SAMIC, the South African Military and Industrial Complex, was not included in the published volume. On another note, I find sweet the complete unawareness of the coming mobile phone revolution.

2 In passing, it is worth mentioning that Vella Pillay served as a member of the GLEB Board quite apart from being asked to manage the MERG process.

the post-apartheid record of 'conversion' is not one that was explicitly targeted and, to put it mildly, subject to all of the negative aspects of post-apartheid malfunctions more generally.

Another major influence on the piece, unsurprisingly even in the early 1990s, was thinking around the MEC. This had two aspects. One was to see South Africa's armaments and 'defence' activity more generally as belonging part and parcel to the MEC (think SASOL, nuclear power, roads for military vehicles, and beyond to the geography of apartheid itself). The other was analytical. Having felt obliged to characterise South Africa as MEC, I had thoroughly reviewed literature on the MIC, military-industrial complex, especially associated with the USA (alongside other postures suggesting the stability of capitalism depended upon militarism in general and armaments expenditure in particular). Despite my antipathy to the notion of MIC, discouraging use of the MEC for South Africa by acronym association and more, the MIC served as a sort of default test for the legitimacy of the MEC in methodological, conceptual, theoretical and empirical terms. Why should MEC but not MIC be legitimate? As a result, I was fully familiar with the MIC literature.

More specifically, the MEC posture had been used to explain why South Africa had undertaken a particular trajectory in its technological capabilities (dovetailing with its economic trajectory). In particular, it was extremely weak in the production of capital equipment for intermediate and consumption goods as opposed to capacities around minerals and energy (high voltage transmission for example) and, as another exception to prove the MEC rule, those associated with 'defence' with field phones, for example, to the fore. This put me in engagement with the National System of Innovation (NSI) literature, drawing upon its broad compass of factors (and its evolutionary framework antipathetic to mainstream economics and equilibrium) but observing the lack of political determinants. It is impossible to have understood South Africa's NSI without regard to apartheid (and its implications for what is produced and consumed by whom, and how its economic and social reproduction is guaranteed, or not).

As a result, I did publish a piece on the NSI literature drawing upon South Africa as an example (Fine, 1993a). And I also wrote up my thoughts on the notion of MIC (Fine, 1993b). For the latter, in general, I benefitted by having been and being in an environment steeped in the study of 'defence', especially around Ron Smith, his collaborators, such as Dan Smith and Paul Dunne, and his research students such as Tony Humm and George Georgiou. More immediately, much of my research was able to be undertaken rapidly within the officies of the Anti-Apartheid Movement in London, with its collections of materials understandably covering the apartheid regime's production and use of force.

Last, and by no means least, my organising motivation for framing the Chapter was to see part of the post-apartheid dividend as deriving from conversion in the specific context of economic and social reconstruction along the lines of the UK post-war Labour Government. Hence my appeal, in section 6 below, for *From War on the People to the War Effort to Provide Basic Needs*. All observed in the breach but hope springs eternal.

Summary of Conclusions and Recommendations

- Economic analysis of military spending in the Third World has led to a number of hypotheses concerning its economic advantages and disadvantages. Applying these in detail to the South African economy leads to the conclusion that the disadvantages totally outweigh the advantages and the latter are practically non-existent and could be better obtained through more direct methods rather than by negligible spin-offs from military to civil production.
- The use of the military to engage in a war against the majority of the people of South (and southern) Africa must be transformed into a 'war effort' to provide basic needs for the mass of the people. In this, the ethos of eradicating the effects of apartheid must replace the latter's current dominance over much of the institutional and ideological organisation of South Africa, and this will prove a material force for economic and social change.
- Conversion from military to civil production is gaining increasing attention around the world. This will provide a growing pool of economic and technical research which can be used in South Africa in dismantling the apartheid armed forces and its equipment and redeploying the freed resources to meet basic needs. Research needs to be initiated to keep up with the latest developments and their relevance for South Africa.
- Reductions in military expenditure will, as a result of its high-capital intensity, lead to significant opportunities for employment and income growth in the more labour-intensive goods and services meeting basic needs and for extension of infrastructure to the mass of the population.
- In order to bring about successful conversion, extensive and detailed state intervention will be necessary to provide for new orientations in marketing, technology, management and product development. Particular emphasis should be given to serving agriculture and rural industrialisation, as these are current priorities and have suffered from the urban and industrial biases that are consolidated by military procurement.

- Privatisation of military procurement must cease as this leads to potential closure and to loss of productive resources.
- High technology capability (in R&D, capital goods manufacture and work skills) and infrastructural services are heavily concentrated in military procurement and the Minerals-Energy Complex. Their wider role and transformation must be incorporated into any plans for conversion and may serve both to support the economic needs of the mass of the people as well as to focus selectively on high grade products and export opportunities.
- A policy of developing arms exports must cease together with an end to continuing and newly proposed major military products.
- Conscription other than possibly for community, technical and professional service for the nation should be suspended, thereby releasing much skilled labour for civil employment. Militarisation through cadet training in schools must cease as must big business support for the military through charitable donations.
- Major products designed for security purposes such as SASOL, Koeberg and Mossgas must be reassessed.
- Research links between the military and the universities must be suspended together with the publication and propaganda role of the military.
- Sufficient information must be made available on military procurement so that alternative economic policies can be formulated.
- South Africa has inflicted appalling economic losses on the southern African region (estimated at $4 billion for Angola alone, for example). Demilitarisation must be accompanied by regional cooperation, coordination and development with a concerted effort on the part of South Africa to correct the imbalances created by its economic and military aggression.

1 Military Expenditure and Economic Development[3]

There has in the past been a neglect of the study of the relationship between military expenditure and economic development. Studies of the latter abound more recently with the use of variables such as GDP per capita, the share of

3 In the original draft, there were some references not cited in the text. These were Anon (n.d), Cawthra (1986), Cock (1989), Costello, Michie and Milne (1989), Dunne and Smith (1990), GLC (1985b), Landgren (1989), Matthews, R. (1989), McWilliams (1989), Michie (1990), Quigley (1989) and Simpson (1989). They are listed here to indicate literature consulted, and possibly intended to be cited. But see also Preamble.

government expenditure, the dual economy, etc but these have not tended to cut across and isolate the specific role of military expenditure, even though it forms a, if not the, major part of what is conceived to be development aid in many cases. Fortunately, this situation has begun to change from the mid-seventies onwards. With the collapse of assured growth following the end of the post-war boom, interest has been aroused in why growth rates differ between different countries. The relatively poor growth performance of those with high levels of military expenditure such as the United States and Britain – experiencing catch-up and being overtaken by competitors – stands in sharp contrast to those with low levels of military expenditure such as West Germany and Japan. Subsequently, the relationship between military expenditure and economic development has been explored in the more general context of the Third World.

In an extremely useful book, Ball (1989) summarises what has been learnt theoretically and empirically from what is now a wide range of studies of the relationship between military expenditure and economic performance. Her conclusions are reproduced in full with some explanatory notes in brackets [], p. 389:

The potential positive effects of security expenditure (are):

- improvement of the government's tax-collection effort [through acceptance of security effort]
- expansion of aggregate demand
- creation of dual-purpose infrastructure
- substitution of security assistance [ie foreign aid] for domestic financing, increasing the resources available to the civil sector
- stimulation of certain industrial sectors
- limited manpower training

The potential negative effects identified included:

- curtailment of some kinds of public investment
- reduction of expenditure in the social sector (for instance, education and health)
- contribution to trade imbalances
- reduction of foreign exchange available to the civil sector
- increase in indebtedness
- aggravation of inflationary tendencies
- exacerbation of biases against rural development
- transfer of inappropriate technology
- use of economic aid to support the security sector
- withdrawal of technically skilled manpower from the civil sector
- distortion of R&D effort.

In addition, Ball argues very cogently for the contingent applicability of these conclusions – that their presence or not is highly dependent upon the specific character of an individual country under consideration. They are not universal laws. Moreover, any empirical conclusions are hedged by the quality of the data available.

2 Is South Africa a Military-Industrial Complex?

How relevant are these conclusions to the study of the South African economy? Consider, first, whether they should be assessed in the framework of South Africa seen as (containing) a military-industrial complex, as in Frankel (1984), Grundy (1988) and Matthews (1988) for example. Two particular factors need to be borne in mind in the application of the term to South Africa. The first is the presence of the major blocs of capital which lie outside or, at most, on the fringes of any identifiable complex elite (containing the military). This is what has been termed the Minerals-Energy Complex in other EROSA papers. Based on mining, electricity, transport, etc and the close relations between highly concentrated monopoly capital (as in Anglo-American) and state enterprises (such as ESKOM, SATS, ISCOR, etc), this core section of the South African economy (and also with its ownership and control across finance and other sectors) is much more influential than any fusion between industry and military. This is not to say the Minerals-Energy Complex is independent of the military – nonsensical given the migrant labour system and oppression more generally – nor that it does not itself engage in military production and interchange of personnel with ARMSCOR and government agencies. Rather that it borders on the ludicrous to suggest that, for example, the world's major gold producer and the world's most electricity-intensive economy should have been a product of the decision-making of an equal partnership between military and industry. The military has attempted to guarantee the security of industry but it has not determined its primary direction.

Second, whilst this is often left aside in many accounts of the complex, the presence of apartheid has meant that any identifiable complex has been totally incapable of wedding the majority of the population to its project of militarisation and hence incapable ultimately of undermining 'civilian' checks and balances to its power as is required by the theory of the military-industrial complex. The apartheid regime has, of course, attempted to win the white population to this ideology but, as evidenced by the current crisis and the long-standing struggle against racist and oppressive government, there has not been and could not be any serious attempt, let alone success, in incorporating the non-white population to such goals (although South Africa has been of strategic military importance to foreign powers). Increasingly, sections of the white population and the international community are opposing the South African apartheid project.

Thus, any discussion of the economic role of the military, whether seen in the context of a more general military-industrial complex or not, must recognise, first, that it co-exists primarily with a minerals-energy not a broad manufacturing complex; second, that any economic spin-off effects from the military (whether positive or negative) have to be seen in the context of majority hostility to the military itself, a significant economic factor, even if difficult to quantify in its strength and implications.

This serves as a useful starting point for adopting the fruitful approach suggested by examining in practice for South Africa the conclusions of Ball reproduced above. For her, propositions on the effects of military expenditure can be set against the specific features of the South African economy and society. Before doing this, however, a number of reservations are in order. First, it has been implicitly assumed that South Africa is a third world country; indeed, Ball conforms with this view in constructing a table that shows the shares of military in government expenditure. This is not the place to enter the debate on whether South Africa is or is not part of the Third World (with ideologues wishing to claim that it is when stressing the problems to be confronted and denying it when wishing to point to developmental success). Rather such categorisations in the context of the effects of military expenditure are hopelessly inadequate in the case of South Africa. For, inevitably they lead to the use of aggregate or average statistics (such as share in government expenditure) which conceal the basic parameters of the economy and society – that such expenditure, as marked in health, education, etc is heavily skewed in its use for the imperatives of apartheid, and from which only a minority of the population gain any service in the form of 'national security'.

A second problem is the availability of information. Under the National Supplies Procurement Act of 1970, it is illegal to reveal:

> any information in relation to the acquisition, supply, marketing, import, export, development, manufacture, maintenance or repair of, or research in connection with armaments.

This, together with similar proscriptions on information concerning oil supplies and the wish to evade discovery of breach of the arms embargo, means that it is difficult to assess the current economic linkages supporting and depending upon military provision, let alone assess the options in a post-apartheid society.

Third, discussion of the role of military expenditure has been almost exclusively oriented around the issue of the effect of armament embargoes (along with the economic cost imposed by the apartheid regime on the southern African region). To what extent has this undermined the ability of South Africa to obtain the arms, technology and components that it requires? What have been the economic costs of the embargo? Has it unwittingly led to the creation of a particularly strong and indigenous armaments industry? These issues have been highly contested. Paradoxically, those that oppose sanctions have generally adopted the view of ineffectivity in that the arms embargoes have had the perverse effect of strengthening the productive capacity of the arms industry and hence of the economy, whilst also claiming that more general sanctions are only effective by harming the economy and the non-white population and hence are undesirable. Here there is a clear problem of logical consistency in moving from cause to effect across the two arguments. Whilst, however, much information has been learnt about armaments provision as a result of these debates, it has not been predominantly concerned with economic effects and prospects. Although technical and other linkages have often been prominent in discussion, their overall impact has been difficult to assess.

There is, however, an important positive factor in analysing the (potential) economic role of resources previously devoted to military expenditure. This is the attention that has increasingly been given over the past fifteen years or so to the problems of conversion – that is of mobilising for civil purposes the resources that could be released from military expenditure. This will be taken up later.

3 South Africa's Economic Impasse[4]

Before assessing the role that economic resources currently devoted to military expenditure could play in a post-apartheid South Africa, it is first necessary to take a view of the economy's current problems and how they are related to military expenditure. The concern here will be primarily with economic problems in a narrow technical sense without wishing to imply that other factors – such as the role of trade unions, internal and regional conflict, urbanisation, rural decline and international pressures, etc – are either non-economic or irrelevant, secondary or independent of those factors that are considered.

---

4 The term, "economic impasse", was coined by Laurence Harris as leading member of EROSA.

The South African economy is recognised to be in a structural crisis by a wide variety of authors although the exact causal parameters are a matter of dispute. The symptoms of crisis are, however, clear enough to all. There has been an inability to generate sustained growth over the 1980s so that unemployment has grown along with population, and there have even been periods of negative growth in the level of net investment. This is in part due to foreign disinvestment (although South African corporations have also sought to locate investment funds abroad), the inability to raise foreign capital – especially following the debt squeeze – and the increasing domestic costs of seeking internal security and stability whether through 'reform' or repression.

The inability to sustain growth is associated with at least one major linkage. South Africa has an extremely poor capacity in the capital-goods sector. Consequently, any period of growth leads to the need to import capital goods so that productive capacity can expand. This is much more important than the effect of increasing imports through direct consumption out of higher incomes. As a result, increasing capital imports to sustain a period of expansion leads in the short term to deterioration in the balance of trade as the imports are needed as inputs prior to the production and sale of any exports. Usually, such short-term trade deficits could be covered by borrowing until growth (of exports and foreign exchange earnings) provides for a positive rate of return with which to repay the debt or interest upon it. Clearly, such borrowing facilities are not generally open to the South African economy and, even if they were, other aspects of the crisis of apartheid bring into question the ability to generate a (foreign exchange) surplus. In short, the technical dependence of the economy on capital imports renders growth unsustainable, even where an economic surplus could in principle be generated, because of the restrictions on access to foreign borrowing (the need for which is intensified by capital outflows).

It is crucial to recognise, however, that this problem is not universal across the economy as a whole. Mining, in particular, especially gold, has developed its own capital goods sector. Not only does gold earn 40% of export earnings (with coal a further 20%), it is predominantly self-sufficient for inputs, only having a 5% import dependence (of what may, nevertheless, be strategically important inputs). With the increase in the price of gold and coal in the 1970s, the economy was able to enjoy a period of limited expansion but this was predominantly based upon the earnings of the Minerals-Energy Complex and served to conceal the extent of the weakness of the manufacturing base, particularly in the harsher global competitive climate for manufacturing exports.

4 South African Military Expenditure – Any Advantages?

Against this economic background, what economic role has been played by military procurement in easing or intensifying the identified constraints? Consider the factors put forward by Ball and listed above. First the potential advantages.

- It may well be that the burden imposed by a military budget, and the ideological justifications associated with it, has made the collection of taxes easier. But this can only be so for the 'sacrifices' made by the tax-paying population, predominantly whites; this can do little to resolve the impediments to growth insofar as the rationale of the apartheid economy is to privilege whites. Moreover, a major part of taxation is potentially payable by the corporate sector and it is extremely unlikely to forego substantial profits willingly to bolster the apartheid regime except to the extent that it is forced to do so. Then, the sustainability of private capital is itself brought into question as profitability is eroded by taxation.
- The idea that aggregate demand is expanded by military procurement and hence occupies otherwise idle resources has long been one current within Marxist economics and has become more widely appealing in the context of Keynesian analysis of deficient aggregate demand. Its applicability in general has been strongly disputed on theoretical and empirical grounds (with higher military expenditure associated with poorer economic performance through crowding out of investment) and its relevance for the South African economy is even more dubious. For, has military expenditure made up for deficiencies in overall demand in the rest of the economy? Apart from the contrary evidence provided by high levels of inflation, the experience of the South African economy over the past two decades has been one of extraordinary growth in demand through expanding expenditure in the public sector for which military expenditure has hardly been a necessary adjunct. Thus, for example, the state sector accounted for almost two-thirds of the total level of investment in the economy over the period from 1974 to 1989, much of this in state-owned industries such as ESKOM. Indeed, as the crisis has bitten deeper, this level of state investment has been seen as a source of economic strain and there has been retrenchment in public investment as in the postponement of capital projects. Thus, it is far from clear that the military has provided expenditure opportunities in the absence of alternatives.
- There is no doubt that the military has been a source of some infrastructural development. But its creation of favourable economic linkages must

be doubted given its major role in oppressing the majority of the population rather than in providing the public utilities through which smaller-scale businesses and more general economic activity such as transport, distribution and marketing could prosper. South Africa is notably peculiar in the extent to which it has not only a highly skewed distribution of income, but also a corresponding absence of a developed informal and small-scale sector. Far from adding to the infrastructure available to the vast majority of the population, the military's role in supporting apartheid has been to undermine its emergence and growth. On the other hand, there probably has been some contribution to infrastructure serving the minority and big business, but the net direction of support probably runs in the opposite direction with infrastructure such as the highly sophisticated systems of transport, electricity and telecommunications serving the Minerals-Energy Complex, industry, finance and agriculture being overburdened by the costly support required to meet specialised military needs.

– It is irrelevant to suggest that aid has been made available for military expenditure and that this has released resources that would otherwise have been taken at the expense of the civilian sector.
– The idea that military procurement has initiated and strengthened certain sectors is possibly the most appealing argument in favour of military expenditure in South Africa in terms of generating some positive economic impact. This could work through a number of mechanisms. First, military procurement might create in conjunction with non-military needs a sufficient level of demand that a domestic industry for the products concerned could be created. With a few exceptions, this seems highly unlikely. The overall level of domestic demand for the vast majority of industrial products is either sufficient in itself to support manufacture – possibly with trade protection – or, as is more generally recognised, with limited purchasing power for the majority of the population and trade restrictions through sanctions, domestic markets for many products are too limited relative to scale economies even with the addition of military procurement.

Indeed, second, influence may run in the opposite direction, with secure markets for the military leading to subsequent provision for the broader domestic market. Here it is much more likely that the costs of providing for the military are still not covered by the extra demand from the non-military. In some cases, such as the benefication of minerals and the development of special alloys, the continuing exhortation of the mineral sector to make further progress suggests that spin-off from the military has not been extensive.

Third, there is the argument that military procurement runs from serving the domestic market to the generation of exports. The extent of armaments exports by South Africa remains disputed although some put it as high as R1.8 billion in 1987. Another estimate suggests R2 billion over the past thirteen years. On a rough calculation, this is equivalent, leaving aside the import cost effects of inputs on the balance of payments, to the price of gold having been $8 per ounce higher in price on average over the entire period. During this time, the price of gold fluctuated between $35 and $900 per ounce and had an average price somewhere between $300 and $400. This puts the export impact of armaments into perspective – at most at 2% of gold's contribution, small compared to the changes occurring simply through the volatility of the gold price.

But perhaps more important in denying the demand effects of spin-off from the military either for arms or related sectors is the evidence of selective current defence cuts on the fortunes of the supplier industries. There has been retrenchment and rationalisation of both ARMSCOR subsidiaries and private contractors suggesting that demand for their products, whether on domestic or export markets, is far from buoyant.

Fourth, there is the idea that military procurement stimulates the economy through technology transfer and development. More generally, there is increasing doubts about the extent to which the military is a source of technical spin-off with most developments, for example, in electronics with civilian applications being developed within the civil sector. In order to assess this any further, it is necessary to examine in empirical detail both the extent to which technical capacity *within* arms production has been developed and the extent to which it passes such capacity *onto* other sectors. In fact, both of these processes seem to be extremely limited as is indicated by the attached text[5] in which add-up engineering is estimated to be the exception and the more important indigenous design and production remains an exception and is essentially confined to small arms (and all of these engineering capabilities are attuned to aircraft, armoured vehicles, missiles and small arms, each of which has limited application to the civilian sector). Moreover, each of these modes of technological up-grading is liable to absorb vast quantities of resources when of significant application even if confined to the military sector, and particularly in aircraft manufacture.

- It is claimed that the military, through conscription or the professional force, can give rise to higher levels of discipline and literacy, etc and to the creation of more specific skills in engineering, etc. In the case of South Africa, it seems most likely that the conscript army of white males at an age of peak

5 Not included nor even identified in retrospect!

employment will have acted as a significant drain on the (skilled) labour available to the economy despite high levels of unemployment amongst non-whites and also that the military will command more skilled personnel in its permanent force than it creates itself. Whether the non-white personnel in the armed forces rejoin the civil labour market with enhanced employee attributes that are not already available is a moot point. There seems no particular reason for South Africa to depart from Ball's (1988, p. 330) conclusion:

> In general, one must conclude that the claims made for the armed forces as a source of technical and administrative training in the Third World have been overly optimistic.

In addition, such skills as are obtained are often unduly dependent, as a consequence of their military origin, upon hierarchical forms of control, lack of initiative and flexibility, and geared towards unduly high standards of technical proficiency (fail-safe syndrome).

In assessing the potential advantages of military procurement, it must be borne in mind that those few that have been positively identified are not necessarily best pursued through the military. You do not have to burn your house down to keep warm, beneficial side-effect though it may, temporarily, be. Thus, whether concern is with demand, infrastructure, civil spin-off or employee training, it is not necessarily optimal to pursue these through the indirect method of promoting the military. As Ball concludes for training, p. 332:

> Although the civil economy does undoubtedly benefit to some extent from military training, it is always less expensive and more efficient to train people directly for jobs in the civil sector. The purpose of the military training should always be to promote the effective functioning of a country's armed forces. The argument that military training can benefit the civil sector should never be used as an excuse for substituting military training for civil sector training.

And as Sen (1987, p. 45) argues for deficient demand:

> Even when aggregate production is demand-constrained (with the resource constraints being 'slack'), for example, in situations of Keynesian unemployment, the demand expanding role of defence can be taken over by more fruitful forms of public spending.

5 The Overwhelming Disadvantages

These two sorts of comments begin to point to the disadvantages of military procurement in pre-empting policies that can more positively and directly contribute to economic progress. In terms of the list above from Ball:

- Far from creating otherwise deficient demand, military expenditure appropriates resources that could otherwise be made available to develop infrastructure, for example in providing decent electricity and water for the mass of the people and in developing the transport, distribution and marketing networks which are necessary within the mixed economy for the wider spatial and regional spread of economic activity and progress.
- Military expenditure is also a drain on resources that could begin to serve the basic needs of the mass of the population in food, clothing, housing and education.
- Having identified the balance of trade as a severe constraint on the sustainability of economic growth, and whatever the level of armaments exports, the need to import technology and components to serve the armaments industry is an impediment to growth.
- The same applies in its negative effects on the availability of foreign exchange, and through increased indebtedness and inflationary pressures.
- Within development policy, there has often been a bias towards both the urban and the industrial sectors. In the context of the apartheid economy and non-white agriculture, this has reached extreme proportions and is only intensified by the growth and extent of military expenditure which has no significant linkages to the rural economy. Yet this, in the context of the question of land and survival itself, is one of the key political and economic issues of the coming period.
- Technology transfer through the military is possibly the most inappropriate for meeting the basic needs of the mass of the people. First, it tends to be of high-tech military components with built-in foreign dependency and guaranteed obsolescence. Second, there are limited spin-offs to the civil sector. Third, where these do exist, they are liable to be appropriate only to the current needs of the apartheid economy with a Minerals-Energy Complex at its core and of limited benefit in meeting those industries and technologies that can promote employment and growth around fulfilling the basic needs of the mass of the population.
- Clearly, the role of the apartheid military machine has been to deny the economy the advantages of genuine economic aid and to distort the use of precious resources in R&D and skilled labour away from more productive employment.

In short, Ball's conclusions appear to apply particularly severely to the South African economy, p. 382/3:

> It is extremely difficult for developing countries to attain the two main economic objectives of domestic arms production: the promotion of industralization and the reduction of foreign exchange outlays in the defense sector. For domestic arms production even to be contemplated, a certain industrial/manpower base must already be in place. Most developing countries do not have a sufficiently diversified industrial sector, enough qualified manpower, the necessary production equipment, or adequate supplies of special raw materials to support a military-industrial sector of any size. Because of this weak industrial base, design and production capability must be purchased from abroad, and this frequently entails substantial outlays of scarce foreign exchange. Having established arms production facilities, Third World countries often find that these cannot be operated at full capacity, further increasing costs.
>
> An additional problem is the relative lack of linkage between the civil and military-industrial sectors. The civil sector either cannot produce the necessary inputs in large enough quantity, cannot produce items of sufficient quality, or simply cannot produce the items at all. This means that Third World arms producers either must manufacture these components themselves or must rely on imports. In-house production invariably raises the cost of weapons while imports make additional demands on scarce foreign exchange resources.

So far there has been consideration of the impact of military procurement in a relatively narrow economic framework. In a more general context, it has sometimes been claimed that the military can be an agency of modernisation although this is usually employed as an argument within political theory. It is clearly fallacious for South Africa as far as the mass of the people is concerned, since the military has served as a central support of apartheid which has held millions in the southern African region in conditions of poverty and repression. Consequently, other factors need also to be taken into account, those involving the ethos dictated by the military and which goes beyond the influence of ideology and politics alone. For example, the military is intimately involved in commissioning university research and in publishing propaganda on its own behalf. Each of these activities is not only wasteful of resources in reconstructing a post-apartheid South Africa, but each also supports attitudes, behaviours, and creates institutional environments, linkages and rigidities that are liable to obstruct economic and social progress.

More generally, however strong it may be, the military imperative tends, first, to dictate a logic of its own in terms of the choice of, and commitment to, particular projects and then, second, for these to become cemented in place over and beyond any meaningful economic rationale. As Ball (1988, p. 357) concludes:

> No one, not even the most ardent supporter of defense industries, would deny that the industrialisation process would be better served by investing directly in the civil sector. When it comes to making a calculation of the relative costs and benefits of defense industrialisation, however, the political and military justifications weigh heavily in the balance, and even though the economic costs alone might seem quite high, governments are loathe to abandon their defense-industrial sectors.

For example, in the UK there has been a continuing commitment to nuclear power derived initially from weaponry requirements and then from the pressure emerging from indigenous research interests before residing in the hands of the power stations suppliers. In France, source of the Koeberg reactor, the situation has been even more sharp, commonly parodied as involving a (nuclear) state within a state.

For South Africa, similarly expensive projects such as SASOL, Koeberg and Mossgas have been developed in the interests of security. They have absorbed enormous capital resources and skilled personnel. In the case of SASOL, for example, one recent estimate places its cost of producing petrol at £2.20 per gallon compared with a world price equivalent to £.70 per gallon (and a production cost of about £1.00 per gallon for liquefaction of coal from a new plant in North Wales). For a post-apartheid economy an assessment will have to be made of the continuing commercial viability and use of such projects.

6 From War on the People to the War Effort to Provide Basic Needs

An assessment has been made some of the ways in which military procurement has held back and distorted development in South Africa. In a calculus of advantage and disadvantage the one is overwhelmingly outweighed by the other. This might suggest that the productive capacity associated with military procurement is liable to be of even more limited value in a post-apartheid society seeking to serve non-military needs rather than those derived from the oppression of the majority by the minority.

This would be a serious mistake. The resources associated with the military have an enormous potential in the provision of basic needs, whether directly, or indirectly through the ability to generate high quality goods that can earn foreign exchange or enhance civil industrial production. Whilst it has been argued that the economic and other linkages between the military and industry (and society more generally) have been both damaging and a reinforcing support to the skewed and stagnant apartheid economy, these linkages can be positively transformed by the realisation of new goals and methods both for military and civil production and for the relation between the two.

For, whilst military procurement has been associated with an ethos of what might be termed a war against the people, the general and detailed military aspects of this must be dismantled as part of a negotiated settlement. But exactly the same applies to economic aspects. At the general level, the war against the people must be transformed into a war for the provision of basic needs. This is not merely some polemical device nor an ideological imperative. In times of war, with the support of the majority of the population, not only are great sacrifices often made, but also there is a commitment to eliminating profiteering on the one hand, and poverty on the other. The war effort to meet basic needs must command the fullest support – just as, for example, measures such as works canteens, nurseries, rent controls, and price controls and rationing of basic consumer goods were adopted in the UK during the second world war and, with such a level of popularity, that a reforming Labour Government was elected after the war to sweep the welfare state into place.

At a lower level of detail, immediate measures that might be taken include the suspension of conscription (other than for community, technical or professional service if considered desirable), the suspension of research links between universities and the military, and the suspension of publicity by the military other than that agreed by negotiation. The training of military cadets in schools must cease (estimated at 170,000 in 1983). Nor should 'charitable' donations to military by big business be permitted (targeted at R1 million per annum). In short, there is an old ethos to be rooted out and destroyed, and a new one to be created in the economic and social planes as well as in the military arena. Otherwise, war by other means will persist rather than peaceful commitment to eradicating poverty and oppression. After all, it must be recognised that the military does do all that is required to meet basic needs – it procures food, transport, clothing and shelter but also employs sophisticated means of destruction and oppression rather than of production and liberation.

7 Conversion at the Macro Level

This is all very well at the humane level of generalities but how is it to be implemented in practice? First, research is now advanced around the world in examining the effects of reduced military expenditure. Previously, it has been a response to the increasing capital intensity of military production so that even increasing levels of military expenditure have led to reductions in employment as more sophisticated hardware has been associated with fewer jobs to manufacture or assemble it. Consequently, there has been a need to find ways of redeploying to civil production those workers and facilities that have been lost to military production.

On the other hand, recent changes in the super-power relations have also reinforced interest in the conversion of military to civil production in view of the prospect of a more stable detente and apparent commitments to reduce arms expenditure. In response, initiatives are being taken such as planned research at the University of California, sponsored by its congressional delegation, into the effect of defence cuts on the state's economy, and Daimler-Benz has set up an Arms Conversion Unit at its military aerospace subsidiary. Further, a study of the UK, for example, has found that a cut in defence expenditure to fifty percent of its current level by the year 2000 would lead to a higher growth rate by 1.5 percent per annum and a fall in unemployment of 376,000, given a compensating increase in government spending across other expenditure programmes.

These increases in employment result from the higher capital-intensity of defence expenditure and through the macroeconomic effects working via a relaxed constraint on the balance of payments and increased levels of investment. As Ball (1988, p. 163) reports:

> Recent econometric research suggests that security expenditure has a negative effect on economic growth in developing countries, either because security spending competes with investment … or because it dampens the savings rate.

A similar exercise for South Africa would arguably give rise to much greater proportional effects as a result of relaxation on borrowing requirements and the trade deficit if defence expenditure were cut. These effects would be immediate and the employment linkages from the more labour-intensive provision of basic needs would be that much greater because of their even lower call upon capital in South Africa relative to the UK, given the closer levels of capital-labour intensity for military procurement.

Such macroeconomic effects can be calculated on the basis of different scenarios according to the macroeconomic model employed, the rate of decrease of military expenditure adopted and, in practice, depending upon the availability of the necessary data to make the calculations. In the war effort to provide basic needs, there can be no monopoly of information which, after the monopoly of property and state violence, is perhaps the most important lever of oppression. Release of information and access to data appropriate for economic forecasting and policymaking must be negotiated. Sensitivity over past deeds and present security arrangements must be rejected as reasons for lack of access to the basic materials necessary to formulate a negotiating position, let alone to formulate and implement policy. This applies equally to more detailed information at company and sectoral level and to strategic information concerning technology, etc.

8 Conversion at the Micro Level

Whilst such macroeconomic exercises are important, they are limited by two factors. First, the structural relations of any model based on past performance will be inappropriate and potentially pessimistic when utilised to represent the economic possibilities released by the abolition of apartheid. Second, and a related point, large shifts out of military expenditure are themselves comparable to a structural (model) shift in the workings of the economy. If defence expenditure is replaced by other categories of government expenditure, the forecast results will presume that the productive capacity of the one is harmoniously realised in the expenditure on the other.

This is the classic swords to ploughshares syndrome. Evidence of unemployment following armaments retrenchment suggests that the creation of alternative, let alone increased, employment is far from automatic. How can it be guaranteed that the decline in military procurement is more than matched by growth in the civil sector? Again, the issue of conversion has received a growing level of attention in recent years, often at the level of the firm, plant or locality affected, and new technology appears to make transitions easier and fuller in choice. The general conclusion is that such transitions, and even ones resulting from increasing capital-intensity of arms production in the absence of overall cuts in defence spending, cannot be left to market forces. This is not, as some might expect, because conversion requires state aid to bring about enormous technological leaps to enable factories producing fighter aircraft to change to production of kidney machines. In general, the problem of conversion is not technical in the sense of equipment, process or product. Rather the problem is in making the economic and social adjustment to the environment of civil as opposed to military production – in creating new methods of marketing, management, etc. Most of the components used for military production are potentially of use in civil production.

An early example was provided by the Lucas Aerospace combined Shops Stewards Committee in 1976. As Didsbury (1989, p. 38/9) reports:

> Ideas for alternative products were invited from the workforce, leading to 150 proposals in five main areas: transport, renewable energy sources, oceanics, remote control systems (telechirics) and medical equipment.

And success was achieved at Marconi Instruments in Fife, p. 41:

> A switch was effected from military simulation trainers to training equipment for train drivers and expert equipment for the treatment of asthma.

The obstacles to civil production often arise out of the industrial structure of military production. This tends to be bimodal in size distribution, a few very large companies sometimes with diversified production into civil markets; and a larger number of smaller companies whose contracting or subcontracting forms their main area of activity and upon which they become reliant. Generally, military production is highly profitable with certain profitability and is based upon poor levels of scrutiny and full cost mark-up. For the large companies, a military division may have linkages with other divisions geared to civil production. But there then tends to be a subsidy running from the military to the civil production. As and when military production is reduced, there is a negative knock-on effect to civil production where it exists and which becomes unprofitable and contracted rather than expanding to compensate for the lost military orders. For the smaller companies, more likely to suffer the effects of retrenchment in practice, similar effects lead to closure.

In the case of South Africa, many of these features are reproduced. The state-owned ARMSCOR has nine major subsidiary and employs more than 20,000 workers to produce arms. But the private sector is responsible for as much as 70% of defence production. ARMSCOR subcontracts to more than 1000 private companies (and total defence-related employment is claimed to be connected to 100,000 jobs in total). Of these companies, 400 would not be able to exist without defence orders. A small number of the companies involved, and major suppliers, are part of the conglomerate industrial structure and/or effectively affiliates of multinationals.

What are the alternative ways of handling decreases in military expenditure? First, the state must supply the necessary market demand for alternative products for the firms concerned to tide over an adjustment period and to allow marketing, management and design, etc to be developed. Second, technical and managerial support is required at an enterprise level to provide for this. Third, and especially but not exclusively for the larger enterprises, strategic emphasis must be placed on meeting basic needs. Infrastructure can be developed, as part of a broader economic strategy, in line with the contribution by both the military and the corporations. To give a simple example, much of the coal now produced by SASOL could be redeployed to meet some of the fuel requirements of the mass of the population. But this would require a distribution and marketing network to be set up for which, for example, the conversion of armed vehicle to coal truck production would be important. In this way a more economic return to the project to produce diesel engines indigenously may be obtained – its having been targeted to be 80% strategic and 20% economic but described as 111% strategic and minus 20% economic.

More generally, it will be necessary to formulate a whole series of enterprise, sectoral and strategic plans for the conversion of military to civil production in coordination with the wider transitional use of basic productive resources. This may include coordination of skills, R&D and capability in capital goods manufacture across military and civil production for, as has been suggested, within the military and the core of the Minerals-Energy Complex are to be found the most successful examples of manufacture and lack of technological dependency. All of these arguments point to the need for substantial state economic intervention, and possibly ownership. Accordingly, privatisation of military procurement should cease immediately as this tends to expose productive resources to closure rather than to conversion. Considerable emphasis should be given to developing appropriate technology and products to aid small-scale farming and rural industrial development.

Some conversion projects will involve production and processes that are not designed immediately and directly to serve basic needs but which can do so indirectly or in conjunction with provision for high quality export markets and a narrower segment of the domestic market. In telecommunications, for example, SAPO has high capability, a stagnant domestic market serving predominantly saturated white demand, and a highly concentrated structure of equipment supply subservient to the affiliates of multinationals enjoying high levels of profitability and almost entirely exhausting the domestic electronics industry. This situation could be transformed, for example, in view of the military's highly sophisticated development of field telephones that could be adopted for use across South Africa until more permanent cabling infrastructure is installed. More generally, a post-apartheid government could negotiate improved deals and joint ventures with an increasing variety of foreign firms, thereby drawing upon and extending its current strengths in telecommunications whilst diversifying into broader selected areas of electronics.

Similar considerations do not apply to a continuation and development of the production of arms for export. Given the stockpile of arms available following the end of repressive measures, South Africa will be in the fortunate position of not being dependent upon military aid from donor countries, this being a source of political, technological and economic dependence, and of domestic elites, over time. It is extremely unlikely in a post-apartheid context that development of armaments for export could show a net economic benefit, given high competitivity, rapid technological change and obscolescence, and import dependence. Arms standing at the top in manufacturing exports not only is an indictment of civil manufacturing performance, it also exposes the economy to uncertainty in its foreign exchange receipts. Even if, as seems unlikely, a profitable trade balance could be earnt, basic needs and limited economic linkages dictates that this avenue not be pursued. Major projects to develop and manufacture armaments must be curtailed immediately.

CHAPTER 4

Privatisation and the RDP: A Critical Assessment

Postscript as Personal Preamble[1]

This Chapter is the first of two on privatisation, separated by a few years in the mid-1990s. It is a reaction against the emergence of privatisation as a preferred policy in principle from at least some leading sections of the ANC-led government as early as 1995. It takes the incompatibility between privatisation and the RDP as its implicit starting point (despite acknowledging the dilution of the RDP) but locates privatisation in terms of the continuities in policy with, and failure to remedy, those of the outgoing apartheid regime. The later Chapter 8, drafted for COSATU, is still making reference to the RDP even in 1997 but the emphasis is much more focused upon the comprehensive case against privatisation and for public enterprise.

Unsurprisingly, in light of its association with Mrs Thatcher from the late 1970s onwards, I had long studied and combatted privatisation. I have continued to do so, not least as it has grown in breadth, depth and forms (Fine, 1989a and b, 1990a and b, 1997e, 1999a and 2020; Fine and Hall, 2012; Fine and Poletti, 1992; Bayliss and Fine, eds, 2008 and 2020; and Bayliss et al. 2016). Interestingly, whilst the role of finance appears heavily in the account, financialisation does not appear at all. Its time was yet to come, alongside its increasingly intensive and extensive attachment to privatisations (and even continuing public sector provision). We all know from where privatisation derived, in the first phase of neoliberalism and its shock therapy. It is now entrenched in the third phase of neoliberalism in which financialisation is to the fore, and the state's resources are deployed to support the private financial sector to underpin its own rewards and the private sector provision of public services – on the bizarre grounds, even in the wake of the Global Financial Crisis of 2007/8, that this is preferable to direct public provision because the private does better (with state support and subsidy to providers and their financiers).[2] Where will it end?

1 Originally published as Fine (1995a). Note exact sources for quotations, missing in the original, could not always be found and so are not always able to be given.

2 For the trajectory of neoliberalism through its three phases, see Fine (2025a).

1 Introduction

Recent proposals, particularly those emanating from Thabo Mbeki, to privatise state corporations in order to finance the Reconstruction and Development Programme (RDP), present a stark reminder of just how far ANC economic thinking appears to have shifted over the last few years.[3] Under an unprecedented ideological assault from big business and the media, initial commitments to public ownership, as derived from the Freedom Charter, first gave way to a compromise around 'the mixed economy' and 'growth through redistribution'. These terms now seem to belong to the distant past, with the RDP being diminished both in its content and in the means to implement it. It scarcely seems credible that a privatisation programme, that was substantially brought to a halt by popular and organised resistance in the late 1980s, should now be warmly embraced, so quickly, by the Government of National Unity (GNU).

The purpose here is four-fold. First, the general arguments for and against privatisation are briefly assessed in order to show how limited is the case for privatisation in terms of both the content and the scope of the factors brought into consideration. Second, the privatisation programme of the previous government is assessed in order to identify the underlying economic and political factors involved. This is done, third, in order to see how these factors have changed so that government can and does once again put forward privatisation proposals – only now, paradoxically if not perversely, with greater confidence of success. Finally, the likely impact of a privatisation programme is assessed against its supposed goals of financing and furthering a progressive social and economic reconstruction. Those less interested in the theory and the past might simply jump to this last substantive section, which is intended to stand alone even if at the expense of a little repetition from the earlier sections.

2 Some Theoretical Considerations

Privatisation involves a range of different policies, each potentially implemented in different ways. First, however, it is worth distinguishing between privatisation and deregulation (or liberalisation) of the economy. Privatisation involves the selling-off of state-owned assets to the private sector or the withdrawal of the state from certain areas of economic activity to allow the private sector to take them over. Typical examples might be the selling of shares

3 See Fine (1995b) for a recent discussion.

in a state-owned company, or the company as a whole, or the ending or scaling back of state provision of services such as education, health or cleaning and catering.

In each case, conditions concerning the ability of the state and private enterprise to engage in economic activity will have been transformed. But this can also be brought about independently of privatisation, as in deregulation. Thus, even if Eskom, for example, is not sold off, statutory or other obstacles to the private generation of electricity might be weakened. On the other hand, once privatised, Eskom's near monopoly in electricity supply might be preserved for the private sector. In the first case, there is deregulation without privatisation and, in the second, privatisation without deregulation.

The primary concern here is with privatisation of large-scale, state-owned enterprises and not with deregulation nor with other forms of privatisation. This is not because the latter are unimportant. Deregulation of transport, for example, is on the agenda and should be considered in conjunction with the potential splitting-off for privatisation of some of the assets and activities of SATS, in part prepared through its reorganisation as Transnet. Similarly, the privatisation of health services and of education is of enormous economic, political and social significance.[4]

However, the theme that connects these various activities together, of expanding the private sector at the expense of the public sector, is almost certainly less significant than the differences in the activities concerned and the differing economic and political conditions that more generally determine their roles and outcomes. Consequently, to include all areas of privatisation and deregulation together would tend to force extremely diverse areas of activity into a superficial and erroneous uniformity. Nevertheless, the analysis that is offered here may have implications at a general level for those concerned with specific instances of privatisation and deregulation that are not encompassed by the sale of large-scale state-owned enterprises.

As privatisation has come to the fore over the past decade, so it has been complemented by a newly-emerged economics literature. This falls into two parts. The first, what Fine (1990a and b) has dubbed the new synthesis, argues that ownership as such does not matter. What is more important than whether an enterprise or sector is in public or private hands are the conditions governing its competition and regulation. Irrespective of the validity of this proposition, the way in which it is justified is open to criticism. For it depends upon a sequence of erroneous or dubious propositions that impede a fuller

4 See the discussion in MERG (1993).

understanding of the role and determinants of public sector economic activity and its relationship to the private sector.

In particular, it requires that: the more firms there are, the more competitive and efficient is the sector; industrial economics is primarily confined to the consequences of optimising behaviour according to the conditions governing supply and demand, thereby leaving aside the role of institutions, structures and collective or other forms of behaviour; uncompetitive industries can easily be divided into natural or artificial monopolies according to the presence or not, respectively, of economies of scale; the act of ownership is essentially a residual claim to revenue after all costs have been covered, rather than a fierce contest to guarantee profitability that ranges over a complex variety of economic and political conditions; analysis can be focused upon static conditions concerning resource allocation rather than the dynamic creation of comparative advantage; the case for state intervention arises out of market failure where the potential failure of the state would be less damaging; other instruments of government policy, whether at the macro- or micro-levels, can be presumed to have guaranteed full employment, equitable distribution, optimal growth rate, etc; the economy can be considered in isolation from the broader factors associated with the exercise of economic and political power; and, finally, industrial policy should be made up of competition policy (ease of entry and exit) directed at artificial monopolies and regulation (of prices) for natural monopolies – rather than considering a fuller range of measures to promote successful industrialisation.

The second approach to the issue of privatisation addresses it more in terms of informational issues, thereby often seeking to complement the other approach by suggesting this is where ownership does matter, and that private is superior to state ownership in this respect. This is supposedly so because of principal-agent problems – that, if the private sector is to be regulated for goals other than its own, who is to monitor the regulator? – and, in the absence of perfect and symmetrical information for all, private agents will know better what are their own interests and how to pursue them. Essentially, each of these arguments takes as axiomatic that the market and private ownership can work perfectly in the absence of informational imperfections so that, even in their presence, there is a prejudice against state intervention.[5] It has to deal with more layers of informational imperfection as well as with more layers of

5 For a thorough rebuttal of this view in the context of industrial policy more generally, see Chang (1994).

conflicting motivation, as state officials are required to act in the general, and not their own, interest.[6]

These may be seen as unduly abstract analytical considerations. They are matched by other postures that are equally far removed from reality. For, a further feature of the debate over privatisation is the common belief that the private sector has performed better than the public sector. Even by the criteria of operation of the private sector (leaving aside social goals and constraints that have governed the public sector over and above commercial considerations), this remains unproven and the evidence is mixed. There are difficulties in making comparisons of like with like, clearly the private sector sample will be biased by survival (those going bankrupt will not form part of the sample), and privatised companies are liable to have been rendered profitable or to have more than usually favourable prospects in order to guarantee the sale of shares.[7] In addition, the difference in performance between public and private sector companies *within* an economy is liable to be closer than the differences in performance between both taken together and the companies, public or private, of other countries. In other words, although not supporting the proposition that ownership as such does not matter, the difference in performance between the public and private sector will be heavily influenced by other factors than ownership alone.

In contrast to the 'synthesis', then, privatisation needs to be examined from an entirely different perspective, in which it is possible to incorporate the factors that are otherwise notably absent. The approach adopted here is to see privatisation as a different form of *intervention* by the state (and not simply its withdrawal) in promoting the restructuring and accumulation of private capital. Thus, although it is accepted that privatisation signifies a policy break with the past, it can still represent considerable continuity with what has gone before. Specifically, as has been argued for the UK, for example, privatisation has symbolised and sustained the lack of coherent, long-term industrial policy,[8] an experience in common with South Africa.[9]

---

6 For a critical assessment, see Rowthorn and Chang (1992) and Chang and Singh (1993). See also Cook and Kirkpatrick (eds) (1988).

7 For a review of the evidence on public and private sector performance, see Chang and Singh (1993).

8 In particular, in the energy sector, for example, it has signified a persistence in favouring nuclear power at the expense of the coal industry, of fuel consumption at the expense of conservation and energy efficiency in use, and of lack of coordination across sectors involved directly and indirectly in the provision and use of energy. See Fine (1989 and 1990a). See also Fine and Poletti (1992) on the privatisation of British Steel.

9 For a full discussion of the lack of coherent industrial policy in South Africa and the reasons for it, see Fine and Rustomjee (1996).

In this light, a number of different (types of) factors can be used to explain the pressures behind privatisation. First, previously developed patterns of public and private ownership across the sectors of the economy may be rendered inappropriate by changes in technology. This has been particularly so with electronics, a generic technology with the potential to forge linkages across a wide range of previously separate activities. The most notable illustration is provided by information technology in which communications (often under public ownership) and office equipment (usually under private ownership) have been forged as information technology, with data processing and transmission increasingly inseparable. More generally, whilst the redrawing of barriers between the public and private sector may be driven by technological change, the process of diversification or fragmentation across sectors, for whatever reason, may impart a pressure for privatisation.[10]

Second, privatisation may be stimulated by the presence of high levels of unemployment or other labour market conditions in an attempt to affect wage levels or other changes in working conditions without directly implicating the role of the state as employer (although the power of the state as an employer can often be more effective than the private sector in undermining wages and working conditions). This is important in the contracting-out of public services but the preparation of companies for privatisation necessarily depends upon the state as employer, with significant change often achieved *prior* to a sale to the private sector.[11]

Third, privatisation can be prompted by the presence of otherwise idle finance which can be used to purchase state assets or to engage in productive activity on a relatively short-term basis until more profitable opportunities arise (if recession gives way to boom, for example). The latter is especially characteristic of contracting out of public services which were often historically undertaken by the state or local government precisely because of the failure of the private sector to deliver.

Fourth, privatisation is a shift in ownership which may both reflect and further the exercise of economic and political power. Quite apart from the conditions under which the sale takes place (which may favour those purchasing as well as those financial capitals that arrange the sales), as indicated in the

10 Significantly, in South Africa, as previously in the UK, this has prompted the separation of postal and telecommunication services, the better to introduce 'market forces' into each.

11 The most dramatic case in the UK has been the coal industry, with employment falling over a decade from over 200,000 to a few thousand only. The same, if less severe, drop in employment occurred in the steel industry prior to privatisation. Employment levels have also tended to continue to decline following privatisation.

second point above in the context of the labour market, privatisation shifts the conditions under which capital operates and is open to economic and political conflict. Thus, there is usually popular opposition to privatisation of health services on the grounds that they are liable to be less readily available even if, in principle, redistributing compensation could be paid to treat the poor. For the capacity to guarantee provision is liable to be politically less open under private than under public provision. Similarly, privatisation of public assets removes them from some forms of political power, and is desired by large-scale capital if the state's policies are not considered secure (as was the case with the prospect of an ANC government).

Fifth, privatisation through the selling-off of assets involves a reorganisation of the state's finances which can potentially relieve pressures on the state's budget deficit in the short run – but only at the expense of long-term prospects except in the unlikely event that the privatisation itself directly or indirectly enhances the state's finances.[12] It must, however, always be borne in mind that the financial motives underlying privatisation are not simply some neutral technical exercise in macroeconomic management. Rather, it involves a particular response to the economic, political and ideological pressures upon the state, favouring some at the expense of others both in the content of policy and in the way in which it is conducted. At the end of the day, privatisation is liable to be about favouring large-scale corporate capital and its counterparts in the financial system.

3 Privatisation and the Demise of Apartheid

It is against this analytical framework that I will assess South Africa's experience of privatisation. As a potential policy measure, it rose rapidly to prominence in the mid-1980s.[13] This appears to represent a dramatic reversal of the policies adopted in the 1970s when public sector investment, especially in ESKOM, ISCOR and SASOL, proved to be the driving force behind the economy, accounting for as much as two-thirds of the country's gross investment. The economic stagnation in the 1980s was as much a consequence of the decline in public sector as private sector investment.

12 It has recently been revealed that the privatisation of British Coal entailed the government writing-off a debt of £1.6 billion, being paid back at the rate of £100 million per annum, in return for a sale price of under £1 billion!

13 For some of the South African literature at the time, see Crankshaw (1986), de Beer (1987), Hofmeyr (1988), Innes (1987), McGregor (ed.) (1987), Mahadea (1988) and du Plessis (1988).

Why was there this shift in policy and what was its impact? For some, privatisation is a policy whose time had arrived, not just in South Africa, but in a global context. It is associated with the fuller release of market forces, both in the socialist east as well as in the capitalist west, as an antidote to the over-extension of state economic intervention and expenditure. At the ideological level, the supposedly beneficial forces of the market and individual incentives are set against the presumed corrupt and inefficient bureaucracy of the state.

Casual evidence seems to support the view that privatisation is a significant if not overwhelming economic development in recent years. The most favoured example is the United Kingdom, but denationalisation has also been adopted across a wide range of other advanced countries as well as in many developing countries. This global spread of an apparently uniform policy is, however, seriously misleading. The economies of the east and west, for example, are substantially different from each other and there is no underlying economic or political force or mechanism that has yielded an apparent coincidence of economic policy. Within the west, privatisation has covered a wide range of differing economic activities and has been adopted for a variety of different reasons.

To draw a parallel between South Africa and other countries in this context then is to make a serious mistake. For its peculiar economic and social structures, encompassing the apartheid system, but also heavy state economic intervention, a peculiar industrial structure, and a high level of concentration of ownership of capital, has set it apart from other countries. In addition, the question of privatisation did not simply arise in the context of an otherwise neutral policy choice between public and private ownership, between the state and the market, it was rather a product as well as a response to the crisis of the apartheid regime itself. To some extent, it concerned the issue of how apartheid would strive to survive; it also concerned the economic, political and ideological conditions which would be confronted after the anticipated demise of the apartheid system.

As an economic measure, privatisation within South Africa had two main motives; one was to raise finance to boost government revenue, the other was to strengthen the position of corporate capital (although, as will be seen, these are not always compatible with one another) and to bolster a paralysed economy. This is not to suggest that other motives and effects were entirely absent, but they were of secondary importance – which is why the privatisation programme was relatively short-lived. In short, Harold MacMillan's accusation against Mrs. Thatcher, of selling the family silver (in her case to bribe the electorate), is a more apt description of the South African Government, as it attempted to find the funding for the survival of apartheid. As a *Standard Bank Review* (1987) put it at the time:

> Privatisation may therefore come to be seen as a very desirable method of funding increases in government expenditure with little or no pain.

In 1984, the Committee for Economic Affairs of the President's Council published a Report entitled *Measures Which Restrict the Functioning of a Free Market System in South Africa*. It did envisage a certain degree of "privatisation of government controlled undertakings" but these were mainly so that "trading activities of administration boards in their territories be undertaken progressively and as rapidly as possible". Indeed, the Report goes out of its way to list seven reasons why there *should be* state economic intervention, apart from enhancing "political stability", and is generally favourably inclined towards it despite observing the increasing share of economic activity then being undertaken and controlled by the state.

A year earlier, the Kleu Report (1983) of the Study Group on Industrial Strategy was produced. It had been set up almost six years earlier. Whilst looking for a commitment to no further expansion for state-owned production, it gave a positive sign of approval to state enterprise, "the South African Railways and Harbours, the Electricity Supply Commission and the Postal Services are examples of enterprises where government ownership can be justified on the basis of efficiency".

When the Government ultimately produced its response to the Report in a White Paper of 1985, attitudes had begun to change but not to an enormous extent except through a retrospective reading, "the State does not wish to compete with the private sector. In fact, the Government is *firmly committed* to allowing the private sector to develop its full potential and to privatising organisations in the public sector in an acceptable way with full cognisance of all hidden costs and subsidies".

By August 1987, with the publication of a White Paper, *Privatisation and Deregulation in the Republic of South Africa*, there had been a distinct change of emphasis but there were still no concrete proposals. The spirit of the White Paper was to respond to the growing size of the state sector by privatising activities where it could, and it listed a number of measures of privatisation and deregulation which had already been adopted. These were all relatively minor and predominantly concerned with localised government services. Nonetheless, there was recognised, apparently for the first time, that state-owned assets made up a potential source of revenue, to be drawn upon reluctantly – in 'apartheid-speak' – to provide for the system's survival:

> The Government also does not favour selling public sector enterprises or assets to the private sector just to obtain the non-recurring additional income from the proceeds. The Government is prepared, however, to consider the sale of assets in appropriate cases if it is convinced that this will be in the long-term interest of the Republic's inhabitants.

The White Paper was itself a response to a Discussion Paper prepared for the President's Conference in November 1986. The delay and some administrative reshuffles, together with an apparent concern in the White Paper for the interests of, and the potential obstruction by, state employees led those in favour of privatisation to be pessimistic about the Government's resolve. By February, 1988, these fears seemed to have been proved wrong. In the Budget package, sweeping measures for privatisation were announced, embracing all of the major state-owned corporations with the exception of those concerned with armaments. What had produced this rapid turnaround of policy?

The simplest explanation, paradoxically, would be that the Government had been slow to respond to policies that were both novel and had proven successful elsewhere. It is important to recognise, however, that even Mrs. Thatcher's Government had only recently turned privatisation policy into one of denationalisation. Such proposals had not been present, for example, in the Tories' 1983 election manifesto. Rather they had been embarked upon in the wake of the perceived success and popularity of (local government) council house sales and, to a lesser extent, the privatisation of local authority services.

Thus, the South African Government's privatisation plans do indeed have to be seen as a relatively rapid and dramatic break with the policy of the past – certainly in terms of the proposals themselves. This break is especially sharp in view of the crucial role that the state had recently played in the economy. It would appear to have posed in principle, if not necessarily in practice, a reduction both in state intervention in, and control over, the economy. Whilst it is normal in many countries for activities such as electricity, transport and iron and steel (if not something like the SASOL complex) to be undertaken by state enterprises, the significance of these for the South African economy is what is out of the ordinary.

It might be argued then that the change of policy came out of the mounting political pressures upon the state to moderate its economic role and the gathering support for free market ideology. This is again unsupportable. For the ideology of privatisation within the South African context is not new. State production had long been associated with the supposed dangers of communism (and was often coupled with a critique of the high concentration of ownership and monopolisation within the economy). This is, for example, the message to be found in A. D. Wassenaar's *Assault on Private Enterprise*, published in 1977, and is posed even more clearly by McGregor (author of the South African *Who Owns Whom*):

> There is a fine line between communism and socialism and South Africa's concentration of control in the public and private sectors makes us the nearest economy to socialism outside Russia.

It is scarcely credible that such sentiments could have commanded widespread and increasing support and form the basis for a shift of policy towards privatisation (even if such views do obtain a greater prominence as privatisation comes on to the agenda). The same is also true of the less dramatic anti-statism which views government as bureaucratic, inefficient and overspending. No doubt this intellectual currency had gained political support but not to the extent of prompting major privatisation plans.

If the privatisation plans did not come out of newly discovered economic policies nor out of significant changes in the balance of anti-statist feeling, it was in the changed economic circumstances that the roots of the move to privatisation must be discovered. Of paramount importance was the debt freeze of 1985. This made it increasingly difficult for the state to finance its own activities. For it placed the mobility of foreign capital at risk. And, although the debt freeze and other measures were designed to restore financial credibility, the continuing crisis of the apartheid regime made only too clear the probability of a debt freeze being reimposed – if ever lifted – once financial difficulties recurred in the absence of a political settlement. Yet the regime's dependence upon foreign capital, although modest by international standards, was deepening until the debt freeze, with the ratio of external debt to GDP rising from 6.4% in 1980 to 27.1% in 1984. In 1987, $8.5 billion of this foreign debt was owed by the Government and its corporations and $14 billion by private banks and companies. Interest on public debt rose from 4.9% of Government expenditure in 1975/6 to 14.2% in 1985/6.

Thus, creditworthiness in terms of the ability to raise loans formed the primary motive for privatisation. In a sense, the state as guarantor of loans had lost its credibility. Consequently, its own productive assets rather than its word in the form of government bonds were being offered as collateral. In short, the privatisation programme represented the selling-off of the family silver in order to raise the funds to finance the apartheid regime.

In this light, the privatisations do have some resonances with similar measures taken in other countries, although not with those in the UK. For the privatisations in Nigeria, Mali, the Philippines, Mexico, Brazil and Tanzania have been forced through by the IMF along with austerity programmes as a condition for its making loans. This is exactly what happened in South Africa although it was not so explicitly formalised nor dependent upon IMF conditionality.[14] Significantly, for example, the privatisation measures were announced to the accompaniment of a proposed freeze on public sector wages and a revision to the tax system designed to cast its net wider and deeper through the introduction of VAT in 1989.

4 What Were the Proposals?

After the Budget Speech of February 1988, there was a much clearer commitment to the selling-off of state enterprises but the details of policy remained unformulated or undisclosed. By July, more details had emerged along with a great deal of speculation. First, the Government stated the intention of retaining 51% ownership of the enterprises, thereby illustrating that revenue was the prime motive, for continuing state majority control does not release the presumed advantages of market forces.

Second, the same motive was revealed in the policy of the Government to retain the income from the sales – rather than allowing the enterprises themselves to use it for investment purposes. In the words of Finance Minister, Barend du Plessis:

> The emphasis should also be on the opportunity offered by privatisation for the release of government funds at present locked up in these enterprises. Such release of funds could be used for alternative purposes by government.

Third, whilst it was claimed that the funds generated would be earmarked for priorities – capital expenditure rather than current expenditure, to reduce the state debt followed by infrastructural funds for the 'developing areas' and to promote small businesses, this is seriously misleading. For the Government has a pool of revenue from which expenditures are made. Ideologically, it might wish to argue that the receipts from privatisation are not, in some sense,

14 It has become a popular myth that post-apartheid economic policy was conditional on, or complicit with, funding support from the IMF, offering one motive and rationale for the turn in economic policy towards neoliberalism. This is simply false as I insisted upon at the time as no loan was ever taken although one was arranged. This was subsequently documented in detail (Padayachee and Fine, 2019).

being wasted. But there are always strains on the Government's budget as a whole and it is purely propaganda to argue that some extra revenue is being used for one particular purpose rather than another.

Fourth, speculation concerned which state enterprise would be privatised first, although a state share in SASOL I had already been sold.[15] There were two favoured candidates, each with very different characteristics, ESKOM and ALUSAF. But each illustrates the importance of the revenue motive. ESKOM, with fixed assets valued at over R35 billion, had already long been highly active and successful in the market for international finance. Loans from abroad grew at 64.1% p.a. from 1974 to 1982, during which there had been a flight of private sector capital from South Africa. It had been able to command long-term loans (unlike most other loans which had often been more short-term) and, symbolising its creditworthiness, it issued the first Euro-Rand bond. ESKOM had been equally successful in negotiating loans in the domestic market. In short, it had issued the most treasured of South African securities on both domestic and international financial.

The Government hoped to use this credibility to raise finance through the selling-off of its assets. That the revenue motive had been paramount is demonstrated by the common belief that ESKOM had already achieved high levels of efficiency, and that little was to be gained through subjecting it to market forces. Thus, as one commentator put it as late as 1987:

> The privatisation of ESKOM does not seem to be on the cards for the foreseeable future. The organisation is run well and provides a reasonable service. ESKOM is also technically innovative ... There are, however, areas

15 The choice was given by the following:
Assets of Major Public Enterprises, 1986

Company	**Fixed assets R million**
Eskom	35,664
SATS	18,614
Post Office	8,297
Land Bank	7,939
ISCOR	3,894
IDC	3,058
Armscor	1,706
Alusaf	500
Foskor	126

See McGregor (ed.) (1987) for these and other assets with a potential for privatisation such as government-owned land and buildings.

> which government appears to consider sacrosanct, e.g. the privatisation of ESKOM.

In addition, over the previous few years, ESKOM had gone through a reorganisation that had, amongst other changes, led to the loss of 10% of its staff, thereby leaving little potential room for further cost savings of this sort, except in line with increased productivity or decreased demand.

The importance of ESKOM as a borrower from international and domestic money markets is in part due to its bonds having enjoyed certain tax privileges (akin to those offered to insurance companies and pension funds). The announcement of its future privatisation led to speculation that these privileges would be withdrawn, and the value of its stock fell accordingly. To restore ESKOM's financial status, the Government immediately announced that there would be no detriment to existing stock and, in ESKOM's own words:

> The minister's announcement countered much of the uncertainty and should enable ESKOM to fund itself during the transition phase from a public to a private organisation.

The second favoured candidate for early privatisation was ALUSAF, the partially state-owned aluminium producer, with assets estimated at R500 million. It was operating profitably, with exports at 50% of its output. Situated close to Richards Bay, it was less liable to be subject to a rise in transport costs or disruption. Thus, the attraction of ALUSAF as a candidate for privatisation was its apparent secure profitability.

In the event, the privatisation programme passed over both ESKOM and ALUSAF, and incorporated much less promising assets such as ISCOR and SASOL. However, even if some of these assets had been sold, it does not necessarily mean that an equivalent level of finance overall would have become available to the Government. A useful starting point in recognising this is to envisage the capital market working in some ideal way. In this case, the Government ought to be able to raise whatever finance it likes by issuing Government bonds (although it might raise the rate of interest as it borrows more by doing this). Consequently, if it attempts to sell off state-owned assets as well, those who wish to save will see this as equivalent to holding bonds. Accordingly, what the Government gains in privatisation it loses in the bond market.

Arguments such as these have been used to criticise the privatisations in Britain if they are seen as serving any purpose in relieving financial constraints on the government. Whilst, of course, the measured government borrowing requirement may be reduced, the net effect on financial markets is not measured by this alone. But, of course, the capital markets never work in this ideal fashion, particularly in South Africa. Indeed, the privatisation programme is an explicit recognition of this as the Government considered that its productive assets offered a greater sense of security to potential lenders than its own bonds. Was this then liable to be a source of expanded credit?

First, it must be recognised that assets may be purchased for one of three reasons – to make a short-run capital gain (in anticipation of the share value rising in the early future); to balance a level of return in the long run against a level of risk; and to secure productive assets that can be integrated with those already owned.

Second, there is the question of who will buy the assets concerned. There are three broadly defined potential customers – foreign investors, small-scale domestic savers and the large-scale shareowners. The motive for each will depend upon the level at which the shares are offered. To the extent that the price is lowered, clearly the Government will realise a lower level of revenue. There were other factors depressing the price likely to be achieved, not least the reduced confidence in the stock markets around the world, following the crash of October 1987, and the sheer size of the transactions coming on to the market all at once if they were to have any financial impact for the Government.

In addition, the Johannesburg Stock Exchange had not recovered as well as other financial centres, following the crash of October 1987, because of lack of confidence in the price of gold. Investors in privatised utilities in the developing and developed world had also offered a wide and increasing choice of investment possibilities, with an estimated $50 billion of assets already privatised (from 55 enterprises) in the first five years of the 1980s and a further 2000 with value of $130 billion planned for sale by the end of the century.

All of these circumstances severely limited the prospects for South Africa to benefit even in the short term from the revenue to be gained from a privatisation programme. Either too many shares would be sold, depressing the price, or finance would be crowded out from purchasing other shares or making other forms of saving (including government bonds).[16]

This is all on the presumption that a state-owned company is sold off in one go. If, however, ESKOM, for example, were sold off in tranches, then there would be an existing price on the stock market following the sale of the first

16 In the case of the UK privatisations, for example, the evidence is that many small-scale savers simply withdrew money from a building society to purchase privatisation shares, resold the shares at an increased stock market valuation and then put their money back into the building society (to await the next privatisation).

tranche. This price will tend to be reduced by further sales of shares and, in any case, this would tend to eliminate the expectation of a higher share price post-privatisation as a motive for buying. Further, given the sanctions campaign, the trend of disinvestment and the instability of the apartheid regime, there were few reasons for believing that simply substituting productive assets for Government assurances would suffice to increase the expectations of a secure long-run rate of return on South African shares.

ESKOM officials, for example, are reported to have consulted the British electricity supply industry which was then preparing its own plans for privatisation. They dealt with a checklist of thirty or so key items. But none of these would have been able to counter the continuing boycott of South Africa by overseas institutional buyers (nor the reportedly cold shoulder that the ESKOM delegation received from bankers and stockbrokers).

Consequently, there was little chance of privatisation yielding floods of foreign investment. Nor was there liable to be an enormous expansion of domestic saving, particularly in view of stagnant income levels amongst the white population. Thus, the success of privatisation depended upon the large institutional investors and whether they would be prepared to increase their funding of the apartheid regime in return for a stake in what were state-owned institutions.

It seems, then, that for a substantial privatisation programme to have materialised, the support (probably in advance to guard against an unsuccessful flotation) of the major corporations would have to have been secured. This may have been motivated by the availability of financial surpluses, the fear otherwise of higher taxation, and to procure previously state-owned assets prior to the emergence of an ANC government. On the other hand, the corporations may have preferred to export as much finance as possible, whether legally or not, and to continue to rely upon their close coordination with state corporations even though not directly owning them. Whilst estimates differ, (illegal) capital flight from South Africa may have been as much as 7% of GDP in the period leading up to 1988 (Rustomjee, 1991). This is hardly indicative of commitment to domestic investment by large-scale private capital. And, further, if privatising ESKOM and ALUSAF, the state would have lost ownership of the companies best able to borrow on domestic and international markets without being sure that a net increase in funding would have been available to the economy.

The exact process by which the privatisation programme was actually brought about is a matter of speculation, at least until official records become available. It proved much less in practice than would have been anticipated from the scope of the policies being peddled after the debt freeze. The estimated gains in short-term revenue may have been limited, and the large-scale corporations may have resisted being embroiled in a privatisation programme from which it had little to gain – given its already secure integration with state corporations. Further, private capital may have feared the intensification of industrial conflict if compromised in a privatisation programme and the prospective threat of renationalisation with less than full compensation. What is striking, however, was the lack of any impetus to privatisation deriving from the imperatives of production, productivity and investment. It was a strategy for survival, reflecting the limited extent of commitment to coherent industrial policy making and reorganisation that had long been characteristic of the apartheid regime.

5 First Time – Farce; Second Time – Tragedy

In the previous sections, it has hopefully been established that the major motive for embarking upon a privatisation programme in the 1980s was to bolster the ailing apartheid regime's short-term finances. The chances of success even for this limited aim were remote. And, quite apart from potentially exposing even further the weaknesses of the country's finances should a privatisation issue have failed, the policy might also have backfired in generating considerable popular and industrial unrest.

Moreover, if the reversal of policy stance, from promoting state enterprises to privatisation, is put in proper perspective, it can be seen to represent a continuity in serving the interests of large-scale capital. State enterprises had played a major role in building up the mining and energy sectors and much of the large-scale industry around them, such as heavy chemicals and mineral processing.[17] Privatisation would have transferred state assets to the large-scale corporations at low prices and potentially beyond the reach of a prospective government.

In the event, only one major denationalisation was implemented, that of ISCOR. This proved successful in that the issue was oversubscribed by more than four times, and investors won an immediate ten per cent premium over the fixed selling price of R2 per share. Subsequently, this premium was eroded, a factor discouraging further denationalisations. Significantly, ESKOM, the most valuable state corporation and the most amenable to attract investors, had been 'prepared' for privatisation but was not sold.

17 This is discussed in Fine and Rustomjee (1996) in terms of a Minerals-Energy Complex, straddling large-scale public and private sector corporations.

The formation of the GNU serves more to change the circumstances within which a privatisation programme can be launched than it does to change its impact beyond the higher price that might be obtained for the family silver. The irony is that, having beaten off the apartheid regime's privatisation programme, the ANC is moving to re-introduce it in the more auspicious circumstances for potential investors that are provided by the constitutional settlement. Whilst the cover for doing so is in order to provide finance for the RDP (as opposed to the apartheid regime's faltering finances), this is based on a fallacious perspective. For the reconstruction of the economy depends upon a long-term strategy and vision, not one of short-term management of a putative financial crisis. The net effect of a privatisation programme will be to consolidate the power of large-scale corporate capital and to undermine the capacity to deliver economic and social policies that constitute the RDP. Why is this?

6 Privatisation Is Not Reconstruction

Comparative experience suggests that active state intervention and ownership is essential for, if not guaranteeing, successful economic and social reconstruction. It is worth noting that the nationalisations that took place of the 'commanding heights' of the British economy after the second world war (coal, rail, electricity, gas, etc) were prompted by the success of war-time control as well as by the abysmal record of the industries before the war when in private hands. Paradoxically, the very success of the state sector in reconstructing these industries over the post-war period is what has enabled them, even if mistakenly, to be returned to the private sector over the past decade.

In some respects, the same is true of the South African economy although many of its industries have been nurtured from scratch under state tutelage. In addition, the task has yet to be completed. For South African industrial development has been and remains seriously deficient. This is despite the misleading view that primary production (agriculture and mining) has become less important to the economy. In fact, South African industry is seriously distorted, continuing to rely heavily upon the processing of primary materials (as in steel, SASOL, and food industries, for example) and the manufacture of consumer goods, primarily for privileged white consumers, at domestic prices that are not internationally competitive. A major weakness of South African industry is the relative absence of productive capacity in intermediate and capital goods. This has a negative impact on the economy in a number of different ways:

(a) Economic expansion leads to growing imports of these goods and so creates balance of payments pressures.
(b) Up- and down-stream integration of economic activity is poorly coordinated, whether in the provision of mutually reinforcing access to finance, markets and technology.
(c) Employment generation, broadening of the skill base, and the opportunities to diversify into new sectors of industry are severely constrained.

These weaknesses of South African industry are not accidental nor are they simply the consequences of apartheid. Rather, they reflect the inheritance of *past* mistakes in economic policies, although these policies were designed to build up large-scale Afrikaner capital and integrate it with large-scale 'English' capital. They also reflect the way in which the private sector, dominated by a few multinational corporations of South African origin, *continues* to be committed to a speculative and international orientation with little or no regard to the industrial reconstruction of the domestic South African economy.

More specifically, South African industry has suffered from stagnation in investment since the early 1980s, whilst South African corporations have engaged in:

(a) capital flight,
(b) speculative purchase of industrial and other assets as disinvestment was prompted by international sanctions, and
(c) heavy lobbying for policies to promote their interests, whether materialising under the previous apartheid regime or the current GNU. This is most notable, for example, in the pursuit of state-subsidised mega-projects and the pressure for privatisation, in part to undermine the state's influence over the economy as well as to obtain productive assets cheaply.

In short, South African industrialisation has been a *failure*, despite some notable achievements on the basis of a distorted development, and this is a consequence of the continuing failure of both the state and the private sectors. Nor is the failure of the private sector a consequence of the role of the state. Indeed, at least over the past twenty years, state economic policy has been driven by the interests of large-scale South African capital. It follows that the solutions to industrial weaknesses do not rest upon the withdrawal from state industrial intervention and reliance upon the market (by which is meant, in practice, a few large-scale corporations). Rather, there is the strongest possible case for more extensive industrial policy of a different type and with different objectives.

For example, the recent experience and successes of the Newly Industrialising Countries, NICs, such as South Korea is now widely recognised to have been the result of extensive and concerted state economic intervention to create internationally competitive industries. Even the World Bank has been forced to concede, after years of asserting the opposite, that successful industrialisation has been heavily dependent upon active state policy (although it seeks to retrieve its ideological stance by arguing that the state has undertaken initiatives that the market would have brought about had it been working perfectly!). Specifically, in the South African context, the World Bank has accepted that public sector investment has the effect of crowding in, not crowding out, the private sector, a point heavily emphasised by the MERG (1993) Report. Consequently, concern should be less with the false dichotomy between the role of the state and the role of the market, since both necessarily interact with one another. It is more important to identify the policies that it is necessary to undertake and the means by which to achieve them. Privatisation is an abandonment not only of policy but of the scope of potential policy.

Nor can it be defended on grounds of raising finance for implementation of the RDP. There are a number of equally simple fallacies in this stance as well as further drawbacks:

1) As Harold MacMillan eloquently remarked of the UK privatisation programme, this would be a matter of selling off the family silver. To the extent that the South African privatisation programme gives up one physical asset (the public corporations) for another, it has done nothing to raise extra revenue. It would necessarily forego the revenue that would accrue on an annual basis from the public corporations and would be forced to borrow in order to make up the difference (or cut expenditure and raise taxes). This it could do, if thought desirable, to fund the RDP directly.
2) Inevitably, the privatisation programme would be wasteful in transforming the state's physical assets into finance. The process of privatisation is itself expensive in terms of consultancy fees, advertising, share issues, etc and can cost up to 10% of the value of the revenue raised.[18] Experience suggests that in order to guarantee a successful privatisation, in terms of a complete and assured sale, the share price has to be set at a level below real worth, partly because most companies' shares are usually only sold piecemeal and not all at once (except in a take-over or merger which tends to raise the share price). This is widely reflected in the immediate rise in a privatised company's shares following flotation, and has the

18 Almost R1 billion has been spent over the past ten years simply to *advertise* the British privatisation programme.

effect of rewarding those who are already in the advantageous position of being able to afford to purchase shares, further consolidating inequality in wealth. In addition, privatisations place unusually large demands upon financial markets and tend to crowd out the availability of finance for other investments.

3) There is no evidence nor guarantee that the finance raised through privatisations will in fact be earmarked and used for progressive policies, such as the RDP in the South African case. In fact, the funds simply become a general part of government revenue, and it can always be said that whatever is spent on the RDP came out of the privatisation fund. Further, funding the RDP out of privatisation revenues is to concede the principle that its policies are contingent upon a successful raising of revenue so that they are always a hostage to the more general fortunes of the economy and the state's finances. Moreover, those supporting privatisation as an economic policy more generally are usually conservative in economic outlook and will be prepared to sacrifice the RDP, and even to abandon it, whether privatisation is successful or not. In short, the RDP should take priority as an economic policy and not be made contingent upon a privatisation programme. The record is that privatisation goes along, and builds up a momentum, with other regressive, 'market-led' policies. This is especially so for the UK, for example, where privatisation has witnessed the most dramatic redistribution of income and wealth in favour of the already wealthy – exactly the opposite of what is required in South Africa.

4) Privatisation is not itself a simple policy to implement, like buying or selling food in a supermarket. It requires assets to be identified and valued, for finance to be raised, for the conditions under which the company will operate under private ownership to be determined, etc. This has two important drawbacks – the first is that scarce resources and skills in management and government, etc will be commandeered to implement the privatisation programme when they could more usefully be used to implement the RDP directly. Interestingly, one of the first arguments used against renationalisation is the demands it would place upon the legislative programme of the government concerned. Exactly, the same applies to privatisation in the opposite direction. The second such drawback of a privatisation programme is that it will strengthen what are already bloated institutions in South Africa dealing in the speculative buying and selling of financial assets. What is needed is financial institutions primarily geared to the raising and directing of funds into productive investment.

5) Policies to finance the RDP out of a privatisation programme are not only doomed to failure for the reasons given, since privatisation can only change (and worsen) the balance of the state's finances, but are reactionary in suggesting, erroneously as has been shown in the MERG Report, that the major constraint on implementing the RDP is the availability of finance. In short, institutional and political effort needs to be put into the RDP, rather than undermining it by a privatisation programme.

Apart from rejecting privatisation as a means of funding the RDP, there are arguably even stronger reasons for opposing privatisation more directly in terms of its broader impact on economic policy. As has already been indicated, the major problems with South African industry are:

1) Lack of investment
2) Lack of capacity in intermediate and capital goods
3) Lack of integration across different sectors of the economy

A privatisation programme will only worsen these problems. Evidence of privatisations elsewhere, and especially in the UK where the programme has lasted longer and cut deeper, is that:

1) In the period leading up to privatisation and subsequently, the main priority is to ensure short-term profitability rather than long-term industrial restructuring. This is inevitable given the transfer of the assets to the private sector. It leads to major closures of capacity and huge job losses irrespective of the wider implications for the short- and long-term functioning of the economy as a whole.
2) Not surprisingly, in diversifying from their previous role of providing, however effectively, a public utility, privatised companies seek to engage in financial restructuring, mergers and acquisitions, and international operations that do not have any direct bearing upon domestic industrial regeneration nor upon meeting the basic needs of their customers. In Britain, the privatised electricity utilities have now just become more readily open to acquisition. The first hostile bid has been made by a conglomerate which wishes to set the utility's profits against its own short-term losses, thereby gaining by not paying almost R1.5 billion of taxes on the utility's profits. In other words, industrial restructuring becomes driven by strategies that have nothing to do with reconstruction and development (tax farming and engineering). And, it is precisely such shenanigans that are characteristic of the South African financial system and its failure to develop satisfactory finance for industrial investment. Privatisation will consolidate, not address, these weaknesses.
3) Privatisations tend to create private monopolies. These need the closest possible regulation. In general, regulatory bodies do not have sufficient

powers to enforce appropriate strategy upon the companies concerned being confined to prices and other conditions concerning delivery of services. Regulation of this sort can be considered as an abandonment of industrial policy to an indirectly accountable body with limited powers and information – it cannot determine levels of investment, research and development, training programmes, collaboration across sectors, export performance, etc. In addition, effective regulation requires the use of a highly skilled and scarce workforce which would be better deployed in formulating and implementing industrial policy directly. It will also be continually engaged in counter-productive legal and other wrangles with the privatised companies over its exact powers and the interpretation of its rulings, with the companies consistently exploiting their wealth and power to ensure precedence of private profitability over public provision of basic needs.

4) Privatisation will create a company ethos of self-advancement and personal gain rather than of public service and meeting of basic needs. Those currently in charge of public corporations will be in a powerful position to exploit the need for their cooperation should privatisation proceed. Such a scandal has already emerged in the UK where more than fifty directors of previously publicly-owned utilities have each made more than R5 million more in salaries, share options and pension rights than they would have before privatisation. At a lower level, whilst workers will often gain on a much smaller scale from share options, these gains do not persist and may even be set against wages. Small-scale share ownership in a privatised company is no substitute for broader participation in determining corporate policy. In addition, worker shareholdings necessarily reinforce existing inequalities between workers. The better and the more secure your job in a privatised corporation, the more the shares you are liable to gain. Those that remain in the public sector, let alone women, for example, scraping a livelihood in the rural areas, are proscribed from participating in this putative form of redistributing wealth.

5) The latter is but a particular example of a more general and crucial point, particularly germane in the South African context. Privatisation will inevitably lead to a further consolidation of wealth and power in the hands of the large-scale conglomerates who are the only ones capable of financing the purchase of public corporations. In terms of benefits to individuals, these will accrue disproportionately to those few who are already extremely wealthy.

7 Concluding Remarks

Debate on privatisation in South Africa has been marked not only by sudden and extensive shifts in the balance of opinion but also by a lack of sophistication and depth. At the end of the day, support for privatisation is probably more motivated by a sense of political compromise than by a sense of practical and principled purpose. The vast majority's desire for redistribution is to be appeased by tying this perverse form of reconstructing ownership and control to an ephemeral mechanism for financing state expenditure on their behalf. More substantively, it is intended to satisfy big business whether as the direct beneficiaries in taking over ownership, or in terms of a symbolic commitment to both private enterprise and fiscal responsibility. With the financing of the RDP contingent upon the revenues derived from privatisation, the GNU has internalised the conditionalities imposed by the World Bank and IMF even without the benefits of a negotiated loan in return for these backward policies.

Such efforts to court the elusive goal of business confidence is a recipe for disappointment as has been dramatically revealed by recent events in Mexico. Do all they want and they can still let you down. Whatever the motives or reasoning underlying the privatisation programme, they are seriously deficient in logic and ethos. Indeed, privatisation does not offer the means of realising the RDP, nor does it merely represent its erosion and redefinition. It is its antithesis – consolidation of, and continuity with, the economic power and policies of the past.

CHAPTER 5

From Equal Pay and Minimum Wages through Public Works to Income Support

Postscript as Personal Preamble

As explained in the opening Chapter,[1] I was asked in mid-1995 to join the Presidential Labour Market Commission (LMC) as an international expert advisor. I was surprised by this given the post-MERG environment but also because, with a few exceptions, I had not worked concertedly on labour market issues and did not have a reputation as a labour market expert, international or otherwise.

Nonetheless, the exceptions were significant in and of themselves – although I have no reason to believe that anyone involved in my appointment knew of them – and in the role I played on the Commission. Most important analytically and informing my thinking had been my work on segmented labour markets (SLM), something that had engaged my interest as an alternative to mainstream labour economics (Fine, 1987, 1990c, 1993c and 1994b).[2] More fortuitously than otherwise, I also came across the SLM approach as part of the trappings of the post-fordist framing of labour markets as flexible-specialisation.[3] It was heavily promoted at the Greater London Council by Robin Murray who headed the Industry and Employment Branch having taken on the role from being at the Institute of Development Studies (IDS) at the University of Sussex. I also came across the flec-spec approach in teaching the economic and social history of Britain at Birkbeck, alongside Jonathan Zeitlin, one of its leading proponents. A more significant input from my own working at the GLC in the mid-1980s

1 Where there is some select account of the LMC itself.

2 Note that the first contribution ran to well over one hundred pages. At the time, the SLM approach, preceded by the (dual) DLM approach, was firmly rejected by mainstream economics for being atheoretical and merely descriptive. Only after labour market economics was taken up by economics imperialism in its second phase of market as informational imperfections was SLM analysis embraced by the mainstream – with a vengeance. See first two volumes in this series (Fine 2024a and b).

3 My reservations over flec-spec, and its application to South Africa by the Industrial Strategy Project, ISP, are aired in detail in Fine (1995). ISP was spearheaded by Raphie Kaplinsky, also from IDS, University of Sussex.

was my being a contributing editor to the *London Labour Plan* (GLC, 1986). This covered a wide range of labour market issues.

I drew freely on the SLM literature, which I much admired especially for its insistence upon the social structuring of labour markets. But I was equally critical for two major reasons. First is its tendency to see the structuring of labour markets (for example, occupational segregation) by what might be termed the intersection of supply- and demand-side factors although these are broadly and socially cast to include non-economic factors. I was more inclined to see this in terms of economic and social reproduction around differential access to the labour markets and under what conditions. Second, and more important, has been my emphasis on not just the structural separation of one labour market from another but that labour market segments, whether within sectors (employers) or across them ('professions' or 'trades'), are differentially segmented internally. Segments are structured from one another as well as structured differently in and of themselves. Interestingly, what brought this home to me was when I was studying South African labour markets and, in particular, the broad segment of domestic servants as opposed to the equally broad segment of (migrant) mining labour. They are simply distinctive labour markets from one another as well as being segmented from one another.

Such influences from SLM analysis were also complemented by my work for the UK's National Union of Mineworkers (NUM). Two issues were prominent in this scholarly activism. One, unsurprisingly was how to assess the economic and social costs of unemployment (brought about, for example, by pit closures) and whether this warranted subsidies to keep them open. Drawing on a methodology developed by Andrew Glyn, I undertook such calculations for specific closures under judicial review which had been promised during the strike to persuade pit deputies (with union NACODS) not to join regular workers attached to the NUM during the strike of 1984/85. After the strike was (won and) lost, we actually won one review only for its decision to be ignored if, putatively, "taken into account" by management in coming to the same ex ante decision on a verbal loophole to the astonishment of all and sundry (Fine, 1990a). There were few other reviews as the threat of loss of more generous severance pay was used as a deterrent if the workforce elected for a review.

The second main issue on which I worked for the NUM was to prepare evidence for an equal pay claim for female workers (canteen and cleaners). This led to a major review of comparable worth legislation in general and how the National Coal Board had systematically gone about avoiding its intentions. At least, after nearly ten years, we won this case in 1990, with back pay to be paid to those against whom there had been adjudged to have been discrimination albeit some beneficiaries dying in the interim (Fine, 2023; and O'Donnell, 2023, although each drafted many years earlier).

This explains why I prepared major pieces of work for the Commission on equal pay/comparative work. Minimum wages were sufficiently prominent on its agenda that I also undertook a major study on its literature and operation in practice. Amongst other issues, I also drafted short pieces on contract compliance (to meet labour standards), public works for employment creation and income support, the former reproduced at greater length in Chapter 6, and the latter two here as Sections 2 and 3, respectively. Both the long pieces on comparative worth and minimum wages were pillaged for my subsequent book on labour markets (Fine, 1998a),[4] alongside the SLM and other work, so that they can be consulted in slightly updated forms there. Nonetheless, the summary for comparative worth and its lessons for South Africa are reproduced here as Section 1, as not appearing in the later book, whereas the minimum wage chapter did not include a summary nor application to South Africa.

Is it possible that the work on comparative worth (equal pay) had an impact in South Africa? I have no direct evidence to believe so although there was soon legislated the Employment Equity Act 55 of 1998, with many amendments subsequently. I have only casually followed up its consequences. The lessons I sought to draw do not seem to have been learned, the main one being that the more comparative worth is made a legal matter, the more it will be obstructed by the greater legal resources available to employers. Yet, as adjudged by Ebrahim (2016), by contrast to South Africa, "It is clear that the United Kingdom has a more than adequate legislative framework in the form of the EA [Equity Act], which is able to give effect to the principle of equal pay for work of equal value."[5] From my own experience in the 1980s, this is the opposite of the case unless prepared to wait upon ten years and commit huge resources to winning. Nor does the situation seem to have improved in the intervening period given a case just settled in favour of the female workers of Next, the clothing retailer, which took six years to resolve (involving 3500 workers and £30m in back pay, Hooker, 2024).

I have no evidence that my efforts on minimum wages had any effect. Only a decade later was a concerted campaign fought and won for a national minimum

4 I only (re)discovered this and recovered my memory of thirty years before after preparing the two chapters for publication and, then, searching for the old LMC files – which are in wordperfect – to check on some conversion glitches, found them essentially to have the same names as the later book chapters.

5 See also Mabathoana (2019) for a similarly positive, and false in practice, assessment of the UK legislation.

wage in South Africa. It was spearheaded by a former doctoral student of mine, Gilad Isaacs, together with Neil Coleman, who have gone on to form the Institute for Economic Justice, with a Basic Income Grant (BIG) as their next major mission (I would have preferred them to have gone for a national health service worthy of the name, with reservations over BIG implicitly expressed in Section 3 in this Chapter). But it has led me to puzzle over what made the minimum wage campaign successful in South Africa in the context of so much failure otherwise.[6] To some extent my own contribution was pushing against a door opened by the work of David Card and Alan Krueger that empirically showed how raising minimum wages was not at the expense of employment.[7] It was simply a matter for me of dealing with those who sought to restore the conventional wisdom that raise the price of something and the demand goes down (i.e. minimum wages must decrease employment). In a nutshell, my response was that labour markets do not work in this way and, in addition, those arguing for negative impacts of minimum wages on employment could be parodied as suggesting that if you take away all the factors that make for a positive impact then the impact is negative. Now, no one can argue against that tautology.

1 Propositions Concerning Comparable Worth: Summary[8]

The Problems

Comparable worth legislation (or equal pay for work of equal value) is intended to deal with direct discrimination in the labour market. In principle, the idea is

6 For a comprehensive account of what makes for minimum wage legislation, how it is administered and set at what levels and with what range of coverage, see Konopelko's (2023) PhD thesis completed under my supervision. It conforms with my own inclinations as far as South Africa is concerned – it required extensive scholarly research and support in favour beating out mainstream opposition, a successful and unremitting media campaign in face of hostility, support from trade unions, and sponsoring from a major politician in power (President Ramaphosa as it happened).

7 The work of the two is remarkable for progressive mainstream economists having a major impact on a specific issue (if to be followed by the Piketty phenomenon on inequality, in turn in the wake of the wide spread of issues covered by those such as Joe Stiglitz and Paul Krugman with limited impacts upon policy despite popularity and prominence). Krueger went on to become a chief economic advisor under Barack Obama but died (by suicide) in 2019, too soon to share the Nobel Prize for economics with Card in 2021.

8 The longer paper does not follow the order of this summary. As mentioned in the Preamble, it was updated for inclusion as a chapter in Fine (1998a). See also Fine (2023) for an account of its earlier application to equal pay for female canteen workers in the British coal industry.

that two workers who contribute broadly comparable work in terms of 'worth' (and not necessarily in the content of the job itself) should receive the same pay (and fringe benefits, etc) and, in particular, that differences by race or gender alone should not justify differences in pay. Because of what is often extreme occupational segregation, equal pay for identical work is not an effective option as it would have little purchase for many workers. Consequently, it is what workers do that has to be compared in order to be able to make equal pay legislation operative.

In practice, comparable worth raises a number of problems. First, there are pay differences between workers irrespective of race and gender, even where comparable worth might apply. Two white males, for example, doing exactly the same job in different firms might be paid differently for a variety of reasons, often referred to inappropriately as market forces. In addition, different workers will have different characteristics and different tasks for which pay levels might justifiably differ, irrespective of differences by gender and by race. How then are we to untangle outcomes in the labour market and determine when equal worth is being contributed but not being paid?

Essentially, all the other problems derive from this issue. For, second, to make a comparable worth claim, a 'comparator' has to be chosen for a comparison to be made with the appellant. Who is an appropriate comparator? In the case of race, a black worker would make a comparison with a white worker. But who would be eligible for the latter? In general, in deference to market forces, choice of comparator is restricted to someone in the same place of employment. But even this is extremely ambiguous. Does this imply the same employer, the same location of employment (or 'plant') or even the same bargaining structure? Whatever the answer given, whether the range of comparators is broad or narrow, employers can potentially manipulate their organisational structure to evade or minimise the impact of comparable worth legislation. Women-only or black-only workplaces would, for example, be unaffected by comparable worth if the same workplace were used as the basis for selecting comparators. On the other hand, if the same multi-plant employer is used, then this raises the issue of whether workers, in what are potentially very different local labour markets, should be paid the same. This might be especially important for state employees, whether at national or local level. When should these be considered to constitute the same place of employment for comparable worth purposes?

Third, given the choice of a comparator, how should the comparison be made across the different tasks involved? In practice, this has proved the least problematic, since there is now long experience in what is termed job evaluation schemes. Nonetheless, these can be far from neutral, both in recognising what constitutes skills and in rewarding them, with a potential for prejudice against the skills brought to work, for example, by women which are undervalued.

Fourth, how is comparable worth legislation to be implemented in practice? There is the choice between tying it formally to the legal system or incorporating it more informally within the industrial relations system (although there can be some overlap between the two). The apparent advantage of a more formal and legal basis is the supposed certainty and precision involved, especially as case law and precedents accumulate over time. The disadvantages are the delays and costs involved which can be manipulated by employers in particular to evade the intent of comparable worth.

Fifth, given a comparable worth judgement has been made, how are its implications to be extended to other sections of the workforce? Whilst comparable worth is essentially based upon comparisons between individuals, it almost inevitably has relevance for other workers in the same or similar circumstances, even if class actions are permitted and have been won. Will other workers need to bring their own cases, replicating earlier proceedings, or will they be subject to the same favourable judgements by extension and, if so, how?

Analytical Principles

Whilst the previous section has laid out practical issues attached to comparable worth, these do themselves reflect a more fundamental analytical issue which it is important to reveal and debate. It concerns differences over how the labour market functions. It is essential to take a view on this, even if implicitly as is often the case, because, only then, can an assessment be made of the likely effects of comparable worth.

One approach to the labour market, which underpins much discussion of comparable worth, is the notion that there is sharp division between market and non-market forces and, within the market forces (often referred to as supply and demand, for example), there are legitimate determinants of differences in wage levels as well as those that should not be allowed – for which discrimination is one example. Essentially, the idea is that in an ideally functioning labour market, individuals would be paid according to their own employment characteristics (what work they can contribute and how much it is demanded), however these might have been determined in the first place. Consequently, comparable worth legislation seeks to ensure that individual workers are paid what they would be in the absence of discrimination.

This does involve, however, identifying and netting out the various factors, other than discrimination, that have influenced wage levels. This might include an attempt to determine the 'normal' forces of supply and demand

and, by default, the 'abnormal' discriminatory factors. In practice, however, wage bargaining is so much a departure from the laws of supply and demand (with presence of trade unions, bargaining structures, technical change, etc) that appeal to supply and demand is merely a terminological renaming of the problem of what is allowable as non-discriminatory. This approach, because it tends to believe in a 'natural' rate of pay for the job, leans towards a formal and legalistic approach to comparable worth, allowing legislation and precedent to settle the circumstances under which comparable worth claims can be made and justified.

In short, the supply and demand approach to comparable worth has the advantage of focusing upon the determination of wages at the level of the individual (with the intent of revealing presence of discrimination or not) but is hopelessly out of touch with the realities through which wages are determined in practice. The alternative is to accept correctly that wage determination, and labour market outcomes more generally, are socially determined through a variety of factors and specific institutions. Explanations have to be structured, not only between market and non-market forces but also within each of these spheres of activity. As a consequence, for the purposes of understanding wage determination, the sharp separations between market and non-market forces, and between legitimate and illegitimate incidence of market forces, are invalid. The various factors involved interact in an integral and complex fashion to yield labour market outcomes for which the impact of discrimination cannot necessarily be simply and fully isolated.

Those taking this approach tend to see comparable worth as a support to those who are disadvantaged in the labour market by virtue of race and/or gender. Consequently, they will tend to seek more informal institutions in implementing comparable worth so that it can be both more accessible and more effective for the disadvantaged. The approach has the advantage of reflecting the socioeconomic determinants of labour market outcomes but, inevitably, at the expense of providing an account of the level of discrimination experienced by an individual, the level at which comparable worth legislation tends to be pitched (in making comparisons between individuals).

What each approach reveals in its own way is the tension that exists in comparable worth legislation between recognising the social or structured determinants of wages, on the one hand, and the outcomes for individual employees, even if taken in groups, on the other hand. This is a tension that can only be resolved practically and pragmatically in terms of the legislation adopted and the way in which it is implemented. Its effects will depend upon other wide-ranging determinants which lie outside its scope. By the same token, its impact will be uneven across both employers and employees.

Implications for South Africa[9]

The context within which South African labour market policy is being reformulated reflects the broader goals of the RDP set against the apartheid heritage of severe pre- and post-entry oppression of black workers. Comparable worth is designed to deal with post-entry discrimination – that is, given workers are in employment, are they being paid the appropriate wage by comparison with one another? It is not directly concerned with why black or female workers enter the labour market from a disadvantaged position as a result of inherited disadvantage in education, health, welfare, transport, etc. There must, however, be a presumption that labour market discrimination has led to considerable post-entry discrimination that should be corrected – that is black and female workers have much to gain from comparable worth exercises and these should be a major component of the current restructuring of labour markets even as the RDP hopefully narrows inequality in pre-entry labour market conditions over the longer term.

This suggests that comparable worth legislation is in part required as a one-off exercise to correct the major distortions inherited from the past. As such, as initially formulated and implemented, it may be inappropriate for the necessary and continuing comparable worth legislation of the future – after an initial phase of equal pay adjustments have been made. Consequently, whatever comparable worth legislation is put in place, it should be reviewed annually for its direct impact and efficacy and, after a five-year period, for its continuing relevance for the restructuring of labour markets more generally.

As observed, critical responses to comparable worth legislation have fallen at two extremes. One occupies a *laissez-faire* stance and perceives it as undue interference in the (objective) workings of the market, thereby allowing public servants to make subjective judgements about levels of wages. Such ideology is totally out of touch with the realities of how (labour) markets function in general and with the intent of the RDP in practice. It is, however, complemented by a critique that sees comparable worth as incapable of redressing labour market inequality satisfactorily and as unduly favouring those workers best able (often already the better-off) to make use of the legislation and, thereby, undermining the pressure for more fundamental change. As it were, equal pay legislation becomes hi-jacked by professionals or others well-placed in the labour market, at the expense of a broader scope incorporating the lower paid. It is also possible that equal pay can occupy undue attention relative to other, possibly more

9 This is taken from the full report, not the summary, as longer and not amended nor reproduced within the later labour market book (Fine, 1998a).

fundamental, aspects of labour market inequality – such as unemployment and pre-entry labour market conditions.

These are serious points but they can be positively embraced in the design of comparable worth legislation and in its practice. It must be recognised that comparable worth can only have a limited, if significant, impact, contingent upon other aspects of labour market functioning – as has been observed, equal pay is more effective in the presence of trade unions, collective bargaining, and the active participation of women negotiators. Thus, equal pay will inevitably favour those who are in secure, organised employment. Whilst this has to be accepted, comparable worth strategy can still be oriented as far as possible to support as many as possible in lower paying occupations. There is no reason to believe that this must prejudice those who do not benefit directly from equal pay legislation. There may be off-setting deterioration in their working conditions, but it is more reasonable to assume that there will be a positive trickle-down or demonstration effect. Even if not, the indirect effect of equal pay on one set of workers is only liable to disadvantage others in conjunction with, and through, a range of other factors that will not remain the same and which will be open to other forms of government support – from minimum wage legislation to employment creation schemes.

From the UK experience, and elsewhere, it is apparent that the more comparable worth is tied to a formal legal system, the more ineffective it is in speed and cost of deliberation. Excessive legality also tends to favour employers with their greater access to funds and legal advice. In addition, formal legal systems, however well-intentioned, because of their necessary precision whether by statute or case law, inevitably open up the potential for abuse through evasion. Consequently, informal rather than strictly legal procedures should be adopted for the implementation of comparable worth policy. It is necessary to rely upon informed and guided judgement rather than the court of law.

Fortunately, this approach already conforms with proposals in the draft Labour Relations Bill, 1995, designed for industrial relations and collective bargaining more generally. This Bill, however, whilst committed to the principles of the RDP, scarcely mentions discrimination. Whilst no provision is made for equal pay legislation, responsibility for comparable worth can readily reside with the Conciliation, Mediation and Arbitration Commission. Given its other responsibilities, this should provide for considerable economies of scale and scope – although whether there should be a separate division for comparable worth remains open. Most of the issues being covered by the Commission will require considerable expertise in those necessary for comparable worth decisions, specifically the role of (the structure of) collective bargaining, job evaluation schemes, grading and wage scales. It is also crucial that comparable worth be applied to fringe benefits with which the Commission should develop expertise.

More specifically, the Commission would need to determine the criteria under which comparisons would be allowed to be made, whether by race or gender. If these were set in stone by legislation, they are open to manipulation by evading employers. Nor is there any reason why the criteria for comparator should be the same from one set of jobs to another. It will be necessary to build up a set of principles and precedents. These will dovetail with the pursuit of equal opportunities, however strongly on either side of the industrial relations divide, through the normal course of collective bargaining.

Whilst this may add to the burden of the Commission's work, it will be able to choose priorities in its comparable worth deliberations. Although no case should be allowed to linger indefinitely, the Commission would be able to take account of the number of workers involved, their existing levels of pay (with a priority to considering those on low pay), the extent of unjustified differentials on a preliminary analysis, and the potential implications for other cases not directly affected. An important starting point would be within the public sector itself, where government can be prevailed upon to fund and implement the necessary wage adjustments without undue opposition for commercial or other reasons (such as ideological resistance to equal pay). This would then potentially create a model and precedents for adjustments within the private sector. In this light, it might be worth addressing at an early stage sections of both white- and blue-collar workers within the public service, even though the former might be considered relatively favourably placed in wages and conditions, in order to develop a portfolio of experience and precedents.

As a statutory body, but not subject to legal process as such, the Commission would be able to make broader decisions concerning the implications of its judgements. It could award pay increases for similar circumstances without the necessity of further cases being brought before it. This would have the advantage of avoiding delay in the adoption of comparable worth by employers affected in principle by the Commission's judgements.

The Commission could also be pro-active. Either as a matter of its own focused research or arising out of its experience more generally, it would be able to identify particular sections of the workforce where it felt comparable worth was being substantially violated. It could investigate and make awards accordingly even where a case was not initiated by employees.

In putting forward these proposals, it is necessary to be mindful that the Commission is already required in the draft Labour Relations Bill to exercise considerable discretion in meeting the needs of the RDP, and that undue wage awards might be counterproductive in removing the very jobs that they are designed to enhance. In extending the Commission's, or some other body's, responsibilities to comparable worth, there is no reason to believe that the weight of judgement required will be unduly greater.

2 Some Notes on Job Creation Programmes

In assessing the potential and actual impact of job creation programmes, it is crucial to take account of both direct and indirect effects. In general, the indirect impact can be calculated through multiplier effects, whether on employment, balance of payments, government deficit, etc. In doing this, it is important to recognise that multipliers will differ at different levels of economic activity and by region, sector, etc. They are hard enough to calculate in the first instance and should be treated with considerable scepticism. In particular, care must be taken to ensure that the infrastructural and institutional capacity exists to deliver the programmes and their presumed multipliers and not to assume that they will spring up out of the need for them. Further, it is possible for multipliers to be negative, especially if job creation is also job displacing – just supporting one set of workers to do what would have been done in any case by others.

Notes prompted by Dalgleish et al. (1994), see also the special issue of *International Labour Review*, vol 131, no 1, 1992, for coverage of some of the issues associated with employment generation and, in particular, the tensions between targeting those most in need, the institutional capacity to deliver, and the imperative to engage decentralised participation:

Transport is a potentially important source of employment creation; quite apart from the short-term jobs created directly by construction, there are those of repair and maintenance and of operating transport systems. In addition, the indirect effects include a positive impact upon secondary employment generation through local firms that might themselves have been created or consolidated by the initial infrastructural investment. There is a clear case for close coordination between the Departments of Transport and Labour in order that the implications for employment of transport policy and projects are taken fully into account.

There is considerable scope for the development of small local firms and community businesses around waste collection, recycling and energy conservation. In much of South Africa's 'First World' urban environment, lessons and policies can be drawn from the developed countries, where projects that are viable by both economic and social criteria would prove even more so at lower levels of wages in job creation programmes. Employment could be created in collection, sorting and distribution of waste materials, the construction of recycling facilities, the marketing of reprocessed materials, and in the manufacturing companies using secondary materials to produce new products.

In the United States, 10% of waste material, 20 million tons, is recycled annually creating over 43,000 jobs. In South Africa, through collaboration with mining companies, it might also be possible to generate higher level jobs devoted to developing and using new technology for the environment. In the Ruhr, for example, 100,000 new jobs have been created in 1,000 small and medium enterprises in the development around clean technologies and waste management equipment.

With the growth of schooling and other educational institutions, the collection of waste paper for recycling will become more viable. A coupon scheme could be employed in which schools are accredited and rewarded for the paper delivered. Similarly, with the growth of tourism, there is the possibility of recycling organic waste from hotels, gardens and water purifications plants. This could be used to produce high quality compost.

In short there is a need for coordination between the Departments of Employment and the Environment in which locally based environment audits are linked to job creation programmes. In some cases, collaboration with the Department of Trade and Industry will be essential.

Housing programmes involve both new construction and rehabilitation, repair and maintenance. Apart from the direct employment created, much of this will also involve a range of other economic and social activities for community development, including the provision of skills and coordination and management of housing services. These can form the basis for employment generation, within each of the private and public sectors and in the relationships between them. Again, there is a need for coordination between the Departments of Employment and Housing.

Notes prompted by UNCHS/ILO (1995):

Housing provision, like much other socioeconomic infrastructure, has the potential to raise productivity indirectly – with less absenteeism, ill-health, stress, etc. It also generates employment and income both directly and indirectly through multiplier effects, notionally liable to be in the region of 2, with low-income housing and employment relying less on imports. It is important to recognise, however, that the macroeconomic effects of a large housing programme are liable to be complex and different according to the nature of the programme itself (although the quote that follows is preceded by an assertion of the harmful effects of heavy subsidies and direct government provision of housing), p. 34:

> Good policies (from the macroeconomic viewpoint) are those which improve the supply of key inputs to housing (a skilled labour force, a sound and functioning regulatory framework, and the efficient supply of building materials, land and finance at prices people can afford) and ensure their efficient use.

Whilst it is generally recognised that economies of scale do prevail in the provision of on-site services and in constructing large numbers of houses, and that public sector might surpass private sector performance, p. 46, such large-scale delivery systems may not be available. SMEs are perceived to have some compensating advantages in (i) using labour-intensive methods (ii) knowledge of local conditions (iii) potential to grow from a small-scale using local skilled and unskilled labour (iv) using local materials. See page 48/9 for scope to shift activities from the public to the private (SME) sector.

The extent of employment creation, both direct and indirect, depends upon choice of product, technology and production methods. Policy should be geared towards making these as labour-intensive as possible without entirely sacrificing commercial considerations. For example, Soweto's engineering department has experience in using smaller-scale locally manufactured concrete trenches, capped with concrete planks, in place of larger stone water pipes that require mechanical handling and off-site manufacture. Similarly, a programme of servicing and replumbing 56,000 plots has been broken up into a large number of small-scale labour-intensive contracts. This does, however, require the development of expertise and capacity in programme management.

There is also potential for labour-intensive production in building materials such as stone quarrying, tiles, brickmaking and cement blocks. The viability of these depends upon the choice of construction technology and design and access to markets.

The development of housing and attached infrastructure should incorporate other indirect influences upon job creation. As already mentioned, how waste services are organised can affect the potential for job creation through waste recycling, and housing itself is often used as a site for informal, self-employed production and not simply as domicile. Home-based enterprises (HBEs) have the advantage of supporting those with least access to formal labour markets, although they tend to be characterised by poor levels of income and working conditions.

Notes prompted by Sen and Ghosh (1993):

Much of the literature on the generation of rural employment observes, particularly in the context of rural industrialisation, just how great are the constraints upon effective and sustainable job creation. The reasons are lack of entrepreneurship, absence of rural credit, undeveloped local markets, absence of adequate infrastructure, overcentralisation of authority and institutions, urban bias in policy making, and lack of availability of appropriate technology and skills. As a consequence, not surprisingly, the tension for policy in job creation is often that those most in need – women located in rural areas – are the most difficult to support.

In South Africa, the trend has been towards decline in the numbers employed in agricultural itself. This might be tempered for a short time by a variety of measures associated with land reform but growth in agricultural employment is not liable to be sustained. Nonetheless, employment can best be encouraged through policies that support double-cropping, investment in major and minor irrigation works, flood control and drainage, land levelling and other rural infrastructure.

In India, poverty alleviation in rural areas has taken the form of government provision of jobs. The impact of this has tended to be underestimated. Although it only makes up about 5% of total employment in rural areas, the government's contribution to employment is as much as 20% both of total non-agricultural rural employment and of the increase in total rural employment over the 1980s. Further, 60% of *regular* non-agricultural jobs are provided by government and 80% of increases in such jobs.

To a large extent, these figures reflect the high and growing level of casualised employment in the rural areas, whether in agricultural work or not. South Africa has similar features where self-employment in agriculture is not a viable option by itself for the majority of the predominantly female workforce, and wage income, however insecure, is the main source of livelihood. This points to the crucial importance of public sector employment programmes in the rural areas as a means of poverty alleviation. Nothing else is liable to be as effective.

Such programmes will not necessarily directly benefit those most in need. Whatever the intention, secure public non-agricultural employment will be preferred over casualised agricultural employment by those already in jobs. Those holding localised control over the disbursement of public funds are liable to use them to benefit those already in employment, such as upper income agricultural workers, as a form of political patronage. This can, however, lead to a trickle-down mechanism, less through the demand and employment generated by public expenditure, and more through the jobs that are released in agriculture by those who benefit from the job creation programmes. In other words, the labour market position of those worst-placed is liable to be strengthened indirectly by employment creation schemes.

Obviously, this is a generalised commentary that needs to take account of differences across localities. The Departments of Agriculture and Labour should collaborate over rural job creations schemes, even if non-agricultural employment is involved, in view of the likely impact on working conditions within agriculture.

3 Some Rough Notes on Income Maintenance Programmes (IMPs)

The vast majority of the economics literature on Income Maintenance Programmes (IMPs) has been focused upon developed countries. This has had a profound impact on the sorts of assumptions, often implicit, that have been made and which are entirely inappropriate for developing countries and especially for South Africa where levels of poverty and unemployment are so high. First, it is presumed that the proportion of those in poverty and in need of income support is relatively small given that the majority of the population will have access to income from employment even if as dependants. This also implies a small but significant number of relatively well-defined and identifiable categories of the population 'at risk' – the unemployed, the disabled, children in households without an earner, senior citizens, and those (and their dependants) in employment but on low wages.

Second, there is a presumption of effective administration of IMPs through the institutions of the welfare state, including an effective taxation system, and hence an administrative knowledge of incomes, to which tax/benefit adjustments can be made with limited potential for, or impact of, fraud. This tends to generate studies of why benefits are not taken up, rather than the extent of abuse, although benefit fraud and dependency often figure prominently in political ideology and as an explanation for the imputed presence of the 'work-shy' and high levels of unemployment.

Third, the household is often taken to be relatively stable (except where IMP is specifically concerned with single parents, etc). In addition, although there are exceptions in practice in the targeting of benefits and in the form that they take (who gets paid for what), the household is usually perceived as equivalent to an individual so that intra-household access to, and use of, benefits are neglected. But, as Sainsbury (1993) shows in a comparative study of the UK, USA, the Netherlands and Sweden, there are substantial differences in the types of benefits to which men and women have access, with men most likely to benefit from social insurance schemes. Women are more likely to be subject to means-tested benefits via their husbands' entitlements derived from the latter's higher levels of labour market participation – with Sweden favouring women more in their own right than in the other countries. In this context, Sainsbury (1993, p. 90) concludes:

> Entitlement through labour market status leads to the exclusion of women (as well as other vulnerable groups such as young people, the handicapped, and immigrants) to the degree that they are not economically active. It is thus imperative to provide an adequate minimum for persons outside the labour market, and, if one wants to avoid social control and stigma, an alternative which is not means-tested.

In addition, there is the danger of an income support system proving to be indirectly discriminatory as in contributory schemes and/or earnings-related benefits (such as pensions) where higher (male) earners are bound to be more amply recompensed. In short, p. 92/3:

> Universalist policies where entitlement is a right of citizenship generally work against a pattern of sex segregation in access to benefits, whereas policies based on labour market status and contributions encourage sex segregation in the access to benefits. Without programmes based on citizenship, women's only alternative is to rely on means-tested programmes which entail social control and dependency.

Fourth, partly reflecting the methodological individualism of neoclassical economics and its current analytical fashions, the theoretical focus has been upon benefit system design in the light of informational problems and work incentives. More specifically, government is presumed to have limited knowledge of individual earning capacities, and this opens up the possibility for individuals to rely upon the benefit system out of a preference to avoid work when they need not do so. I will take this up in more detail later.

Fifth, much of the literature is partial in scope. Primarily concerned with the relationship between benefits and work incentives. There is a neglect of knock-on effects, ranging from the fiscal implications of expenditure and the macroeconomic implications of the implied redistribution of income.

Sixth, there is a political economy of IMP literature in which those who might benefit have indirect powers to influence policy through the ballot box or social disruption. They must not, however, press too hard or they will undermine the incentives of the better-off to comply in funding the IMP. By the same token, the better-off are perceived to judge the level of support for an IMP that will provide for social stability. Clearly, such horse-trading is a highly simplified understanding of the political process.

In short, as Atkinson (1987, p. 783) concludes in his wide-ranging survey of income maintenance and social insurance (although his praise of economic analysis can be questioned):

> One of the insights offered by writers from outside economics is that the role and function of income support can only be fully understood in the context of a particular society. Economic analysis is valuable because it can be easily transported across national boundaries and provides a common language with which to discuss problems, but it must always be applied with the aid of background knowledge of the institutions involved and how they operate on the ground. A second-year student can see that a rise in unemployment benefit may reduce the incentive to work (in the simplest neoclassical model), but to judge whether the effect is likely to be important in a particular situation, one has to study the way in which the benefit is administered, the constraints to which the unemployed are subject, the prevailing social norms, and the nature of the labour market. Superficial application of micro-economic analysis, not taking account of such real-world factors, has done a great deal to discredit economics.

In this light, the best way in which to gain from the existing literature is through a critical appreciation of the factors involved in IMPs. I begin with what has been constituted as the standard problem in the literature even though this does not, especially in the South African context, raise the most important issues directly.

The standard problem is to devise income support at least overall fiscal cost in order to guarantee that each individual/household attains a minimum level of income. The most sophisticated treatment of this problem is Besley and Coate (1995) upon which I draw freely. It is first assumed that individuals fall into groups with different earning capacities. If government has full knowledge of these earning capacities for each individual, it can design a 'first best' income support scheme at minimum cost that subsidises those who earn below the minimum level and which does not raise anyone above that level. Also, except for those with zero earning capacity, by making a certain level of earned income as a precondition for income maintenance, it is possible to make recipients work harder than they would in the absence of support. The point is to use the income support in part as a mechanism of 'self-help'.

None of this is possible if, realistically, government does not know individual earning capacities, even if it does know the distribution of earning capacities across the economy – that is, the number of individuals earning each amount, if not who they are. In this case, if, for example, government attempted to operate the first best scheme, those capable of earning just above the minimum level would have an incentive not to do so and take the higher benefit and work less. This leads to a more complex 'second best' IMP in which the two groups of recipients/non-recipients are supplemented by a third intermediate group who receive benefit which takes them above the minimum, apparently leading to a waste of fiscal expenditure. However, should their benefit be cut to bring them down to the minimum, then they would work less and claim an even higher benefit to bring them up to the minimum.

This situation arises because of the inability to target or 'screen' earning abilities perfectly. Indeed, the only way of screening benefit recipients is in the offer of income support itself. As a result, in order to minimise the fiscal cost of the universal minimum, it is necessary both to support some at a rate that raises them above the minimum and, in addition, some will be supported who could earn above the minimum in the absence of the IMP. Further, some in receipt of benefit will work less than in the absence of the IMP. Clearly, inferring this after the implementation of the IMP might lead to the conclusion that the intermediate group should be denied benefits. But this can only be done by increasing the total cost of the scheme (as members of the middle group switch with less work to the lower group) or by lowering the minimum standard.

The political acceptability of the second-best optimal outcome to the lower and upper groups must be seriously examined. Both will observe that transfers to those whom they might consider are undeserving – for the lower group because they are themselves worse-off, and to the upper group who would prefer fiscal transfers to target the lower group.

Besley and Coate add a further dimension to their IMP by allowing for workfare in which income support is contingent upon undertaking public sector work. This allows the second best to be moved closer to the first best because the offer of workfare can be used as a second screening device to sort between earning capacities of households. In this case, four groupings emerge. The lowest group engages in private and public sector work, remuneration from the latter just bringing them up to the minimum. This implies a 100% tax for them on private sector earnings, but more such work would be compensated for by a reduction in public sector work obligations. The second group with higher earning capacity would not engage in workfare but would receive income support. A third group would not engage in workfare but would receive income support to take them above the minimum. Finally, a fourth group would simply rely upon private sector earnings. Once again, the political acceptability of this outcome must be questioned, especially as it can be shown that the public sector wage offered must exceed the private sector wage and must rise with private sector earning capacity. This is necessary in order to guarantee incentive compatibility – to minimise the adverse effect on the overall cost of the programme due to individuals hopping between groups.

As is apparent, such analysis is complex even on the basis of drastic simplifying assumptions – not least the capacity of government to vary the level of income support and workfare requirements and of individuals to vary the level of private sector earnings (by hours worked) whether engaged in workfare or not. For reasons of institutional convenience and political acceptability, much simpler schemes are inevitable although this carries the implication of only attaining the minimum for all at a higher fiscal cost.

I will return to this later after considering other effects of IMPs that have been highlighted in the literature. First, extending the previous discussion of work effort and incentive compatibility, account can be taken of the broader impact upon labour market participation, as in retirement and training and education. A guaranteed income may encourage early retirement, or lesser work in retirement, as well as withdrawal from work for education and training. It may also reduce saving as provision for the future is less necessary. Further, the levels and form of income support will affect household formation in the widest sense, including the incentives for migration, co-habitation, divorce, marriage, and fertility. Thus, for example, a guaranteed income to women (with dependent children) might support separation from a male partner and reduce overall income available to the household. Such issues, even if primarily in the context of work incentives, have been examined in the wake of socioeconomic experiments with guaranteed income in select local areas in the USA and Canada – see Hum and Simpson (1993) and Anderson and Block (1993) for a survey and competing views. Finally, workfare can be construed as a form of (negative) payment in kind as compared to income support. More generally, payment in kind, as in food programmes, is an alternative or additional form of support to IMPs. This has received considerable attention in light of programmes such as Food Stamps in the USA, and how they interact, for example, with Aid to Families with Dependent Children (AFDC), aid to families with dependent children.

In view of the earlier discussion, each of these factors should not simply be seen as an added complication. Rather, they represent alternative mechanisms for screening the population in response to incentive compatibility. A rice ration of poorer quality, for example, as opposed to its monetary equivalent, is liable to target the poor as the better-off prefer higher quality rice or other foods.

This raises the central issue, given the likely fiscal resources available, of whether incentive compatibility and screening are liable to be that important, given the numbers of those in poverty and the level of a feasible minimum. High levels of unemployment and poverty are such that the design of maintenance programmes, whether in income or kind, and the identification of targeted groups, are far from difficult. In a perverse way, the extent of income support required and the wide range both of categories of the population and types of programme that could be used are positive factors in minimising the impact of screening, targeting and incentive compatibility. Institutional capacity to deliver is much more of a problem. This is not to suggest that knock-on effects are unimportant. But these can also be drawn upon constructively – as in the well-known use of pensions, for example, as a secure source of income employed for a variety of household expenditures and dependants. In this case, the social minimum is liable to be underestimated.

In short, the use of an IMP as a labour market policy appears to be extremely limited. Rather, the goals and targets involved are almost certainly more readily attainable through traditional policy measures such as public works, pensions, and subsistence in kind as in the "Mandela sandwich" for school children and welfare provision more generally. A purer scheme based on income benefits alone and broadly applicable is liable to be excessively costly at any effective minimum and to be subject to severe incentive compatibility problems for the large numbers of workers around the level of the minimum. There would also be considerable problems of the political acceptability of fiscally efficient schemes, with a potential bias towards favouring those who are not most in need.

CHAPTER 6

Industrial Policy and South Africa: A Strategic View

Postscript as Personal Preamble[1]

Bordering on the length of a small book, this Chapter brings together a number of streams of my work, put to the service of how to go about formulating industrial policy in general and for South Africa in particular. One of the most important points is that industrial policy needs to be sector specific and what I have termed vertical – linking production upstream and downstream to consumption (and even disposal itself). In terms of debate at the time within South Africa, this was, to some extent, pushing against an open door. Exactly the same position was being promoted by the Industrial Strategy Project (ISP), a major research programme[2] with strong links to the trade union movement (and to Alec Erwin who was to become Minister of Trade and Industry in 1996). But, as already observed in the previous Chapter, my position on sector policy was very different from the flec-spec approach attached to the ISP (although the ISP did allow airings for other positions in occasional sectoral studies, inevitable where flec-spec could not apply especially around heavy industry).

Significantly, my commitment to sector policy had different origins than flec-spec, arising in part, admittedly, from working for the Greater London Council (GLC) and its London Industrial Strategy (GLC, 1985a), and its own efforts to revive the London rag trade (small clothing producers). But the London economy, dominated by the City and finance, and with large-scale industry long since departed, was totally inappropriate as a model for industrial strategy for South Africa except, even then where appropriate, around the margins. The main source for my sectoral focus came from studies of consumption in general and of food in particular (with a major research project on

1 This working paper was prepared for COSATU and issued under the auspice of the National Institute for Economic Policy (Fine, 1997a), the paper successor to the MERG process which continued for a number of years and, at this time, thanks to the extraordinary energies of Jaya Josie and then Asghar Adelzadeh. The presentation of main points inevitably leads to some repetition of the content of the body of the paper. Thanks to Asghar Adelzadeh, Costas Lapavitsas and John Sender for comments during drafting.

2 See ISP (1995) and Fine (1995) for a critique.

foods and the UK's diet ongoing as this Chapter was being drafted, Fine et al. 1996; and Fine, 1998b).[3]

At the time, the Global Commodity Chain (GCC, subsequently, Global Value Chain, GVC, and Global Production Network, GPN) approach was also emerging and strongly promoted sectoral analysis (often, if subsequently, married to the flec-spec approach). Once again, I departed from this approach because of its ill-fitting imposition of ideal types of GCCs or the like on particular sectors (retail-led, production-led, etc). Unsurprisingly, the more the GCC/GVC/GPNs have been studied, the more ideal types are needed as well as more factors along the chains or networks to be included – the approach has been very slow on consumption itself, other than it should be flexible and, with flec-spec, niche, and even slower on financialisation (as opposed to who appropriates surplus along the chain of provision). My critique, though, was not simply empirical and looking for an improved and enlarged scheme for classification but rejected the latter altogether on the grounds that sectoral developments needed to be located within their particular context and industrial policy defined accordingly rather than being straitjacketed into off-the-shelf ideal types. Each chain (or system of provision, SoP, in my own terminology) is distinctive by sector, time and location and needs to be contextually and concretely specified as such (an energy system as opposed to a food system or a housing system).[4]

In addition, the context itself is not simply intra-sectoral and 'vertical' but also 'horizontal' to incorporate the nature of the South African economy itself, its insertion into global conditions, and the challenges that these pose in terms of addressing (un)employment, inequality, poverty, productivity increase, economic and social infrastructure, regional development, etc. To a large degree, there was a common understanding that South African industrialisation had failed – inescapable given miserable levels of manufacturing investment, and

3 Thus, to understand (policy for) food, and patterns of its consumption, it is essential to trace the sector from its origins in agriculture (and before) through to its retailing, preparation and beyond. Prior to the food study I had researched the relationship between consumer durables and female labour market participation. For a retrospective account and full background to what follows, see Bayliss and Fine (2021).

4 Note that, whilst dwarfed by the GCC/GVC/GPN approach in prominence, the (alternative) SoP approach has attracted a significant and growing following (Bayliss and Fine, 2021 for an overview of its origins and continuing trajectory), described early on by Leslie and Reimer (1999, p. 405) as "the most comprehensive elaboration of production consumption relations". See also Jackson et al. (2004, p. 8). It has also been applied to public provision (Fine, 2025a), especially in the wake of neoliberalism and financialisation, and, in more recent years, it has been taken up as a way of understanding, and remedying, environmental crises through the prism of the determinants of consumption.

lack of international competitiveness of manufacturing despite, or because of, considerable use of protective tariffs. But why there was that failure and its very nature was subject to considerable dispute with corresponding differences over how these problems should be addressed. This will be covered in detail in other Volumes on South Africa to follow. What is highlighted in this Chapter is the failure of the South African financial system to generate sufficient investment despite or, once again, because of its high level of sophistication. Close attention is also given to tariff policy, and the goal of reducing effective rates of protection, showing that the whole exercise of defining EPRs, measuring them, and deducing that reducing them is beneficial is fundamentally flawed.[5]

The intellectual climate at time of writing is that the Washington Consensus is suffering a crisis of legitimacy but the Post-Washington Consensus, spearheaded by Joe Stiglitz at the World Bank as Chief Economist until he was sacked, is just around the corner – although it did little to put industrial policy on the agenda (other than to correct market, informational and institutional failures in broad terms).[6] Also imminent, and so absent from consideration, was the Asian crisis of 1997/98. This had the effect of dulling the shine of the East Asian NICs as exemplars. But what I have called the Developmental State Paradigm (DSP) was also off the agenda in South Africa at that time.[7] Nor had environmental considerations yet thrust themselves to the fore.

5 But I have also argued there is a positive side to (demonstrating) this flaw. It means, unlike EPR calculations, industrial policy has to take account of unemployment, economies of scale and scope, dynamic change, presence of multinational corporations (and inter-affiliate trade), levels of risk in relation to capital-intensity, imperfect competition in input and output markets, and the presence of non-traded goods. In a study for Mozambique, I also pointed to the significance of smuggling – for which tariffs are irrelevant as they are not paid. On a lighter note, searching comprehensively for the literature on EPR brought up many contributions on condoms just as searching on labour segmentation yielded much on Caesarians.

6 Industrial policy was (re)placed explicitly on the World Bank agenda by Justin Lin (2012). But it was in a flawed way, explicitly designed to limit its scope and instruments (Fine and Van Waeyenberge, 2013, for a critique). The more recent rediscovery of (the new) industrial policy is best seen in similar terms and as a leading aspect of what has been dubbed the third phase of financialised neoliberalism (Fine, 2025).

7 Only being hauled from off-stage ten years later in a desperate attempt to relaunch the Mbeki Presidency. Establishment hostility or, more exactly, neglect of the DSP in South Africa no doubt had its rationale in the hostility to state interventionism. Although progressive in its thrust, and a major thorn in the side of the Washington Consensus (industrial policy against the market does work and is necessary), I had my own doubts about the DSP as a way of understanding the South African economy. This is expressed in Fine and Rustomjee (1996) and in many continuing contributions (Fine, 2003, 2007, 2010a and b, 2012a and b, 2016b; Fine and Pollen, 2018; Fine et al. eds, 2013; and Ashman et al. 2010).

As mentioned though, with whatever influence through the ISP, sectoral policy has been, and remains, at least discursively, on the policy agenda and has been heavily signalled as such, by the Department of Trade and Industry not least through the various iterations of its IPAP (Industrial Policy Action Plan) programmes.[8] What also stands out alongside the dogged commitment to sectoral policy is its limited scale, scope and (successful) impact in practice. Why and how this should be so will be covered in later Volumes as this one is concerned simply to establish that alternative policy approaches and policies were available. Suffice it to observe for the time-being that, some hopes are placed in the text that follows upon the appointment of Alec Erwin as Minister for Trade and Industry in 1996 (until 2004),[9] and my co-author of the MEC book (Fine and Rustomjee, 1996) was appointed as Director General to the Department in 1995. Whilst Zav(areh) and I may have had some differences, we were pretty much on the same page both analytically and policy-wise. He is a trained and experienced chemical engineer with qualifications in development studies and a PhD in Economics on the MEC (under my supervision at SOAS). He dedicated his full energies and more to his job as DG. He has continued to serve the public purpose with distinction in many roles, and resigned from a private sector post when he felt it was not committed to that purpose. His contract as DG was not, however, renewed in 2000, and he was replaced by Alistair Reuters who had previously held the role of Deputy Director General for cooperatives (and served for five years as DG before resigning and becoming a very successful businessman across many sectors). Counterfactually, if Zav's contract had been renewed and sectoral industrial policy pursued with vigour in practice, how different might and must things have been in terms of the nature and content of policymaking to come, both within the DTI and in its relations and coordination with other arms of government.

Otherwise, in retrospect, this Chapter represents a major coming to terms with industrial policy if far from a or my final world. Subsequently, as covered in later Volumes, I have debated South African industrial (and other) policy

8 Currently, though, as reported in ITAC (2022, p. 8), "At the start of the sixth administration, the President, Mr Cyril Ramaphosa, called for a re-imagined industrial strategy". But this seems to involve continued commitment to sectoral strategy, "As part of the Government's Re-imagined Industrial Policy, a number of industry Masterplans have been signed, including in the automotive sector, poultry sector, clothing, textile, footwear and leather sector, and sugar sector", p. 19. Imagined, or re-imagined, is the operative word.

9 Alec also served as Deputy Minister of Finance from May 1994 to April 1996, during which he may have been socialised into less state interventionist positions than previously. After the DTI, he served as Minister of Public Enterprises from 2004 until 2009.

in response to contributions and postures that share one thing in common, a failure to get to grips with South African realities, especially as far as the central role of the Minerals-Energy Complex is concerned (with financialisation also increasingly coming to the fore). I have also contributed more generally to debate, especially around the DSP and the World Bank (see earlier footnotes), and on behalf of UNCTAD (Fine, 2011; and see also Fine and Mohamed, 2023). Overall, the literature has become much richer in depth, scope and progressive intent in some respects although less in others (public ownership and major interventionism still tend to be shunned in deference to private industrial and financial interests) with new technologies and environmental considerations much more to the fore (and more acknowledgement of the global organisation of production and its implications for national policies).

Presentation of Main Points

Introduction

For almost two decades, debate over industrial policy for developing countries has been dominated by the agenda set by the World Bank and the IMF. This has pitched the state against the market, with the Washington Consensus heavily favouring the latter and breaking with an earlier traditional dependence upon industrialisation led or heavily influenced by the state sector. More recently, longstanding theoretical and empirical criticism of the Washington Consensus has begun to have an effect, particularly in the light of the experience of the East Asian NICs, for which state economic intervention has been shown to have been both necessary and highly effective.

To a limited extent, South African current industrial policy has incorporated this shift in emphasis towards more reliance upon the state. Nonetheless, policy remains marked by the market-led approach. This is particularly inappropriate as the South African example demonstrates that the state versus market approach is itself misleading as the state must in part work through and with the market, not only in the provision of basic needs and social and economic infrastructure but also in industrial policy. Moreover, due account must be taken of the economic and political interests that are influential upon the state as well as the capacity to formulate, implement and monitor policy. Such issues tend to be set aside when relying upon the more nebulous capacity of the market to deliver what is required.

It would be unfortunate if South Africa continued to be unduly influenced by a market ideology when this is itself being steadily eroded by new initiatives and thinking in development and industrial policy. Indeed, South Africa could itself take a lead in the formulation of a new agenda for industrial policy, to its own as well as to the advantage of other developing countries, especially those in Africa which have been least affected in practice by the new currents in development policy.

Whilst South African industrial policy has rejected exclusive reliance upon the traditional supply-side measure of simply getting the prices right, it has not developed supply-side policies far enough in depth and scope by way of alternative. Welcome acknowledgement of the spill-over effects of industrial clusters and the benefits of social and economic infrastructure does not in principle provide sufficiently for policy formulation which needs to be worked out in detail for individual sectors and their vertical integration, against the background of a systemic strategy for South African industrial reconstruction.

In particular, there is a need, first, for expertise to be developed in industrial policymaking in which due account is taken of full social cost benefit analysis in the light of the strategic objectives of the RDP. The main goal must be the secure provision of basic needs for the vast majority, whether through growth, employment or redistribution. This may be associated with a number of intermediate goals, as in macroeconomic policy to generate business confidence and economic stability, the funding of various mega-projects to generate foreign exchange and knock-on employment, and reform of trade policy to induce competitiveness.

Second, however, it is only a first step to assess these factors in principle, it is also necessary to ensure that the benefits do indeed accrue in practice. Thus, mega-projects for example, designed to generate foreign exchange do not necessarily contribute to more fundamental goals if the earnings are freely invested abroad.

Third, the formulation, implementation and monitoring of policy needs to take account of the vested interests that can influence the policy process and to be assured that strategic goals are being met by including them within contracts where appropriate. Apart from the normal requirements around price, quality and delivery times, these might include wages and working conditions as well as employment levels, export targets, technology transfer and provision of training and adult basic education, etc.

The limited progress made with social plans for the gold mines is indicative of extreme weakness of industrial and other policymaking in South Africa. No serious calculation seems to have been made of the relative merits of mine closures or downsizing, of maintaining the mines for the benefits they bring in employment, multiplier effects and foreign exchange earnings, or of retraining and redeploying a skilled and organised workforce for other employment.[10] What is true in this instance, where the leading issues involved are transparent to a degree, is even more disturbing in other cases of industrial policymaking where neither the capacity exists nor is the attempt being made to come to decisions grounded in an overall strategy incorporating full impact analyses, taking account of sequencing, dynamic economies of scale and scope as well as the more direct and observable effects.

In the first instance, three separate issues are involved in rectifying this situation. The first, readily overlooked and treated as secondary, is organising the systematic collection of adequate data for the policy process. Without such data, it is neither possible to formulate policy adequately nor to monitor its effects. Second, government departments must have the skills and motivation to carry out the necessary policy work. Third, there must be the determination to overcome, or incorporate, the interests of the powerful conglomerates in formulating, implementing and monitoring policy. These three aspects must be carried forward together with, for example, data collection responding to the impact analysis of policy work, and policy responding to and informing the strategies and activities of the conglomerates.

The discussion indicates that industrial policy should not be narrowly conceived, as trade or competition policy for example, as has previously occurred in South Africa as elsewhere from time to time. Rather, as a range of factors and policies impinge upon industrial performance, these need to be taken into account in the specific context within which they are being assessed. How industrial policy is defined, quite apart from how it is formulated, implemented and monitored, will reflect competing economic and political interests. It is imperative that working people bring their perspectives to bear upon the policy process, otherwise it is liable to be partial in content and place important decisions outside the scope of government and public scrutiny.

The Economic Background

South African industrial development has been and remains seriously deficient. A major weakness of South African industry is the relative absence of productive capacity in intermediate and capital goods. This has a negative impact on the economy in a number of different ways:

(a) Economic expansion leads to growing imports of these goods and so creates balance of payments pressures.

10 See discussion of Stals in a footnote in Chapter 1.

(b) Up- and down-stream integration of economic activity is poorly coordinated, in terms of the provision of mutually reinforcing access to finance, markets and technology.
(c) Employment generation, broadening of the skill base, and the opportunities to diversify into new sectors of industry are severely constrained.

Further, South African industry has suffered from stagnation in investment since the early 1980s, whilst South African corporations have engaged in:

(a) capital flight, much of it illegal (estimated to be as much as 7% of GDP),
(b) speculative purchase of existing industrial assets as disinvestment was prompted by international sanctions, and
(c) heavy lobbying for policies to promote their interests, whether materialising in the past under the previous apartheid regime or currently under the newly elected democratic government. This is most notable, for example, in the pursuit of state-subsidised mega-projects and the pressure for privatisation, in part to undermine the state's influence over the economy as well as to obtain productive assets cheaply.

Some key aspects, then, of the South African economy are:

1) A lack of capacity in intermediate and capital goods.
2) An aged capital stock, reflecting limited investment in the past.
3) Declining shares in critical world markets for manufactured exports, especially those in which other successful developing countries have been prominent.
4) A lack of integration across sectors.
5) Limited skills and employment opportunities for the workforce, complemented by poorly trained and inadequate management.
6) A highly concentrated pattern of corporate ownership which straddles the economy as a whole and not just industry.
7) An institutional structure and governance that continues to reflect the economic and industrial imperatives of the past.
8) There is a highly skewed distribution of economic and industrial activity both within South Africa and across the southern African region as a whole.

It is crucial to recognise that these general characteristics of the South African economy differ in weight from one sector to another and within sectors, and that these factors are integrated with one another in different ways depending upon the sector concerned. Clothing and telecommunications, for example, have obviously evolved along quite separate paths and pose different policy challenges despite their common origins within the South African economy. In addition, it is important to recognise that the South African economy enjoys certain advantages – such as large-scale public and private sector corporations, an extensive if unevenly delivered infrastructure, and, especially important, the capacity and prospect of delivering such social and economic infrastructure to a varying degree.

Industrial Strategy

COSATU should consider that the following be given the highest priority in the direct and indirect formulation of industrial policy:[11]

(a) Meeting of basic needs;
(b) Generation of employment;
(c) Education and training;
(d) Sectoral policy;
(e) Infrastructural provision and measures to ensure economic and social spin-offs;
(f) Reform of the financial system to secure finance for industry;
(g) Monitoring and control of foreign investment flows, particularly those outward investments by the conglomerates of South African origin;
(h) Minimum labour standards and the narrowing of wage differentials;
(i) Macroeconomic policy;
(j) Regional integration within South Africa and across the Southern African region;
(k) Restructuring of state assets; and
(l) The reform of the institutions for making industrial policy so that the allocation and coordination of responsibilities across government departments is rationalised, coordinated and coherent.

Some of these are already high on the government's agenda but others are not. Even where they are high on the agenda, this is not always with sufficient detailed attention to their impact on industrial policy, as is the case for macroeconomic strategy, for example.

In relative terms, again without commenting in detail on the policies adopted, too great an emphasis has been placed on the following:

(a) Promoting a spurious business confidence, which remains elusive, constrains consideration of more effective and more certain policymaking, accords priority to a minority of opinion makers and business interests, and does not guarantee a calculable and positive return.
(b) Promoting small business which is imperative but should not be at the expense of distracting attention from policymaking for large-scale

---

11 Future presentations have explicitly added the environment and, what was more taken for granted, inequalities across race and gender.

business on whose fortunes small businesses will probably depend much more than any other single factor.

(c) Promoting privatisation, especially as a source of revenue, since this merely transfers ownership, at a cost, without otherwise formulating constructive policy.

(d) Competition policy in the absence of a broader strategy for industrial and corporate restructuring, since this merely limits the scope of operation of big business without addressing the role of economies of scale and scope.

(e) The promotion of mega-projects at the expense of ensuring their overall economic and commercial viability since these may generate foreign exchange and downstream processing but the net benefits to the economy have to be shown and made to accrue.

In short, COSATU should see its role as first shifting the industrial policy agenda to give top priority to those issues of most importance to working people and, then, to ensure efficient, effective and equitable policies are adopted within that agenda.

Implementation and Monitoring

One form in which the implementation and monitoring of policy can be effectively pushed forward is through contract compliance. As a major customer of industry, government can impose a number of conditions on its suppliers over and above the traditional concerns of price, quality and delivery time. Contracts may usefully incorporate requirements on the development of education and skills, security of employment, and the development and sharing of technology, quite apart from trade union recognition, affirmative action, and observance of general government policy and specific sectoral policy, such as export targeting. A contract compliance strategy with three separate arms is required: one concerned with compliance in the narrow sense of meeting contracts effectively in the absence of corruption and profiteering; one concerned with the employment and other impacts of businesses such as export and training levels; and the last to promote the role and interests of consumers.

More generally than through the government's own procurement, there is a tripartite institutional structure for the implementation and monitoring of industrial policy, including industrial corporations themselves, financial institutions and government. Together these incorporate a financial system, broadly conceived. International evidence suggests that the nature of a financial system is crucial in determining the levels, composition and effectivity of investment. Despite some positive aspects, in the capacity of conglomerates to generate finance for investment internally, the South African financial system has functioned in practice like a market-based as opposed to a banking system, a feature which is generally acknowledged to be deficient in promoting appropriate industrial investment and policy, especially in a developing economy in transition.

Despite the discrediting of the de Kock reforms of the South African financial systems in practice and in principle, together with a complete change in domestic and external circumstances and in economic objectives, no serious consideration has been given to relations between finance and industry, and the capacity of government departments to coordinate and innovate in the formulation of policy. This is despite:

1) Inadequate provision of finance for industry.
2) Inadequate coordination of investment across sectors.
3) Inadequate formulation, implementation and monitoring of sectoral strategies.
4) Inadequate coordination across government departments and other agencies.
5) Corporate strategies that are inconsistent with the policies required for industrial reconstruction.
6) Macroeconomic policy that is unduly influenced by short-term financial rather than longer-term and other economic imperatives.

Consequently, it is recommended that an investigation into industrial policy be undertaken with a particular but not exclusive emphasis upon the role played by finance for industrial investment. The inquiry should address:

1) A review of past, present and prospective sources of finance for investment together with the design of an appropriate system of data collection so that policy can be soundly formulated.
2) A review of past, present and prospective institutional arrangements governing the relations between finance and industry, covering both macroeconomic and microeconomic issues, distinguishing between different sectors and enterprise scale and type of ownership.
3) A review of past, present and prospective methods of, and personnel capacity for, the monitoring of investment in both the public and the private sectors, as well as how the two interact. Particular attention needs to be paid to the coordination of policy across government departments.
4) A review of past, present and prospective levels of capital flight, legal or illegal, and the regulatory and fiscal initiatives which might stem damaging outflow of capital.
5) Consideration of formalising financial monitoring of industry through policies such as directed credit for successful promotion of exports and other strategic objectives.

6) Institutional initiatives to strengthen the role of Task Forces in sectors such as automobiles and clothing/textiles and to introduce them into other sectors.
7) How new sources of finance can be used to raise substantial additional capital for the developmental financial institutions, such as the IDC and DBSA, so that they expand their operations where social exceed private returns.

This review should also explicitly address the role played by direct foreign investment, drawing upon best practice in assessing the net impact of such investment according to a full social cost-benefit analysis. There can be no presumption that the overall impact will be significant relative to what needs to be provided from domestic resources, and investments need to be carefully assessed on a piecemeal basis in the light of sectorally-specific circumstances and outcomes. The undue courting of direct foreign investment will be damaging to policymaking more generally, and will engender support for policies that could even weaken investment from domestic resources as pressure builds for deflationary policies to allow for the lifting of exchange controls on capital movements.

Trade policy in South Africa has in general pursued trade liberalisation beyond the level even required by the developments arising out of the Uruguay Round. This is despite the potential for negative impact on the industries concerned and the failure to formulate and put adequate supply-side policies in place prior to liberalisation. The justification for, and impact of, trade liberalisation has rested to a large extent on the calculation of effective rates of protection (EPRs). These are, however, ill-founded conceptually, in practice in how they have been calculated, and as a guide to policy in their imputed effects. In particular, they take no account of dynamic and static economies of scale and scope, excess capacity, capital-labour intensity, market structure, presence of multinationals, skill requirements of the labour force and management, developments in world markets, product differentiation and quality, commercial risk, age structure of capital stock, the differential impact of non-tradeables, and the substitution between capital and labour in production in response to changing input prices. In this light, it is inconceivable how EPRs can justifiably be used as the basis for industrial policymaking of which trade policy is an integral part. Doubts must be equally strong over their usefulness for measuring macroeconomic impacts on employment, inflation and growth.

Rather than assessing trade independently of industrial (or supply-side) policy, the two must be integrated with neither logical nor sequential priority attached to trade policy. Exactly the opposite is occurring in South Africa in practice. The process of dismantling protection has preceded the election of the ANC government. It is gathering momentum. That it does so appears to reflect a lack of conglomerate commitment to the restructuring of many industrial sectors, with a preference for a strategy of global reorganisation of productive investment. Accordingly, it is essential that appropriate *sectoral* industrial strategies are put in place, insisting upon cooperation from large business if necessary, prior to any further trade liberalisation.

1 Introduction

The debate over industrial policy for the last two decades has been dominated by an agenda set by the World Bank and the IMF in the context of stabilisation and structural adjustment policies. The main thrust of the position adopted by the international financial institutions (IFIs) has been two-fold. On the one hand, industrial policy has been subsumed under or at least subordinated to deflationary macroeconomic targeting. On the other hand, industrial interventionism itself has been criticised in deference to market-led policies – of getting the prices right, whether for goods, money (the interest rate) or the exchange rate. Measures to promote domestic industry, from tariff protection and import-substitution more generally through to advantageous access to credit and public ownership have been condemned.

The debate that these postures have prompted is aptly summarised in terms of the state versus the market. The IFIs have leaned considerably, if not falling over, on the market side. Both on theoretical and empirical grounds, however, they have been heavily and successfully criticised. That criticism reached a pinnacle with the publication of the World Bank's own assessment of the East Asian Miracle (World Bank, 1993). In deference to the weight of scholarly evidence that had demonstrated that the success of the newly-industrialised countries (NICs) had been heavily dependent upon extensive state intervention, including getting the prices wrong, the World Bank's study had concluded that these interventions were in fact market-friendly (what the market would have done in the absence of imperfections) and, in any case, were not open to replication in other countries. This had the simple effect of outraging critics even further, leading to further accounts of the way in which state intervention, and industrial policy in particular, had been central to the performance of NICs.[12]

12 See, for example, the special section in World Development edited by Amsden (ed.) (1994). For a review of the literature for its relevance for South Africa, see Fine and Rustomjee (1996, Chapter 2).

The critical literature has also been constructive in two separate ways. First, in the light of accumulating evidence from country studies, it has been able to uncover in some detail the different ways through which active industrial policy can be successful, whether it be targeting of exports, preferential access to credit, coordinating expansion across vertically integrated sectors, etc. Second, by the same token, it has revealed that successful NICs do not constitute a single model. They are highly diverse, both in their patterns of industrialisation and in the type of industrial policy through which their success has been achieved. This leads to the important conclusion that specific policies cannot be readily replicated from one country to another with exactly the same effects, certainly not without taking account of comparative differences. It does not mean, however, that there are no lessons to be learnt from the experience of others. Rather, attention has to be focused on strategic considerations and on the tasks that industrial policy needs to address as well as the ways of accomplishing them.[13]

The last point has to a large extent led to a different and primarily separate branch of the literature. That referred to already has been concerned with what are the appropriate policies to be adopted by the state. There is often an implicit assumption that, once identified, these policies can be effortlessly put in place by the state. However, there can be no such presumption. For, quite apart from whether the state has the capacity to formulate and implement the desired policies, it may not have the political power to do so. Such concerns have led to a different focus – leaving aside what are to be the policies themselves, does the state have the strength to carry them out?[14]

The notion of the strong state has also proved elusive. It has at least three separate components which do not necessarily coincide with one another, and each of which can be examined under a number of different elements. First, there is the general capacity of the administration – does it have good governance, the skills, efficiency and capacity to carry out policy? Second, there is the issue of the extent to which the state is able to resist or rise above the representation of particular political and economic interests, whether they be from different classes or from within the state bureaucracy itself (as in corruption). Third, there is the extent of the state's economic activity itself, its strength within the economy.

13 For a discussion of the lessons for African industrialisation to be learnt from Asian experience, see Stein (ed.) (1995).

14 In the context of the literature on the developmental state, Fine and Rustomjee (1996) refer to those concerned with the appropriate policies as the "economic" school, and those with the capacity to carry them out as the "political" school. See also Fine and Stoneman (1996).

The most facile way of answering questions concerning the developmental state is to argue that market-led policies are the ones that can by-pass the political problems arising out of state intervention. However, once again, the literature has shown that such conclusions are not just wrong but that they are also simplistic. The political processes through which state policy is decided are complex and diverse. They, along with the balance of interests which are represented, cannot be spirited away by an illusory reliance upon market forces. Even such a stance would require a strong state to resist the pressures for discretionary interventions that arise from interest groups.

It follows that, whilst all agree with the need for 'good governance', its presence in practice, especially in the context of industrial policy, depends upon a judicious sensitivity both to the policy requirements themselves and the feasibility of achieving them in the light of underlying economic and political interests. As a result, it is far from clear that the analytical agenda set by the IFIs in the past, irrespective of their success in debate and practice, is appropriate. The clash between state and market is not necessarily fundamental as is most apparent when particular policy issues are examined. Rather, as for each of the constituent elements of the RDP, for example, the issue is not one of state versus market, or public versus private, but how the two can be functionally integrated. Such integration means that the state must play a leading and active role albeit one dependent upon the interests that it represents, as well as the determination and skill with which it represents them.

Significantly, over the past few years, a shift appears to be taking place in the thinking of the IFIs. They have become much less confident in their policy framework in principle and with the results of their policies in practice. To some extent, this has been due to the weight of evidence that has been presented against them. But it has also reflected shifts in the sources of aid, with Japan emerging to a position of prominence. Japan's orientation has been very different from what has been termed the Washington Consensus. For the latter would require Japan not only to deny the known realities of its own economic history, in which the state has played and continues to play a crucial and extensive role in industrial policy, it would also undermine the activist policies that Japan seeks in other countries as a complement to many of its own strategies for direct foreign investment which is increasing rapidly.

Indeed, the World Bank study of the East Asian miracles was commissioned by the Japanese even if the content was not entirely to its satisfaction.[15] The

15 See Wade (1996) for a full account of these issues.

pressure for a change in thinking, however, is slowly but unevenly finding its way into the IFIs. At one extreme, the reaction is stronger than the challenge to the received wisdoms. This appears to be so in eastern Europe, for example, where the introduction of what are perceived to be market forces and privatisation has been pursued disastrously as an article of faith.[16] On the terrain of debate, there are still those arguing that the problem is not with the IFIs' policies but with the failure to implement them. This leads to attempts both to exert influence over governance itself, within the limits set by proscriptions on IFIs' political interference, and to train indigenous elites that will 'own' and promote the desired policies themselves.

With respect to South Africa, the position and influence of the IFIs have been mixed. None can doubt their heavy presence, the flood of policy documents and advice, nor the growth of their direct and indirect impact upon government through a variety of channels. On the other hand, government has occasionally sought other sources of advice, and the peculiarity and prominence of the South African 'adjustment' has induced both caution and some innovation on the part of the IFIs. They have been willing to recognise that public sector investment can crowd in the private sector and have called for a land reform. Nonetheless, whatever the merits of their particular proposals in these and other areas, advice on macroeconomic and industrial policy remains rooted in past principles and practices, with little by way of concession to the crumbling of the Washington Consensus upon which they have been based.

To the extent that South Africa remains responsive to such guidance, it would be a triple misfortune. First, it would be tying itself to a policy framework and policies whose sell-by-date had already passed but which have continued to be peddled because of institutional inertia and for want of the full development of alternatives.[17] Second, South Africa can itself play a major role in displacing

16 On an anecdotal level, in a speech on infrastructural provision in Azerbaijan in November, 1996, having first disowned any responsibility for the low risk rating reported for the country in *Euromoney*, the representative of the EBRD promised, to thunderous applause, the "wherewithal to drive privatisation to its last point", suggesting that the example of Albania should be followed into which foreign investment had flowed after a Coca-Cola plant had been established. In fact, the wherewithal offered over a number of programmes was in the region of $150 million, not all disbursed and subject to conditions. By comparison, in an earlier speech, the Deputy Minister for the Economy had indicated the economy needed US$22 billion for modernisation of the economy, nearly 150 times the wherewithal. Over previous years, whilst awaiting privatisation and investment, Azerbaijani industrial output had fallen by 60%.

17 In addition, the conventional wisdom based on getting the prices right has necessarily left unexplored the various other sorts of industrial policy that might be supported. It has also

the Washington Consensus and in developing more constructive alternatives to fill the void that is being created by the increasingly transparent sterility of the state versus market approach that has marked the outlook of that Consensus and many of its critics. It would be a shame, given their past record, if the IFIs themselves simply took on the responsibility for the new policy frameworks and initiatives. They would be marked by the weight of the past traditions as well as a simple shift along a one-dimensional understanding of state versus market. Third, then, this opens up policy potential not only for South Africa itself but also for the Southern African region and for Africa as a whole. For it is notable that, eastern Europe apart, application of the Consensus remains at its strongest in Africa where, indeed, it is least appropriate.[18]

Significantly, and not surprisingly, the shifting balance against the Washington Consensus has been felt across a number of policy areas, and analytical misgivings in the context of development have been reinforced by a new wave of literature mainly evolving in the context of the developed economies. One area dealt with at some length in this Report is that of the relations between finance and industry, for which financial liberalisation is no longer seen as a panacea. In addition, trade policy is also covered in some depth. Once again, the new international trade theory has played a major role in questioning trade liberalisation dogma in the light of developmental externalities, economies of scale and imperfect competition.

Similarly, new developments in labour market theory have criticised the notion of labour market flexibility as having been too readily associated with reducing real wages and undermining working conditions. Both theoretical and empirical evidence has been used to show that labour markets do not work in such simplistic fashions, that flexibility is extremely complex and multi-faceted, depending upon the interaction of labour and other markets and institutions. Further, flexibility at one level, in pushing down wages, for

---

been wedded to the idea that manufacturing has been unduly advantaged by powerful urban elites, at the expense of rural and agricultural interests and social and economic infrastructure more generally. Accordingly, as observed by Riddell (1993), manufacturing has been of the lowest priority in allocation of foreign aid. In sub-Saharan Africa its share fell from less than 12% at the beginning of the 1980s to 7% by the end of the decade, with the prospects of this trend continuing. Nothing could illustrate better the unsuitability of advice on manufacturing emanating from the donor agencies. It is not their priority either in theory or in practice.

18 See Fine and Stoneman (1996) for a review of the assessments of the experience of structural adjustment and stabilisation policies in Africa. See also Mosley et al. (1995) and White (1996).

example, can adversely affect systemic flexibility – by discouraging labour market turnover, lack of training, and failure to adopt new technology and more capital-intensive and productive investments.[19] The most striking example of the turning back of conventional wisdom is the explosive growth of literature on the impact of minimum wages. Representatives of South African business would do well to take note of the increasing difficulty that orthodox economists are experiencing in demonstrating that there is anything other than a negligible impact of minimum wages on employment levels, and whether it is negative at all.[20]

Other major issues within the labour market, apart from unemployment, include the levels of skills, education and training, and the extreme inequality in earnings. Whilst most policy emphasis has been upon the skill level of workers in general, and the shortages of particular skills, there is considerable evidence that the skills of management are often seriously lacking and that levels of remuneration are unnecessarily high.[21] This raises, in the context of affirmative action, not only the raising of the general levels of skills as well as narrowing the disparities in access and provision, but also whether existing skills are being properly measured and rewarded. For reasons of efficiency as well as equity, it is important that proper job evaluation schemes be introduced into South African employment and that pay scales, grading and other components of the pay package, or benefits, be based equitably upon them. This not only has the effect of encouraging the efficient deployment of labour, motivating the workforce, and pricing skills appropriately, it also often serves as an important trigger to more general evaluations of the efficiency of work organisation, thereby inducing productivity increase. Job evaluation exercises should begin in the public sector immediately, in part as a component of affirmative action, and be encouraged and supported in the private sector, ultimately as a policy requirement.[22]

Another area of progress in economic analysis, of considerable relevance to developing economies and to industrial policy, has been the new (endogenous) growth theory. It seeks to explain why divergence in growth rates should persist

---

19 See LMC (1996) and also ILO (1996) which demonstrate the considerable degree of flexibility that is characteristic of the South African labour market. See Fine (1998a, Chapter 4) for a more wide-ranging review.

20 Also see LMC (1996) and ILO (1996) for the South African evidence, and Fine (1998a, Chapter 9) for an assessment of the literature.

21 See ILO (1996) and Wood (1995).

22 See Fine (1998a, Chapter 8) for a discussion of job evaluation in the context of equal opportunities.

over long periods of time despite mobility of capital. It shows how the growth process can be cumulative, either through the externalities between investing and innovating firms or through the positive difference between public and private rates of return that arise out of various sorts of economic and social infrastructure. Significantly, throughout the debate on growth and redistribution, none of this literature was referenced. The same remains very much true today. It is particularly marked in the formulation of macroeconomic policy, where the short and long runs are illegitimately separated from one another, and the short run is seen as deviations around a trend that is more or less given by fixed production possibilities and the proportion of resources devoted to investment. The cumulative impact of public sector expenditure is not incorporated, necessarily leading to negative crowding-out rather than positive productivity effects. Nor is any proper account taken of the monopolistic structure of the economy.[23]

There is a very big difference between identifying these theoretical arguments, and their empirical and policy application to other countries, and applying them to South Africa, particularly to industrial policy. This will be demonstrated in some detail below in the case of finance for industry. However, the difficulties must be overcome if the policy process is to advance beyond discredited theories and policy frameworks. Three conditions need to be fulfilled before this can happen. First, it is impossible to translate such abstract theories into policy practice in the absence of reliable, comprehensive and up to date statistical surveys of manufacturing and other data. What can be achieved depends upon the current industrial structure, skill and employment levels, machinery in place and its age composition, product market structure, capacity utilisation, etc. Only with information on these factors in place will it be possible to assess potential and the mechanisms for achieving what is proposed. Otherwise, unfounded and untested assertions will flourish, become part of conventional wisdom, and unduly influence the policy process in ways which will be self-confirming in their selection of evidence and even in their effects on industrial performance.[24]

---

23 For a critical assessment of macroeconomic theory in the light of the failure to address these issues adequately, see Fine (1998a, Chapter 2). Damania and Madsen (1995), for example, construct a model, testing it successfully on twenty-two OECD countries (those other than Iceland, Yugoslavia and Turkey), which finds counter-intuitive results from raising the interest rate as a result of allowing for strategic behaviour by monopolies. See also Madsen (1995).

24 For detailed arguments of the same sort in the context of the labour market, see ILO (1996). Its work had the effect of questioning the meaning and lack of flexibility in the labour market, of pointing to the depressing effects of overtime, of critically assessing

Second, government has to have the capacity to carry out the necessary policy analysis. The evidence is overwhelmingly depressing in this regard. Even where the sorts of theoretical points mentioned previously have been acknowledged, they have rarely been quantified and factored into policymaking. This is most apparent in the current downsizing of the gold industry. The implications of closures and redundancies are well-known. There are multiplier effects on domestic industry and on the demand effects from the expenditure of wage revenue. There is the need to provide for those made redundant, and those who depend upon the wage revenue. There is loss of foreign exchange that would be earned by gold sales which would ease the balance of payments. As is well-known, considerations such as these have led the NUM to demand a social plan for the mining industry. This does not seem to have been matched by any careful and comprehensive social cost-benefit analysis of the various options, even though this is a standardised procedure that could be readily adapted to South African circumstances.[25] Failure to have proceeded in this way, in principle and practice, is almost certainly sadly indicative of a lack of application of such policy work in other areas, such as trade and infrastructure, where full impact analyses are notable only for their absence.

The Industrial Development Corporation (IDC), for example, has created employment for 41,000 workers over the past five years at a direct cost of R463,000 per job. Within this figure, the R1.4 billion spent on SMEs has given rise to 26,000 jobs at a cost of R54,000 each in capital expenditure.[26] Now, these dramatic differences in capital expenditure per job in a labour surplus economy might well be justified on a whole series of grounds over and above those of commercial viability, not least the indirect jobs created through linkages and multiplier effects and the foreign exchange generated through export earnings. But these do have to be demonstrated through a full cost-benefit analysis of prospective impact, and that supporting policies put in place guarantee that the benefits do accrue and the costs are not exceeded.[27]

This might be due to lack of skilled capacity within government. If so, this needs to be urgently acknowledged and rectified. Of course, lack of skills, in government as elsewhere, is a general and, at times, genuine complaint and

---

the notion of jobless growth and high and undifferentiated levels of unemployment, etc. Whilst all empirical issues, sensible theoretical and policy discussion is dependent on the quality of data availability.

25 For discussion of such an analysis for the closure programme for the British coal industry, with a case study included, see Fine (1990a).

26 See BDM (1996).

27 For a discussion of the need to reform the IDC in light of its investment record, see LMC (1996).

excuse. In the interim, before such skill shortages can be made good, it is necessary that tasks to be done and the training to be given be prioritised. It would appear that insufficient priority is being given to these tasks and skills because they are not recognised as sufficiently important by government in its current policy framework. A third condition for putting more soundly based policies into practice is the commitment of government to do so. Apart from collecting data and providing skills, it needs to motivate its own civil service and to overcome opposition from civil society, and not least corporate capital. For the latter is liable to resist some of these proposals as a matter of principle – as potentially opening the way for more extensive intervention in the economy. Whilst employers would appear to have little to fear from a fully informed civil service, competent to undertake full cost-benefit analysis of its activities, it could well prefer to pre-empt, rather than to cooperate with such an extension of government capability even though it could itself benefit from more effective industrial policy for the domestic economy. Irrespective of the stance of big business, the extension of the power of government to determine and deliver well-informed and effective policies is imperative.

2 Defining Industrial Policy

Specifying the scope and content of industrial policy is extremely difficult. Almost any economic policy of any significance is liable to affect industrial performance and, consequently, can be considered to constitute a component of industrial policy. Even those who would seek to minimise the role of industrial policy, in view of a favourable stance on the market and a general aversion to state intervention, can be interpreted as adopting an industrial policy of a particular type. 'Getting the prices right', by moving towards free trade for example, and providing macroeconomic stability, through reducing budget deficits, represent particular analytical and policy stances towards what is deemed liable to make industry prosper. At times, if not always, such policies are adopted with industrial development in mind. It is argued, for example, that there is no case for promoting domestic industry through protection at the expense of imports, or that macroeconomic stability is more important than undue expansion in aggregate demand.

By the same token, deliberately getting the prices wrong, through protection or subsidies, and using government expenditure to promote industry, even directly through investment in state enterprises, can be considered to be more traditional and common components of industrial policy. Moreover, kick-starting the economy through government expenditure will also create enlarged markets for domestic industrial production, both directly and indirectly through multiplier effects. However, as previously observed, the sensitivity of industrial performance to a whole range of influences means that policies which affect research and development, training and skills, regional distribution of economic activity, etc and which may have been adopted for other purposes, under different rubrics, or by ministries other than that of trade and industry, also qualify, at least in principle, as industrial policies. Even where such interventions do emanate from concerns other than those directly related to industry, their impact upon industrial performance may be more important than in their intended or initiating purpose. Such side-effects are, for example, especially important in the case of macroeconomic policy, which is intended to govern overall levels of demand, interest rates, and the exchange rate – all of which are important to industrial performance. The same also applies, for example, to industrial relations and labour market policy which are more readily seen to have an effect on industrial performance rather than as components of industrial policy itself.

As a result, it is necessary neither to take a fixed nor a limited view of what constitutes industrial policy even though this is what has happened traditionally – in South Africa as elsewhere, in policy as well as in academic discussions. The result in defining and debating industrial policy is that only particular, if shifting, elements have, from time to time, been brought to the fore whilst others have been neglected or omitted altogether.[28]

Why this should be so and why certain components of industrial policy should be prominent at certain times and circumstances and not in others are not always easy to disentangle. Often it is a consequence of intellectual or policy fashions. An equally important influence, however, are the interests of those who are affected by industrial and other policies. Some can clearly have an interest in keeping some issues off the industrial policy agenda just as they can have an interest in highlighting other issues. Thus, prior to dispute over the conduct of industrial policy, there is the matter of determining what it is and, equally important, how it should be settled – whether within the orbit of government institutions explicitly designated to make industrial policy, or not, through governmental forum, or even outside government altogether. It used to be said, for example, that the United States did not need an industrial policy for the electronics sector whilst it had IBM!

28 For a recognition of this point, see Chang (1994) who offers a particular response in defining industrial policy as sectorally targeted. For a different view, see Fine (1997d) who considers that the definition should be left open according to context.

These remarks are borne out by considering the way in which industrial policy has been defined in South Africa, especially during the apartheid era. According to the Industrial Development Corporation, even as late as 1990, industrial policy is perceived to have been primarily implemented through the use of protection, something which it now deplores as detrimental to industrial performance; for the IDC (1990, p. 1), "the terms 'trade policy' and 'industrial policy' are used synonymously and interchangeably". This narrowing down of the definition of industrial policy is particularly ironical in view of the fact that the IDC was itself one of the main instruments of industrial policy through its investment strategies – through which SASOL, ISCOR and other large companies were built up.

In addition, it is not simply industrial policy that is narrowly defined by the IDC in terms of the policy instruments employed. The strategy underlying industrial policy is also narrowly understood. For the IDC states that, "for almost 70 years, the industrial development policy of successive governments was based on import replacement". In short, despite itself having been extremely active in industrial policy in a variety of ways and with a variety of objectives, the IDC chooses to limit the definition of industrial policy to trade policy, linked to a corresponding strategy of import-substituting industrialisation. This has the further effect of leaving aside other contributing factors to industrial performance, not least the oppressive labour market policies adopted under the apartheid system and, possibly more conventionally understood as industrial policy, the building up of heavy industry around mining and energy.

The purpose of this commentary is not so much to indict the IDC for having defined industrial policy and strategy too narrowly, but rather to illustrate how its definition of industrial policy, and the definitions of others, are far from neutral precisely because of what is included and what is excluded. At different times, different policies come to the fore – the role of small businesses, the promotion of exports, the need to introduce more competition by breaking up large-scale conglomerates, the pressure to privatise, etc. The particular prominence of these issues at different times needs to be treated with considerable caution. For the setting of the policy debate will tend to promote some interests at the expense of others, and to exaggerate and generalise the significance of certain policies to the exclusion of others.

What the experience of industrial policy demonstrates is that the shift in policy fashions is a reflection, however appropriately, of different industrial problems at different times. The problems and solutions tend to be generalised. So, just as a wide range of different economic policies can have an impact on industrial performance, so such impacts are liable to be very different from one economy to another and from one sector of the economy to another. For some economies or sectors, finance for investment may be the problem, whereas for others this may not be so compared to the availability of markets, the skills of the workforce, etc. It follows that the definition of industrial policy, drawing upon the wide range of options available, should be specific to the problems to be addressed – which themselves need to be identified and justified. By the same token, COSATU should be prepared to refuse to accept the particular definition of industrial policy that emanates from its negotiating partners, since this is liable to be limited or skewed in scope and content.

A related but different point concerns the way in which industrial policy tends to be understood purely in terms of the instruments adopted by government, however much these are focused and narrowly or widely interpreted. By contrast, the position adopted here is that industrial policy needs to be set in a much broader context. It requires an assessment of the economy and the place of industry within it, both in terms of structure and dynamic. This is the only appropriate basis on which industrial policies can be formulated. The formulation of policy, however, requires the specification of goals, objectives or strategies. Attention must be paid to how and whether the policies can be implemented, through which mechanisms and institutions, and with whose participation. Finally, provision must be made for assessing the impact, and hence success or failure, of the policy processes – with corresponding provision for the revision of policy in the light of outcomes.

Just as the definition of industrial policy can reflect different interests and outlooks, so the same applies to the assessment of the economy, the formulation of priorities, and how policy is to be implemented and monitored. COSATU is liable to bring a different view to bear on each of these aspects than its partners in negotiations.

The Economic Background

South African industrial development has been and remains seriously deficient. This is despite the misleading view that primary production (agriculture and mining) has become less important to the economy. In fact, South African industry has a skewed structure in terms of the composition of output, continuing to rely heavily upon the processing of primary materials (as in steel, SASOL, and food industries, for example) and the manufacture of consumer goods at domestic prices that are not internationally competitive and for a market structure of demand that reflects the uniquely inegalitarian distribution of income. A major weakness of South African industry is the relative absence of productive capacity in intermediate and capital goods. This has a negative impact on the economy in a number of different ways:

(a) Economic expansion leads to growing imports of these goods and so creates balance of payments pressures.
(b) Up- and down-stream integration of economic activity is poorly coordinated, whether in the provision of mutually reinforcing access to finance, markets and technology. At times, protection or (transfer) pricing policy has led to domestic manufacturers only obtaining access to South African produced inputs at prices above those prevailing on world markets and available to competitors.[29]
(c) Employment generation, broadening of the skill base, and the opportunities to diversify into new sectors of industry are severely constrained.

These weaknesses of South African industry are not accidental nor are they simply the consequences of apartheid. Rather, they reflect the inheritance of *past* economic policies, although these were successfully designed to build up large-scale Afrikaner capital and integrate it with large-scale 'English' capital. They also reflect the way in which the private sector, dominated by a few multinational corporations of South African origin, continues to be committed to a speculative and international orientation with little or no regard to the industrial reconstruction of the domestic South African economy.

More specifically, South African industry has suffered from stagnation in investment since the early 1980s, whilst South African corporations have engaged in:

(a) capital flight, much of it illegal (estimated to be as much as 7% of GDP),[30]
(b) speculative purchase of industrial assets as disinvestment was prompted by international sanctions, and
(c) heavy lobbying for policies to promote their interests, whether materialising in the past under the previous apartheid regime or currently under the newly elected democratic government. This is most notable, for example, in the pursuit of state-subsidised mega-projects and the pressure for privatisation, in part to undermine the state's influence over the economy as well as to obtain productive assets cheaply.

In short, South African industrialisation has been a *failure* relative to the performance of other middle-income developing countries, despite some notable achievements on the basis of some sectors around mining and energy, and the limited scope of success is a consequence of the continuing failure of both the state and the private sector. Nor is the failure of the private sector a consequence of the role of the state. Indeed, at least over the past twenty years, state economic policy has been primarily driven by the interests of a few large-scale

29 For the chemicals industry, see Crompton (1995). See also Wood (1995).
30 Estimates vary considerably. For a review, see Wood (1995).

South African conglomerates. It follows that the solutions to industrial weaknesses do not rest upon the withdrawal from state industrial intervention and reliance upon the market (by which is meant, in practice, a few large-scale corporations). Rather, there is the strongest possible case for continuing an extensive industrial policy of a different type and with the different objectives as defined by the RDP (in its initial version).

Some key aspects, then, of the South African economy are:[31]

1) A lack of capacity in intermediate and capital goods.
2) An aged capital stock, reflecting limited investment in the past.
3) Declining shares in critical world markets for manufactured exports, especially those in which other successful developing countries have been prominent.[32]
4) A lack of integration across sectors.
5) Limited skills and employment opportunities for the workforce, complemented by poorly trained and inadequate management.[33]
6) A highly concentrated pattern of corporate ownership which straddles the economy as a whole and not just industry.
7) An institutional structure and governance that continues to reflect the economic and industrial imperatives of the past.
8) There is a highly skewed distribution of economic and industrial activity both within South Africa and across the southern African region as a whole.

It is crucial to recognise that these general characteristics of the South African economy differ in weight from one sector to another and within sectors, and that these factors are integrated with one another in different ways depending upon the sector concerned. Clothing and telecommunications, for example, have obviously evolved along quite separate paths and pose different policy challenges despite their common origins within the South African economy. In addition, it is important to recognise that the South African economy enjoys certain advantages – such as large-scale public and private sector corporations, an extensive if unevenly delivered infrastructure, and, especially important, the capacity and prospect of delivering such social and economic infrastructure to a varying degree.

---

31 For discussion of South African industry, see ISP (1995) and Fine and Rustomjee (1996). See also Fine (1997d).

32 See Wood (1995) and Moll (1990).

33 See ILO (1996) and the survey on which it drew, and Wood (1995).

3 Industrial Strategy

In formulating industrial policy, it is essential to retain a grasp of a broader industrial and economic and social strategy. This is so for three separate reasons. First, industrial policy is subject to considerable conflict, not surprising in its representing different interests. It is essential to retain a hold on what those differences are, especially as negotiations take on a more detailed form. Second, as already observed, the scope of industrial policy is frequently unduly narrowed down to particular issues. Third, the initial goals of industrial policy often become displaced onto other objectives which take on an undue priority of their own – whether it be 'competitiveness', employment creation, or obtaining investment at any cost without assessing the broader implications and impact.

Moreover, government is subject to a range of economic, political and ideological pressures. Some of these are directly antagonistic to working people and the trade union movement, others are indirectly so. Many of these pressures, particularly those originating from big business and international agencies, are also unrepresentative in any democratic sense. Consequently, it is legitimate for COSATU to press for its own industrial policy perspectives, partly in response to its own sectional interests, partly on behalf of working people more generally, and partly as a programme for more extensive and rapid political and economic reform of a society that continues to be marked by the ravages of the apartheid regime.

Nor is it simply a matter of COSATU occupying a legitimate position at the bargaining table and representing its own and other interests. The continuing economic and industrial structures inherited from the past, and the general lack of capacity to formulate, implement and monitor programmes, imply not only that there are genuine differences within policy debates but also that different constituencies have different capacities for creating priorities in the attention to, and formulation of, policy. Moreover, big business and international agencies are particularly adept and well-organised in pressing for some policies rather than others, shifting both the policy agenda and the content of that agenda.

Further, industrial policy is not simply trade or competition policy as often narrowly and traditionally seen in the South African context. Rather, it is at the rough end of a range of policies that can affect industrial outcomes in complex and varied ways from sector to sector and from region to region. This is true, for example, of labour market, macroeconomic and technology policy as previously argued.

As a consequence, and irrespective of its own policy positions and differences with government and business, COSATU should consider that the following be given the highest priority in the direct and indirect formulation of industrial policy:

(a) Meeting of basic needs.
(b) Generation of employment.
(c) Education and training.
(d) Sectoral policy.
(e) Infrastructural provision and measures to ensure economic and social spin-offs.
(f) Reform of the financial system to secure finance for industry.
(g) Monitoring and control of foreign investment flows, particularly those outward investments by the conglomerates of South African origin.
(h) Minimum labour standards and the narrowing of wage differentials.
(i) Macroeconomic policy.
(j) Regional integration within South Africa and across the Southern African region.
(k) Restructuring of state assets.
(l) The reform of the institutions for making industrial policy so that the allocation and coordination of responsibilities across government departments is rationalised and coherent.

Some of these are already high on the government's agenda but others are not. Even where they are high on the agenda, this is not always with sufficient detailed attention to their impact on industrial policy, as is the case for macroeconomic strategy, for example.

In relative terms, again without commenting on the policies adopted, too great an emphasis has been placed on the following:

(a) Promoting a spurious business confidence, which remains elusive, constrains consideration of more effective and more certain policymaking, accords priority to a minority of opinion makers and business interests, and does not guarantee a calculable and positive return.
(b) Promoting small business which is imperative but should not be at the expense of distracting attention from policymaking for large-scale business on whose fortunes small businesses will probably depend more than any other single factor.
(c) Promoting privatisation, especially as a source of revenue, since this merely transfers ownership, at a cost, without otherwise formulating constructive policy.

(d) Competition policy in the absence of a broader strategy for industrial and corporate restructuring, since this merely limits the scope of operation of big business without addressing the role of economies of scale and scope.

(e) The promotion of mega-projects at the expense of ensuring their overall economic and commercial viability since these may generate foreign exchange and downstream processing but the net benefits to the economy have to be shown and made to accrue.

In short, COSATU should see its role as first shifting the industrial policy agenda to give top priority to those issues of most importance to working people and, then, to ensure efficient, effective and equitable policies are adopted within that agenda.

4 Implementation and Monitoring

As important as the formulation of policy is how it will be implemented and monitored. The choice of particular policies does not guarantee that they will be adopted at all nor in the way in which it was intended. In addition, policy can never be specified in complete detail so that there is always flexibility in interpretation and in practice. It is crucial then who participates in the implementation of policy and how. Clearly, government will play a major role in general but its role will depend upon the institutions with which it works, the capacity of those institutions and their staff, and the way in which policy is carried out in view of staff motivation and the pressures to which they are subject by interested parties. It follows, as in the formulation of policy, that the interests of labour need to be represented in the implementation of policy – although there is a danger to be avoided, as in other areas of representation, that this does not involve inflexible compliance so that trade unions, for example, lose their scope for independent action. As already discussed before, but it warrants repetition, the success of the policy process requires the regular collection of industrial data, at sufficient level of detail, and open to critical assessment.

Ideally, implementation and monitoring of policy should overlap considerably. This is not always so since industrial policy is based upon the assumption that the private sector will respond in particular ways to the policies adopted. The anticipated is often not the actual outcome because the private sector does not respond in the way required by the policies. One reason, then, for insisting upon monitoring is to ensure that policies are delivered as intended, with the potential for penalties where this is appropriate. If subsidies are provided for job creation, it is as well to confirm that jobs have indeed been provided where the subsidies have been paid. Another reason is to check whether the intended effects are materialising even where they are not required by the policy itself – do export subsidies induce higher levels of exports or simply transfer resources to those who would have exported anyway. Finally, monitoring is essential to keep abreast of changing circumstances and in order, accordingly, to refine understanding and policy.

One particular role that can be played by monitoring is in ensuring that broader goals are targeted and achieved whenever government intervenes through industrial or other policy. This will be illustrated below in the context of contract compliance although it does not have to be confined to this area.

Contract compliance concerns the conditions that are attached to business that is undertaken on behalf of government. It is the formal aspect of what is expected from the private sector, although the informal aspect may be as or even more important.

Over the past fifty years, for example, the National Party Government has systematically used its policies to privilege some sections of the population, building up their power and wealth both in the private sector and through public provision of welfare and other services. From the moment that it came to power, the Government turned as much business as possible over to its favoured citizens, even beginning with its own bank accounts as these were used to bolster the Afrikaner financial sector.

The present Government has a different constituency – now including the majority making up the black population. But it would be a mistake to repeat or copy the policies of the past and simply hand business over to some of the Government's supporters irrespective of their capacity and efficiency. Yet it is necessary to recognise the important role that the Government plays not only as a producer through its nationalised industries, not only as a provider through its welfare policies, but also as a customer in the goods and services that it purchases from the private sector. It is a duty to ensure that these are procured efficiently and fairly but also in a way that is consistent with the goals of the RDP. It is the Government's responsibility to ensure that the favouritism, inefficiency and downright corruption of the past are rooted out, and replaced by a system of public procurement that is effective and functional for the sort of economy and society that is being sought through reconstruction.

Industrial policy, as already observed, has been traditionally conceived in the South African context as being organised around trade policy or around the state versus the market. These are much too narrow for much more else is involved in the fortunes of industries, not least the quality and standardisation of products, the size, security and distribution of customers, the level of technology and research and development, the availability of finance, and the wages, skills and working conditions of the labour force.

Public procurement has a significant impact on each of these. At times government will be a sole customer; at other times it will be a, if not the, major customer. As such it has a powerful ability to direct and to promote industrial development. It is, as it were, the state working through the market in a way that ought to be applauded by the free marketeers. If the market is to work competitively for the economy's benefit, then it is necessary that customers ensure they get what they want – and government is a very big, if not the biggest, customer.

What is needed? This can be divided into three broad areas – cost, quality and conformity to economic and social aims. In the case of cost, concern is with the traditional content of contract compliance – do we get what we pay for at a reasonable price? Whilst long-term, secure contracts whether for large projects (such as infrastructure provision) or for repeated supplies, such as office equipment, can provide the security for suppliers to build up strategic planning and cost-effectiveness, it is equally open to be a source of the featherbedding of inefficient producers with guaranteed contracts.

It is generally acknowledged that South African procurement has been riddled with unchanging contracts that have been turned over, with limited competitive tendering and even less turnover in suppliers themselves. In this respect, the new government has the opportunity to shake up what has been too comfortable a relationship between government and certain sub-sectors of industry. This does not simply mean making the market work; it means making government make the market work. One arm of contract compliance, then, must be strengthened, the one concerned to ensure the delivery, on time, of goods and services of the level of quality and at a price appropriate for government as large-scale customer. Penalties must be effective where there are breaches in contracts.

But, from labour's perspective, there is no point in securing contract compliance if this is at the expense of the workforce. Indeed, contract compliance should ensure that it includes the wages and conditions of the workforce – are required wage levels being met, are trade unions recognised, is provision of training and adult basic education adequate, what is the gender and ethnic composition of the workforce and how does this correspond to employment hierarchies? Although this will differ from one sector to another of the economy, it will be appropriate for such matters to be part and parcel of the contract governing public procurement. Equally, depending on the sector concerned, it will be appropriate for penalties to be imposed for non-compliance.

These might vary from fines, through to being struck off from an approved list of suppliers – with a corresponding stain on the company as far as other, private customers are concerned.

Further, it may be important to link government procurement to other areas of industrial policy – export performance is now recognised to have been one of the most crucial areas of compliance imposed by the South Korean government upon its private corporations. More generally, contracts may usefully incorporate requirements on the development of education and skills, security of employment, and the development and sharing of technology.

Partly as a customer in its own right and as the guarantor of the consumers' well-being, contract compliance also needs to address the quality of goods and the service provided. Quite apart from price and availability, it would include health considerations, for example, in the case of foods. Again, it might be appropriate for government to proscribe a supplier from being involved in public procurement if it proves unsatisfactory either in public or private sales. In this respect, it will be important to promote the role of consumer organisations and for them to be closely allied to public procurement agencies where appropriate.

In short, a contract compliance strategy with three separate arms is required: one concerned with compliance in the narrow sense of meeting contracts effectively in the absence of corruption and profiteering; one concerned with the employment and other impacts of businesses such as export and training levels; and the last to promote the role and interests of consumers. The purpose is not to lay down more layers of bureaucracy when administrative resources of the right type are short in supply, and when it is urgent that public procurement in so many areas needs to get moving. In addition, such contract compliance needs to be sensitive to sectoral as well as to geographical differences, including the tier of government at which such functions should be carried out. Nonetheless, now is the time to put into place the mode and methods of government that are to be carried forward, and such policies can make a significant contribution to the efficiency of industry and the efficacy of industrial policy. Further, the policies around contract compliance need to be formalised and implemented at each level of government, with central government taking the lead and supporting the activity at lower levels.

Currently, there are proposals to link public procurement and tendering to a ten-point system in which extra points are allocated for meeting non-commercial criteria. Thus, for example, a premium of up to 13.64% would be paid on government contracts (17.65% for building and engineering contracts). Points would be allocated on the basis of price and ownership, with black firms receiving a premium of ten points (but only two points for those owned by women). Other RDP points would be allocated according to provision of training, and it is also suggested that sureties be waived on smaller contracts, with larger contracts broken up to allow smaller firms to participate more readily.

Whilst these proposals are welcome in principle, it is not clear that they go far enough, that they have the right emphasis, nor that their intended effects will materialise in practice. The points system is essentially an attempt to skew the award of contracts according to the equivalent of a pricing system for desirable characteristics of tendering firms. It is not clear, however, that this is sufficient in implementing and monitoring contract compliance. Rather, those responsible for compliance may need to develop skills and experience that are sensitive to the non-commercial goals involved as well as the peculiarities of the activity for which there is contracting. The points system has also clearly been motivated by the wish to promote small black-owned enterprises. But there are other criteria that are as important, not least the interests and gender and racial composition of the workforce. Further, in practice, there is the possibility of paper observance of criteria in order to do well on the points system. All of these issues need to be addressed in order to ensure that contract compliance is both effective and not subject to abuse.

5 The Macroeconomic Environment

General Considerations

From the previous discussion, an important conclusion to emerge is that it is crucial not to take a narrow nor fixed notion of industrial policy. Industrial performance itself, as well as the impact that can be made by different types of policy, is highly dependent upon a range of factors that vary by time, place and sector. Generalisation is as dangerous as it is attractive – offering solutions that are oversimplified and insufficiently targeted.

Nonetheless, there are general considerations that need to be taken into account. Perhaps the most important, especially in the South African context, is the level of investment upon which industrial performance is so dependent. A high level of investment is liable to provide for a more rapid rate of growth and for greater employment creation. But much more is involved than this when consideration is given to the dynamic effects of investment and growth. Through a variety of overlapping mechanisms – scale economies, externalities, economic linkages, spill-over effects, learning by doing, research and development, education and training, evolving entrepreneurship, etc – investment and growth have the potential to be self-sustaining and mutually reinforcing.

This has led some to refer to virtuous circles in the growth and investment process, with high levels of productivity and growth in the manufacturing sector underpinning the capacity to provide for the continuation of success in economic performance. By the same token, the counterpart to a virtuous circle is the vicious circle of low levels of investment, growth and productivity increase.[34]

One of the key challenges to developing countries is to determine the conditions and corresponding policies that make for a virtuous as opposed to a vicious circle of performance. The issue has been extensively debated, if not always explicitly and directly in these terms, in view of the successes associated with the East Asian NICs and the comparative failure of many other countries.[35] Can the East Asian NICs be emulated and, if so, what are the key policies that need to be adopted? Is it possible simply to copy their strategies, policies or institutions, or must they be adapted or changed for other economies in different circumstances?

The answers to such questions are not easy to provide. This is for a number of reasons. First, in line with the virtuous/vicious circle syndrome, it is difficult to disentangle cause and effect since all favourable, or unfavourable, factors in economic performance tend to be correlated with one another. Second, not always recognised, there are considerable differences amongst the East Asian NICs themselves, so it is not simply a matter of identifying and adopting one set of their uniquely successful policies and approaches. Third, underlying conditions and policies associated with the NICs have shifted over time.

In the light of such considerations, the approach adopted here might be termed systemic.[36] It recognises that different economies function in different ways – depending upon their institutions, industrial structure, political processes, international economic relations, etc. It is necessary to uncover what functions are being performed and with what effects as well as examining how these might be improved. In this respect, piecemeal policy, or even a bundle of policies, is liable to be ineffective, even counterproductive, unless it is complemented by an appropriately functioning economic system.

34 For a discussion in the context of regional development and the role of multinational enterprises, see Young et al. (1994).

35 For debate over the NICs in the context both of industrial policy and the market versus the state, see Amsden (ed.) (1994). See also Fine and Rustomjee (1996, Chapter 2).

36 For the conclusion that such an approach is necessary in view of a comparative perspective, see Stewart (1996). See also Brautigam (1994).

Although somewhat vague and abstract, this commentary is particularly apt in the South African context. For whilst the South African economy has traditionally been seen as systemic, however well-specified, by reference to the system of apartheid, there has been a drift since the formation of the democratic government away from this sort of understanding. Early discussions focused on the role of the mixed economy; some emphasis has been given to the relationship between growth and redistribution; ultimately, however, the package of aspirations that make up the Reconstruction and Development Programme became adopted as the strategy for economic policy. But, both in principle and in practice, this has increasingly been undermined and displaced by a range of conventional and conservative stances around economic policymaking.[37]

Prospects for Investment

From the perspective of industrial policy and the central role to be played by investment, the weakness of the Government's position stands out sharply in its macroeconomic policy, especially GEAR. The purpose here is not to assess GEAR as a macroeconomic policy even though it does have considerable weaknesses.[38] Rather, it is to assess the prospects for investment, especially in the light of potential for industrial performance. In this respect, GEAR is to be commended for placing emphasis on the need to raise and to sustain the level of investment in the economy. Beyond this, however, it is sorely deficient for three reasons.[39]

First, the macroeconomic strategy for investment is heavily oriented around the targeting of business confidence, although this has been complemented by a number of microeconomic inducements such as tax holidays. This is unsatisfactory since business confidence is itself highly elusive quite apart from being subject to sudden and arbitrary changes, as in the Mandela illness factor for example. Further, quantifying the responsiveness of investment to macroeconomic strategy, especially where it depends upon speculation around the impact of business confidence, adds another element of uncertainty. In short, the macroeconomic strategy is almost certainly unduly optimistic about the levels of investment that can be generated by the policies proposed particularly, irrespective of the validity of the macroeconomic analysis itself, as

37 For debate over the evolution and content of ANC economic policy, see Nattrass (1995) and Fine (1994a).

38 For a review of evidence on the causes and effects of investment, and the uncertainties attached to them, see Bond and Jenkinson (1996).

39 See Calvo et al. (1994) for a critical assessment of relying upon capital in-flows in the context of Asian and Latin American countries. Many of the policy implications are also relevant to South Africa.

relatively little attention has been paid to the supporting mechanisms that ensure that investment in manufacturing will materialise.

This is hardly surprising given that the main orientation of GEAR is to hit macroeconomic targets, such as the fiscal deficit, with an implicit presumption that doing so will suffice to induce appropriate levels of effective investment. Second, then, this is seriously open to question since capital flows suffer many leakages before they are translated into productive investments. Macroeconomic stability, for example, especially if based on high interest rates, can induce an inflow of foreign capital or, perhaps, higher levels of domestic saving. However, these can lead to the growth of both short-term and financial assets without there necessarily being any corresponding addition to productive assets. If, for example, there is a stock or property market boom, or a wave of acquisitions and/or mergers, saving may increase without any corresponding growth in real investment. Moreover, the more assets are short-term and liquid, the more the potential there is for speculative instability, reinforcing the need for a vicious circle of austere macroeconomic policies.[40]

The preceding discussion concerns the way in which saving and capital flows are composed in terms of the balance between financial and productive assets and the balance within financial assets. This issue will be reviewed below in the light of the contribution of financing domestic resources for industrial investment. However, third, it is also important to examine the composition of industrial investment itself. Overall levels need to be disaggregated into their separate components. This can be done in a number of ways – the most important being by sector and by region. Given that much of the weight of the economy's capital stock is in sectors such as mining, energy and associated heavy industry, the prospects for investment are far from encouraging since investment opportunities are limited, especially in gold mining which is acknowledged to be in decline because of deteriorating availability of quality ore reserves. Also, to the extent that investment does take place in such sectors, employment creation may be limited because of high capital-labour ratios. Further, for the overall level of investment to be secured in other sectors, currently of lower weight within the economy, it would be necessary for them to exhibit exceptionally high rates of growth from a relatively low base. And, as already suggested, there is the question of what the resulting regional distribution of economic activity would be – whether more equitable and, if so, whether the relatively growing regions would have the capacity to absorb such high levels of investment in particular sectors.

---

40 For a critique of GEAR, see ILO (1996) and Adelzadeh (1996).

The Financial System and Finance for Investment

One of the key issues in determining the level, composition and effectiveness of investment is the role played by the financial institutions in mobilising and deploying funds. Broadly, there are three different approaches to this issue.[41] First, the real resources approach is macroeconomic in content, examining the resources required to generate a given growth rate and highlighting, in the context of a developing country or one in transition, the need for foreign investment to supplement domestic saving to close the gap with domestic investment requirements. Whatever its analytical merits and practical scope for application, this approach is necessarily concerned with macroeconomic modelling and policymaking and, as such, lies outside the direct scope of this Chapter. In addition, it necessarily sets aside what is of central relevance – the institutional and systemic efficacy with which finance is mobilised and deployed.

The second approach is one of financial liberalisation. Placing its faith in the general virtues of the market, it seeks as much deregulation of the financial system as is perceived to be consistent with macroeconomic stability in the belief that this will lead to existing financial markets functioning more efficiently as well as encouraging financial deepening, the creation of a fuller range and use of financial assets in line with saving and investor needs. In this approach, market-determined interest and exchange rates play a central role.

The third approach examines financial *systems*, recognising a structural separation between those that lend and those that borrow money. This separation can itself be explained by the productivity of specialisation – in various aspects of finance as opposed to productive entrepreneurship – but the distinguishing analytical content of this approach is in the informational asymmetries and uncertainties that surround financing. First, if I am to lend money, how am I to know who is a good and who is a bad risk? Second, how am I to be sure that the loan is being used for the purpose for which it has been made? Third, how am I to guarantee that the borrower, who is in a better position to know, is accurately reporting firm performance and prospects. Nor are all the problems on the side of the lender. For a borrower needs to know that a lender will tide a firm over an unforeseeable and unfortunate time of difficulty rather than, for example, forcing bankruptcy and collecting on any arrangement for default collateral. Fifth, what is to happen in the event of an unpredicted or unpredictable outcome, one not covered explicitly by contract? Who is to bear the unforeseen losses or gains and how?

---

41 As outlined in Harris, J. (1994).

Despite its apparent novelty, the financial systems approach lies within the mainstream, even if not vanguard, of orthodox neoclassical economics. It has yielded a range of remarkable results, not least the eclipse of the financial liberalisation approach which is merely a special case of a financial system in the absence of contractual costs and of informational asymmetries and uncertainties. In the light of the financial systems approach the alternative of the financial liberalisation approach is fatally deficient in two telling respects. First, it is incapable theoretically of addressing the specific role played by finance since it treats it as one market amongst many.[42] Second, not surprisingly, the financial liberalisation approach has a limited ability to explain the emergence of different financial systems, how they function empirically, and how they might be improved other than by deregulation.[43]

More constructively, the financial systems approach is able to show, first, that a deregulated financial system, leading to financial deepening, can be inefficient since the degree of certainty and efficacy of contracting can be enhanced by imposing financial regulations. Second, it points to the importance within the financial and industrial system of the methods of monitoring investment prior to, during and after the application of funds; further, traditional monitoring devices such as stockholder meetings, threat of takeover, and dependence on external finance have weaknesses as well as strengths.[44]

42 For Stiglitz (1985, p. 134), in the traditional, financial liberalisation approach, "Banks are like suppliers of pencils or toilet paper; each supplies a necessary ingredient in the production process of the firm, and there is no more reason to ascribe control to banks than to suppliers of other inputs." Note that Stiglitz sees the polar opposite of the toilet paper view of banks as the Populist one of the late nineteenth century that considers, "that banks were running the country". He concludes that "economic theory ... is more consistent with what I shall loosely refer to as the Populist view ... Shareholders do not control the firm, and managers do not necessarily act in their interests". Quite apart from its implications for the role of banks, consider the significance of the conclusion if the firm is understood as the economy, shareholders as the general populace, and managers as the government!

43 As Mayer (1987, p. xv) concludes, "Corporate finance is at a crucial juncture. The elegance of traditional models of corporate finance stands alongside a stark empirical failure to explain many, if not most, aspects of behaviour." Note that he continues, "As a consequence, the finance literature is in a state of transition. A search for alternative theories is in process and much attention is being focused on the inclusion of problems of imperfect information. But modelling is complex and the general relevance of most theories appears limited at the moment."

44 See Stiglitz (1985). Stockholders find it difficult to organise collectively and meetings are stage-managed by better-informed management. Apart from the costs that can be imposed by an incumbent management, those contemplating takeovers need to distinguish poor performance and poor circumstances in evaluating a firm – doing so may incur investigative costs from which others benefit in following a share-purchase lead

Third, deregulated financial systems can lead to short-termism at the expense of long-term commitment on the part of finance in the goals of growth and productivity increase.[45] Fourth, unregulated financial systems can lead to inefficiently high rates of interest, discouraging productive investment and, paradoxically, reduce the rate of return to lenders as only ever more risky borrowers are prepared to borrow.[46] Fifth, a resolution of all of these problems is in part possible through the closer collaboration between contracting parties, rather than reliance upon the anonymity of deregulated market forces, so that reputation can be built into and support long-term financial arrangements. Consequently, how banks relate institutionally to industry is of crucial importance.[47]

On the basis of these theoretical propositions, the financial systems approach has generally been inclined towards favouring bank-based financial systems – those most notably, if not exclusively, associated with Japan and Germany.[48] For these, banks, often a main bank in the lead, are presumed to have an intimate interaction with the firms to which they lend, monitoring performance intensively, providing long-term finance and, most important, securing long-term plans for restructuring in times of 'distress', reflecting a systemic reputational effect, or implicit contract, on both sides. The bank is prepared to take a huge risk with a poorly performing company which, in turn,

(free-riding). Reliance upon external finance as a disciplining device is limited to the extent that managers can deploy retained profits.

45 For Stiglitz (1985, p. 147), "Keynes, in the *General Theory*, expressed a concern that investors in the stock market were merely concerned with short-term gains, not the long-term returns. Today, increasingly, similar allegations are brought against the managers of many of America's largest enterprises: the heads of these enterprises are financial experts, not production experts. Their job is to allocate capital. And their perspective is not unlike that of the Keynesian investor: they wish to find under-priced assets, just before those assets are discovered by others, so that they can reap a short-term capital gain. Their behavior is not surprising: what incentive do they have to be concerned about the long-term prospects of the firm of the productivity of the economy?"

46 For a discussion of this Stiglitz-Weiss result, see Mayer (1987, p. v) Note that a knock-on effect is liable to be increased demand by savers for existing financial assets, thereby artificially inflating their prices.

47 As Mayer (1988, p. 1183) concludes for the UK, "The distinctive feature of successful financial systems is their close involvement in industry ... The fundamental challenge that faces any institution or government that can affect the practice of finance is to encourage the emergence of closer relationships and to direct the wealth of talent that has now been concentrated in British financial institutions into direct participation in corporate activities."

48 Classic references within the financial systems approach are, respectively, Corbett (1987) and Cable (1985).

during better times, does not take advantage of the possibility of turning to other banks or sources of finance and imposing competition for its banking business.[49] The systemic outcome can be one of lower interest rates and higher levels of long-term industrial investment. This is in contrast with the so-called market-based system which is supposed to be typical of the USA and, especially, of the UK, for which a greater proportion of funds is obtained through internally-generated finance (retained earnings) and anonymous external funds, more likely on a short-term basis even if competitively determined.[50]

Given the strengths of the theoretical results of the financial systems approach, and its sounder correspondence to empirical evidence in the functioning and structure of financial markets than is allowed for by the financial liberalisation school, it would be natural to expect the drawing of immediate policy conclusions – to move towards a bank-based financial system. Such a conclusion is, however, both premature and insufficiently nuanced for the following reasons.

First, although technically sophisticated in both a modelling and statistical sense, the financial systems approach is extremely crude in its characterisation of a financial system. For theoretical purposes, banking is construed in terms of a set of archetypical assets (short- and long-term, for example, or overdrafts as opposed to equity) and regulations concerning the extent of liberalisation of the financial system and the degree of state intervention through monetary policy. Correspondingly, the market as opposed to the bank-based system is readily and correspondingly associated with the predominance of different types of assets and regulations. In practice, however, the distinction between

---

49 As Mayer (1988, p. 1179) puts it, "The bank that takes a current loss in the hope of a future return is reliant on a more advantageous arrangement not being presented to the firm. Ex ante the bank would like to commit itself to a loan that specifies the terms of future finance, thereby encouraging the firm to undertake the investment. Ex post there will be an incentive for the firm to renege on this finance. Conversely, the company that is currently seeking rescue finance will be ex ante willing to commit itself to one bank but ex post be tempted by more competitive offers. These are all examples of the central conflict between commitment and competition."

50 For Mayer (1988, p. 1183), dovetailing with a quotation from a previous footnote, "A primary characteristic of a market-based system is an arm's length relation between investor and firm ... the basic requirement of a market, that investors be treated equally, acts against the close involvement of any one party. This separation between investor and borrower reflects a variety of historical, sociological and institutional factors and for that reason, if no other, there is no panacea ... the apparent attractions of intensifying competition in financial markets may have to be resisted. The benefits of competition may only be attained at the expense of longer-term economic prosperity."

the two forms of banking is not so sharp, nor does it readily translate unambiguously into different types of assets and regulations.[51]

Second, by the same token, the theory is based upon a variety of functions, undertaken in sequence over the lifetime of investment projects. Purely in the relations between finance and industry, this involves screening proposals, constructing contracts with terms and conditions, monitoring outcomes, and dealing with them when they fall outside contractual stipulations. Once again, such functions do not necessarily correspond consistently with one another along a single dimension of continuum between a market and bank based financial system.[52] A short-term loan, for example, in the form of an overdraft, may be readily rolled over by a bank with a longstanding industrial customer. This is typical of Japanese but not of UK banks, for example, rendering it difficult to distinguish the two banking systems empirically if purely examining the stock and form of bank credits to industrial enterprises.

Third, the requirements made of the financial system differ over time and, more specifically, at different stages of economic development. Financing trade on a short-term basis, for example, is more important during industrialisation and, it has been argued, the virtues of the bank-based system are less significant once large-scale corporates and conglomerates have been established along with the capacity to command sufficient long-term finance from a variety of diverse sources. This insight has been used to explain why an economy

51 For Mayer (1987, p. iii), "It is commonplace to draw a distinction between 'market' and 'bank' oriented financial systems. The distinction is usually drawn on the basis of a number of characteristics of the financial systems of countries. The size of equity and bond markets, the equity holdings of institutions and individuals, and gearing proportions of the corporate sector are often quoted as distinguishing characteristics. Within this framework, Japan and Germany, and slightly less clearly France, are regarded as being 'bank oriented' financial systems, and the UK and the US are market based systems.

In fact the criteria mentioned above do not provide anything like a sharp classification of the five countries. The UK and the US do indeed have large equity markets. But so too does Japan. The equity holdings of financial institutions of Japan and Germany are large but so too are those of institutions in the UK. It is true that the equity holdings of institutions in the UK are concentrated in pension funds and life insurance firms and those of Japan and Germany are primarily in banks, but it is not clear what the significance of that distinction in the context of the bank/market classification is supposed to be. On gearing, it is virtually impossible to obtain internationally comparable estimates. As a consequence, many of the stylised facts of corporate finance, for example, that Japan has a higher level of gearing than most other countries, have been challenged." See also Corbett and Jenkinson (1996).

52 Thus, encapsulating many of the points made here, for Corbett and Jenkinson (1996, p. 72), "The result of our research leaves us doubtful that aggregate international data can be used effectively to test many of the new theories of corporate financing."

with a bank-based financial system, such as the Japanese, has been willing to embark upon financial liberalisation.[53]

Fourth, the character of the financial system is not purely dependent upon the terms of its structural separation from industry and how they interact with one another. Nor are the intrinsic structures and functions of these two components invariant since there are different types and dynamics of industry as well as of finance. Moreover, each and their interaction are dependent upon broader socioeconomic factors. In Japan, for example, the system of life-time employment and welfare benefits through corporations has been an important constraint since corporate or affiliate bankruptcy implies unacceptable social and economic costs on the workforce. Consequently, industry and finance are themselves constrained to restructure corporations in distress.[54]

Recognition of the broader context within which financial systems operate is indicative of a serious weakness within the financial systems approach itself. It does have considerable merit, as outlined, in its capacity to highlight the weaknesses of the financial liberalisation approach; to address empirical variation and complexity in financial systems; and to propose policies in principle to regulate the financial system. However, it does so on the extremely narrow and technical basis of informational asymmetries, incentive compatibility, and the costs and difficulties of monitoring. Further, the modelling is usually conducted within an equilibrium framework even if the outcome is not always efficient in the absence of government intervention. Apart from traditional assumptions about supply and demand, the theory is highly dependent upon given economic conditions concerning what information is available to whom, at what cost, and what are the costs of producing and undertaking transactions, etc. No account tends to be taken of distributional considerations – who owns what property – except in so far as it affects the costs of monitoring.

It must be doubted whether such assumptions are appropriate for any economy, let alone one like South Africa which is in the process of reconstruction. To be more specific, three issues can be brought to the fore. First, the financial systems approach has depended upon a clear definition of, and distinction

53 Lapavitsas (1997) shows that the extent of Japanese financial liberalisation, even if it can be interpreted as a move away from a bank-based system, has been exaggerated and, to the extent that it has occurred, it has been disastrous in precipitating the financial crisis that emerged at the end of the 1980s. In a variety of forms, long-term main bank relations have been retained, and there is a continued confidence that the government will intervene in case of an industrial and/or banking crisis.

54 Hence, as Lapavitsas (1997) argues, because bankruptcy was not a possible resolution of the Japanese financial crisis of the late 1980s, so fraud and accumulation of bad debts intensified.

between, real property in physical assets and the financial assets with which they are funded. Indeed, the theory is concerned to examine how the one is best served by the other. However, especially during economic transition, property rights are themselves subject to transformation. What a physical asset is able to yield is dependent upon the financial conditions in which it operates and vice-versa. If, for example, government does change financial regulations, this affects the relative value of financial and real assets both according to the uneven ways in which they might have interacted in the past as well as in the ways in which they interact in the future.[55] It can even blur the distinction between different types of assets.[56]

Second, except in the terms already covered, such as monitoring, incentives, etc, questions of power and politics are more or less avoided. Consider, for example, a situation in which finance and industry are inappropriately coordinated through the market. This might be because a number of industrial sectors need to be expanded simultaneously to accrue economies of scale and scope to an extent beyond the resources of a single financial institution. In the case of Japan, for example, the state has undertaken a number of measures to secure such coordination – through its own industrial policies, targeted and cheap credit, and its guarantees to the banking system. Once in place, no financial institution has an incentive to withdraw from funding its share of industrial expansion, given it is assured that others are also involved. On the other hand, there is a low-level equilibrium, lacking coordination, if none of the financial institutions is funding investment.[57]

On the other hand, the state may be required to enforce such transactions since each of these may not be the best course of action for individual banks or firms even with the assurance that others have so proceeded. Consequently, none of the transactions occurs without state direction, even though the economy (and its agents) can be better off when all rather than none act in

55 This point tends only to be acknowledged in passing in the financial systems literature. For Stiglitz (1985, p. 135), a footnote is used to point out that the efficiency of information-constrained economies can be improved by government intervention but whether this is politically feasible is left open.

56 For Mayer (1988, p. 1181), in view of banks' interventions when they loan, "What is formally described as debt in Japan has all of the characteristics of equity finance and what elsewhere is deemed to be equity participation is much more akin to debt." See also Corbett (1987, p. 32), "Yet at the point of bankruptcy the characteristics which distinguish debt from equity *ex ante* are reversed *ex post*. Debt then has many of the characteristics of equity since control over assets is transferred to creditors."

57 Consequently, this is technically known as the assurance game, although this is a particular application to the relations between finance and industry.

concert.[58] A simple example is the requirement that all banks should contribute collectively to a central bank reserve to provide for security against random fluctuations or speculative movements. But each bank would wish to avoid participating just as we would all prefer to pay no taxes. Similar considerations can apply to proscribed assets for the purposes of generating domestic investment and macroeconomic stability and to controls on flows of capital to protect the balance of payments.

What is not readily recognised in the financial systems literature, however, is that each of these solutions, whilst potentially beneficial to all concerned, has the effect of rationalising the role of the state in intervening in finance and the financing of industry. It can, thereby, provide the momentum for more extensive intervention which either finance, industry or both have an incentive to resist. In other words, the preservation of a particular financial system may take precedence over improvement within that system, especially where the redistribution of property or property rights may be involved.[59]

Third, as a generalisation of the second point, interests within the financial system have an incentive to block or to promote particular non-financial policies according to their more or less favourable direct and indirect impact. For example, a highly interventionist industrial policy is liable to be opposed by a financial system which is threatened by the implications for priorities in the way in which finance is raised and deployed, quite apart from the potential strengthening of both industrialist and working class economic and political strength. The same can clearly apply to the opposition to expansionary macroeconomic policy in so far as it gives precedence to welfare at the potential expense of conventional conservative macroeconomic targets which are

---

58 For two agents, this situation is formally known as the prisoners' dilemma; for many players, the isolation paradox.

59 Thus, Cable (1985, p. 130) argues that the UK would benefit from a move towards a German banking system incorporating internal capital markets but that, "The introduction in Britain of bank lending on German terms would involve long-term structural changes rather than a mere short-run behavioural adjustment … the German model suggests that some redistribution of existing property rights would be involved and in any event changes in company law would be required." Interestingly, Stiglitz (1985, p. 148) argues that two institutional innovations have the greatest potential for overcoming the problems of long-term monitoring, "To have control effectively exercised, those exercising it must have a strong incentive for doing so. There are two institutions that have such incentives: banks and unions (as representatives of workers)." In the literature, almost without exception, the latter suggestion has simply been overlooked. But note the long-term interest that Japanese workers have in corporate performance and survival through the implicit contract for life-long employment, supported indirectly through the financial system and its tripartite relations between banks, industry and government.

conducive to profitability in the financial sector. Moreover, the financial sector has considerable power to impose penalties on the economy if it opposes policies by virtue of its capacity to generate and to reflect loss of business confidence.[60]

In short, the financial sector is not necessarily sharply distinguished from the real economy, it requires coordination and discipline by the state, and it can pursue economic and political interests within a given system of regulation that are inefficient within that system in order to forestall more fundamental change. Further, then, from both a theoretical and empirical standpoint, the elements that make up a financial system are complex and historically and socioeconomically specific. This means that simple lessons cannot be drawn from comparative experience. Not surprisingly, as already observed, given the shifting orientation of the literature away from the financial liberalisation approach, there is a ready-made conclusion of the desirability of moving towards a bank-based financial system along the lines of Japan or Germany.[61] However, the exact nature of a move towards a bank-based system is not readily discernible either in the reform of the financial sector itself or

60 This is one of the themes of the debate over British financial institutions in whether they have starved British domestic industry of funds for investment as well as dominating economic policy through economic and political power. See Ingham (1988) for a late contribution to the debate, but also Fine and Harris (1985). Zysman (1983) offers a comparative perspective, emphasising the importance of understanding a financial system in the broad sense, as discussed later, p. 80, "First, the structure of the national financial system affects the capacity of the national policy executive to intervene in the industrial economy. Second, since the financial system is a constraint on action and an influence on the power relations in the economy, it is an element shaping the arena for industrial and economic politics." Consequently, p. 94, "The British and French case studies are crucial to our evaluation of this argument. When British bureaucrats confronted an entrenched market financial system, they were *not* able to turn it to their purposes of modernization. In France, conversely, the character of the financial system presented the political modernizers with valuable weapons."

61 Thus, for Singh (1992, p. 45), "There is evidence as well as strong analytical grounds for believing that … negative features of the stock-markets (speculation, lack of long-term investor commitment to corporations, short-termism) may play a significant role in putting the stock-market dominated economies of the United States and the United Kingdom at a competitive disadvantage in relation to countries such as the Federal Republic of Germany and Japan. These unfavourable aspects of the stock-market are likely to be particularly important in third world countries with undeveloped stock-markets and high volatility of share prices." However, Singh adds a note of caution in the light of experience in developing countries over the past twenty years, especially in those economies suffering from macroeconomic instability, where it is necessary to guard against the potential for corruption or 'crony capitalism', the dangers of promoting domestic oligopolies through preferential access to finance, and inadequate overall banking regulation.

also in its relations with and the reform of other institutions in the economy more generally.

This does not imply that no lessons can be drawn from comparative analysis – only that the benefits of the Japanese banking system have in part necessarily been uniquely Japanese and cannot be simply emulated elsewhere. However, with sound theoretical principles and a sensitivity to historical and empirical comparative differences, it is possible to examine how a financial system might be favourably reformed or restructured. Certainly, the financial liberalisation approach does not have the capacity to undertake this task since it presumes a common, liberalised outcome as the most effective financial system and only addresses historical and comparative differences in terms of the pace and sequence of reform in achieving this single goal.

Unfortunately, the financial systems approach is only marginally superior for drawing lessons from comparative experience. As observed, it is capable of yielding remarkable results about the potential need for government regulation and intervention but only on the basis of the narrowest of theoretical foundations. Paradoxically, the simplicity and elegance of these results is also the source of their weakness. For it renders the analysis incapable of addressing the complexity, variety and, at times, key causal elements of financial systems in practice.

However, whilst the new financial systems approach has brought the issue of the relations between finance and industry to the fore within orthodox neoclassical economics, it has not essentially created any new results. For its conclusions replicate what have been a longstanding component of an older institutional analysis that has examined the relations between finance, industry and government on a broader canvas. Such accounts have been more descriptive than the formal models of the financial systems approach, and this has allowed them to be more wide-ranging and country and circumstance specific, although they have also more recently incorporated the insights and terminology of the newer approach.

Not surprisingly, the two types of work are broadly consistent with one another, although the more descriptive is more wide-ranging. Essentially, the Japanese-type bank-based system is once again perceived to be preferable, especially for a developing economy.[62] This is in part in order to promote and coordinate industrial development but without neglecting three major

62 As Aoki and Patrick (1994, p. xxii), for example, conclude, "A basic conclusion of this study is that banking-based systems in most cases are the most appropriate for industrial financing until a rather late stage of a country's economic and financial development." See also Patrick (1994).

practical problems – soft budgeting in which enterprises are not subject to sufficient financial discipline; rent-seeking or corruption in which undue influence is exerted through economic and political interest groups; and the scarce availability of the skills necessary to monitor investment decisions from inception to fulfilment.[63] However, the designation between financial systems as market- or bank-based is not readily applicable, with France for example as the archetypal mixed system.[64] This is in part due to the mix of financial assets involved but also because of varying systemic connections between industry and finance.[65] It also reflects the need to focus on the functions to be carried out by the financial system and how these might be most effectively achieved by orientation towards the Japanese model.

In particular, ex ante, interim and ex post monitoring of investment can be coordinated. The social costs of replicating monitoring are avoided if the monitoring is undertaken by a single bank or authority – compared to many different external agents investigating the market position of firms and speculating upon them. Mutually reinforcing complementary investments can be readily coordinated. Firms or sectors in temporary difficulties can be rationalised and restored through a longer-term banking relationship, avoiding the social costs of short-termism and liquidation of productive capacity. Further, as a banking system, there is the scope for keeping the interest rate low and rationing credit according to priorities and performance.[66]

One of the major empirical results that emerges is that the monitoring of firms by banks under the Japanese system is particularly prominent when the firms are under duress. It can even be argued that the emphasis on monitoring at other times is exaggerated, no doubt because of the focus on monitoring in the context of informational asymmetries that has been prominent in the more modern literature. Otherwise, it would be as if the banks were effectively undertaking or duplicating the various functional tasks of productive entrepreneurship. This only seems to be so at times of major restructuring, particularly in what would otherwise be prospects for downsizing.

But it would be a mistake to see the distinctiveness of the Japanese banking system as one that merely allows for intensive monitoring at particular points. For, this leaves unaddressed how the monitoring is undertaken in advance of

63 See Aoki and Patrick (1994, p. xxix).

64 See Aoki et al. (1994, p. 36) for example.

65 For Aoki et al. (1994, p. 35), referring to the Japanese financial system but of comparative relevance, "The characterization of the main bank system as (1) a nexus of main bank-firm relationships, (2) delegation of reciprocal monitoring arrangements among main banks, and (3) discretionary regulatory relationships, is admittedly stylized and static."

66 See Aoki (1994, p. 128/9).

such difficulties, at other times. In the Japanese context two further factors are crucial. One is the traditional strength of, and commitment to, industrial policy by the state, including its monitoring of industrial performance. The other is the corresponding commitment of the state to the banking system, not least in its role of promoting industrial investment. This suggests a subtle analytical point – that the financial system can itself be viewed in two different ways. It can either be seen narrowly as the financial institutions and activities alone or, more broadly, as the system by which industry (or the economy more generally) is financed which will involve consideration of the interaction between financial and other institutions and how they mutually undertake financial functions.

Now consider the South African financial system against the background of this extensive analytical discussion. Its financial institutions are usually described as having evolved upon the UK model and, hence, to be market-based.[67] The leading financial institutions are the few, highly concentrated commercial banks with branch networks, holding short-term assets and liabilities. Until recent deregulation and liberalisation, inspired by the deliberations of the de Kock Commission during the first half of the 1980s prior to the debt freeze of 1985, there were distinct specialist institutions, such as building societies, discount houses and merchant banks, dealing in specific asset markets. In addition, whilst the JSE plays a relatively minor role in raising capital for investment, the corporate ownership of company shares has become dominated by the leading savings institutions such as insurance companies.

These features of the financial system would suggest, from the narrow version of the financial systems approach, that limited capacity exists for the monitoring of investment finance. Nothing could be further from the truth in view of the concentrated, corporate and conglomerate ownership of South African capital that straddles *both* financial *and* industrial enterprises. In principle, the problems raised within the financial systems approach should not be a problem for the South African economy, since the German solution of internalising capital markets has been taken to its logical conclusion of mutual ownership! It is remarkable how little attention, if any, has been paid to the role of the South African financial system in raising finance for investment.[68]

67 See MERG (1993, Chapter 8).

68 In keeping with tradition, in the latest of a series of books on the South African financial system, the role of the financial system in generating finance for (industrial) investment is scarcely mentioned (Falkena et al. eds, 1995). Although recognising something unusual, the only substantive comment straddles the borders between tautology and complacency, Uys (1995, p. 41), "In comparison with the experience of most other countries, the financing surpluses recorded for the private non-financial corporate enterprise sector

Yet, there clearly are problems in the level, composition and productivity of investment.[69] But this cannot be said to be due to the nature of the financial system narrowly conceived. Nonetheless, it is heavily influenced by the role played by corporate conglomerates. First, as already argued, whilst they are responsible for the ownership of the vast majority of South African manufacturing, their core businesses remain in and around mining and energy. They have displayed relatively little interest in exploiting the economies of scale and scope that could arise out of vertical and horizontal integration. Indeed, their oligopolistic command of manufacturing can discourage new, including foreign, investors not simply because of the need to break into highly concentrated markets but also because of the difficulty of negotiating joint ventures with competitors in vertically integrated activity. This can be so of exclusively domestic investors. Intense competition between highly concentrated domestic capital can lead to oligopolistic divisions between sectors, stagnation of investment and failure to coordinate investments and engage in joint ventures.

This is not an issue of knowledge and monitoring but of market power. Its presence within highly concentrated goods markets can lead to negative effects being reproduced in financial markets and vice-versa. At times, for example, there is 'socially wasteful' competition in property markets, with over-supply and inflated prices for office blocks whilst, in many sweated industries, the counterpart is too many small firms with insufficient investment, training and research and development.[70] Thus, oligopolistic competition in financial markets can result in these being overextended for some assets at the expense of other assets altogether.[71] In the presence of oligopoly, financial services will

---

during most of the years under review were rather unusual ... (due in part to) the dominant position of mining and industrial houses in the economic structure of South Africa. The mining and industrial houses manage and invest large amounts of their own as well as of their group companies' retained earnings within their own group or in associated companies. In view of their substantial overall financial means, the mining and industrial houses, as a major finance and investment sector, contribute very considerably to the South African private corporate sector's ability to provide for its own financial needs."

69 This argument is made by Harris, L. (1994). He merely concludes, p. 10, "Bank-industry links along German or Japanese lines may generate dynamic or static production efficiency in some circumstances, but in South African circumstances they appear not to have done and may even be a brake on economic growth." This is left hanging without further causal commentary. Instead, Harris suggests that the banking system may have better, reverse asymmetric information than small investors about the prospects for the economy. In addition, he makes the case for a small payments system and calls for new measures to finance state debt. See also Garner (1993).

70 For the notion of socially wasteful competition, see Chang (1994).

71 This has been shown by Atkinson (1995) for consumption goods where the rich rewards to be made at the high quality end of a market can crowd out provision of a cheaper

not only be inefficient but will not produce a full range of financial markets, those serving small-scale transactions for example, even if liberalised and deregulated. This can be true both of small-scale financial services as well as, even if to a lesser extent, of finance for industry more generally.[72]

Of course, the conglomerates are liable to claim that their high level of concentration does allow them to coordinate investment and this is, indeed, reflected from time to time in joint ventures and in interlocking patterns of ownership. However, they are liable to be equally quick to claim that they are not so coordinated when it comes to oligopoly in goods markets, and charges of restricting output and raising prices. This is to suspend disbelief. Oligopoly does allow for coordination of markets as well as of investment. The exact mix will vary across time, sector and corporation. Further, such outcomes will dovetail with the oligopoly within the financial system. To some extent, this explains why foreign MNEs can be loath to establish affiliates and make new investments given that they are aware that their immediate competitors, in the markets in which they intend to serve, will also have a powerful command over locally available inputs, including finance, as well as the scope for diversification.

Second, and more important, the conglomerates' strategic vision is globally oriented so that there is a greater concern to invest abroad than to restructure and regenerate South African industry. It is difficult to conceive how industrial policy can be adequately formulated, let alone implemented, if no account is taken of South African productive investments abroad when the corporations involved are mainly responsible for South African domestic production. The narrow financial systems approach has heavily neglected the role played by foreign capital markets and investment since this is just one more angle on the same asymmetric information problem. But, in the context of South African conglomerates, it is crucial both in its investment and financial strategies.

Third, given that the strategic interests of South African corporations lie in globalising their operations, it follows that the policies being used to promote business confidence and macroeconomic stability are highly inappropriate. For business confidence, like strategy, will be closely tied to the conglomerates'

---

standard quality for mass consumption – although the reverse is also possible. This is, of course, relevant for South African consumption goods.

72 It is arguable that a paradox of financial liberalisation in practice is that it leads to greater concentration amongst financial institutions, greater instability and hence calls for state intervention, and higher costs of finance, with the proliferation of asset markets not necessarily broadening the net provision of the scope of financial services. These are all the opposite of the intended outcomes. South Africa's financial history over the past decade is a telling illustration!

capacity to move capital internationally. The more the government's strategy succeeds, the greater will be the demand for more liberalisation and the more will be the movement of capital and potential employment out of the country. This has implications not only for macroeconomic policy, with encouragement for the adoption of standard stabilisation policies. It also in part explains a lack of enthusiasm for, indeed considerable opposition to, extensive state intervention on the supply-side of the domestic economy, which could lead to a rolling programme of reforms.

Fourth, to a large extent, the previous points concern the ways in which the South African financial system is active in the initiatives that it takes. In level, composition and orientation, these initiatives are inadequate. It cannot be expected to reform itself nor to promote investment in industry appropriately unless it is induced or even forced to do so. Success will depend upon the new policies implemented by government, both in the demands that it places upon the financial systems and the means with which it ensures that they are realised. Such initiatives cannot be expected to arise spontaneously from the interests and activities of a powerful class of industrialists, since industry is primarily incorporated within conglomerates which also exercise control over the financial system.

Nor can a sufficient lead be expected to be successfully pursued by organised labour. It has neither the capacity nor the power to raise the levels, composition and coordination of industrial investment. Rather, it has been forced on the defensive against the consequences of the economy's poor performance in its attempts to maintain what are poor and inequitable levels of employment, wages, skills and working conditions. Perversely, the legitimate and symptomatic pursuit of such concerns in response to the failures of the financial system is too readily taken to be the cause of that failure, leading business and others to demand lower wages and limitations on state initiatives both within the financial systems itself and to promote growth, employment creation and redistribution.

Finally, recall that the South African financial system is often compared with that of Britain, with a highly developed range of financial services and a corresponding set of financial institutions and regulations. There is some truth to this claim, although the international competitiveness of South Africa in financial services has yet to be fully tested. Whatever the extent of the parallels, the British financial system is not one to emulate, not least in the context of reconstruction. It has long been recognised that the British financial system has the following weaknesses as far as domestic industry, as opposed to the fortunes of the City itself, are concerned. These are:

1) An emphasis on international mobility of financial assets at the expense of domestic investment, particularly in industry.
2) Reliance upon short-run speculation and borrowing and lending, leading the economy to be particularly vulnerable to economic downturns and plagued by inadequate long-term investment in domestic industry.
3) Priority in policy making to the objectives set by international finance, particularly at the expense of government expenditure and policies more favourable to industrial reorganisation.
4) Limited coordination between the provision of industrial finance and the implementation of long-run policies for industrial development.

Significantly, exactly the same characteristics are to be found in the South African financial system. They are all the more inappropriate given that the financial system is attached to a developing rather than a developed economy, and one aiming at major reconstruction.

There is an urgent need, therefore, to reform the South African financial system with three particular goals at the forefront: to finance expanded government capital expenditure at the lowest possible cost; to provide for industrial investment, possibly through the state, and to forge a closer relationship between industry and finance; to subordinate financial policy to the goals of the RDP rather than to those dictated by an elusive business confidence which, even if met, is likely to consolidate the problems of low levels of uncoordinated industrial investment. Significantly, public scrutiny of the South African financial system as a whole has been virtually non-existent since the de Kock Commission completed its deliberations in 1985.[73] Its policies have proved disastrous in practice, geared towards entirely different domestic and international circumstances and were motivated by the continuing imperatives of the apartheid regime. Moreover, that Commission's analytical framework was exclusively oriented around the increasingly discredited financial liberalisation approach with little concern for the functioning of the financial system as a whole, especially in its capacity to generate and deploy finance for industry in practice except through market-led solutions.

73 For a standard review of South Africa's financial system, see Falkena et al. (eds) (1995). As observed previously, this and its predecessors, such as Meijer et al. (eds) (1991), are notable for their neglect of the issue of critical discussion of how finance is made available to industry. A major exception to this feature of the literature has been the work inspired by MERG. See MERG (1993, Chapter 8) but especially Rustomjee (1993). He shows how limited has been the traditional analysis of the determinants of industrial investment, not least the work of the World Bank, for relying upon inadequate data, and inadequate and empirically unfounded investment function theory.

In this light, what are the prospects that the South African policies will successfully address the issues involved in investment finance? There are some positive signs. The inadequacies of the financial system, both narrowly and broadly conceived, have been recognised and have begun to be addressed in a number of areas. These include the promotion of small-scale enterprises, housing, rural finance and, if more as a private sector initiative, big black business in the form of the reorganisation of the JCI mining house. Further, the spatial development initiatives, SDIs or corridors, represent a significant attempt to coordinate between different government departments, such as transport and trade and industry, together with governmental agencies, such as the IDC and the Development Bank of Southern Africa (DBSA), and domestic and foreign capital. In addition, the change of personnel at ministerial level between finance and trade and industry (Trevor Manuel and Alec Erwin) holds out some prospects for functional coordination between the two departments. Further, the Ministry of Finance in its *Framework for the Transformation of the National Development Finance Institutions* has streamlined the institutions involved, allocated them specialised functions, and established a Coordinating Council to promote joint ventures amongst both private and public investors.[74]

However, these initiatives, whilst more than exceptions that prove the rule, point to the continuing weaknesses of the South African financial system and the failures to address and resolve them. The issue is what will be coordinated between trade and industry and finance, and within what financial system, and not just how well such coordination proceeds. First of all, for example, the breadth of the initiatives being undertaken is insufficient. At one extreme, for example, longstanding proposals for provision of small-scale popular banking have been neglected in practice. At the other extreme, the policy of independence of the Reserve Bank has been maintained in deference to its symbolic importance to business and financial confidence.[75] The effect, however, is more than symbolic given that the Reserve Bank in many different ways is one of the most conservative institutions inherited from the apartheid period and is unlikely to initiate reforms that undermine its traditional role within the existing financial system. Further, allowing the inherited financial system to continue to operate in its traditional ways has proved disastrous in the health sector, where it has promoted a dramatically expanding, commercially-based,

---

74 See BDM (1996). The institutions involved are to be the Land and Agricultural Bank (L&AB), the IDC, the DBSA (infrastructure), the Khula Enterprise Finance Corporation (SMMEs), and the National Housing Finance Corporation.

75 See MERG (1993, Chapter 8).

private health system, with its well-documented attendant features of inefficiency, over-treatment and inequity.

Second, even for those initiatives which have occurred, they have been insufficiently driven by what is termed supply-side considerations. As has become transparent in the case of housing, for example, the provision of subsidised loans to low-income households has been insufficient to unlock the blockages to housing supply. This highlights the need not only to ensure the provision of finance but that it is coordinated with industrial and other policy to ensure effective investment.[76]

In this respect, once again, there are some encouraging signs. The DTI has rejected the World Bank view of structural adjustment programmes in which, infrastructural environment aside, the supply-side of the economy is simply construed in terms of ensuring that prices are right. Rather, especially in the areas of education, training and skills, in research and development and technology, and in promoting the externalities that accrue from clusters of industries and vertical integration, strategic thinking and policymaking has gone beyond the narrow confines of the supply-side as conceived under a market-led ideology.

However, this raises the question of whether the supply-side initiatives, as understood by the DTI, go far enough. The evidence from trade policy, discussed below, and from the restructuring of state enterprises (privatisation), covered in a separate document, suggest that the DTI has been unduly influenced by, if not totally accepting of, the conventional wisdom of the international financial institutions. In addition, whilst concerned with the appropriate issues of industrial policy in principle, these have not been pursued in sufficient detail in practice in policy proposals themselves (how much investment, output, employment, trade, etc and to be achieved over what period) nor in the means to achieve them (who will do what and how). There is also the issue of with what determination and methods will government seek to guarantee the desired outcomes.

This is not all purely a deficiency within and of the DTI alone. It also reflects the non-financial institutional framework through which industrial policy is made and which has also been primarily inherited from the apartheid regime without substantial reform. In particular, industrial policy is being made or heavily influenced by a number of separate departments and agencies which tends to undermine coherence and consistency. Thus, trade and industry, finance, telecommunications, transport, public enterprise, etc

76 Arguments along the lines presented here have been made in more detail both for health and housing in MERG (1993, Chapter 4). For housing, see also Bond et al. (1996).

all have significant influence alongside the IDC and DBSA. Further, each of these institutions tends to be marked by hierarchical management and a continuing workforce not necessarily skilled nor motivated to address new goals and methods. In practice, this has meant that much of the content and methods of policymaking have been retained – especially the coordination of mega-projects around mining and energy, and the strong influence exerted by access to Cabinet.[77]

The continuing intractability of this institutional heritage has been dramatically revealed by the fate of the RDP Office which was charged with, and failed to deliver, the programmes attached to reconstruction despite universal support from participating ministries and departments and ready availability of finance in many instances. In part, these problems were ones of coordination, and the outcome is all the more significant in that the goals of the RDP were not only uncontentious but also did not directly challenge the entrenched powers of large-scale business. Equally telling is the redistribution of the bulk of the RDP Office's specific functions to the Deputy President's Office and to the Ministry of Finance. For the latter, there is no reason to believe that any greater role can be played than the holding of the purse strings. For the former, there is the potential for highly centralised executive decision-making replicating, paradoxically, the model of the apartheid regime.

It must be doubted whether such methods applied to industrial policy will work sufficiently or successfully. To do so would require executive powers that border upon the authoritarian. Even so, the investigative and policymaking capacity of other departments and ministries would need to be duplicated in order that decisions can be made and implemented. And there is little indication that, irrespective of the depth and scope of the interests within the Deputy President's or President's Offices that there is the political will and capability of carrying through substantial change in the content and mode of policymaking. Rather, the concentration of executive powers is liable to be more readily associated with the continuing functioning of the current financial system and smoothing over the problems with which this will be associated.

The fourth, and ultimately decisive, negative feature of the current financial system is the role being played by corporate capital and the failure of policy to recognise and address this. Many of the aspects involved have been outlined above. To these must be added a more over-arching feature – that the prospects for the more encouraging aspects and initiatives already mentioned are themselves limited to the extent that the core and driving force of

77 For a discussion of these issues in greater detail, see Fine (1997d).

the economy, namely large-scale corporate capital, is not integrated into strategic policymaking, especially where there are potential conflicts of interest. These cannot be overcome by ignoring them. Policy for housing, SMEs, etc quite apart from industrial growth and development, are primarily dependent upon the role played by these conglomerates. Whether it be macroeconomic policy, infrastructural provision, availability of technology, competition policy, employment creation, or whatever, South African corporations hold the most powerful position in terms of resources and capability. They must be made to use them in ways which are determined by the majority through government. Significantly, for example, the streamlining and coordination of development finance institutions discussed above is notable for its exclusion of mainstream financing through the major conglomerates except on a voluntary basis in joint ventures.

Of course, traditionally in the trade union and socialist movements, for the Freedom Charter, and in the early ANC policy proposals for a post-apartheid economy, public ownership and further nationalisation have been seen as the only guarantee of the required outcomes in financing investment. This is an arguable position but it is not the only one, and it reduces the policy debate to the simple discussion of the most desirable form of ownership and not what will be done with that ownership. As the discussion presented here, starting from the relations between finance and industrial investment, has revealed, the issues are much more complex. They involve how policy is to be formulated, implemented, coordinated and monitored, quite apart from or, more exactly, in conjunction with how it is financed. One conclusion is, however, clear – that the current South African financial system, broadly and narrowly conceived, is in urgent need of reform. This does not necessarily involve the creation of new institutions. In principle, government departments and ministries, agencies such as the IDC and the DBSA, and corporate capital itself are more than adequate to undertake industrial policy. That they have not done so has been shown to be indicative of the following inter-related characteristics:

1) Inadequate provision of finance for industry.
2) Inadequate coordination of investment across sectors.
3) Inadequate formulation, implementation and monitoring of sectoral strategies.
4) Inadequate coordination across government departments and other agencies.
5) Corporate strategies that are inconsistent with the policies required for industrial reconstruction.
6) Macroeconomic policy that is unduly influenced by financial rather than other economic imperatives.

Consequently, despite the proliferation of Commissions and investigations across many areas and with uneven success and impact upon policy, it is recommended that an investigation into industrial policy be undertaken with a particular but not exclusive emphasis upon the role played by finance for industrial investment. The inquiry should address:

1) A review of past, present and prospective sources of finance for investment together with the design of an appropriate system of data collection so that policy can be soundly formulated.
2) A review of past, present and prospective institutional arrangements governing the relations between finance and industry, covering both macroeconomic and microeconomic issues, distinguishing between different sectors and enterprise scale and type of ownership.
3) A review of past, present and prospective methods of, and personnel capacity for, the monitoring of investment in both the public and the private sector, as well as how the two interact. Particular attention needs to be paid to the coordination of policy across government departments.
4) A review of past, present and prospective levels of capital flight, legal or illegal, and the regulatory and fiscal initiatives which might stem damaging outflow of capital.
5) Consideration of formalising financial monitoring of industry through policies such as directed credit for successful promotion of exports and other strategic objectives.
6) Institutional initiatives to strengthen the role of Task Forces in sectors such as automobiles and clothing/textiles and to introduce them into other sectors.
7) How new sources of finance can be used to raise substantial additional capital for the developmental financial institutions, such as the IDC and DBSA, so that they expand their operations where social exceed private returns.

What body should carry out this inquiry is left open. It is important that it should proceed quickly, with the necessary powers of investigation and with independence from those directly affected by its deliberations. It might, for example, constitute a separate working group of the Financial and Fiscal Commission or be set up under the auspices of NEDLAC.

Direct Foreign Investment

The three issues of the level, asset composition and sectoral (and regional) distribution are particularly sharp in the case of foreign flows of capital. In order to assess the prospects for South Africa to be especially benefitted by in-flows of direct foreign investment, it is worth examining the global patterns of direct foreign investment.[78] A number of strong features were apparent by the beginning of the 1990s. First, direct foreign investment in global terms is essentially a first world business. As much as 95% of its volume is sourced from the industrialised countries which also received 80% of in-flows as 'hosts'. Moreover, just nine countries (the USA, Canada, the UK, the Netherlands, France, Italy, Switzerland and Japan) have been responsible for providing almost 90% of direct foreign investment, and they have also hosted over two-thirds of the associated capital stock. Of these, the USA provided 18% of direct foreign investment during the 1980s, 18% from the UK, and 17% from Japan (a total of 53% for these three countries alone). These were hosts, respectively, to 44%, 15% and a negligible share of direct foreign investment.

In other words, South Africa will be competing for direct foreign investment in the context of well-established and highly concentrated patterns of stocks and flows that primarily locate developing countries in a marginal position. Indeed, between 1960 and 1985, the developing countries' share of direct foreign investment as hosts maintained a steady level of around 25%. But by 1990, this had fallen to 18%. This is despite a remarkably rapid growth of direct foreign investment at 33% per annum between 1985 and 1990 which suggests such growth has been associated with concentration of flows within the developed countries rather than a global spread more favourable to the developing countries.

Second, however, these aggregate figures tend to conceal shifts in the patterns of flows. Most important has been the decline in the USA as a source of direct foreign investment, its rise and that of western Europe as a host, and the rise of Japan as a source. In the 1980s, the USA's share of capital stock owned abroad fell from 43% to 26% but its inward stock of foreign-owned capital rose from 17% to 27%. The corresponding figures for the 'big six' in Europe (UK, Netherlands, France, Germany, Italy and Switzerland) were a rise from 40% to 44% for outward share and from 32% to 34% for inward share. Japan's share of outward stock rose from 4% to 12%, its inward share stagnating at around 1%. Thus, whilst the emergence of Japan as a source of direct foreign investment and the relative decline of the USA are marked, these have not been at the expense of the continued concentration of direct foreign investment activity being confined within the industrialised countries.

Third, though, associated with the success of the East Asian NICs, there has been a small but significant rise of direct foreign investment from these countries. Altogether the overseas ownership of capital stock by Hong Kong,

78 The following account draws upon Renshaw (1993).

China (Taiwan), South Korea and Singapore was approximately $23 billion which needs to be set against a world total of approximately $1,500 billion. However, much of this investment has been concentrated in the Asian-Pacific Rim where Japan's direct foreign investment has often been outweighed by the combined contribution of the four tigers. This has been associated with a virtuous circle of economic integration within the region which does not bode well for the prospects for attracting direct foreign investment to the southern African region.

Finally, whilst these figures are already dated being confined essentially to the 1980s, the most important change in the 1990s for its impact upon the flows of direct foreign investment is liable to have been the collapse of the east European centrally planned economies. Contingent upon their realising political stability and renovating infrastructure, they will offer considerable and varied prospects for foreign investors in view of the skills of their workforces, the size of their potential markets and their geographical location.

More recent figures have been provided by the World Bank for the 1990s, set against longer-run trends and generally accepting uncritically the benefits of globalisation, simply defined as increasing trade and international finance relative to output (World Bank, 1996b). Between 1991 and 1995, world trade at 6.1% per annum grew more than 4% faster than world output. But foreign direct investment in sub-Saharan Africa only made up 0.9% of GDP between 1993 and 1995 (and 0.4% for the Middle East and North Africa taken together). This compares to over 3.1% for the much higher GDP of East Asia. Not surprisingly, it is found that just eight developing countries accounted for over two-thirds of direct foreign investment between 1990 and 1993, with half receiving little or none and increasingly dependent on declining levels of official aid for domestic capital formation. Equity flow into stock markets is the most volatile form of foreign investment, having grown ten times between 1990 and 1993, but then halving over the next two years.

Set against global trends, then, the prospects for a surge of direct foreign investment into South Africa are bleak.[79] Of course, it could be argued that South Africa will form an exception because of its unique history and current progress and that even a very small share of direct foreign investment from a very large total can have a major effect. But this would need to be established in much greater depth than through the pursuit of a nebulous business confidence even if supported by a variety of goodwill missions and investor conferences. Paradoxically, because the prospects for direct foreign investment are

79 See also UN (1995) and Carim (1994) for discussion of prospects for Africa and South Africa, respectively.

so limited, attracting it almost becomes an obsessive goal and mark of success. This is an instance in which underlying and fundamental strategies and objectives become displaced by others which are both indirect and potentially inappropriate.

Indeed, so important can direct foreign investment become as a symbol of success that its positive net impact is taken for granted. Much too much attention has been placed on the policies which have an impact on the inducement to invest – too little on the actual effect of that investment.[80] This is especially so over the last twenty years as the general attitude towards foreign investment by both developing and developed countries has shifted dramatically. Previously treated with suspicion, as a source of exploitation, and as a potential threat to independence, MNEs are now positively courted not least in the light of a more market-friendly ideology.[81]

A review of the evidence on impact of direct foreign investment, especially in developing countries, paints a much less rosy picture. Consider employment for example. MNEs are estimated only to have provided 70 million jobs across the world in the mid-1980s, three-quarters of these in their own home countries.[82] Of course, this does not take into account jobs created by indirect effects such as local multipliers and subcontracting, and employment by MNEs' affiliates in developing countries can constitute a significant share in manufacturing – in one sample of countries, it ranged from 14% to 58% with an unweighted average of 22%.

Even so, care has to be taken in distinguishing between the number of jobs *attached* to foreign MNEs or new direct foreign investment and the *net* creation of employment.[83] Despite the rise in direct foreign investment observed earlier, its total contribution to employment is stagnating or even falling in line with increasing capital-intensity and productivity increase. The net effect of direct foreign investment on employment depends upon the direct and indirect impact. If, for example, the direct foreign investment is simply used to buy into an existing firm, then no new jobs are created. On the other hand, even where this is not the case, domestic firms may be downsized or even eliminated by the competition from the direct foreign investment.

80 See Wilkins (1994) for a discussion of this in a historical context.

81 For an index of this in terms of the demise of expropriation of foreign affiliates as a policy instrument of developing countries, see Minor (1994).

82 This casts doubt on the idea of globalisation as being all-conquering, with the vast majority of MNEs still primarily attached to a country of origin. See Koechlin (1995).

83 Apart from Renshaw (1993), the following draws upon Buckley and Clegg (eds) (1991) and Caves (1996) as well as the other references cited below.

Of course, the processes highlighted in the previous paragraph can be seen as the beneficial workings of the market mechanism. Labour resources displaced by direct foreign investment can be employed elsewhere. This is hardly appropriate for developing countries, such as South Africa, where there are large reserves of surplus labour. Further, the potentially limited net impact on employment is the counterpart to the same effect with respect to investment itself. There tends to be a presumption that direct foreign investment is new investment brought from abroad which adds to the availability of domestic resources. Nothing could be further from the truth, as is revealed by international evidence.

First, even if a MNE does make a new investment, this does not necessarily mean an overall addition to overall domestic investment.[84] The required finance may be raised from domestic markets at the expense of the availability of credit to domestic firms. The creation of a new affiliate may crowd out domestic producers. This applies not only to those in direct competition with the MNE. For the latter may also source its inputs from other affiliates abroad at the expense of domestic supply.

Second, especially for manufacturing, the increasingly preferred method by which MNEs are undertaking direct foreign investment is through acquisition or joint ventures which do not, in themselves, create any new investment directly. What MNEs are seeking is investment in well-established and successful domestic industries rather than to restructure those in decline or to create new potential.[85] Further, there is evidence that MNEs that invest by acquisition bring fewer benefits than if entering otherwise.[86]

Third, how direct foreign investment affects overall investment in the future will depend upon what happens to the earnings that are made from the earlier investments. It is arguable that MNEs are more liable than domestic firms to wish to shift profits abroad and to have the mechanisms for doing so, through transfer pricing and use of licensing agreements for example. Consequently, the extent to which profits are ploughed back into the domestic economy is open to question.

It follows that the net impact of direct foreign investment on overall investment is highly uncertain. It is liable to be less than would be estimated on the basis of gross figures alone as direct foreign investment may crowd out

---

84 See Caves (1996, p. 233), "The quantitative finding that industrial MNEs are unimportant sources of net capital inflows is clearly established."

85 As Caves (1996, p. 226) comments, "MNEs have been entering LDC markets more and more frequently by buying out local firms; indeed, this mode of entry is more common the larger the supply of 'good' local firms to buy."

86 See Pigozzi and Bagchi-Sen (1991) but also Williams (1995 and 1996).

local producers, local use of finance, and may lead to remittances abroad. These considerations, however, need to be located in a more general discussion of the net impact of direct foreign investment. As already indicated, the net impact on employment is not always positive in case of the adoption of capital-intensive techniques. There can also be an impact on the composition of the workforce. For intermediate and consumption goods, for example, employment tends to be relatively low-paid and unskilled. It can also involve the assembly of imported inputs. This is especially so for low-cost production for export. In other words, where high employment and exports are liable to result, they tend to be associated with high import content, limited skills and low wages. Moreover, although MNE affiliates generally pay wages that at least match those already being offered in the domestic economy, they tend to spread the wage distribution, especially through higher internal differentials.

Where production is for domestic consumption, MNEs prefer to have a guaranteed market with few or no competitors, thereby potentially undermining competition policy and the development of other indigenous producers. Significantly, with high market competition in domestic markets, MNEs are liable to transfer more high-level production to affiliates as they are forced to do so. This is especially so where skilled labour is available. Consequently, transfer benefits through affiliates depend upon and reinforce existing favourable or unfavourable conditions in the domestic economy. Further, the low-wage, limited value-added export opportunities are precisely the ones for which there is a great deal of competition between, and even within, LDCs to attract foreign investment. The result can be bidding rounds between, even within, countries, with subsidies and other concessions undermining the long-term benefits and often the long-term presence of foreign companies. Favourable taxation and macroeconomic policies appear only to have a limited long-term impact and are difficult to sustain.

Subsidiaries of MNEs are more likely to import licenses and expertise, etc, from their parents but this does not necessarily lead to technological or entrepreneurial spin-offs to the domestic economy if dynamic economies remain internalised within the corporation. Paradoxically, Japanese firms, which are noted for high levels of affiliate ownership at the expense of joint ventures, can otherwise bring benefits to the domestic economy because of their careful supervision of quality control in locally sourced inputs from subcontractors or suppliers.[87]

87 For discussion of the issues covered in the previous paragraphs, see Kumar (1994), Blomstrom et al. (1994), Kokko and Blomstrom (1995), Anderson and Holmes (1995), Thomas and Friberg (1994), and Munday et al. (1995).

In summary, three broad conclusions can be drawn about the impact of direct foreign investment for developing countries. First, it can be positive in providing additional resources, in creating employment, in serving export markets and in generating dynamic economies of scale through technology transfer, skilling the workforce, and forging linkages with the domestic economy. However, it can also displace domestic investment, production and employment, seek out oligopolistic domestic markets, suck in imports, erode domestic economic linkages, and exploit low-wage labour and induce self-defeating competitive bidding in order to attract inward investment.

Second, the role played by direct foreign investment is both fluid and varied. Generalisations about direct foreign investment can be made taking into account the sector, countries of origin and destination, and other factors but there are always exceptions to such rules.[88]

Third, it is not simply that the impact of direct foreign investment is complex across a range of potential criteria – such as net investment, net employment creation, net effect on technology transfer, economic linkages and skill composition, net shift in the balance of trade and payments, etc – but that meeting one criterion usually has to be traded off against another. Manufacturing for exports, for example, can be low-wage assembly work with a high import content and much competition from alternative sites.

Finally, then, industrial policy towards direct foreign investment needs to incorporate a judicious balance. On the one hand, it requires a systemic understanding of overall impact in the context of an industrial strategy (drawing on industrial strengths, addressing weaknesses, and ensuring the meeting of objectives). On the other hand, only a case study approach can unravel the complex net effects of inward investment. Such an approach is also necessary in order to target maximum benefits and to ensure that they do materialise in practice.[89]

In short, as is the case for domestic investment, foreign direct investment induces a large number of direct and indirect effects on the economy – in finance, output, employment, technology, spillover effects, the balance of payments on both current and capital accounts, on wages and conditions of work, and on political and social life more broadly. The net impact of these effects is

88 See Jenkins (1995) for the mixed experience of the South Korean, Brazilian, Mexican and Taiwanese car industries.

89 As Dunning (1992, p. 357) concludes in the context of MNE investment in Europe: "In summary, depending on the type of inward direct investment, the extent of the existing foreign investment stake, the sectors in which it is made, and the home and host countries involved, its policy implications are liable to differ."

difficult to discern and to determine in advance, especially in a dynamic context. Consequently, it is imperative that the impact of both foreign and domestic investment be closely monitored and coordinated in a strategic fashion. Such is the lesson to be drawn from successfully industrialising NICs, for which mutually beneficial outcomes have been induced through policy towards foreign firms rather than simply assuming that they must accrue.[90]

6 Trade Policy

With the completion of the Uruguay Round of GATT and the formation of the WTO, there is pressure upon developing countries to liberalise trade and, in particular, to allow open access of imports to domestic markets. Arguments in favour of such policies have been consistently found to be inadequate on both theoretical and empirical grounds. There is practically no country in the world which has industrialised without the benefit of sustained protection of domestic markets. In addition, the pressure for liberalisation has especially come about as developed countries have found it to be to their benefit. Consistent with past practice, they have continued to impose protection themselves when considered to be to their advantage, as most notable, for example, in the case of the European Community, not least in its protracted negotiations with South Africa.[91]

The policies or strategies associated with liberalism in world trade are that world prices should be taken as a target to be rapidly achieved unless a large

---

90 For a careful and balanced summary of the literature, in the context of Malaysia, see Rasiah (1995). He concludes, p. 205/6, "In the absence of pro-active regulation, foreign firms can harm efficient local firms ... This calls for developing economies to approve only beneficial firms and impose conditions from time to time so as to shelter the growth of efficient local firms. It may mean government allowing foreign firms only in selected industries or vertical stages. Governments need a dynamic machinery with an efficient bureaucracy to scrutinize firms in terms of their relative potential to generate benefits for host-economies. Objective appraisal methods with economic foresight that address dynamic and complementary influences are essential. Hence, instead of simply relying on conventional methods of approving firms based on their potential for generating investment and employment in static terms, government should pay more attention to their potential role in generating dynamic spillover effects." For consideration of the spillover impact of foreign direct investment on Moroccan domestic industry, see Haddad and Harrison (1993). They consider that the positive effects have been exaggerated and more research on "case studies could help to identify why foreign investment generates positive spillovers in some countries but not in others", p. 71.

91 For an account of the negotiations and the unreasonable and self-interested positions being adopted by the EU, see Reports of the Portfolio Committees for 1996.

market is commanded; where active trade policy does persist, it should be broadly neutral between exports and imports, and certainly not favour protection at the expense of export promotion as is presumed to be common; and the instruments of trade policy should be limited, with interventions in a 'market-friendly' form, modifying prices through tariffs and subsidies, rather than the use of quantitative restrictions such as import quotas licences.[92] The theoretical case for such policies is extremely weak, as has been amply demonstrated most recently by models which take into account the presence of economies of scale and scope, externalities, learning-by-doing, imperfect competition, and even by reference to an economy that has a non-traded sector (a crucial feature for South Africa with its high level of services and goal of providing for basic needs). At times, these factors can be interpreted within a static framework but they are as, if not more, important, within the context of the dynamics underlying productivity growth which is essential to retain or enlarge export potential.

In the absence of sound orthodox theoretical arguments for trade liberalisation, attention has shifted to what are termed "political economy" considerations. Questions are raised about the capacity of government to intervene in practice, especially selectively, with the appropriate policies even if it is accepted that they exist in principle. This view is based on the suggestion that such policies are difficult to identify, require considerable capacity to implement and, most important, open the way for government to be captured by economic interests pursuing inappropriate protection or subsidy. There are serious deficiencies with this stance. First, if government has limited capacity to formulate appropriate policy, this needs to be taken into account but also to be rectified. It is not a reason for abandoning policy altogether. Second, if there are powerful economic interests, these need to be recognised by government. There can be no presumption that the market mediates between such interests either neutrally or efficiently. Indeed, the pressure for a more market-friendly trade policy is itself the consequence of particular economic and political interests – as much at a national as at an international level. Finally, especially for developing countries, changing the structure and composition of the economy – to shift the balance, for example, towards industry and exports – can require the creation of the corresponding interest groups where they did not previously exist. The state can play an important role to support the growth of

92 The following draws upon Helleiner (ed.) (1994 and 1995).

such groups, as is already apparent, and readily accepted, in South Africa in the case of small-scale and black business.[93]

In many ways, even if in a more sophisticated way and with a fuller range of factors, the debate over trade policy simply revisits 'infant industry' arguments whilst, however, complementing previous discussion with 'political economy' factors to which I return below. Beforehand, consider the empirical evidence. First, there is little to suggest that trade policy is itself an important determinant of industrial performance and, even so, a positive role will derive from export expansion (through export performing requirements, for example) as much as from import liberalisation.[94] In any case, the export expansion itself can depend upon the availability of finance for imported inputs.[95]

Second, at least as important as trade policy have been the other elements of industrial policy, such as research and development, and the impact of technology transfer and the scale and growth of domestic markets. Also important has been the macroeconomic environment, especially the level and stability of the exchange rate, the level of domestic demand and real wage restraint. At a more detailed level of targeting, favourable access to credit can be used to promote exports, especially to complement low levels of domestic demand relative to scale economies.

---

93 The theoretical case arises in the context of the developmental state, with the classic case study provided by South Korea for which large-scale conglomerates were created through state intervention. For South Africa, there is the precedent of large-scale Afrikaner capital which was formed over the post-war period. See Fine and Rustomjee (1996).

94 As Helleiner (ed.) (1994, p. 31) concludes, "On the basis of currently available evidence, it is difficult to escape the conclusion that trade policy has *not* been the major influence on productivity growth in manufacturing that many analysts have said that it should be. Such associations as there have been between productivity growth and trade phenomena related to the probable positive role of manufactured export expansion, and *not* to import liberalization." See also the review provided by Edwards (1993) who concludes on the mixed results in favour of trade liberalisation, p. 1389, "Much of the cross-country regression based studies have been plagued by empirical and conceptual shortcomings. The theoretical frameworks used have been increasingly simplistic, failing to address important questions such as the exact mechanism through which export expansion affects GDP growth, and ignoring important potential determinants of growth such as educational attainment. All of this has resulted … in unconvincing results whose fragility has been exposed by subsequent work."

95 For a discussion in an African context, see Kirkpatrick and Weiss (1995, p. 298) who conclude, "If there have been some modest benefits from adopting trade liberalisation measures, these must have come from aspects of the policy-reform package other than real devaluation. The obvious candidates are higher import levels ensuing from the additional finance attached to structural adjustment loans … and efficiency gains stimulated by greater external competition."

Third, because of the significance of stability in the macroeconomic environment and the structure of incentives to industry, it is hardly surprising that liberalisation beyond trade, to capital markets, has not been favourable to industrial performance. The impact of speculative movements of capital can discourage long-term investment; and attempts to stabilise capital movements and the exchange rate then lead to high interest rates further discouraging domestic economic activity. Whilst devaluation can increase international competitiveness, this is liable to be short-term as capacity is switched to serve export rather than domestic markets, and without necessarily adding additional capacity. Such short-term outcomes also depend upon devaluation leading to a reduction in real wages (through the increased cost of the import component of consumption). It is questionable whether this is desirable let alone sustainable over the longer term.

Fourth, it is crucial not to view trade policy in very crude terms as supporting or penalising either exports or imports. In practice, trade policy involves a very wide variety of complex instruments with an equally varied set of outcomes depending upon how the trade policies interact with other policies and factors in the specific economic conditions in which they operate. Consequently, trade policy should not be seen in isolation from other policies and as a bias in one direction or another. Rather, it needs to be situated carefully in a sectoral context. As is currently recognised in South Africa in the phased levels programmes for reducing protection for textiles, clothing and motor vehicles, no simple trade formula or policy is appropriate. But, even more important, the process of restructuring industries, both vertically and horizontally, needs to range far beyond considerations of trade policy alone and to recognise how the structure and functioning of sectors are very different from one to another – by virtue of technology, markets, sources of finance and ownership, vertical integration with other sectors as well as established historical patterns, most evident, for example, in the case of the South African heavy chemical industry with its heavy reliance on coal-based oil through the SASOL complex.

Finally, at a firm level, favourable export performance in developing countries can be associated with larger scale, higher levels of productivity and capital-intensity, and a low ratio of value added to gross value. This suggests, in line with much MNE activity discussed previously, that export performance in LDCs can be highly dependent upon limited processing of previously, possibly imported, inputs. Consequently, even where such positive export performance is associated with trade liberalisation, the net benefits for the economy in terms of employment, balance of trade and payments, and economic linkages and spin-offs are liable to be limited and possibly negative.

In short, the factors underlying appropriate trade policy are not only varied and complex but require trade-offs to be made. Macroeconomic conservatism, for example, in order to provide stability for potential investors and exporters, could prove to be a self-defeating exercise if the level of domestic demand is insufficient to support scale economies. Certainly, however, there is no rationale for accepting the general case in favour of trade liberalisation, and the merits of trade policy need to be examined at a detailed and specific level. Given infant industry considerations, the sequencing as well as the content of policy is crucial, especially as trade, macroeconomic or other policy could kill off infants or even adolescents before they have the opportunity to attain maturity.

Against this general background discussion, serious deficiencies are apparent in the Government's trade policy.[96] Trade liberalisation has proceeded much further than has been required or could have been negotiated.[97] Supply-side measures to compensate for the resulting competitive pressures or to promote successful restructuring have been limited and lacking appropriate coherence and sequencing with trade reform. Further, such has been the pace of South Africa's trade liberalisation that there are liable to be intensified problems of economic integration with the southern African region in view of the lack of compatibility both in economic and industrial development and in trade policy regimes.

The Ineffectivity of Effective Protection

Many of these points are confirmed by close and critical scrutiny of the analysis of South Africa's trade policy that has emerged from the IDC.[98] This offers an account of the phasing out both of tariff protection and GEIS (a government scheme subsidising exports). Figures on changing tariffs indicate the extent to which import duties are being lowered well beyond the levels required by GATT. For the phasing out of GEIS, it is recognised that there will be a varied and possibly serious impact on some sectors for which supply-side measures

96 For much of what follows, see Bell (1993 and 1997).

97 Bell (1997, p. 77) suggests that, "South Africa's trade policy reforms entail a good deal of unilateral import liberalisation, going beyond the commitments entered into in the unilateral trade negotiations. South Africa's trade policy thus is apparently being determined by the economic philosophy of the country's own policymakers, rather than by such negotiated commitments."

98 See Havenga (1996).

will be urgently required. These are simply left unspecified in anything other than general terms![99]

The IDC analysis provides a sector-by-sector breakdown of the incidence of nominal and effective protection. Nominal protection simply reflects the tariff or other advantage granted to domestic producers over importers on the basis of selling price alone. The effective protection rate, EPR, also takes into account the impact of such trade policy on (imported) input prices and costs of production since tariffs on imported inputs affect domestic competitiveness negatively as much as tariffs on final output are supportive. For the purposes of examining the impact of trade reform on (international) competitiveness, the EPR is the appropriate measure rather than nominal protection. The IDC calculations of EPRs do have some features to recommend them. They do incorporate a full general equilibrium model of the economy so that certain interactive effects between sectors are included.[100] They also work with full data of value added within sectors, comparing outcomes at domestic and world prices, rather than simply relying upon ratios of world and domestic prices.[101]

On the basis of its multi-sectoral general equilibrium model, estimates are made of the impact of the new trade regime upon sectoral output. Leaving aside basic metals, it is found that nineteen out of twenty-one manufacturing sectors will suffer a *fall* in output![102] Even so, it is calculated that GDP and employment will increase by 0.3%, reflecting the more than proportionate improvement in non-manufacturing output as a result of cheaper imports and inputs. This is attached to an incredible fall in the price level by 4%. Whilst an improvement in output by 0.3% is small but significant, no sensitivity analysis

99 Havenga (1996, p. 6) *closes* a section, rather than opening a discussion, with the statement that, "It has to be accepted that the phasing out of GEIS will mean substantial losses for some sectors, and government policy will need to pay close attention to alternative support measures, both for those sectors that are losing GEIS benefits and for those sectors that did not benefit from GEIS. The introduction of supply-side measures is especially important in this context." In practice, there is reason to believe that GEIS merely served as a subsidy to large-scale producers who would have exported anyway (Fine, 1997d).

100 For a debate over the importance of this issue in the context of trade policy in interwar Britain, see Kitson et al. (1991) and Capie (1991).

101 See Conway and Bale (1988) for a technique for calculating EPRs when full data are not available on value added. Effectively, they extrapolate from countries for which value added data are known. The implication is that the EPR does not remain fixed even for fixed prices for different stages of development, suggesting the same may be true for more than marginal changes in output at the same level of development. If so, as discussed later, this places the whole calculation and use of EPRs in doubt.

102 The exceptions are rubber and motor vehicle components. Note that Holden et al. (1996) argue that overall levels of effective protection still remain significant.

is provided. This suggests that important sacrifices are being made in the vast majority of manufacturing sectors with relatively small and uncertain returns across the rest of the economy. Further, the overall increase in employment is not neutral across different sections of the workforce. It has been calculated that trade policy from 1985 has been biased against labour-intensive industries and against those that employ proportionately more black workers.[103]

It should also be borne in mind that the increase in output by 0.3% only refers to the *impact* of trade reform on the *level* of output. It is a once and for all improvement and is not sustained as a *permanent* increase in growth performance itself.[104] Indeed, the model under which the EPRs are calculated *precludes* the incorporation of any long-term impact of trade reform on the growth rate, an issue taken up later in detail.[105] It is equally misleading, indeed wrong, to label the fall in the price level as a fall in inflation[106] since the impact on prices, like that on output, is a shift in level, is not sustained, and is once and for all.

The results of the IDC exercise should not, then, be taken too seriously as indicative of what will happen nor as the basis on which to formulate policy. The sort of model being employed is peculiarly inappropriate for the task that it sets itself for a number of reasons. The critical inadequacies of deploying measures of EPRs divide into three sequential sorts. First, are there sound theoretical reasons grounds on which to measure EPRs in principle, especially if it is to be used as a guide to (the impact of) policymaking? Second, assuming that EPRs are well-defined as guides to policy, how well have they been calculated in practice? Third, setting aside the first two points, are the imputed effects of shifting EPRs liable to materialise? The following discussion deals with these issues in turn, although they do overlap and inform one another.

103 See Bell and Cattaneo (1997, p. 26/7), "There has thus been a shift in the sectoral composition of exports, not only away from labour-intensive industries in general, but away from black and Asian/Coloured labour-intensive industries in particular ... It was found, too, that in 1985–93 import penetration ratios increased proportionately more in the most labour-intensive industries ... by far the most significant adverse effects on employment occurred in the ultra-labour-intensive category of manufacturing sectors." Similar effects are anticipated from the current policies projected forward.

104 See Havenga (1996, p. 36) who suggests, on the basis of entirely separate empirical work, that the impact effect will have been attained within about two years, leaving aside changes in capital stock which have not been modelled.

105 For this reason, it is totally misleading for Havenga (1996, p. 13) to claim, "The higher growth in imports relative to exports has a negative effect on the trade balance (but) *The resulting overall impact on economic growth (real GDP) is nonetheless positive.*" (emphasis in original).

106 As in Havenga's Table 4.

The theoretical assumptions on which EPRs are measured are highly restrictive. They take much too much as given. Even over a five-year period, the production and other conditions on which the model is based are bound to change. There is even a perverse and inconsistent logic in the method taken as a whole. For the very purpose of shifting EPRs is to bring about a change in conditions in production. This is the rationale for the liberalisation and the supply-side measures themselves that are intended to temper the effects of, and to benefit from, trade reform. The idea is that together they should bring about a substantial improvement in supply-side behaviour and hence productivity and output performance.[107] These changes ought to be taken into account, something which is admittedly difficult other than at a detailed sectoral level.[108]

Essentially, there are two different aspects to this problem. On the one hand, as mentioned, the method of comparative statics which is employed takes no account of the impact of any accompanying supply-side measures. On the other hand, nor does it allow for endogenous productivity growth (or decay) as a result of the economy's path between equilibria. Now, however, such endogenous growth effects are well-established. Indeed, they are the main basis on which mainstream economic analysis has been able to explain the variation, rather than convergence, in growth performance across countries.[109] Recent literature has emphasised how trade policy and endogenous growth are intimately linked. Broadly, there are two opposing effects, with a dual and mirror-image relationship to one another, depending upon whether enhanced output or input conditions promote endogenous growth. Reserving domestic

107 As Havenga (1996, p. 17) correctly puts it, "The negative effects of trade reform ... should be ameliorated by the battery of supply-side measures which are being designed and implemented. These measures will assist the industries to revitalise themselves and become competitive on both domestic and international markets ... When the industrial support measures are implemented to assist investment and restructuring towards export competitiveness, the pressure from trade reform should be utilised to ensure a long-term competitive and growing industrial sector." But these good intentions and outcomes undermine the basis on which EPRs are calculated!

108 Put another way, as by Havenga (1996) himself, the model rests entirely upon comparative statics in which, it should be added, rather too much remains static in the comparison. For a laughable exposition of the results in these terms, see his Annexure X.

109 For coverage of the issues, see Barro and Sala-i-Martin (1994). A neat combination of endogenous and convergence models with application to OECD countries is to be found in Targetti and Foti (1997). Reference to endogenous growth models is notable for its rarity in application to the South African economy. For an exception, see Holden (1993, p. 227) who concludes, "An increase in productivity can be achieved through better technology and the introduction of new ideas as well as through better education. It is in this area that a role for the state could be envisaged; in particular, subsidisation of private firms undertaking R&D for the purposes of exports should be high on the agenda."

markets for domestic producers or promoting exports can induce productivity increase on the basis of dynamic economies of scale and scope.[110] To the contrary, trade liberalisation can also induce productivity increase through the greater availability and cheapness of imported inputs.[111] It would not appear to make sense to discuss trade reform, and EPRS, separately from, and prior to, supply-side measures and other factors and effects associated with productivity increase. In short, the comparative statics method of the IDC simple sets aside both exogenous and endogenous sources of supply-side change, even though these ought to be the object of policy for which trade policy is an interactive aspect.[112]

In this context, a related but separate point concerns the technical details of the IDC's model. It is based upon fixed input-output technology for each sector. Accordingly, the impact of changes in tariffs for the techniques of production is precisely *nil*.[113] Rather, all adjustment takes place through the shift of economic activity *between* sectors on the basis of given technology in response to incentives induced by the shift towards world pricing in inputs and outputs whether production be for domestic use and consumption or for exports.[114] This is extremely restrictive, and possibilities for substitution between capital and labour in practice imply that the measure of EPRS will be inaccurate. Even in a three-sector general equilibrium model with substitutability in production,

110 See Fine (1996b) for a simple model and some reference to the literature. See also Krugman and Smith (eds) (1994), Edwards (1993), Kitson and Michie (1995), Dornbusch (1992) and Rodrik (1992), for example.

111 See Venables (1996, p. 179), "It may be the case that trade liberalisation triggers a dramatic expansion of output and possibly also a reduction in imports. This arises as import liberalisation lowers costs in downstream industries, expanding their output, and triggering a 'big push' of industrialisation."

112 Other assumptions made in the IDC calculations, and not discussed elsewhere in this Chapter, include fixed real government consumption (despite RDP programme), slack labour markets for all categories of labour (despite skill shortages), endogenous balance of trade with no balance of payment constraint (despite a deterioration in the balance of trade), given tax rates, fixed exchange rate, and fixed gold production (even though other mining is the sector that is by far the most advantaged by the tariff changes) (Havenga 1996, p. 12/13).

113 See Havenga (1996, p. 9) who explicitly recognises, "The production structure is the same when producing at domestic prices and world prices (by using the same I/O-table in domestic and world price calculations)."

114 This implies, for example, that labour as well as other resources move without friction between sectors. In the context of structural adjustment, this has often been brought into question. For a review, with special attention to the labour market, see Agenor (1996). Note that the IDC assumes constant post tax wages despite the reallocation of labour between sectors (Havenga, 1996, p. 12).

the introduction of a third non-traded sector to complement import and export sectors suffices to undermine conventional measures of EPRs.[115] These comments are particularly apt for the South African economy since it is generally acknowledged that it suffers from excessively high capital-intensity in some sectors so that trade or other policies should positively encourage changes in the allocation of capital both within and across sectors rather than taking sectoral capital-intensity as *given* and as the basis on which to formulate trade policy and measure its effects.

A final theoretical reservation concerning the measurement of EPRs is the condition of perfect competition upon which it is based. Again, there is a paradox in that under such conditions, the patterns of trade that are observed throughout the world would not be possible since economies would specialise in their well-defined sectors of comparative advantage. Trade of the same commodities in both directions simply could not occur between countries. Accordingly, trade theory needs to be modified to take into account the market imperfections without which observed trade patterns are impossible. The immediate implication, however, is that EPRs, calculated as if the world and domestic economies were perfectly competitive, are unacceptable.[116] It is as if, for example, we measure the impact of a domestic sales tax on prices and output without regard to whether the industry is competitive or monopolistic in one way or another.

There are, then, considerable conceptual and theoretical issues even in defining levels of EPRs. These are compounded by practical and empirical difficulties. Very careful account, for example, needs to be taken of the role played

115 See Bureau and Kalaitzandonakes (1995, p. 279) whose study of the impact of EPRs on European agriculture draw them to the following conclusion, "The empirical results demonstrate that maintaining zero input-output substitutability – a restriction embedded in all common protection measures – can lead to false results about the level of protection across countries and time." See also Milner (1994) for a similar application to Barbados. He concludes, p. 587, "The traditional classification of trade strategies into 'import substitution' (IS) and 'export promotion' (EP) is based on the traditional two-sector trade model. In the context of a three-sector model – including non-tradeables ... the evidence indicates that ex post classification of trade strategy may differ significantly from the ex ante or intended strategy."

116 See Greenaway and Milner (1987, p. 38) who suggest of traditional EPR calculations, "This analysis is based upon assumptions such as product and production homogeneity, non-increasing returns, arms length trade, and small open economy country conditions. Relaxation of some or all of these assumptions has direct implications for effective protection analysis under any type of trade flows. As is now widely recognised, however, relaxation of these assumptions is also likely to be associated with intra-industry specialisation and exchange."

by the capital stock and investment. As is recognised in the literature, EPRs should be worked out net of depreciation allowances,[117] and distinctions must be drawn between X-inefficiency in the use of capital (under-utilisation and ineffective use of capacity),[118] and the cost of capital (usually interpreted as the interest rate).[119] High interest rates, an old or dated capital stock and substantial excess capacity are all liable to result in unduly high measures of EPRs as these factors would all reduce competitiveness. These are endemic features of the South African economy and should be addressed by policy, not overlooked in calculating EPRs as the basis for policy. In addition, indirectly related to the treatment of capital is the variation in the riskiness of investment across sectors. A higher tariff on inputs, for example, implies more capital will be advanced until a return accrues with sales. This distorts the impact of tariffs across otherwise equivalent sectors through making the riskier investments less attractive.[120]

An entirely different practical aspect in measuring EPRs is the use of world prices as a reference point.[121] These can be inappropriate in case of heavy internal transport charges for example, with the impact of this non-tradeable being crucial as are other internal factors other than tariffs, such as domestic taxes and subsidies, that might affect the wedge between domestic and world prices.[122]

117 The IDC model assumes that the capital stock remains fixed in each industry (Havenga, 1996, p. 12), neglecting the issue of depreciation and replacement cost as well as of shifting capital intensity.

118 See Holden et al. (1996, p. 61) whose discussion of South Africa's comparative advantage recognises that, "There is substantial excess industrial capacity: the typical shift rate is 1.3 on average and machines are idle on Sundays and many holidays."

119 See Ettori (1992) for a full discussion with application to India.

120 See Eldor (1984 and 1986). From the former, in conclusion, p. 235, "If the tariff on the final good is greater (smaller) than the weighted average tariff on the traded inputs, then the effective protection increases (decreases) as one moves from an industry with a low risk … to an industry with high risk."

121 As Havenga (1996, p. 9) makes explicit for the IDC calculations, "The world prices are equal to the domestic price less tariffs. Thus, the tariff is the only measure influencing differences in domestic and world prices."

122 See Rousslang and To (1993) for discussion of Canadian imports from the United States. Byerlee and Morris (1993, p. 805) find, "While world reference prices based on current trading status often represent a reasonable approximation of the prices which would prevail in domestic markets in the absence of policy distortions, under certain conditions their use can lead to incorrect estimation of the degree and sometimes even the direction of protection … Data from Pakistan are presented to illustrate how failure to consider these conditions can result in misleading policy recommendations." Further, p. 812, "The probability that policy distortions will alter the trading status of a commodity increases the closer the country is to self-sufficiency in that commodity. Once the country's trading

Let us now suspend disbelief and set aside the conceptual and practical problems of accurately defining and measuring EPRs. How well do they serve as a guide to policy by suggesting outcomes which ought to be pursued for their beneficial effects or complemented by other policies to moderate their ill-effects? Implicit in the earlier discussion, and what ought to be made explicit in the policy debate, is that such policy analysis is crucially dependent upon the use of counterfactuals. What would happen in the absence of tariff changes, what would happen with them? Hence the impact of tariff reform is deduced. Now, all of the points already made are heavily destructive of the counterfactual basis upon which the IDC has calculated EPRs. What they show is that the economy does not work in the way that is suggested by the restrictive assumptions that have been made.

By the same token, the inferred comparative static impacts are unacceptable even if the calculated EPRs are well-defined and empirically accurate in some sense – an impossible eventuality, since exactly the same conditions that distort the calculation of EPRs also suggest that they should *not* be used as a simple, an *exclusive*, nor *independent* object of policy. For example, much trade is internal to multinational enterprises, involving tied markets between affiliates engaging in transfer pricing. This applies to those importing to, and exporting from, South Africa. Such considerations imply that there is a role for tariffs which depend in part upon how competitive are the domestic markets within which the multinationals operate.[123] Similarly, irrespective of the presence of multinationals, imperfect competition may be endemic with variations in the quality of output and intra-industry trade (making EPRs difficult to measure

status is altered, the degree of potential distortion in conventionally estimated protection measures increases the larger is the wedge between the import and the export parity prices. The wedge, which is comprised of the costs involved in shipping a commodity between the domestic production or consumption zones and world markets, can be particularly large in case of commodities characterized by a low value: weight ratio … The wedge can be especially large in big countries with high internal transport costs."

123 For a theoretical analysis, see Itagaki (1983). He concludes, p. 449/50, "Even if MNEs operate under perfectly competitive conditions, because of the foreignness of the MNEs the host country has an additional reason for manipulating its trade policy … this causes the optimal effective rates of protection to differ significantly from those derived in previous analyses … in contrast to the traditional prescription of the optimal policy for a small importing country, complete free trade is no longer the first-best optimum for the importing host country, even if the supply price of the imported good is constant and perfect competition prevails. Moreover, international monopoly by the MNE causes the meaning and the definition of effective rate of protection to differ from the one employed in the previous analyses, and also influences the optimal effective rates of protection for an additional reason, that is, distortion due to monopoly."

because of the need to disentangle the gap between world and domestic prices according to the role of quality, oligopoly, tariffs, etc).[124]

A slightly different way of illustrating these and other points is by reference to the formula for the EPR itself. As a *ratio* of value added at domestic prices to that at world prices, it is necessarily *scale-independent*. It makes no difference how large or small is the absolute level of economic activity concerned. This could be steel or it could be tiddly-winks. The very simplicity of the formula demonstrates that it has no direct concern for dynamic and static economies of scale and scope, excess capacity, capital-labour intensity, market structure, presence of multinationals, skill requirements of the labour force and management, developments in world markets, product differentiation and quality, commercial risk, age structure of capital stock, etc. Quite apart from failing to incorporate these factors in its definition, the EPR is measured inappropriately by exclusion of these and other factors such as the differential impact of non-tradeables, and the substitution between capital and labour in production in response to changing input prices. In this light, it is inconceivable how EPRs can justifiably be used as the basis for industrial policymaking of which trade policy is an integral part. Doubts must be equally strong over its usefulness for measuring macroeconomic impacts on employment, inflation and growth.

In short, it is erroneous to presume that shifts in effective rates of protection act in a relatively uniform, linear fashion within economic sectors, simply serving to shift output marginally in unambiguous directions in response to the induced raising or lowering of prices. This takes no account of the competitive structure of industries and the role of strategic behaviour (by both domestic and foreign firms) for which differential pricing in export and domestic markets can be crucial in the presence of economies of scale and scope and market imperfections.[125] At best, the IDC model is a very poor guide to anything other

124 See Greenaway and Milner (1987, p. 51), "Welfare-raising non-zero effective protection is a genuine possibility in the presence of intra-industry specialisation and exchange … Given the prevalence of intra-industry trade, the circumstances where such welfare improving intervention is perceived as feasible may be relatively widespread. If nothing else this is likely to strengthen arguments for policy coordination."

125 For a simple account of this now standard relationship between trade and industrial policy, see Fine (1996b). In the context of South Africa Holden et al. (1996, pp. i–ii) report, "Although the manufacturing sector as a whole shows little evidence of the exercise of market power, sub-sectorally there were found to be important differences. Overall returns to scale were found to be increasing in manufacturing. Import penetration and exports as a share of production, failed to affect growth in productivity, and the proportion of skilled workers had a positive impact on productivity growth. Productivity growth in metals, chemicals, agricultural equipment, and iron and steel was shown to benefit from an increase in the proportion of output exported. The penetration of imports had

than a summary of extrapolated, but questionable, marginal changes in the economy, and it is unable to pick up critical collapses in sectors which result from shifting disadvantage in protection, and/or strategic withdrawal or entry by dominant domestic and importing foreign firms, respectively.

The IDC does, presumably inadvertently, only recognise these issues cursorily and marginally in the extreme form of reference to 'dumping'. Unfortunately, dumping in theory – where those importing charge a lower price in export than in their own domestic markets as a way of covering fixed costs – is treated as a readily identifiable pricing strategy which can be countered by punitive tariffs, themselves allowed under the safeguard duties of the Marrakesh agreement. Nothing could be further from the truth in practice. There is no sharply defined import price level, or watershed, at which market competition becomes unfair. Rather, there is a continuum of market effects according to the strategic behaviour of both domestic and foreign firms – and any formula for calculating even a rough boundary between what is and what is not allowed will need to be impossibly sensitive to changing conditions of supply and demand as the incentive for dumping depends upon accidental or deliberate availability of excess capacity. Moreover, the speed with which anti-dumping measures could be put in place is limited relative to the scale of the damage that could be done in the interim.[126]

Whilst these calculations of shifting levels of protection and their estimated effects should not be taken too seriously as a guide to outcomes, much more significant is that they are presented by the IDC, presumably as a parastatal on behalf of, or with a major influence on, government. Is it accidental that sectors to benefit from the tariff reform are other mining (gold is not included in the study), and non-metallic and basic metals, those with which IDC has so long been involved either directly or indirectly? Is it appropriate for the IDC to undertake this analysis, especially when it is demonstrably incapable of addressing the supply-side policies involved? The lack of progress in such

adversely affected on productivity growth in some industries including clothing and spinning. Increasing returns to scale were found in motor vehicles, knitting, clothing, and iron and steel. Coincidentally, market power had been exercised in motor vehicles, knitting, spinning, pulp, carpets, other chemicals, and iron and steel. Those industries where market power had not been exercised, and where returns to scale were increasing, were rubber, other non-metal mineral products, meat products, machinery, metal furniture and cutlery." Note that they also observe that chemicals, iron and steel and motor vehicles alone account together for 31% of manufacturing.

126 Havenga (1996, p. 34) recognises, "Although the mechanism exists whereby the BTT could recommend safeguard duties, it has never done so in the past. The efficacy of safeguard duties therefore remains untested."

matters is dramatically illustrated by the presentation of the policies designed to replace the phased out GEIS. Apart from standard schemes such as export credits, the main policies seem to be to subsidise the airfares of potential traders! This is a far cry from the carefully targeted and heavily subsidised exports that have proved so effective in the case of the Asian NICs.

More fundamentally, the whole way of going about industrial policy, and the place of tariff reform within it, is entirely topsy-turvy. The starting point must be the detailed, sectoral and strategic considerations that are inevitably set aside by the general definitions, calculations and imputed impacts of EPRs. The latter cannot legitimately be assessed separately either analytically or in policymaking from the full range of considerations that enter into industrial policymaking. Rather tariff reform should be the consequence of, and supportive to, the supply-side measures that logically, and almost certainly chronologically, precede trade reform especially if liberalisation, with serious destructive potential, is under consideration.

The Political Economy of Trade

Liberalisation of trade is often presented as an unwelcome policy that is foisted upon economies by the conditionalities imposed by international agencies. Given that this is not strictly so in the case of South Africa, it is important to understand why trade liberalisation should have been adopted to the extent that it has. A number of reasons can be suggested, and I examine them critically.

First, it reflects a continuity of policy since trade liberalisation is not new, having previously been embraced by the apartheid government. What is new is the form in which the policy has been adopted, with tariff reductions being more prominent as opposed to the removal or reduction of non-tariff barriers. Nonetheless, tariff reform originates in the late 1980s.[127] At that time, there may have been a fear that a newly-elected ANC government, backed by COSATU would be more interventionist and protectionist. Import liberalisation may also have been a way of securing supplies and of putting downward pressure on real wages in anticipation of the future government. But why, then, should the ANC government have adopted and even strengthened these policies initiated previously?

127 Bell (1997, p. 80) observes, "There does not seem to be any fundamental difference between the positions taken on trade policy by the IDC in 1990, on the one hand, and by COSATU (1993), ISP (1995) and the DTI (1995), on the other hand. All take the view that import liberalization through tariff cuts will improve the growth performance of manufacturing and of the economy as a whole."

Second, it is argued that reducing tariffs will raise standards of living, especially for the poor and low paid, by cheapening consumption goods, as in the import of wheat, for example. However, if reduced protection leads to job losses, this is liable to outweigh any impact on poverty through price changes. In addition, the relative benefit on consumption will be greater for those at higher levels of income and consumer spending. If poverty alleviation is the goal, it should be tackled directly and by 'domestic' policies for redistribution or welfare provision. It must be suspected that the welfare argument for tariff reduction is an ex post rationale, with limited attention paid in detail to the net impact and to the relative merits of alternative policies.

Third, trade liberalisation can be seen as a measure to undermine the power of employers, with the aim of forcing them to rely upon methods other than protection to promote their competitiveness. Certainly, the earlier history of South African industrialisation is one in which protection has been extended almost on demand to manufacturers, especially to those of consumer goods. The significance of this factor clearly depends upon the political leverage of the economic interests concerned as well as the circumstances in which that leverage is exercised, a matter to which we return below.

Fourth, as a result of sanctions and the self-sufficiency mentality of the apartheid regime, the new government may have wished to distance itself from a past image of autarky. However, it must be acknowledged that the South African transition to democracy must have been one of the most closely scrutinised and welcomed so that the break with the past could hardly have required the added symbolism of an apparent shift from protectionist to neo-liberal trade policies.

Fifth, concessions with respect to liberalisation may have been motivated by the idea of this allowing for greater room for manoeuvre, or even the necessity for, supply-side measures. In addition, COSATU may have conceded on protection in order to secure strengthened institutional representation in policymaking more generally. Each of these factors merely suggests why concessions may have been made to trade liberalisation. Neither explains why such policies should have successfully emerged to such an extent in the first place.

Finally, there is the pressure for trade liberalisation that comes from international agencies. This has now become so pervasive that its influence can be exerted in a number of ways, both directly and indirectly. Donor aid has been conditional upon trade reform and other measures, and their implementation is taken as symbolic of readiness and success for reform irrespective of their impact in practice. Consequently, private capital is said to reward the example set by official aid which has itself been tied to an unquestioned conventional wisdom. By the same token, policymakers have been subject to a barrage of psychological as well as of economic pressure to conform to standard stabilisation and structural adjustment policies. In other words, what is known as the Washington Consensus, a belief in the virtues of free trade and sound money, has exercised a powerful ideological hold, irrespective of the limited if positive impact of such policy stances over the long term.

From this discussion, we consider the continuity between governments in the weakening of trade protection to be crucial, leading it to go beyond GATT requirements and signifying the overall weakness of representation of industrial capital in those sectors which are not internationally competitive. For it is not just protection policy that has been weak but also the corresponding supply-side measures to regenerate industry. This is not because capital is generally weak, hardly plausible given the highly concentrated structure of South African corporate conglomerates. Rather, its strategic interests have also displayed a continuity – to rely primarily upon mining, energy and their closely related sectors, and the service and financial sectors within the domestic economy and, otherwise, do seek to diversify assets internationally at the expense of industrial diversification and expansion at home.

It follows that the weakening of protection is indicative not so much of the weakness of industrial capital but of its weak commitment to industrial policy and the restructuring and regeneration of industry. A telling episode in the past was the way in which gold revenues were squandered in the early 1980s to allow for the liberalisation of the financial system with subsequent disastrous effects when the gold price fell. The appreciation of the rand and the failure to harness gold revenues for industrial investment and diversification, in contrast to the 1970s when public sector investment was particularly high in state corporations, proved especially damaging to industrial investment and competitiveness.[128] In many ways, we are now witnessing a similar process, albeit in less favourable economic circumstances, in which a general strategy of trade and financial liberalisation is being sought by large-scale South African conglomerates so that they can restructure their operations globally, a goal for which smaller-scale and/or domestic industry can be sacrificed.

In short, in trade as in macroeconomic policy, the neo-liberal agenda has the effect of consolidating the existing weaknesses of South African industry.

---

128 The South African economy suffered from what appears to be a classic case of the resource curse thesis as suggested by Auty (1993 and 1994). This includes the squandering of temporary high primary resource revenues, rather than their investment in industrial diversification and development, together with Dutch disease effects – competitive pressure on industry as a result of an overvalued exchange rate caused by the capital inflows induced by the confidence attached to a mineral-rich economy.

Should the policies appear to succeed or the economy prosper from time-to-time, the result is merely to create the pressure for even more liberalisation, although this is now more likely to be notable in the area of finance than for trade. When the economy fails, the outcome is much the same, but more likely to be realised through the destruction of domestic capacity as aggregate demand is limited by deflationary macroeconomic policy to restore balance of payments equilibrium, reduce budget deficits and defend the exchange rate.

The alternative to this prospect of spiralling decline in large tranches of South African industry is not simply to restore protection nor even to complement this with supply-side measures. Rather, whilst these do signify the appropriate policy response, they will inevitably prove half-hearted and ineffective unless they are backed by consistent, coherent and long-term political and economic pressure. Certainly, the commitment to industrial restructuring and the growth of manufacturing must be as strong as, and even be capable at times of defeating, the globally oriented strategy of corporate capital. Prior to further trade liberalisation, government must be given the powers and form the institutions which can play the role of formulating and implementing industrial policies, including the capacity to coerce large-scale corporations where necessary.

CHAPTER 7

Vertical Relations in the South African Steel Industry

Postscript as Personal Preamble[1]

For reasons, which are put right out there in the first paragraph of the summary, I was asked to come up with some analysis and some proposals by an alliance of steel-user companies within South Africa and the main trade union involved in their workplaces, the National Union of Metalworkers of South Africa (NUMSA). These two bodies were generally at loggerheads with one another over wages and conditions and redundancies, but, on discriminatory pricing policy against domestic users of steel, they forged a common purpose to preserve jobs and, no doubt, profits. There was, however, a back story of some significance. In hand was a proposal to use NUMSA pension funds to support the taking over of the steel industry into public ownership. There was also the prospect of China taking over the industry from coking coal and iron ore through to steel output.[2]

My proposal for a South African Steel Authority should be seen in this light, an opportunistic initiative to create the institutional capacity to develop integrally both steel and its use in industry and construction. I was mindful that public ownership was not an option. Nonetheless, the initiative failed

1 This working paper was jointly commissioned by NUMSA (the main steel trade union) and the organisation for steel-using companies. It was made publicly available issued under the auspice of the National Institute for Economic Policy (Fine, 1997b), the paper successor to the MERG process which continued for a number of years and, at this time, thanks to the extraordinary energies of Jaya Josie and then Asghar Adelzadeh. The presentation of main points inevitably leads to some repetition of the content of the body of the paper. I was paid for this work but used the fee to fund a research assistant, Candice (whose surname I forget). Her support was invaluable and her name lives on in the name I gave to the electronic file of the report.

2 An important wheeler-dealer (and my informant) in all of this was Vella Pillay who, apart from leading MERG, was the longstanding manager of foreign exchange for the London Branch of the Bank of China. He was in a position to know and bring interested parties together.

miserably to gain any traction.[3] The steps not taken at that early stage and opportunity led along a quickstep path to disaster. For, the subsequent fates of steel and its users have been no less miserable bouncing between tragedy and farce (or managing to hold onto both at once) not least with the involvement of the Guptas. But corruption, state capture, or whatever aside, key analytical positions highlighted in the Report are telling, that: the developmental public interest needs to be defined and (be shown to be) pursued; in the South African context, if not more generally, the powers of the Competition Commission and the Department of Trade and Industry were insufficient and insufficiently coordinated;[4] and the public interest has been sacrificed to the global restructuring of domestic potential.

Presentation of Main Points and Policy Recommendations

1. The reasons why this Report was commissioned are relatively simple. It is claimed that steel prices in South Africa are set for some purchasers at levels that are significantly higher than those prevailing elsewhere and especially relative to the export prices paid for South African steel. This sets South African steel-using industries at a competitive disadvantage. Indeed, however apocryphal, the story is told of a Taiwanese company importing refrigerators made with South African steel at a price with which South African producers cannot compete, precisely because of the high proportion of the value of the product accounted for by steel. In addition, unnecessarily high domestic prices for steel undermine downstream activity in steel-using industries even where there is no competition from imports, as in the construction industry. During the course of preparing this Report, ISCOR announced a new pricing structure which raised the price of steel to small manufacturers of window frames by

3 One reason given to me by Vella was that the delegation of white businessmen to China to explore options was considered so racist by their hosts that they simply took no further interest.

4 This is not to blame these bodies as such nor the individuals occupying positions within them. See, for example, report after report from the Competition Commission on steel, for which, through no fault of its own, investigations made and penalties imposed were already outdated as the industry had already moved on. For the DTI, see the scathing criticisms offered by Zalk (2017). See also Roberts and Rustomjee (2009). Note also that the irreducible need to integrate the different arms of policymaking is perversely and unwittingly acknowledged by free trade advocates in arguing that almost any national policy that however mildly supports a sector is open to be considered a form of subsidy/protection, i.e good policy is unfair competition which neatly complements the notion that any policy is undue interference with the perfect workings of the market.

22% whilst leaving the price unchanged for large purchasers. It was claimed that this would harm small township producers and the capacity both to create jobs and to support the house-building programme.

2. In view of these concerns, it is important to make clear what this Report does not attempt to do. It does not attempt to come to a judgement on whether the steel industry has been implementing discriminatory pricing, nor whether this discriminatory pricing, if it does exist, is unduly damaging to domestic steel users or the public and other interests. Nor does this Report, therefore, recommend a different pricing structure or set of pricing principles. Indeed, during the course of investigation, it was often suggested that the fact of discriminatory and damaging pricing was already well-established. The main issue now, it has been claimed, is how to tackle this state of affairs and what to do.

3. Thus, the main pre-occupation of this Report is primarily with process by which policy is formed. In this respect, it has a much wider brief than in forming judgements about pricing. The latter is seen as a specific part of the broader vertical relations between steel producers and steel users. Consequently, this issue is one of how they should interact with one another and, in particular, what role should be played by government agencies and government policy. However, despite setting aside direct consideration of discriminatory pricing as a matter for recommendation, it is subject to review in order in part to establish the scope of issues that need to be addressed by policymakers.

4. The Report begins by considering the experience of anti-dumping legislation across other countries. This starting point requires some justification. By pricing on export markets at lower levels than on domestic markets, the South African steel industry would be opening itself to charges of dumping. A survey of the latter is useful to the purposes of this Report since it necessarily addresses the issues involved in identifying and remedying dumping even if from the opposite, or mirror image, point of view as far as South African steel-users are concerned. For dumping, a foreign country is complaining that it is being damaged by imports at a price lower than is being charged on the importer's domestic market.

5. The literature on dumping falls into three overlapping approaches. The first derives from economic theory. It shows that judgements about predatory pricing are very difficult to draw since, as a result of varieties of strategic behaviour, not least the threat of filing an anti-dumping case in order to impose costs on competitors, and the variety of variables involved in pricing policy, there may be good reasons for price differentials. Furthermore, these differentials are not necessarily disadvantageous to the public interest. Differential pricing may well reflect price discrimination and, hence, a degree of market power in the domestic market of the dumping exporter. Consequently, at the very least,

it is necessary to consider all the factors underlying monopolistic behaviour both in a static and a dynamic context.

6. The second approach draws from political economy, and potentially incorporates the content of the first approach together with an examination of how the economic interests involved are represented politically. This can include lobbying for favourable anti-dumping policies when, for example, the domestic market is subject to recession, or even strategic behaviour to induce government response, as in the threat of plant closures and redundancies. Like the first approach, this suggests that it is particularly difficult to identify where predatory pricing is taking place and that welfare calculations of policy are liable to be inappropriate if not taking account of economic interests played out through both economic and political strategies.

7. The third approach is more descriptive in content, examining the legal and administrative practices through which anti-dumping policy is made. It shows how extraordinarily complex are the apparently simple tasks of identifying and quantifying price discrimination, of making a judgement about injury to private or public interests, and of deciding upon remedial action such as a compensating tariff. As in the other two approaches, a wide range of factors has to be taken into account.

8. One conclusion drawn from the literature in the light of the complexity of anti-dumping legislation in principle and in practice is that it has been increasingly used in the era of trade liberalisation as an alternative form of protection by well-organised domestic producers. Paradoxically, trade policy has been 'privatised' in that it is made by those taking out anti-dumping actions or threatening to do so. For those wedded to free trade and reliance upon the market more generally, this leads to the conclusion that anti-dumping legislation should be abolished. A conclusion of a different type is drawn here, and is strongly reflected within the literature. This is that, because of the complexity of factors involved and the different ways in which they interact with one another, anti-dumping must be addressed on a case-by-case basis. Further, anti-dumping like trade policy more generally cannot be considered in isolation from other areas of policy, most notably competition policy but also industrial policy more widely. It follows that discriminatory pricing on domestic and export markets must be examined at the narrow and detailed level of particular sectors but also on the broad level as far as policymaking is concerned.

9. These general considerations are followed by a brief overview of the world steel industry. It is argued that it is undergoing a complex transition and is subject to rapid change. Demand is highly cyclical but distributed variously across a wide range of products and markets. Supply is in a state of transition

between a competitively advantageous and dynamic technology (minimills) and a more traditional technology (large-scale integrated facilities) that incorporates high levels of sunk costs but which is itself open to some adaptation. Supply is also subject to uncertainty around new sources from the economies in transition and depends upon access to a range of raw materials and other inputs as well as a shifting system of distribution. Finally, the industry is highly politicised and has a long and continuing tradition of state intervention and cartelisation both at national and international levels.

10. The South African steel industry is also briefly reviewed. It is both subject to and reflects developments at a world level. In addition, it is undergoing transition from the structures inherited from the apartheid period. As a consequence, the industry seems to be marked by three strategic considerations. First, there is a shift towards the production of stainless steel, especially for export. Second, there is engagement in the formation of international joint ventures and associations. Third, there is rationalisation of product lines on the domestic market. Although prices are higher than for exports, the aim is to focus on fewer products to accrue economies of scale and to rely upon imports for those products not domestically sourced in sufficient volume.

11. There is no reason to believe from a priori reasoning, from the evidence of those in the steel industry and from ISCOR's own statement of its pricing policy that the restructuring of the industry is adequately responsive to the needs of the steel-using industry nor to the advantage of the South African economy more generally. Indeed, ISCOR and its joint venture trading arm, MacSteel International, have an incentive to reorganise the supply and distribution of steel in order to 'cherry-pick' the most advantageous markets, whether domestic or export, on the basis of price discrimination and without due regard to the broader public interest. Our review of anti-dumping and of the world and the South African steel industries suggests that ISCOR is neither best placed nor best motivated to adopt appropriate strategies for the South African economy as a whole, not least because of the complexities and conflicts of interest involved.

12. Policymaking is in part concerned with whether private corporate strategies and their effects are in the public interest and, if not, how the latter can best be promoted. If private strategies are deemed not to be in the public interest, policy is concerned with how alternative strategies can be formulated and adopted and their objectives achieved. The Report then considers whether existing policymaking institutions are able to undertake these tasks.

13. In the case of the Board on Trade and Tariffs, it is found that it has limited experience in dealing with issues of discriminatory pricing. This is reflected in tariffs on demand until the most recent past and in view of the proposed

review of its own anti-dumping legislation and procedures. The Competition Board has much more experience of dealing with price discrimination and restrictive trade practices. But, whilst it has examined the notions both of public and national interest, along with the BTT, it does not appear to have formulated or even reformulated these to reflect the current imperatives of economic and social reconstruction. Further, even if the Competition Board and BTT were in some sense ideally experienced and functioning agencies, they would not have the powers to induce appropriate corporate strategies for the steel industry both because of their limited powers as well as a lack of coordination with other policies.

14. Despite these reservations about the Competition Board, it has undertaken invaluable reviews of anti-competitive behaviour in the steel industry. Indeed, the sector has been under continual review throughout the 1990s for one reason or another. The Board has found evidence of anti-competitive behaviour in a number of instances and has recommended restrictions on a variety of practices as a result. However, more informal evidence suggests that its findings are merely the tip of an iceberg, and that the steel industry is marked by considerable exercise of market power, with potentially damaging consequences through higher input prices on domestic markets, lower levels of exports and export prices, lower quality and delivery standards on domestic markets, capital flight, tax evasion and avoidance, and premature steel plant closure.

15. This does not imply that simply remedying price discrimination within the domestic market or between it and export markets will be in the public interest or will address the problem sufficiently and appropriately. Of course, the private interests of the steel-users are necessarily represented, at least in the short term, by the benefits of lower prices. However, given that the substantial depreciation of the rand, equivalent to a price reduction on steel inputs relative to competing imports, has not markedly boosted the downstream steel-using industries, it is reasonable to conclude that discriminatory pricing alone is not responsible for the poor performance of such industries.

16. As established by a variety of Cluster Studies for the steel industry, the problems are more deeply rooted in terms of the vertical relations between steel producers and steel-users. There is evidence of individual and collective inefficiency as well as of lack of coordination. The Studies conclude that these deficiencies must be remedied but do not address the issues of why the failures have arisen and how they might be overcome.

17. Other research has addressed these issues and also points to the longstanding lack of vertical integration in much of South African industry both through the failure of private capital and industrial policy. The reasons for

this have shifted over time but currently reflect the conglomerate character of South African corporations, their uneasy collaboration with one another from time to time, the reluctance of foreign investors to engage in joint ventures or stand-alone investments where they are constrained in vertically integrated activity (whether in production or access to local markets for sales or purchases), and the strategic interest of South African corporations in internationalising their operations.

18. In view of the above, there is an urgent need for deploying and, where necessary, creating the capacity for formulating, implementing and monitoring industrial policy. In the case of the steel industry, the weight of evidence considered in this Report suggests that the existing institutions, even if working perfectly in areas of policymaking that are marked by a lack of precision and discretion, are sorely inadequate to the tasks involved. They do not have sufficient powers, they cannot function sufficiently quickly, and nor are they open to appropriate coordination. As a result, it is recommended that a permanent steel authority, the South African Steel Authority (SASA) be established which would take over the responsibilities of the Competition Board, the BTT and other relevant statutory bodies as far as steel-related issues are concerned. It should also command wider powers to regulate the industry and to make policy recommendations. However, no further detailed recommendations are made about the composition and functioning of SASA, although there are implications that can be drawn from this Report if the recommendation is accepted.

19. The case for SASA can be made in two different but closely related ways. First, by analogy with the case made against anti-dumping legislation, industrial policy in South Africa for the steel industry is currently being made by ISCOR. As a result, industrial policy has been privatised and is governed by the strategies adopted by ISCOR. Its private interests do not, cannot and are not designed to coincide with those of the public interest. That public interest is itself poorly represented both historically and currently on behalf of those most liable to benefit from the actual or potential jobs and products that derive from downstream steel-using activity.

20. Second, ISCOR is a utility that was privatised under the previous apartheid regime without the introduction of special regulations. This does not mean that ISCOR's performance has subsequently been purely market-driven, at least until the formation of the new government. For relations between ISCOR and government have remained highly politicised, as reflected in economic policies towards the corporation, including continuing measures of protection and provision of state finance through joint ventures with the IDC. In the context of the politics of steel, it may appear to be strange to describe

ISCOR as a utility since this term is usually reserved for those enterprises providing consumer goods rather than intermediate inputs. However, even this is not universally the case, since electricity generation, for example, is generally recognised to require regulation although it does not serve consumers directly as this is the province of the grid or distribution companies. In any case, electricity and other such utilities serve both domestic and industrial consumers and regulation is generally required for the latter as well as for the former.

21. In short, without quibbling over semantics, ISCOR and the steel industry more generally are best understood as a utility. ISCOR itself directly employs over 40,000 workers, has a turnover of R12 billion and capital assets of R12 billion. It has direct or indirect command over important national assets such as coal and iron reserves and scrap. Its forward and backward linkages within the economy and its impact on macroeconomic performance are highly significant. In this light, the proposal for SASA is far from outlandish. As an individual company, ISCOR more than matches the contribution made by total industry in many developing countries. No second thought would be given to providing for a department of industry in such countries even though the range and scale of production and economic impact may be far less than for ISCOR, or the South African steel industry as a whole, in absolute terms. On the other hand, it is common for steel authorities to be formed, as in the longstanding European ECSC, even if within particular ministries. Further, it is recognised by the OECD, for example, that individual countries need to be represented in international negotiations in order to regulate the industry at a world level.

22. It is anticipated that there will be objections to this proposal on a number of grounds. One is that the formulation and exercise of the public interest by SASA will be against certain private interests. This, however, is precisely the rationale for the formation of SASA. On the other hand, it might be argued that SASA will create a new layer of bureaucracy, an ineffective and inefficient increase in state intervention, and command scarce public resources and skills that might be better engaged in other activities. It is, however, a central tenet of this Report that the current provisions for regulating the industry are ineffective and unnecessarily duplicate uncoordinated policymaking resources across various governmental institutions. Indeed, the industry should welcome this proposal for the scope that it provides for the effectiveness and streamlining of decision-making that it promises to yield.

23. Finally, it must be emphasised that the recommendation for the formation of SASA is steel-specific. It is not a general argument for similar authorities for each and every sector of the economy. In other industries, characterised by different structures and dynamics, existing regulatory provisions and institutions may well be adequate or only be open to marginal improvement.

Whether industries should be regulated by a single authority covering the range of issues, or by separate authorities with generic responsibilities can only be determined on a case-by-case basis. The judgement of this Report is that the evidence for a single authority is overwhelming in the case of South African steel. The recommendation has the advantage of being consistent with, and a refinement and development of, current Government thinking on competition policy as presented in its recent guidelines. It is an anomaly of the timing of the privatisation of ISCOR that it should not have been subject to stronger regulation, including the creation of a corresponding regulatory authority. Had ISCOR been restructured as a state enterprise under the current Government, there seems little doubt that it would have been more fully and specifically regulated. This anomaly must be rectified as a matter of urgency.

1 Introduction

The reasons why this Report was commissioned are relatively simple. It is claimed that steel prices in South Africa are set for some domestic purchasers at levels that are significantly higher than those prevailing elsewhere and especially relative to the export prices paid for South African steel. This sets South African steel-using industries at a competitive disadvantage. Indeed, however apocryphal, the story is told of a Taiwanese company importing refrigerators made with South African steel at a price with which South African producers cannot compete, precisely because of the high proportion of the value of the product accounted for by steel. In addition, unnecessarily high domestic prices for steel undermine downstream activity in steel-using industries even where there is no competition from imports, as in the construction industry. During the course of preparing this Report, ISCOR announced a new pricing structure which raised the price of steel to small manufacturers of window frames by 22% whilst leaving the price unchanged for large purchasers, as reported in *Business Day*, November 13th, 1997. It was claimed that this would harm small township producers and the capacity both to create jobs and to support the house-building programme. In August, 1996, the Cape Chamber of Commerce and Industry met with the South African Iron and Steel Institute, SAISI, to complain of prices to domestic customers at levels up to 60% higher than those on international markets (Business Bulletin, 1996).

In view of these concerns, it is important to make clear what this Report does not attempt to do. It does not attempt to come to a judgement on whether the steel industry has been implementing discriminatory pricing, nor whether this discriminatory pricing, if it does exist, is unduly damaging to domestic steel users or the public and other interests. Nor does this Report, therefore, recommend a different pricing structure or set of pricing principles. Indeed, during the course of investigation, it was often suggested that the fact of discriminatory and damaging pricing was already well-established. The main issue now, it has been claimed, is how to tackle this state of affairs and what to do.

Thus, the main pre-occupation of this Report is primarily with the process by which policy is formed. In this respect, it has a much wider brief than in forming judgements about pricing. The latter is seen as a specific part of the broader vertical relations between steel producers and steel-users. Consequently, this issue is one of how they should interact with one another and, in particular, what role should be played by government agencies and government policy. However, despite setting aside direct consideration of discriminatory pricing as a matter for recommendation, it is subject to review in order, in part, to establish the scope of issues that need to be addressed by policymakers.

The Report begins by considering the experience of anti-dumping legislation across other countries. This starting point requires some justification. By pricing on export markets at lower levels than on domestic markets, the South African steel industry would be opening itself to charges of dumping. A survey of the latter is useful to the purposes of this Report since it necessarily addresses the issues involved in identifying and remedying dumping even if from the opposite, or mirror image, point of view as far as South African steel-users are concerned. For dumping, a foreign country is complaining that it is being damaged by imports at a price lower than is being charged on the importer's domestic market. Consideration of dumping on export markets raises, even if indirectly or in mirror image, the issues relevant to discriminatory pricing on domestic markets as each involves the overall strategic behaviour of the same firms whether in domestic or export markets.

One conclusion drawn from the literature, in the light of the complexity of anti-dumping legislation in principle and in practice, is that it has been increasingly used in the era of trade liberalisation as an alternative form of protection by well-organised domestic producers. It is observed, for example, that more than twice as many cases of dumping were brought in the United States in the 1970s than in the 1980s (Boltuck and Litan, 1991), with an international comparative review provided by the contributions to Steele (ed.) (1996). Paradoxically, trade policy is perceived as having been 'privatised' in that it is made by those taking out anti-dumping actions or threatening to do so. For those wedded to free trade and reliance upon the market more generally, this leads to the conclusion that anti-dumping legislation should be abolished. A conclusion of a different type is drawn here, and is strongly reflected within the literature. This is that, because of the complexity of factors involved and the different ways in which they interact with one another, anti-dumping must be addressed on a case-by-case basis. Further, anti-dumping like trade policy more generally cannot be considered in isolation from other areas of policy, most notably competition policy but also industrial policy more widely. It follows that discriminatory pricing on domestic and export markets must be examined, on the one hand, at the narrow and detailed level of particular sectors but, paradoxically, on the other hand, at the broad level as far as policymaking is concerned.

These general considerations are followed by a brief overview of the world and South African steel industries and how the South African industry has been regulated to accommodate the coincidence or clash of public and private sector interests. It is found that there is scope for considerable intervention but that existing institutions are incapable, even with reform, of undertaking the task. Accordingly, it is recommended that a new authority, the South African Steel Authority (SASA) be established.

2 The Economic Theory of Dumping

The economic theory of dumping has its origins in the contribution of Viner (1923) and seeks to explain, in the first instance, why pricing in an export market should be lower than in the home market. A necessary condition is that the two markets be separate in some sense for, otherwise, the price discrimination would be eliminated by re-export to the country of origin. This is immediately to enter the world of imperfect competition in which, for example, a monopolist would maximise profits by exploiting the difference in demand conditions between the two markets. The classic result is that the elasticity of demand should be higher in the export market or, in other words, the home market of the exporter can more readily bear a higher price without loss of demand (Marceau, 1994).

This simple tale already suffices to raise a number of germane issues. First, even though dumping involves imperfect competition between countries, it must also be characteristic at least of the domestic market of the exporting country. Otherwise, price would be driven down there. It follows that the prevalence of dumping depends upon the competition policy of the exporting country. Second, as imperfect competition takes the form of price discrimination across international markets, this opens the way for product differentiation, or genuine quality differences, to supplement those of price alone. Third, especially if some form of protection is adopted, there is the option on the part of the exporter of foreign direct investment of a more or less token kind as a circumvention strategy, with limited assembly of otherwise imported inputs, as investigated by Azrak and Wynne (1995) in the case of Japanese FDI to the USA and by Belderbos (1997) for Japanese foreign direct investment into the US and EU. He finds that tariff-jumping is significant in both cases but doubly so for the EU as its anti-dumping and tariff measures are more stringently applied whilst the USA has more powerful countermeasures in response to tariff-jumping. It is also found that the impact of tariff-jumping in response to anti-dumping measures can increase market concentration in domestic markets as a consequence of competition from inward investment rather than imports.

These considerations are brought out sharply by Devault (1996) in his attempt to measure the welfare effects of US anti-dumping duties. The effect of such duties is to raise the domestic price level, ultimately at the expense of domestic consumers even if domestic producers gain by the protection involved. To quantify the effects, it is necessary to make some assumption about the factors listed in the previous paragraph even if to set them aside as Devault does in case of imperfect competition. On this basis, he calculates that the gain to US producers of thirty anti-dumping duties has been between $90 and $375 million but that the welfare loss to consumers has between $500 and $800 million, with a net loss to US welfare of about $275 million.

Such calculations clearly indicate the trade-off between public and private interests. Anti-dumping duties raise the price of imports to domestic consumers, incurring a welfare loss. This has to be set against the gains to producers in terms of higher prices and output. In effect, the imperfectly competitive conditions prevailing in the exporter's home market are being extended to the export market, forging a link there between trade and competition policy. As Trebilcock (1990, p. 239) suggests, this is a policy of equal misery in the domestic market. If foreign producers enjoy higher productivity, then why should they not sell in the domestic market at lower prices than domestic producers even if this is, in turn, associated with lower prices than in their home market (Deardoff, 1990). In principle, the two effects between the markets of productivity differences and elasticity differences are being conflated with one another. Further, (the threat of) anti-dumping actions can even facilitate collusion across national boundaries as recognised in EU legislation (Bourgeois and Demaret, 1995), in the trade conflicts over automobiles between Japan and the USA, and especially in semi-conductor trade where minimum prices are set even though extremely rapid productivity increases render these non-binding (Baldwin, 1994).

Significantly, Devault draws the conclusion that the particular mix of these complicating factors requires a case-by-case approach rather than a general one. This is especially so when taking dynamic factors into account for his calculations are based entirely on static welfare gains and losses, and he cites the example of Japan shifting typewriter production to the USA to avoid duties. However, dynamic considerations are much more pervasive and, as observed by Stiglitz (1997), fall into two types as revealed in the more recent literature on dumping. On the one hand, the theory of predatory behaviour is concerned with the strategies adopted by firms in which a short-term sacrifice (temporary lower price) is made in order to accrue long-term advantage (permanently higher price and/or elimination of competitors). On the other hand, the new trade theory argues that productivity can accrue through learning-by-doing or other mechanisms which depend upon early and large market share in which protection can play a supportive role. In this respect, strategic behaviour is also involved but in the context of realising productivity gains and not just imperfectly competitive profits over time on the basis of given production conditions.

Lower pricing initially in order to gain market share later has been examined by To (1994) and Hartigan (1996) in terms of switching costs – where it is costly for a consumer to change from one supplier to another. Both Canoy (1994) and Holmes (1996) construct models in which the strategic behaviour of firms leads them to price low in an initial period in order to raise price later, having deterred other entrants and raised market power. More generally, as Stiglitz (1997, p. 404) concludes:[5]

> New developments in industrial organisation theory, however, suggest … a variety of ways in which predators can prevent entry and thus protect the rents accruing during the second stage. The strategic entry deterrence literature, for example, presents models with irreversible investment, in which firms can deter entry by building excess capacity or investing in advertising. Such activities can be expensive, but they make predatory pricing a profitable strategy by protecting second period rents. Alternatively, predatory pricing itself can be a deterrent to entry: Such behavior may create a reputation for craziness and irrational behavior, and this reputation may dissuade potential rivals from entering in later periods.

5 As chance would have it, I was working critically on models of this kind for other purposes at this time (Fine, 1996b and 1999b).

Stiglitz argues that a domestic may be preferable to a foreign predator since the latter would accrue domestically generated consumer surplus and, in addition, the costs of domestic labour market dislocation would not be borne by the foreign producer.

From an analytical point of view, an even more important conclusion emerges. This is that there is no simple relationship between differential pricing and predatory dumping. For the predatory effects may or may not be strategically chosen and may be counterbalanced by other factors affecting differential pricing. This arises, for example, in the context of uncertain, say cyclical, movements in demand. Anam et al. (1996) show that differential pricing is rational if firms wish to reduce profit variability where uncertain demand is correlated between the markets concerned. More generally, Brannlund and Lofgren (1995), in the context of the Canadian pulp and paper industry, illustrate how pricing depends upon the extent of imperfect competition, the strategic behaviour of firms, the sequencing of the availability of information about market demand, and the correlation between demand in foreign and domestic markets.

The previous discussion has been concerned with strategic (predatory) pricing primarily in the context of given production conditions. New trade theory simply adds to the complications involved by incorporating productivity effects in some way, most notably to those who have already produced most or are 'first-movers'. Identification of predatory pricing remains ambiguous for, as Stiglitz (1997, p. 409) acknowledges, where competitive firms are learning-by-doing, it is legitimate to price below cost in the short run and target long-run costs.

Notably absent, however, from Stiglitz's discussion are non-horizontal forms of competition, as if strategies are confined around pricing and supply alone within a single market. In particular, an important aspect of competition both within and between countries is the role played by vertical integration since this provides the means for tied markets within firms. Baldwin (1994), for example, finds that high prices for imported Japanese semiconductors not only facilitated collusion in this sector but also created an advantage for downstream Japanese electronic products originating from the same companies, both in pricing of inputs and learning effects including spin-offs to other sectors using semiconductors. Cheng and Kreinin (1996) suggest that Japanese keiretsu have in-group supplier preferences to accrue the advantages amongst others of risk-sharing, thereby accounting for higher input prices than on the US domestic market and inducing anti-dumping cases. Bernhofen (1995) finds that dumping can occur for intermediate inputs when the receiving country has lower levels of productivity in downstream activity, with the low input prices necessary to compensate for higher costs and to sustain demand for final output. Finally, Laussel and Montet (1995, p. 55) discuss more generally how vertical integration interacts with trade and other policies, not least state-ownership and domestic procurement, to favour domestic industry against (predatory) imports.

In short, the economic theory of dumping suggests that it depends upon the strategic behaviour of firms whether in a static or dynamic context. In either case, there is no simple relationship between dumping and differential pricing in home and export markets. The factors involved are sufficiently varied and complex in incidence and interaction to warrant investigation at a sufficiently disaggregated sectoral level, and there is a need to disentangle competitive malpractice from efficient business strategy. As Mullin and Mullin (1997) conclude for the monopolistic purchase of iron ore leases by the United States Steel Corporation in 1906, this can represent the successful pursuit of efficiency gains by vertical integration rather than the foreclosure of competition through denial of inputs to potential competitors. But such judgements are often impossible to draw, especially in principle. As McChesney (1996, p. 124) concludes in the context of anti-trust policy:

> Many economists have tried to use structural variables (number of sellers, product homogeneity) to pick out industries where anti-competitive activity was more likely. The results heretofore have not been promising. The problems are legion, not the least of which is separating the higher prices and reduced quantities that reflect unilateral behavior in less-than-textbook-perfectly competitive markets … Empirically, previous researchers have questioned whether government trust-busters are capable of separating anti-competitive behaviour from benign business practices.

3 The Political Economy of Dumping

In the previous section, the economic theory of dumping has inevitably focused upon the strategic behaviour of firms. Not surprisingly, such considerations have been extended to incorporate decision-making around trade disputes themselves. Under what circumstances would firms or an industry bring an anti-dumping case, and how would foreign, importing firms respond to the prospect of anti-dumping charges? Further, the same questions can be asked of government policy to the extent that it represents the interests of the firms concerned. In other words, anti-dumping legislation and practice, and whether and how they are used, become endogenous within the political economy of dumping.

As already indicated, as anti-dumping legislation can facilitate collusion if it leads to voluntary import restrictions and higher minimum prices, and domestic and foreign firms in an industry may have an incentive to collaborate in such protection. More frequently, however, the literature has addressed the issue of anti-dumping legislation being used by domestic firms to pursue their own interests at the expense of foreign imports and domestic consumers. As Stiglitz (1997, p. 420) concludes:

> Statutes offering even the possibility of protection inevitably engender rent-seeking activities that are both direct (e.g. lobbying) and indirect (e.g. manipulating output in order to make a positive injury finding more likely).

These two forms of activity are dealt with in turn.

Direct activities can, in addition to persuading the decisions of authorities to be favourable, be incorporated within the strategic behaviour of firms contingent upon the form taken by anti-dumping legislation. The threat of an anti-dumping case can suffice to dissuade a foreign firm from importing at a low price or at all. As Levinsohn (1994, p. 353) puts it in the context of Japanese car imports to the USA:

> An anti-dumping petition acts as a signal (and credible threat) which leads foreign firms to increase their prices. US firms then do likewise and the new equilibrium entails higher prices and profits.

Staiger and Wolak (1994) posit three different effects in studying whether anti-dumping laws restrict both trade and competition. The investigation effect follows immediately from the filing of a complaint, the suspension effect is the consequence of a voluntary deal on the part of importers during the course of investigation, and the withdrawal effect is the impact of the case if withdrawn before judgement. For the USA, they find that the prospect of a favourable judgement is an important determinant of whether a case is filed or not but that, in addition, firms file for the restrictions on trade that are generated by the investigation effect alone, concluding, "that some firms pursue the process-filing strategy and therefore initiate anti-dumping procedures for the investigation effects alone", p. 53. Stiglitz (1997, p. 411) refers to such effects as harassment cases against importers, with the punitive legal and other costs of defending a case potentially disciplining foreign firms irrespective of the merits of their intended pricing and import levels.

Other contributions to the literature are more sophisticated in the sense of examining the knock-on effects of firm behaviour in response to (anticipation of) anti-dumping actions. It is found that the prospect of voluntary export restrictions (VERs) can encourage increases in exports in order to gain higher quotas, as first suggested by Yano (1989) and Anderson (1992). Further, Marchionatti and Usai (1997) suggest that excess capacity may result as part of such strategic behaviour. In short, anticipation of VERs can, paradoxically, lead to a worsening on domestic markets from imports of the competitive pressures that they were designed to eliminate. Strategic price behaviour can lead to similar results. Hartigan (1994), for example, suggests that, in anticipation of an anti-dumping action, a foreign firm may reduce the difference between the prices in the two markets that it serves. This increases the cost of signalling to the export market that it is a low-cost producer in order to induce domestic producers there to exit. In other words, anti-dumping laws may lead to higher prices in the import market and lower prices in the home market for the foreign firm, but this has ambiguous welfare effects in terms of the impact through the survival prospects of the domestic firms. Hartigan also constructs a model of costly demand switching which, given a one-period time-scale over which an anti-dumping investigation must takes place, leads to low pricing for imports initially in order to grab demand that is not fully retrieved by a subsequently favourable dumping judgement. Paradoxically, GATT legislation against dumping may induce the behaviour of first-mover export subsidies that the legislation was intended to eliminate. Schuknecht and Stephan (1994) come to a similar conclusion in the context of the more general result that import penetration can be encouraged in anticipation of future protection. Anderson et al. (1995) examine the reciprocal lobbying by firms from different countries where each can dump on the others' domestic markets. The outcome can be of the prisoners' dilemma type. For each firm has an incentive to lobby for anti-dumping legislation whatever the other firm does. The result, however, is for the price in own market to be reduced relative to a legislation-free environment, with consumers emerging as net beneficiaries.

A more general synthesis and survey of relevant work in this area is provided by Leidy (1994). Given that trade policy, anti-dumping judgements for example, depend upon the movement of observed economic variables – in order to make a judgement of dumping and to assess the resulting injury – then firms and agents more generally may have an incentive to manipulate their behaviour in order to gain favourable judgements and not simply to affect the behaviour of rivals or to lobby for favourable policies. As he concludes, p. 114:

> Contingent commercial policies like safeguards, unfair trade laws, government-assisted VERs, and the like, have linked the prospect of protection to observable industry characteristics (employment, import penetration, capital spending sales, etc). This linkage may thus introduce a political-influence motive to a firm's economic decisions. Alternatively, in the context of newly legislated trade-policy events, the mobilization of political sentiment for protection may depend on the economic decisions of import-competing firms and their foreign competitors. When, for example, a firm such as General Motors announces extensive plant closings and layoffs timed to highly visible pleas for relief from import competition, there may be more at stake than potentially inflated claims of distress. Plant closings and layoffs beyond what are justified on economic grounds, together with the postponement of significant capital purchasing plans might all be used at the margin to re-chart the course of trade policy.

There are two implications of Leidy's review. First, it suggests that theory of strategic behaviour that sets aside its consequences for policy decisions is inappropriate, "the traditional practice of separating normative commercial policy analysis from positive international political economy is thus ill-advised", p. 115. Second, by the same token, welfare calculations of estimated outcomes will be inaccurate since strategic behaviour relative to other firms will be conflated with strategic behaviour relative to the policy process itself.

Despite these reservations, there is a strand within the political economy approach to dumping which sees it as a policy-determined, and hence political, response to economic circumstances. Given that the investigation and response to findings of dumping are flexible, as will be seen in the following sections, outcomes are perceived to depend upon political and not just upon economic circumstances. Tharakan and Waelbroeck (1994, p. 172), for example, recognise that dumping decisions are 'governed by a complex system of national and international laws', with each decision unique to some extent. They examine how decisions in the EC have responded both to technical variables such as capital-intensity, skill-intensity, and scale economies, and to political variables such as level of concentration and numbers employed (to proxy political influence). They test and support two hypotheses, previously found for the USA: that the technical variables are more significant in determining the finding of dumping or not; and that the political variables play the same role in determining whether domestic industry has been injured by the dumping (which is necessary for countervailing action to be taken). Krupp (1994) finds for the US chemical industry that filing an anti-dumping petition is more likely the greater the chances of success, this in turn depending upon the higher is import penetration and the larger the number of (productive) employees.

The conclusion drawn from this study is that, from a free trade perspective antagonistic to the abuse of anti-dumping legislation as a cover for creeping protection, efforts at reform would be best directed at injury rather than dumping determination since the former is more subject to political influences. Finger (ed.) (1993), amongst many others, has been prominent in arguing for the interpretation of dumping legislation as deploying the notion of unfair trade in rhetoric whilst incorporating simple protectionism in a practice which depends upon political influence. Finger (1991) finds, for example, for US anti-dumping cases in the 1980s, that these have proved disproportionately damaging to developing countries, with three-quarters of cases brought against them leading to restrictive outcomes compared to two-thirds for developed countries. On the other hand, 36% of cases for developed countries have resulted in negotiated settlements compared to 15% for developing countries. This is presumed to be indicative of lesser economic and political countervailing power on the part of developing countries. For internal political influence, Leidy (1997) suggests that anti-dumping activity within the USA is counter-cyclical, with pressures increasing as for other forms of protection, during periods of macroeconomic weaknesses. Gallett (1997) also finds that cartel-like behaviour in the US steel industry is countercyclical, weakening when demand is strong and imports are low. As Stiglitz (1997, p. 411) concludes:

> In summary, the antidumping laws no longer have very much to do with the prevention of predatory pricing. Indeed, a recent OECD [1996] study examining U.S. dumping cases between 1979 and 1989 concluded that conditions were not even conducive to predatory pricing in over 85% of the cases that found dumping or that were terminated or suspended before a final determination. It is perhaps worth stressing that the prevention of predatory pricing, which is itself a more narrow standard than the prevention of price discrimination, which is itself a more narrow concept than preventing below-cost sales. And we do not even conduct our price-to-cost comparisons in an entirely disinterested manner and thus are at least three steps away from a purely predatory pricing rule.

In principle, theoretical and empirical studies of dumping in the context of a political economy approach should include all of the variables and considerations that have marked the economic approach together with other variables and strategies drawn from political factors, in order to bridge the three steps between predatory pricing and anti-dumping policy. This can only serve to reinforce the conclusions of the previous section concerning the complexity and variability of the incidence and outcomes of dumping behaviour and its induced remedial responses.

4 Legal and Administrative Considerations

A third branch of literature on dumping draws upon the previously covered contributions from economics and political economy but is more concerned with the details of practice, especially in the light of legal procedures. It is also to be found that the application of analytical and empirical principles is complex and varied. As Steele (1996, p. 6) suggests, following the new dumping code of practice introduced with the Uruguay Round of GATT and the formation of the WTO:

> [W]hile the overall protocol is governed by the Code, each [country] jurisdiction has its own special features in the manner in which the Code is domestically implemented and applied. Such differences involve both procedure and substance and provide fertile ground for debate as to whether they truly reflect compliance with the new Code, properly constructed … the concept of anti-dumping at first sight is disarmingly simple, whereas in truth it is anything but that.

Such an assessment is confirmed by Vermulst (1997) in the discussion of a series of issues that he raises in examining how developing countries can broach anti-dumping laws. First, the complexity of legal procedures is such that, quoting from UNCTAD, anti-dumping measures have become "the tools of protection of the elite", p. 6. In practice, legislation has two components: that set and interpreted at an international level through the WTO, with precedents currently being established through cases; and that set and implemented at a national level. In this respect, there is a sharp contrast between developed and developing countries, with the national laws and administration of the former well-established and more sophisticated than the international. But the opposite is the case for developing countries which suffer from lack of experience, expertise and financial resources. This limits the capacity of developing countries to deliver policy. Vermulst and Komuro (1997) describe the practical problems of dealing with anti-dumping procedures and legislation as "Navigating Dire Straits". In the context of an otherwise liberalised world trade order, this leads Ostry (1990) and Messerlin (1990) to claim that trade policy has itself been subject to "Privatisation" since individually powerful firms or industries have been able to make policy by bringing actions. And, as noted by Staiger and Wolak (1994) for the USA, the cost of filing an anti-dumping suit can easily exceed $500,000.

Second, the GATT Code concerning dumping rests on determining that it both exists and has caused injury to domestic industry. Given the flexibility of interpretation of dumping, and the need to quantify its effects, assessing claims necessarily draws upon economics, accountancy and legal professionals as well as a political process in view of any reference to public interest. Further, the determination and quantification of injury and the posing of remedies (duties, voluntary agreements, etc) is often split between ministries, with trade and industry best placed to assess impact on domestic industry but finance legally responsible for setting and collecting any duties that arise. Vermulst (1997, p. 9) concludes:

> As far as the day-to-day administration of anti-dumping duties is concerned, it seems advisable to establish a separate department within the Ministry of International Trade and Industry. Key disciplines that could be represented in the department include law, economics and accountancy. It also seems recommendable that the department is structured to be an independent technical entity as far as the conduct of investigations is concerned. However, the final decision to impose duties should probably be made at the political level.

In addition, there are requirements on the speed with which investigations are made and conclusions implemented, placing further demands upon the capacity of anti-dumping administration.

Third, the determination of dumping rests on assessing difference between import and home market price. This is far from simple since it depends upon assessing like with like as far as the goods sold are concerned. As brought out in Beseler and Williams (1986), for example, this involves assessing the quality of goods, as well as 'normal' value, drawing in considerations of how costs of production and conditions of sale are to be allocated including those of advertising, brokering, transport and distribution, services and warranties, and research and development. Account must also be taken of differences in tax regimes and subsidies to domestic industries in the exporting country whether direct or indirect (as in export credits or guarantees). As Marceau (1994, p. 26) concludes:

> (T)he reference to cost of production, variable and full costs, used in domestic predation tests as well as in anti-dumping laws, and the frequent construction of prices and costs of production, are deficient. They ignore legitimate national differences in accounting practices, business traditions and social and legal organization.

Such considerations are prominent and extreme in the case of non-market economies or those in transition where costing cannot necessarily be inferred from 'market' pricing of inputs and outputs. This gives rise to the need for reference to a third comparator country for determination of 'normal' trading conditions or for constructed 'fair' values, and these are obviously open to alternative interpretations.

Account must also be taken of the impact of exchange rate movements on the prices of inputs and outputs, for which Raafat and Salehizadeh (1994) suggest there may be partial and lagged responses by importing firms without this necessarily implying dumping. Such effects are even more difficult to disentangle when a country (of origin) is subject to hyperinflation (Parker, 1995). The issue of inflation is taken up by White (1997) and is linked to depreciation costs. He finds that US investigations have used inconsistent methods that are generally prejudicial to importers. In addition, there is the problem of excess capacity and idle plant and whether the full costs of these should be reflected in imputed value. Further, the discussion so far has rested on a clear demarcation between the two countries concerned but other countries may be involved directly or indirectly in the production and trading of the goods under investigation, giving rise to a whole series of complex issues around rules of origin (Vermulst et al. eds, 1994; and Keizer, 1997).

Fourth, it is one thing to establish differential pricing but another to find that it is associated with and causing injury to the domestic economy and to establish what is the level of that injury and by how much and in what form it should be remedied. In principle, what is required is a counterfactual model of the economy in order to assess outcomes if circumstances were made difference by anti-dumping action or alternative strategies of importers. Irrespective of the analytical and legal requirements of such an exercise, Vermulst's (1997) discussion clearly demonstrates that it gives rise to a process equivalent to an academic research project. Questionnaires must be addressed to interested parties, soliciting details of costs and pricing. The information has to be verified and may even entail site visits. Where sampling is undertaken to reduce survey costs, Vermulst (1997, p. 14) observes, "A statistician should be consulted to ensure that the sample is defensible."

Fifth, in determining dumping and consequent injury, a level and form of remedy has to be decided. This can reflect a number of different criteria – ease of administration and monitoring, to stabilise domestic prices, and to raise revenue, for example. More generally, determination and remedying of injury depends upon an assessment and evaluation of the level and incidence of costs and benefits – in other words, the definition of public interest. For the injury to domestic producers has to be set against the interests and functioning of the rest of the economy. Traditionally, as emphasised by those who see anti-dumping as a new form of protection, the interests of domestic producers have been paramount, although from the beginning of 1995, EC regulation has explicitly incorporated the interests of users and consumers, although these, somewhat illogically can figure more as an afterthought once injury has already been determined. For Bourgeois and Demaret (1995, p. 80):

> The new provision should give a stronger voice to consumers and industrial users ... Whether it will bring changes in the material outcome of anti-dumping proceedings is another matter ... the injury caused by dumped imports tends to loom larger, in most instances, than the loss which consumers or industrial users may suffer as a result of anti-dumping duties ... [But] the analysis of the Community interest comes after dumping and injury findings.

In addition, as emphasised by Sykes (1990), it is also necessary to take account of the interests of, and injury to, (dislocated) labour. For Creally (1992), observing that producers tend to predominate over consumers in defining the EU's interests, a whole range of criteria can be used to establish material injury or the threat thereof – levels of production, capacity, sales, market share, prices, profits, return on capital, investment and employment. More generally, Vermulst (1997) suggests that a public interest clause be included in developing country national legislation in order that the interests of producers do not automatically prevail, as in the USA, when it suffices to trigger anti-dumping action for a determination of injury against them alone to be found. The implication, however, is that the general economic and political impact of decisions needs to be subject to full assessment which, inevitably, within the space for discretion, attaches the exercise of a public interest clause to the wider strategies of economic development. As Vermulst and Waer (1991) observe, whilst

EC practices conform with the GATT Code by limiting anti-dumping duties to the level required to remove injury in contrast to those of the USA and Canada, there still remains considerable discretion in coming to judgements which, in principle, ought to reflect the public interest.

Finally, even when all of these issues have been settled, there remains the problem of circumvention which can arise in response to any form of protection. Foreign direct investment to produce for the domestic market can undermine anti-dumping action, especially to the extent that only limited assembly of imported inputs is undertaken. As Messerlin (1990) reports, this led the EC to adopt 'screwdriver' procedures to prevent Japanese circumvention of anti-dumping duties. Once again, this places the issue within the broader context of vertical integration and also the policy stance towards FDI, requiring further sophistication in investigation and policymaking.

Many of these points are illustrated by reference to US practice in anti-dumping action. Consider, for example, the International Trade Commission, ITC (1997a), judgement on whether material injury had resulted from import of steel pipe from Romania and South Africa. The Commission proceeds on the basis of the Department of Commerce already having determined that imports have been based on less than fair value (LTFV) but must decide on whether US producers have suffered as a consequence. In coming to a judgement, they need to take into account the following factors, "output, sales, inventories, capacity utilization, market share, employment, wages, productivity, profits, cash flow, return on investment, ability to raise capital, and research and development", p. 18. Further, "no single factor is dispositive and all relevant factors are considered 'within the context of the business cycle and conditions of competition that are distinctive to the affected industry'", the latter quote being taken from the Act governing its deliberations. In considering these issues, account has to be taken of captured sales (what proportion of output is used within companies), 'Buy American' restrictions (some customers require its suppliers to have used US-manufactured products as inputs), fungibility (how closely products are substitutable for one another in use), the geographical concentration of markets for imports, the role played by distribution channels and service centres, the cumulative impact or even threat posed by imports taken as a whole from all or all potential importers, and the impact on competition and/or dumping in third markets.

Similar complexity is to be found in the ITC (1997b) consideration of imports of steel plate from China, Russia, South Africa, and Ukraine, with the need also to identify how cyclical peak to peak comparisons are to be identified. Hardly surprisingly, the Commissioners in each of these cases are unable to reach unanimous conclusions so that there are both dissenting views and minority reports. Irrespective of the fairness of the US anti-dumping procedures, these cases illustrate the complexity of the factors that need to be taken into account, and their specificity to particular sectors, when policy is being formulated.

5 The Imperatives of Coordination

From the review of the experience of anti-dumping, then, a number of conclusions can be drawn and developed further. First, whether examined from the perspective of economic theory, political economy or legality and administration, outcomes are extremely complex both in principle and in practice, covering a range of factors and behaviour at a great level of detail. Second, not surprisingly, such complexity is wedded to a shifting weight of each of these considerations from case to case and how they interact with one another. Third, the strategic behaviour of firms is potentially sophisticated and uncertain in face of given legislation and practice. It also can be directed to influence such legislation and practice. Fourth, as concluded explicitly by Bourgeois and Demaret (1995), the appropriate policy mix is highly dependent on case-by-case consideration. Fifth, policy itself needs to be directed at defining, identifying and implementing the public interest and for it not to be privatised according to the strategies of particular private interests. Sixth, agencies engaged in determining and implementing policymaking require skills in economics, accountancy and law; they can be spread across different government departments giving rise to problems of administrative capacity, inefficient duplication of function and lack of coordination and consistency in decision-making.

These issues can be approached in a different way and taken further. As dumping involves differential pricing, it concerns competition policy as is made explicit by the notion that anti-dumping actions raise domestic price levels and may facilitate collusion between domestic and foreign producers. Consequently, for some, it might be argued that anti-dumping legislation ought to be dealt with under domestic competition policy alone, especially as domestic producers can abuse anti-dumping actions for anti-competitive purposes (Ostry, 1990, p. 20).

A more sophisticated position is adopted by Hoekman and Mavroidis (1996). For they recognise that domestic competition policy does not have jurisdiction over the antitrust legislation of other countries. They emphasise that equal contestability in both markets is essential for the subsumption of anti-dumping to antitrust policy. This is rarely met in practice and, in addition, antitrust legislation tends to be more longstanding, sophisticated and precise than anti-dumping which is, consequently, more open to discretionary use of variable interpretation of public interest. In the context of regional integration, in which anti-dumping becomes precluded by common prices across countries, it is transparent that competitive advantage between countries remains uneven in view of differences in antitrust legislation and practice. The same applies where anti-dumping is in place prior to integration so that its abolition is contingent upon harmonisation of antitrust policy.

By the same token, as recognised by Hoekman and Mavroidis (1996), any other factor that affects competitiveness would need to be harmonised across countries for anti-dumping to be justifiably eliminated, whether differences across the putative playing field derive from industrial policy more generally and/or from the exercise of different notions of public interest. Essentially, a similar conclusion is drawn by the contributions to Buiges et al. (eds) (1995), especially Gual (1995) and Bourgeois and Demaret (1995), which seek coordination between the separate areas of trade, industrial and competition policy within the EU.[6]

Such a conclusion is in part driven by a practical definition of the three areas of policy, as they are applied according to EC and national laws. From an analytical point of view, however, this is unnecessarily restrictive, since policy considerations are confined to those defined by specific laws or conventions. By contrast, industrial policy, for example, can be narrowly interpreted as various supportive measures sanctioned on the supply-side but, as argued in Fine (1997a), it is more appropriately understood as any concrete, and potentially shifting, set of policies that are designed to promote industrial development or adjustment. Since industry is potentially affected by finance, macroeconomic, training, research and development, regional as well as trade and competition policy, these have to be considered in conjunction with one another in the light of specific sectors. By the same token, in addressing anti-dumping policy or differential pricing between domestic and export markets, it is necessary

6 Interestingly, similar conclusions are to be found in other work around path dependence, anti-trust and its application to software and EU (and other) policymaking (Fine, 2024c). The general problem is simply illustrated around identifying competitiveness empirically given that each of extreme collusion and 'perfect' competition imply uniform pricing irrespective of how many producers there are.

not only for it to be coordinated with competition, industrial and other forms of trade policy. In addition, these must be incorporated within the widest context of policymaking, both in order that they can be successful on their own terms as well as in the broader goals of industrial development and in defining and meeting the public interest.

It is recognised by those, writing of the need to coordinate different areas of policy for anti-dumping policy to be eliminated, that the prospects for such coordination (of competition policy through contestability) across countries is not in prospect, Hoekman and Mavroidis (1996, p. 49):

> Current antidumping enforcement procedures make no attempt to determine whether markets are uncontestable ... governments [should] put greater effort into determining whether the conditions that are alleged to give rise to 'unfair trade' actually exist, before having recourse to antidumping. The proposal is an exercise in the second-best – clearly the abolition of antidumping altogether, or a return to a strict predation standard, would be preferable from an economic welfare point of view. Realism suggests that achieving this in the foreseeable future is unlikely.

Such an observation neither supports nor undermines the case for anti-dumping action in the absence of other policy coordination, but it does reinforce the case for integrating policies within a country so that the appropriate scope of considerations and interventions can be considered.

This leads to two final points. One concerns the use of policy which, in the case of anti-dumping, can depend exclusively on action taken by private interests, as is so for the EC, for example, which has not been able to investigate anti-competitive trade behaviour on its own (Bourgeois and Demaret, 1995, p. 112). This contrasts with competition policy and, by doing so, biases practice in favour of domestic producers who are already generally reckoned to be unduly favoured for reasons previously discussed. Second, as suggested by Bourgeois and Demaret (1995, p. 113), proceedings should be as open as possible given need for commercial confidentiality, and decisions justified, especially as much political discretion is deployed in determining damage to the public interest and remedying it in the case of anti-dumping duties. The same point is emphasised by Tharakan and Waelbroeck (1994, p. 189) and Vermulst (1997). It is imperative, however, that openness be welcomed both for seeing that justice is done by the letter of the law and also to open the definition and scope of public interest to public scrutiny and accountability.

6 The Structures and Dynamics of the World Steel Industry

Prior to the collapse of the post-war boom in the early 1970s, the world steel industry seemed to be marked by a number of permanent features, as revealed for example, in a series of books by Hogan (1983, 1991 and 1994). First, production has been based on large-scale integrated plants enjoying substantial economies of scale. Second, domestic markets have been protected and have formed the basis for subsidising competition in export markets. Third, because of high fixed costs and the sensitivity of steel demand to cyclical movements in the economy, pricing and profitability have been extremely vulnerable. Fourth, this has encouraged, historically for even longer, the formation of more or less formal cartels across the industry, both within countries and at an international level with greater or lesser state support. Fifth, competitive advantage within the industry has depended upon vertical integration and has involved differential access to raw materials at one end and to markets at the other end of the steel chain. Sixth, with secure demand for standardised products, especially automobiles, shipping and construction, markets have often been served directly by producers. Seventh, the post-war boom did witness the emergence of new producers, most notably Japan, which was a negligible producer of stainless steel in the 1950s but now leads the world. Eighth, not surprisingly, with a buoyant world economy, steel was a rapidly growing sector of the economy.

From the mid-1970s, this situation has changed dramatically, and the world steel industry has been marked by new structures and dynamics although some of these, as will be seen, remain tempered by, and draw upon, the conditions inherited from the past. First, over the 1980s, steel production has stagnated. As Hogan (1994) reports, world production in 1982 stood at 645 million tonnes compared to 714 million tonnes in 1992. This contrasts with the growth between 1966 and 1976 from 473 to 685 million tonnes. Second, this has entailed dramatic downsizing by many of the world's major steel producers, especially the EU and the USA. Third, governments have been heavily involved in restructuring steel industries in view both of the high levels of redundancies involved and the competitive advantage of the business interests that they represent. Fourth, despite the downsizing of the 'traditional' producers, the 1980s has been remarkable for the emergence of significant steel production from developing countries, especially China, South Korea and Brazil, which accounted for 102 million tonnes in 1980 but 214 million tonnes in 1992. Fifth, such capacity has been felt on export markets with developing countries accounting for a mere 9.5 million tonnes in 1980 compared to 27 million tonnes in 1991 (all figures from Hogan, 1994).

To a large extent, the shift in conditions reported in the previous paragraph are confined to those that reflect the changed patterns of supply and demand on the basis of continuing dependence upon large integrated steel production. However, over the two past decades, the world steel industry has been marked by the emergence to prominence of minimills. Before the 1970s, they scarcely existed at all. Following the second world war, the industry was dominated by integrated facilities, with technical change mainly confined to the shift from open hearth to basic oxygen blast furnaces, without this holding back the increasing overall scale of operations. Minimum efficient scale on integrated plants is as much as 3 mtpa, even double that if twin furnaces are constructed to allow for disruptions, especially the relining of the furnaces every seven to eight years. The decline of the old system is indicated by the fact that the only new integrated steel plant to be built in an industrialised country over the past twenty years has been in South Korea, with a capacity of 11 mtpa, although the Ogishima (Keihin) works in Japan, which is the newest integrated steel works in a major OECD country, has been scheduled for conversion to an office park (Crandall, 1996)! Between 15% and 20% of integrated facilities are expected to close over the next fifteen years, although production at the remaining units is liable to rise by more than 2%, *World Steel Dynamics*, July, 1997.

The emergence of the minimill has not only imparted new structures and dynamics to the industry, thereby undermining those prevailing previously, it has also stimulated new structures and dynamics around pre-existing facilities. In other words, it is not simply a clash of production systems and their attendant modus operandi, but also a complex and continuing interaction between the two. Consider the distinctive character of the minimill system, as addressed, for example, in Crandall (1996) and Sander (1996) and, especially for the United States, Smith (1995).

First, minimills depend upon scrap or directly reduced iron (DRI) ore and work with an electric furnace. As a result, they command lower fixed capital costs and minimum efficient scale. Nonetheless, by the 1990s, some of the largest minimills were operating at a capacity of 1 mtpa, or double that with twin furnaces. The capital cost per tonne of capacity for integrated steel producers is in the region of $700 compared to $150 for minimills. With the stagnation of the world steel industry since 1979, the production of the world's largest companies has been scaled back with closures and concentration of output on the more efficient facilities. Between 1981 and 1994, output from the ten largest companies declined from 156 to 129 million tonnes. In the meantime, minimills have become responsible for one-third of western steel production.

It is worth commenting on the relative merits of minimills and integrated facilities for, even if the former have a significant technological advantage, the pace at which and extent to which they are introduced depends on a host of moderating factors. First, as new investments and irrespective of their own intrinsic merits, minimills have been able to incorporate other technological improvements that could prove expensive or impossible in existing integrated plants. These include the continuous processing of the molten steel into products ready for rolling, computerisation and greater energy and environmental efficiency.

Second, although minimills depend upon scrap as a major raw material input, this does not put them at too much of a disadvantage relative to integrated plant. For, if scrap prices rise too high, then the minimills can use DRI ore instead, with its excess capacity available for high enough prices. The use of scrap has declined from 25% in the mid-1970s to a current level between 10% and 12%, ILO (1992). The pricing of DRI ore is itself mainly determined by the price of iron ore, any rise in the price of which would equally have an impact on integrated producers (who would also be affected, even if to a lesser extent, by the price of scrap which they can also process). Clearly, the price of electricity is also liable to be a factor in the relative advantage of minimills. But integrated plant also depends upon coking coal, whose prices are liable to move in line with those of electricity if there is any systematic connection between the two.

Third, labour relations are generally considered to be more advantageous in minimills. This does not necessarily result from the absence or even exclusion of trade unions from greenfield sites or new production facilities. Rather, jobs appear to be more rewarding in a less hierarchical occupational structure with decentralised management. Perhaps most important though is the immanent conflict and tensions that are induced in the integrated plants by their being continually under the threat of closure or downsizing.

Fourth, as far as marketing is concerned, minimills have been able to specialise in particular subsectors, operating at relatively high levels of capacity. In this, there is a contrast with the integrated producers who need to serve a range of product markets but, even so, still tend to be subject to excess capacity. Minimills have also been able to offer high quality products and customer service in terms of delivery times.

Fifth, the financial conditions under which minimills have operated have differed from those of integrated facilities. The latter have usually been attached to very large, well-established companies which, if not state-owned and quoted on the stock exchange, have been subject to the danger of takeover should industry or company performance be depressed. Consequently, financial policy can be induced to lean towards short-termism, favouring declaration of dividends at the expense of long-term investment. Minimills have often been new ventures, not quoted on the stock exchange, and specialising in steel alone as opposed to a portfolio of corporate activities.

The different characteristics of the minimill system have influenced how the world steel system functions, quite apart from displacement effects on integrated facilities. These in part derive from its own intrinsic competitive strategies to be more cost-effective in meeting specific markets; it is also a consequence of the competitive reaction of large-scale producers. It has, for example, been associated with a shift in the structure of marketing, with greater reliance on sales through merchants, both to accommodate the limited product range offered by each of a large number of minimill producers as well as the wider range and larger quantities offered by large-scale integrated producers. In 1968, stockholders accounted for 27.4% of steel sales; this progressively increased to 36.9% in 1978, 51.3% in 1988, and 58.1% in 1995 (Key Note, 1996).

To some extent, this has been a consequence of the previously remarked decline in the sale of homogeneous products to large-scale steel-using industries. Such developments have, however, been complemented by the increasing reliance of the steel industry on the sale of a wider variety of products rather than leaving its customers to process a standardised product. As Key Note (1996) observes, 70% of steel products currently sold have been developed over the past ten years. The development of new products has also been associated with the development of new technology both for minimills and integrated facilities. Minimills have been extending their range of products, with the creation of greater capacity for long as well as for flat products. On the other hand, technology for integrated mills has been addressing the need to cast finished products in a more cost-effective way to compete with the continuing casting of minimills.

One response to excess capacity amongst integrated producers has been the formation of international joint ventures. These have been particularly prominent in the United States, where all of the large-scale companies had entered into alliances with Japanese companies by 1990, other than Bethlehem Steel which had been exploring a joint venture with British Steel (ILO, 1992). The motive for the US companies has been to gain access to the financial leverage of their partners who were also able to offer skills in technology and marketing in return for access to the huge US domestic market. But such joint ventures are not confined to the United States. As Key Note (1996) observes, they have also been prominent in and from western Europe – between companies from Sweden and the UK, Italy and Germany, France and the United States, and Spain, Germany and Mexico, for example.

In the light of these considerations, it is hardly surprising that the advice to steel enterprises from *World Steel Dynamics*, July, 1997, comprises the following elements. No more blast furnaces should be built; alliances must be sought; cost, volume and product mix must all be actively addressed as must product quality and delivery, continuous processing, computerisation, breakthrough technologies, and energy and the environment. Decisions must be made quickly and with a global perspective.

These developments from within the industry itself have been overlaid with external changes that have been of special significance for steel. On the one hand, the increasing liberalisation of trade, most notably, through the Uruguay Round of GATT, has been particularly important to a steel industry that has traditionally taken its own domestic markets for granted. On the other hand, the collapse of centrally planned economies has given rise to a shock increase in capacity seeking sales on world markets.

Not surprisingly, in view of the conditions that have prevailed in world steel markets, anti-dumping activity has been especially prominent and reveals all of the features outlined previously. Glais (1995) provides an overview of developments in the EU, with 14% of anti-dumping proceedings initiated by the Commission between 1981 and 1991 concerning steel. Complaints seem to have been filed on the basis of imports undercutting the price of domestic producers rather than on the basis of comparison with price in the domestic market of country of origin, p. 236. Imports from non-market economies have attracted particular attention, and trade agreements have been negotiated with a large range of countries, with negotiations with the USA being particularly delicate in terms of market access in both directions.

Indeed, half of the anti-dumping cases taken against EU producers have been lost but cases continue to be brought before the US International Trade Commission. The American Iron and Steel Institute continues to campaign vigorously for as much protection as possible (AISI, 1997). Between 1980 and 1989, of the 451 anti-dumping cases filed, as many as 201 concerned the iron and steel industry, the next most prominent sector being chemicals with just 58 cases, followed by food and non-ferrous metals with 16 each (Boltuck and Litan, 1991, p. 3). Further, of 300 countervailing duty cases, 149 were accounted for by iron and steel.

There is good reason, then, to question any presumption that the steel industry has become more competitive through being subject to free trade. It is questionable whether this is the correct way to understand developments. For, with substantial excess capacity in an industry that has been dominated by large-scale producers with strong ties to domestic markets, there will always be a strong element of making of the market, not least because of the so-called natural protection that arises out of transport costs. As Key Note (1996) reports, prices in the United States are 15% to 20% lower than in the EU. Even within the EU's single market there are continuing disputes over subsidies, British Steel planning to take the EC to court in view of its allowing the Irish industry a subsidy of £39 million which it considers will lead it to an output increase of 66% rather than the 25% projected by the Irish.

The impact of liberalising trade is not liable to be absolutely effective because of the broad boundaries between trade policy, dumping and other forms of subsidy. Thus, Fors (1991) complains bitterly over the protection that Sweden has faced against its imports into the United States. Even though, Sweden has itself offered 'good international citizenship' in restructuring its industry along the lines of profitability through private ownership with limited subsidy, it has confronted "producers in the United States ... shopping around for ways to restrict imports of Swedish stainless steel products", p. 30. The threat of legally costly anti-dumping suits can be sufficient to discourage attempts at imports. Further, as Sander (1996, p. 120) reports, domestic steel industries are open to support from state or local community subsidies. In the case of the North Star-BHP project in Ohio, more than $20 million was offered in incentives, across nine different policy measures, equivalent to financial support of almost $70,000 per potential employee.

The issue of trade, then, is complex and not reducible to one of being closer or further away from free trade. This is because of imperfect competition, joint ventures, up- and down-stream linkages, the variety of policy measures involved, as well as the role of strategic decisions about product mix and how it dovetails with differential pricing on domestic and export markets, exactly some of the issues that have been raised in the previous discussion of anti-dumping. On the latter point, the industry is subject to two countervailing trends. On the one hand, the economies of scale in production attached to mass production by integrated facilities of basic steel has encouraged it to be sold cheaply on export markets. On the other hand, possibly taking advantage of the availability of cheap bulk steel, there is the opportunity to specialise in high value added products which also have a comparative advantage in transport costs. More generally, steel can be exported indirectly in the form of finished products as in motor cars or consumer durables, highlighting the inter-dependence between the steel and other down-stream activity.

Also important in the marketing of steel is the role of stockholders who serve as intermediaries between steel producers and users. They may also engage in a certain amount of limited processing. They have the advantage of monitoring quality and ensuring supplies by drawing upon a variety of sources. They have the disadvantage of adding an extra stage in the chain of supply to final product, and it is a moot point whether they reduce the overall stock of steel held. In the context of an oligopolistic industry, supplying a product range to both domestic and export markets, with varying degrees of protection, there is the possibility that stockholders will perform the function of remedying the deficiencies of domestic supply at high cost rather than the associated problems being addressed directly.

Subject, then, to many complications, the situation of the steel industry is one of an older well-established large-scale technology being challenged and displaced by one based on smaller scale production but also interacting with it. In this respect, it is worth examining why some countries have adopted minimills faster than others. At one extreme is the United States which has seen its traditional industry decline and a rapid rise of minimills. Apart from the pressures arising out of cost advantages, an explanation is to be found in the decline of the powerful steel industry lobby, combining the interests both of large-scale corporations and trade unions. As Moore (1994) observes, the steel workforce declined in the US between 1974 and 1992 from 512,000 to 140,000. As already noted, the domestic market had been targeted by foreign firms in the form of imports and joint ventures. The industry's political base within Congress from which to campaign for continuing protection was also undermined by the eventual formation from 1989 onwards by a consortium of previously fragmented steel-users. Other writers, such as Lenway et al. (1996) and Schuler (1996), have also emphasised how the political representations of traditional steel interests have been eroded in the USA.

In contrast to the United States, many of the other major western steel producers have adopted a policy of supporting their large-scale integrated plants through a variety of measures, although these have all involved downsizing. To some extent, an exception is provided by the UK, where the privatisation of British Steel was used to support the continuing finished steel products sectors at the expense of sustaining capacity in bulk steel (Fine and Poletti, 1992). More generally, state policy has involved the goals of stabilising industrial relations whilst reducing employment and rationalising production facilities, promoting joint ventures, upgrading technology at integrated plants (for product quality and mix and for continuous casting), guarding domestic and promoting export markets (Glais, 1995).

The extent, nature and impact of state intervention across different countries has varied in response to economic and political conditions. For example, as Kipping (1995) has found for the French industry, state intervention was necessary to overcome the conflicts of interest between steel producers and users. Less extensive intervention has been required in Germany because of greater corporate links between steel producers and users, emphasising the importance of vertical integration to the formation and desirability of state economic intervention.

This section has served to demonstrate how complex is the functioning of the world steel industry and how rapidly it can be subject to change. Demand is highly cyclical but distributed variously across a wide range of products and markets. Supply is in a state of transition between a competitively advantageous and dynamic technology (minimills) and a more traditional technology (integrated facilities) that incorporates high levels of sunk costs but which is itself open to some adaptation. Supply is also subject to uncertainty around new sources from the economies in transition and depends upon access to a range of raw materials and other inputs as well as a shifting system of distribution. Finally, the industry is highly politicised and has a long and continuing tradition of state intervention and cartelisation both at national and international levels (Dale, 1980, p. 163/4).

7 South African Steel in Transition

The South African steel industry is in a state of transition for two separate reasons. First, it is subject to the conditions operating at a world level which have been described in the previous section. Second, the industry has been built up under apartheid and strongly reflects the pre-democracy economic and political conditions under which it functioned. This included labour market practices which have scarcely been remedied given the backlog of low skills and wages experienced by the black workforce. ISCOR, the key steel corporation within South Africa, has only just appointed the first black member of its management team, and its Annual Report does not include figures on the composition, grading and remuneration of its workforce in order to demonstrate how it is adjusting to economic and social reconstruction.

The inheritance of apartheid, however, goes far beyond the relative conditions experienced by different sections of the workforce. The development of the steel industry under the tutelage of the apartheid government has been highly dependent upon state support, and inevitably dependent upon motives other than economic development alone (Clark, 1994). It has been associated with the key role played by state-ownership, with steel provision in part designed to ensure supplies to domestic industry and to promote industrialisation. Consequently, the industry has been marked by constraints on its international operations. On the one hand, it has developed an extremely wide product range. On the other hand, also partly as a consequence of apartheid and the impact of (the fear of) sanctions, there have been limitations on exporting products, importing technology and forming joint ventures.

The purpose here is not to provide a complete nor a detailed overview of the South African industry. This can be found in Competition Board (1995) for example, and a working knowledge of the sector will be taken for granted. Rather, the intention is to point to some salient features of the industry. For, despite the heritage of apartheid, the South African steel industry enjoys considerable advantages. First, it has an enviable access to raw materials. With the exception of coking coal and nickel, it has abundant supplies of most of the material inputs required for steel production. Indeed, it is a major exporter of iron ore and is the world's largest producer of chrome. In addition, South Africa enjoys provision of the cheapest electricity in the world, not least because of its abundant supplies of coal.

Second, the South African steel industry enjoys considerable technical expertise or the capacity to draw upon it through overseas contracting. I give a few examples, as reported in various issues of *Steel Times International*. ISCOR's Pretoria works have been converted to stainless steel production through the introduction of the world's first Corex plant. The Saldhana Steel project, a joint venture between ISCOR and IDC, will represent a state-of-the-art facility for manufacturing stainless steel. Columbus, a joint venture between Samancor, the IDC and Highveld Steel, is set to be the largest, single-site stainless steel manufacturing plant in the world. Nor is technical expertise restricted to major projects alone. Scaw Metals has installed a third rotary kiln, ISCOR has developed capacity for tin can manufacture, and ISCOR is engaged in contracting out technical advice to a number of projects being undertaken outside South Africa.

A third advantage, as revealed in the previous paragraph, is that the South African industry has a corporate structure that is capable of formulating, financing, implementing and monitoring large-scale projects. Apart from the role played by ISCOR, the IDC has long been and continues to be a major source of finance for mega-projects, especially those around minerals and processing. In addition, South Africa has a highly concentrated corporate structure so that large-scale investments are also feasible on the basis of initiatives taken by its own privately-owned companies, as illustrated by Highveld and Columbus. Further, even if adopted from the previous apartheid regime, state institutions do exist for undertaking sectoral industrial policy, through the DTI as well as through the nominally independent but state-owned IDC.

The combination of these advantages, the inherited structure of the sector, and broader global developments seem to have given rise to a strategy for the industry which focuses on three inter-related components. First, there is a shift towards the production of stainless steel, especially for export. This is reflected, for example, in the conversion of the Pretoria Works and the investments in Columbus and Saldhana Bay. It is also part of a more general strategy to export products with greater value-added. Second, especially through ISCOR, there is engagement in the formation of international joint ventures and associations. Third, there is rationalisation of product lines on the domestic market. Although prices are higher than for exports, the aim is to focus on fewer products to accrue economies of scale and to rely upon imports for those products not domestically sourced in sufficient volume.

ISCOR, in particular, has undergone considerable reorganisation since Hans Smith was appointed as Managing Director in September 1993. Previously, the company had been privatised in November 1989 but had been cushioned by tariffs and other subsidies. Smith has placed individual operations on a commercial footing. As he puts it in the *Steel Times International* of November, 1995, p. 39:

> We became lean and mean by replacing an engineering view of the running the business with a genuine financial and commercial function. We have appointed some thirty chartered accountants in this company over the past eighteen months.

In addition, by forming MacSteel International in a joint venture with MacSteel Holdings, ISCOR has committed itself to consolidating the indirect sale of its output on both domestic and export markets through a single merchant.

These developments raise four issues as far as public policy is concerned. First, whilst it has been emphasised above that the industry has considerable capacity to formulate and implement strategy, it does not necessarily follow that it does so efficiently. The conversion of the Pretoria works to stainless steel has proved in the short term and with hindsight to have been mistaken, with its reverting to production of pig iron. The decision to convert was a calculated risk based on the prospects of future prices for stainless steel which, in the event, proved disappointing.

Second, whilst it must not be presumed that private corporations will always formulate and implement strategies efficiently, even where they do so, a distinction must be drawn between their own private interests and those of others affected or potentially affected by their decisions. Strategies for global profitmaking do not necessarily coincide with the policy goals of government. Such is obviously the case in the formation of cartels and restrictive pricing.

Third, even where public and private interests coincide, they are not necessarily efficiently achieved because of lack of coordination, a theme increasingly emphasised in recent developments in economic theory. This is liable to be of importance where vertical integration is involved, for example – lack of readily available and cheap steel inputs precludes the development of a corresponding downstream manufacturing facility which, in turn, leads to a lack of demand for, and supply of, the inputs concerned.

Fourth, where inefficient management, conflicts of interest and lack of coordination persist, remedial action depends upon the capability and power of government to recognise and to rectify them, unless one is wedded to an unshakeable faith in the market. In other words, the issue is one of government promoting corporate efficiency, forming a view of public interest, and coordinating industrial and other policy. Although these issues are distinct in principle, they are not readily disentangled in practice and informed judgement has to be made over all of them at once, the task to which I now turn.

8 Private and Public Interests in the South African Steel Industry

Although the concern that inspired this investigation does not concern dumping of steel on the South African domestic market, in fact quite the reverse, it is worth reviewing the measures that are in place to deal with dumping. Fortunately, this has recently been reviewed by Blumberg (1996). Prior to 1992, there was anti-dumping legislation in place, but it had never been used since other protectionist measures rendered it unnecessary. Indeed, protection of South African industry had been granted more or less upon request, as reviewed in Fine and Rustomjee (1996, Chapter 8) – so much so that the Minister of Trade and Industry felt able to pronounce new GATT-friendly measures in terms of, "protection on demand is now dead", p. 226. Consequently, Blumberg points to the limited experience of case law, the variable times required to complete investigations, the increasing involvement of lawyers, the mixed responsibility across the Ministries of Finance and Trade and Industry, the ill-defined content of normal value, injury, causation and compensating tariff, and, not least, that the Board on Trade and Tariffs, which has investigative responsibility, is on a learning curve.

It is enabled to go on foreign visits and to undertake its task through questionnaires to relevant enterprises. Moreover, in principles laid out in a Guide rather than in legislation, material injury can include "actual and potential declines in sales, profit, market share, productivity, return on investments or utilization of capacity, prices, margin of dumping, cash flow, inventories, employment, growth, and the ability to raise capital investments", p. 222. Causation can take account of volume of imports, existing tariffs and rebates, the impact of imports and their prices on domestic markets, political influences, the state of the economy, labour matters, boycotts, product quality and range, delivery periods, the technology employed, the utilization of production factors, and the policies of the industry concerning production, marketing and finance, p. 225.

To a large extent, as suggested by Blumberg, these considerations ape those laid down by the GATT Code on anti-dumping. Indeed, she reports that the legislation and procedures involved are to be overhauled, and she has been appointed by the Minister of Trade and Industry to lead the task! However, as has already been suggested in the more general discussion of anti-dumping, whilst this may bring South Africa up to best practice within this area, best is not good enough or, more exactly, appropriate. For, even where anti-dumping is not subject to abuse as a form of protection by other means, its provision is inadequate as policy unless coordinated with other aspects of industrial policy such as competition policy.

For the current investigation, other than in raising relevant causal factors, such considerations may appear to be irrelevant, since current complaints centre on the opposite of the charge of dumping and the need for anti-dumping action. Prices on domestic markets are too high relative to export prices. This might be due, if unlikely, to the fear of anti-dumping cases being filed or to monopolisation on the domestic market. If so, appropriate investigation falls under the auspices of the Competition Board, within the Department of Trade and Industry, which is empowered to investigate price-fixing and other restraints on trade.

The Competition Board, in part through its previous incarnation within the Board of Trade and Industry, is much more longstanding and experienced in practice than the Board on Trade and Tariffs in its dealing with dumping, as is evidenced by its own review of competition policy in 1985 (Competition Board, 1985). This Report, along with others such as Competition Board (1989 and 1991) dealing with specific industries, makes clear that the Board is able to distinguish between public and private interests across a variety of competitive practices, and it has reviewed the experience and criteria of a range of other countries. It has also incorporated the notion of national, as distinct from private or public, interest, although this almost certainly signifies the economic and political imperatives of apartheid.

This leads to two conclusions despite the breadth of experience of the Competition Board. First, whatever its judgements and practices in the past, these will not have incorporated the substance of public and national interest as required by the needs and goals of an economy and society in reconstruction. Second, even if this were so, there is no guarantee that the powers of the Competition Board would be adequate to deal with the broader policy issues raised by its terms of reference which are concerned with pricing and restraint of trade alone.

This is especially so for the steel industry which has been investigated by the Competition Board on a number of occasions. For example, the Board of Trade and Industry (1974) reported on scrap collection and ruled against the monopsony that disadvantaged collectors by fixing prices below international levels, thereby discouraging supply and leading to its leaking abroad. There can, however, be economies of scale in the processing of scrap and benefits from the greater certainty of fixed prices. In current conditions, policy towards scrap is complicated by its being used in different proportions in different production processes and, hence, for example, in leading to greater or lesser advantage to different products and, hence, domestic as opposed to export markets. Further, scrap is a national resource whose international price may not reflect its social value in terms of the domestic capacity to generate employment or even greater foreign exchange if processed prior to export. As will be seen, such issues around scrap have continued to be contested.

More recently, the Competition Board (1995) delivered a report on restrictive practices in the distribution of metal products and scrap. It came to the following conclusions, p. 31/2:

> (T)he Board found that the following practices constituted restrictive practices … which could not be justified in the public interest:
> (a) price leadership in the oligopolistic steel (stainless and other) merchanting market;
> (b) a refusal to supply by persons in an oligopolistic market;
> (c) a refusal by Columbus to deal with scrap merchants other than Tillmor; and
> (d) the collusive purchasing of non-ferrous scrap.

The associated practices were, then, naming specific companies, declared unlawful by the Minister on March 10th, 1995, although one declaration was withdrawn on August 11th, 1995, following corresponding assurances from Columbus.

Significantly, these decisions were reached on a Notice of Investigation by the Competition Board given as long ago as February 28th, 1992. Essentially, as far as iron and steel are concerned, the complaints concern the squeezing out of small users or dealers and/or their disadvantage in pricing as a result of the collusive or cartel-like behaviour of the companies named. Paradoxically, ISCOR does not appear as subject to complaint since it is only indirectly involved through the dealers concerned. This reflects the structure of the industry in which ISCOR might only sell in large quantities to customers directly or to merchants who can charge at high prices to small-scale consumers – and, more recently, ISCOR has opened a large discount for bulk for some of its products.

However, no sooner had the judgement referenced above been delivered – it bears repeating after three years of deliberations – than it was superseded altogether by the decision of ISCOR to pursue a joint venture with MacSteel Holdings to form MacSteel International which would have total responsibility for all of ISCOR's export trade and for a large share of its indirect sales on the domestic market. Not surprisingly, the proposal met with considerable opposition from other steel merchants. On June 14th, 1996, the Minister allowed the venture to go ahead for a two-year period on condition that the Competition Board monitor its practices through provision to it of the necessary information, and that the venture did not engage in anti-competitive behaviour. In other words, the judgements require the Competition Board to be continuously vigilant over the pricing policies of ISCOR and MacSteel International.

During the course of the earlier investigation, it was alleged that some potential witnesses were unwilling to testify for fear of being victimised by the colluding parties. The proposed formation of MacSteel International also gave rise to a series of allegations that have yet to be made public about malpractice or inefficiencies that will arise as a result of the venture or which characterise the functioning of the steel industry more generally. These include the following:

(a) ISCOR threatening not to supply from domestic production (for exports) if merchants engaged in supplying imports for the domestic markets.

(b) ISCOR losing export business and opportunities by excluding other merchants from handling its business.

(c) ISCOR paying unduly high commissions on its merchanting.

(d) ISCOR exposing the South African steel industry to the risks attached to MacSteel's more general trading activity.

(e) The creation of conflict of interest between MacSteel serving ISCOR and serving other steel producers, with the potential loss of ISCOR's export markets to other producers.

(f) The knock-on effects of high commissions and loss of markets can be to render domestic steel capacity unprofitable and subject to closure.
(g) The joint venture will allow ISCOR to transfer profits abroad through transfer pricing in the form of high discounts and reduce its tax obligations and the restrictions imposed by controls on export of capital.
(h) More generally, the venture represents a cartelisation of the steel industry in domestic and export markets, with the capacity to discipline, exploit or eliminate others engaged in the steel business.

Against this background, it is worth assessing ISCOR's own presentation of its pricing strategy, as delivered to the South African Department of Trade and Industry (Robertson, 1997). It begins by drawing a sharp distinction between domestic and export markets. The first is taken as prior ("why do South African primary steel manufacturers produce more than the local market requires?", p. 1) and the second as the outlet for a surplus ("can this excess primary steel be sold profitably into other markets?", p. 1). Such a situation, of capacity surplus to domestic requirements, is explained in terms of historically incorrect anticipation of domestic needs and excessive investment in the past. On this basis, it is argued that exports can make a contribution to profits even if sold at a price lower than in domestic markets.

It must be observed, first of all, that the undue privileging of the domestic market as the target for capacity is entirely arbitrary. Indeed, it is perverse in so far as its perceived priority leads to a justification for the charging of higher prices on domestic markets. With exports commanding more than a third of supply, it makes little sense to see them as a release of excess capacity, and it is irrelevant how capacity levels may have arisen in the past. More important, there are differences in the demand for steel in domestic and export markets, and differences in costs of delivery, but these do not justify labelling the export markets as the ones which should be deemed as benefiting from surplus capacity. It would be equally possible for steel to be sold at between variable and average cost in the domestic market and still contribute to profits. In other words, the pricing strategy and structure does not simply arise out of the need to sell excess capacity on export markets. It is a matter of how much is sold, by whom, to whom, at what prices and with what subsidies or other policies (should government choose to intervene).

Without the lower prices on export markets, it is argued that there will be closures of capacity with detriment through lost investment, jobs and skills, retrenchment costs, supply problems to steel-users, loss of foreign exchange, increased share of fixed costs on continuing production, and multiplier effects on suppliers to the steel industry, p. 8. These are genuine considerations and lead to the suggestion that they have been taken into account by subsidising steel-users who export their products – through the Committee on Secondary Manufacture (COSM) administered by the South African Iron and Steel Institute (SAISI). Over the past four and a half years, this amounts to assistance of R327,671 million which needs to be set against a total of foreign currency earned through export of secondary manufactured steel products of R12, 929 billion, Annexure 3. The subsidy of approximately 2.5% compares with claims of 60% higher prices being paid domestically for some products. In addition, ISCOR has also offered rebates to exporters adding value to steel-based products. This has amounted to a further R1 billion over the past five years, Annexure 4. In short, something around a 10% discount has, on average, been offered in 'assistance' to steel-using exporters over the past five years.

It is worth quoting the presentation's final paragraph in full, p. 13, para 5.3 (sentence numbers added):

> 1. There is no such thing as a two-tier or dual pricing policy for steel in South Africa. 2. Iscor's local price of steel is based on the cost of production, a responsible profit margin policy and local market conditions. 3. This is no different from any other overseas steel producer or listed public manufacturing company in South Africa, with a responsibility to its shareholders. 4. Excess steel, produced because of current (and future) surplus capacity, will be sold at the best price obtainable in other markets from time to time. 5. If this price proves not to be viable, plant will be shut down, workers retrenched, fixed costs reduced and export sales stopped. 6. Then only one steel price in South Africa will exist – that which the market can stand in the face of international competition and substitute products. 7. However, if the local economy grows which results in a better local market for steel (it has been shown over the last 20 years that GDP growth and local steel sales growth match each other closely), then exports of steel by South African producers will reduce accordingly and the high costs of exporting be eliminated. 8. In time, these cost reductions can be passed on to the consumer by way of lower price increases.

The first sentence is false by own admission and is contradicted by the fourth sentence. The second sentence, together with the third, provides four different criteria for pricing steel locally – cost of production, profit margin, local market conditions, and responsibility to shareholders. These are not mutually compatible in all or even most circumstances. Nor does it take account of the export assistance offered. The third sentence is also false in so far as steel and other manufacturing companies can be and have been subject to government regulation and policy. The fifth and sixth sentence are erroneous in their understanding of the steel market. For whatever happens to South African steel capacity, the domestic market will inevitably be subject to imperfect competition and price discrimination between markets. The seventh and eighth sentences presume that general demand must grow in order for fixed costs to be spread and for prices to be lowered. However, were prices to the domestic market to be lowered, this might increase demand and downstream economic activity even if at the expense of ISCOR profitability. Further, the explicit posing of the problem in terms of only meeting exports with excess capacity is in complete contradiction with investments currently under way to serve export markets.

Although the ISCOR presentation is confused, inconsistent and self-serving, it usefully, if often inadvertently, raises a number of crucial issues. First, and foremost, what are to be the objectives of pricing policy? However well-defined they might be for ISCOR itself, there is clearly the potential for divergence between its own private interests and those of others. This is true of the public interest as represented, for example, by employment provision and the earning of foreign exchange. It also holds for the difference of interest between ISCOR and domestic steel-users who clearly prefer lower prices.

Further, second, even where there is no conflict of interest, there can be problems of coordinating and even enforcing those interests in practice. This is apparent in the case of the symbiotic relation between steel supply and use, where the scale of market demand depends upon price, and price depends upon costs in the context of scale economies. It cannot be presumed that ISCOR pricing and supply strategies are the ones that are most beneficial to the economy as a whole even if they are most beneficial to ISCOR itself.

Third, to some extent, this is recognised by ISCOR in principle in terms of its wider responsibilities for employment, etc, and it is also recognised in practice through the export assistance offered to steel-users. However, is such assistance offered at the appropriate level and is it appropriately distributed across the different steel-using sectors? As already implied, there can be no presumption that ISCOR is appropriately suited to make such decisions by virtue of its own private interests and its ability to coordinate such decision-making with wider economic considerations. Nor is there any reason why assistance should only be offered to exporters of steel-using products.

In this context, it is worth observing that the use of such export assistance is, in principle, consistent with private profit-making on the part of ISCOR. Indeed, it can be understood as part and parcel of the dual price strategy used in the direct export of steel. Further, it has the advantage of exporting steel indirectly through the products in which it is incorporated. On the one hand, this may reflect ISCOR's price discrimination in both domestic and export markets for steel as an input for those products which are traded more readily or with more commercial viability (for what ISCOR does, so can other producers on the world market, so that competition becomes fiercer and prices have to be lower). On the other hand, exporting steel indirectly in made-up products has the potential advantage of avoiding anti-dumping actions. However, as demonstrated previously, given the complexity of anti-dumping legislation and practice, it is far from clear that ISCOR is either best placed or most suited to making such policy, even if implicitly. What is certain is that the pricing strategy revealed by the ISCOR document would be interpreted by the United States, for example, as an explicit dumping policy, open to counter-measures. In addition, to avoid such action requires targeting of subsidies to steel-using exports that are not readily traceable to specific products. This, however, places the matter even further beyond the strategic boundaries occupied by ISCOR itself.

Fourth, the ISCOR presentation raises issues of adjustment within the steel industry but only from a very partial perspective. Essentially, it is seen as adjusting to excess capacity, although some reference is made to modernising plant, increasing productivity, reducing costs and rationalising plant and product range. Once again, the emphasis is on the role of domestic supply and demand, with exports easing adjustment. But it is the international orientation of ISCOR that is at least as important as domestic restructuring, as is apparent in the new investments that are being made to expand capacity. These do not figure in the ISCOR presentation.

In addition, careful consideration must be given to the prospective role to be played by MacSteel International which, paradoxically, given the focus on pricing, is also notable for its absence from the ISCOR presentation. It is as if it is implicitly assumed to be a neutral conduit for the transmission of pricing policy. But the joint venture with ISCOR implies that domestic production of steel, whether for domestic or export markets, will be set strategically against the international trading activities undertaken by MacSteel International. In principle, it is possible to speculate that the arrangement could be entirely to the advantage of the South African economy. Domestic production of product range can be rationalised and, otherwise, steel purchased and sold on international markets at the best available prices and terms. However, in practice, as already considered, ISCOR's monopolistic position as domestic producer is complemented by that of MacSteel International as trader. To maximise profitability, the two companies would be expected to discriminate between both sources of supply and demand in order to exploit market power.

There is no reason why such a strategy would coincide with the most advantageous development of either the domestic steel or domestic steel-using industries. On the one hand, there could be a strategy of cherry-picking – merely engaging in, or skewing activity to, the most profitable markets whether as direct producer or trader – on the basis of monopolistic position rather than productive efficiency and broader economic potential. Thus, domestic production might be sacrificed in order to allow for trading profits by MacSteel International on imports. On the other hand, MacSteel International would not necessarily facilitate access of domestic steel-users to the cheapest available steel on world markets in order to boost profitability on domestic supply. In short, the current restructuring of the South African steel industry will inevitably reflect and consolidate its monopolistic structure in ways that do not best represent the development either of the industry itself or the other industries to which it is attached.

9 Conclusions and Policy Recommendations

As already observed, it is not the intention of this Report to investigate these issues in detail and to adjudicate on the veracity of charges of price discrimination and its quantitative significance. What such charges do indicate is a wide range of potential deficiencies in the functioning of the South African steel industry for which remedial action goes far beyond the limited scope for intervention falling under the auspices of the Competition Board and BTT.

Such conclusions are confirmed by the Cluster Studies (IDC, 1997a–d), for the steel and steel-using industries conducted on behalf of the IDC. Interestingly, in view of its 'diamond' approach, such studies focus in part on vertical integration. It is found, for example, that downstream integration in the use of steel is inadequate as reflected in poor quality and regularity of supply and a need to rationalise product range. Nor do domestic appear to follow international prices in response to movements in the value of the rand.

Whilst the Cluster Studies point to the need for such deficiencies to be remedied and for the industries concerned to move to best international practice, they do not explain why the failures have arisen and how they might be overcome. Other research has also addressed these issues and points to the longstanding lack of vertical integration in much of South African industry both through the failure of private capital and industrial policy (Fine and Rustomjee, 1996; and Fine, 1997a and d). The reasons for this have shifted over time but currently reflect the conglomerate character of South African corporations, their uneasy collaboration with one another from time to time on a piecemeal basis, the reluctance of foreign investors to engage in joint ventures or stand-alone investments where they are constrained in vertically integrated activity (whether in production or access to local markets for sales or purchases) by domestic conglomerates, and the strategic interest of South African corporations in internationalising their operations. In addition, Fine (1997a) surveys the goals that can inform industrial policy, the measures that might be used to address them, and some of the economic, political and administrative constraints on the pursuit of the public interest, or economic and social reconstruction, through industrial policy.

In the case of the steel industry, the weight of evidence considered in this Report suggests that the existing institutions, even if working perfectly in areas of policymaking that are inevitably marked by a lack of precision and discretion, are sorely inadequate to the tasks involved. They do not have sufficient powers, they cannot function sufficiently quickly, and nor are they open to appropriate coordination. As a result, it is recommended that a permanent steel authority, the South African Steel Authority (SASA) be established which would take over the responsibilities of the Competition Board, the BTT and other relevant statutory bodies. It should also command wider powers to regulate the industry and to make policy recommendations. However, no further detailed recommendations are made about the composition and functioning of SASA, although there are implications that can be drawn from this Report if the recommendation is accepted.

The case for SASA can be made in two different but closely related ways. First, by analogy with the case made against anti-dumping legislation, industrial policy in South Africa for the steel industry is currently being made by ISCOR. As a result, industrial policy has been privatised and is governed by the strategies adopted by ISCOR. Its private interests do not, cannot and are not designed to coincide with those of the public interest. That public interest is itself poorly represented both historically and currently in the actual or potential jobs and products that derive from downstream steel-using activity.

Second, ISCOR is a utility that was privatised under the previous apartheid regime without the introduction of special regulations. This does not mean that ISCOR's performance has subsequently been purely market-driven, at least until the formation of the new government. For relations between ISCOR and government have remained highly politicised, as reflected in economic policies towards the corporation, including continuing measures of protection and provision of state finance through joint ventures with the IDC. In the context of the politics of steel, it may appear to be strange to describe ISCOR as a utility since this term is usually reserved for those enterprises providing consumer goods rather than intermediate inputs. However, even this is not universally the case, since electricity generation, for example, is generally recognised to require regulation although it does not serve consumers directly as this is the province of the grid or distribution companies. In any case, electricity and other such utilities serve both domestic and industrial consumers and regulation is generally required for the latter as well as for the former.

In short, without quibbling over semantics, ISCOR and the steel industry more generally are best understood as a utility. ISCOR itself directly employs over 40,000 workers, has a turnover of R12 billion and capital assets of R12 billion. It has direct or indirect command over important national assets such as coal and iron reserves and scrap. Its forward and backward linkages within the economy and its impact on macroeconomic performance are highly significant. In this light, the proposal for SASA is far from outlandish. As an individual company, ISCOR more than matches the contribution made by total industry in many developing countries. No second thought would be given to providing for a department of industry in such countries even though the range and scale of production and economic impact may be far less than for ISCOR, or the South African steel industry as a whole, in absolute terms. On the other hand, it is common for steel authorities to be formed, as in the longstanding European ECSC, even if within particular ministries. Further, it is recognised by the OECD, for example, that individual countries need to be represented in international negotiations in order to regulate the industry at a world level.

It is anticipated that there will be objections to this proposal on a number of grounds. One is that the formulation and exercise of the public interest by SASA will be against certain private interests. This, however, is precisely the rationale for the formation of SASA. On the other hand, it might be argued that SASA will create a new layer of bureaucracy, an ineffective and inefficient increase in state intervention, and command scarce public resources and skills that might be better engaged in other activities. It is, however, a central tenet of this Report that the current provisions for regulating the industry are ineffective and unnecessarily duplicate uncoordinated policymaking resources across various governmental institutions. Indeed, the industry should welcome this proposal for the scope that it provides for the effectiveness and streamlining of decision-making that it promises to yield.

Finally, it must be emphasised that the recommendation for the formation of SASA is steel-specific.[7] It is not a general argument for similar authorities for each and every sector of the economy. In other industries, characterised

7 Note that Mazzucato and Gasperin (2023) recommend a holding company across South African of state-owned enterprises in the reasonable goal of (horizontal) coordination between them. But, as with the vertical coordinating role of the SASA proposed here, the subsequent decisive issue would be the political powers and pressures to deliver (and why they are not already in place with or without a dedicated institution for that purpose).

by different structures and dynamics, existing regulatory provisions and institutions may well be adequate or only be open to marginal improvement. Whether industries should be regulated by a single authority covering the range of issues, or by separate authorities with generic responsibilities can only be determined on a case-by-case basis. The judgement of this Report is that the evidence for a single authority is overwhelming in the case of South African steel.

In this respect, the proposal is both consistent with and a refinement of the recent DTI (1997) policy guidelines for competition policy. It is highly critical of past policy and institutions, it widens the compass of public interest to included developmental goals, in part to remedy the inequities of the past, it acknowledges the need to set competition policy within the broader framework of industrial and trade policies, it addresses the problems of both vertical and horizontal integration, it seeks structural remedies where necessary, and it warns against the drawbacks of weak powers and the duplication of procedures across different authorities. Whilst the proposed guidelines do address the issue of competition policy where there are strong links between public and private enterprise, there is no explicit consideration of privatised utilities. Nonetheless, it does advise in case of each public enterprise that, 'a thorough review of the situation is undertaken and the necessary legislative changes prepared', p. 25. It is clearly an anomaly that ISCOR was privatised under circumstances in which appropriate legislation and institutions for regulation and development were not even considered let alone established. This should now be remedied as a matter of urgency both in developing the steel industry to meet South Africa's new needs and in contributing to the development of competition policy more generally through this specific case.

It is one thing, however, to recommend the establishment of a steel authority in principle and another to put it in place with detailed recommendations on how it should operate. It would be fortunate if the model for such an institution could be picked off the shelf from experience elsewhere, whether drawing upon steel authorities in other countries or on authorities for other sectors whether from South Africa or other countries. If this were possible, however, it is almost certain that the need for the authority would not have arisen in the first place. The specific needs of South African steel need to be addressed, and it is important to understand why an ideal model does not exist, although lessons can be learned from the experience of other countries.

The case for the steel authority rests on the need to coordinate policy across a variety of issues, not least pricing and vertical integration. The overall performance of the sector, however, also depends upon levels, location and composition of investment, availability of finance, technological performance, R&D,

skills of the workforce and management, etc, and the institutions devoted to them. Abe and Fitzgerald (eds) (1995) cover the range of institutions involved in Japan's industrial success. If account is taken of just one of these, such as productivity performance, it is apparent that the determinants of outcomes are complex and various. The impact of a single institution devoted to productivity change depends upon what goes on around it. This is the conclusion from the literature on national systems of innovation, for which Fine (1993a) provides an overview, an approach that has been influential in South African technology policy. As Shin (1996, p. 146) shows in his comparative institutional study of catch-up and technology transfer in Germany, Japan and South Korea:

> The efficiency of institutions cannot be assessed separately from contexts ... It can be assessed only by analysing concrete contexts in which these institutions function.

More generally, when addressing industrial policy, it has been recognised that the character of the institutions formulating and implementing policy depends crucially upon the strategy and ethos with which they are imbued, as well as their flexibility, as is demonstrated by the study of Pierre and Park (1997) for Japan's MITI. Similar conclusions are drawn for Norwegian industrial policy in the context of financial provision by Knutsen (1997, p. 126):

> The government gradually built up a network of agencies, organisations and ad hoc committees within the framework of an indicative system of planning, which utilised the financial system to reach major targets in industrial policy ... the specific configuration of national systems for industrial finance contribute to the differing capacities of governments to intervene in the industrial economy.

According to Chang (1997), price regulation is more advanced in the United States than elsewhere because of the relative absence of public sector enterprises. In addition, the functioning of regulation depends upon whether competition is seen as market-based or dynamic and developmental, on the extent of distributional considerations, on the role of the state in creating and not just in regulating markets, and on the politics of regulation. From the experience of India, Majumdar (1996) suggests that the negative impact of regulatory institutions is closely associated with the high levels of x-inefficiency or excess capacity generated. Further, much of the literature points to the need for correspondence between institutions and levels of development. Those institutions that are appropriate at one stage of development may become inappropriate at a later state.

This has been sharply revealed over the last two decades with the greater emphasis on market-led policy, although the policy pendulum is now swinging back to greater intervention. Stern et al. (1995) question not only whether the institutions, that engineered the heavy and chemical industry drive in South Korea, were necessary but whether they proved capable of sustaining successful policy. Kap-Young (1997) suggests not in the light of the collapse of Hanbo Steel, with 5 trillion won of debts, arguing for transparency if not withdrawal of government involvement. Cho (1996) finds the need for new institutions in the light of the privatisation of the South Korean power industry. Similar conclusions are drawn for Amin and Thomas (1996) for Denmark. Nembhard (1996) examines the shifting impact of capital controls, in conjunction with financial regulation and industrial policy, in the industrialisations of Brazil and South Korea.

In short, the institutions for making policy are best seen as conduits. They are the product of country- and sector-specific economic and political factors as well as an influence upon them and outcomes. This is most notable in the work of Douglass North, as deployed by Knutsen (1997) for example, who distinguishes between institutions and organisations, with the former "broadly defined as ranging from organisations and networks of organisations to professions and cultures", p. 107. Similarly, Andreff and Frensch (1997) examine institutions for policy making in the terms in which the developmental state has been understood, revolving around issues of governance, accountability, meritocracy, democracy, embeddedness, etc.

Against this background, the proposal to establish a steel authority in South Africa can be examined in a number of different, if overlapping, ways. First, it can be set in the context of strategic principles. What are the goals that should be set for such an authority? These must clearly conform to those of government, most notably in its economic policies. In view of the earlier analysis, priority must be given not only to the traditional goals of macroeconomic policy – such as balance of trade and employment generation – but also to the pricing of output, vertical integration, product composition, and the provision and coordination of finance for investment.

Second, the authority can be viewed in terms of its functions. As already argued, it should take over the functions that would otherwise accrue to more general statutory bodies – those concerned with competition and trade, for example. In addition, it will need to monitor and coordinate the horizontal and vertical restructuring and growth of the industry.

Third, and most controversial, there is the question of the powers of the authority. Will its role be purely indicative with no powers of enforcement, or will it have the statutory authority to impose targets and/or punitive measures? Short of public ownership, there is a potential conflict between the rights of private corporations and government policy. How should this be resolved? For a number of reasons, there is a strong case for heavy powers of intervention. These include the extent of restructuring required within the industry, the imperative to develop downstream activity, the conflict of interest between the private goals of ISCOR and those of domestic manufacturing development, and the need to establish an ethos of strategic policy making, especially in this sector where privatisation occurred under the apartheid regime without accompanying regulation. Further, it is to be anticipated that obstacles will be placed in the way of strategic intervention through the courts or otherwise unless backed up by the strongest legislation and powers.

The simplest way for these powers to be exercised is through SASA serving as a licensing authority for steel producers. The granting of a licence will depend upon the submission of operational plans. These can be coordinated by the authority and licences granted contingent upon performance (as in exports, employment, investment, etc). The authority will also be able to undertake or promote initiatives of its own.

In effect, this grants the authority almost limitless powers. These must be counterbalanced by a broader political authority. Accordingly, the renewal of licences should be subject to review by the Minister for Trade and Industry, although it is anticipated that this is liable to be a formality in the normal course of events. However, as previously argued, the functioning of the system will be highly dependent upon the strategies and ethos with which industrial policy is made and the responses of the private sector. The exercise of the authority's powers in practice cannot be pre-determined but, as indicated, it is wise in the first instance to err on the side of excessive powers in order to ensure that its functions can be carried out. If these powers are excessive, they need not be used and they may be denied by ministerial intervention.

Finally, there is the issue of the composition of, or participation in, the authority. Here, a delicate balance has to be struck between competence and independence. The authority should be governed by a commission that has a majority of those with no direct connection with the industry. It should gather together existing expertise and functions from government. It should include representatives from other government departments and be housed within the Department of Trade and Industry. There should also be representatives from the steel industry itself, from trade unions, corporate finance, and the IDC.

CHAPTER 8

Privatisation and the Restructuring of State Assets in South Africa: A Strategic View

Postscript as Personal Preamble[1]

In some respects, this Chapter can be viewed as an update on Chapter 4 although the message is much the same as far as privatisation is concerned, and for the same reasons – Don't do it, ownership matters, and public ownership can do more and better than private. What stands out in the case of South Africa, however, is how constrained has been privatisation (in the form of denationalisation) in the post-apartheid period especially given the presence of huge state-owned corporations such as Eskom and Transnet. Major privatisations have, though, included Telkom (2002), SASOL (2000), and parts of the steel industry (2002) that were not (or could not be) privatised under apartheid in 1989.

I wish I could say that the continued ownership of utilities such as Eskom has been marked by successful performance. This has been far from the case with excess supply of electricity at the beginning of the post-apartheid period giving way to well-established rolling programmes of scheduled blackouts at the time of writing. Transition from the most energy- and coal-intensive economy in the world to greener pastures has also stalled. It is more than tempting to wonder how much better things would have been if privatisation had been undertaken on a larger scale although various forms of commercialisation have been imposed on continuing state enterprises. Even so, as can be seen in the previous Chapter in case of steel, outcomes under privatisation are not necessarily successful.

What remains puzzling, though, and, arguable, a prior question, is why there was not more privatisation. An answer can be speculated in terms of push and pull factors. Changes in ownership always reflect a corresponding shift in whose interests are served and how. The major restructurings of the South African economy in the post-apartheid period have taken the form of globalisation, financialisation and incorporation of a black elite into

---

1 Thanks to John Sender for comments during drafting, and to participants in a COSATU Workshop on an earlier draft. Kate Bayliss played a major role in drafting Section 3. It eventually morphed into a contribution within Bayliss and Fine (eds) (2008).

ownership. Eskom and Transnet are, to a large degree, non-tradeable in their production, heavily indebted and far from readily subject to incorporation into global infrastructural ownership.[2] Despite its (supply) failings, Eskom has always offered preferential deals to private capital as bulk purchasers in the form of cheap electricity. It is also subject to considerable strife both from its workforce and from its (domestic) customers. It is unclear why and which private corporations or funds would willingly pull Eskom into their portfolio. On the other hand, why would domestic elites throw away the opportunities that come in the form of management positions, and control over masses of funds and contracts. In short, under continuing state ownership, everyone is a winner apart from the mass of the population. Nor can it be presumed that privatising, if achieved, would have made things better, not least as the same (or different) interests that prevail under public ownership would have sought similar benefits albeit under different conditions and scrutiny but not necessarily superior results.

As mentioned in the Preamble to Chapter 4, my work on privatisation precedes and follows that presented in this Volume. It has always sought to chart the shifting incidence, forms and effects of privatisation, as well as how it has been promoted, opposed, or viewed indifferently, by discourses whether scholarly, popular or in targeting policy. For mainstream economics, everything has been thrown at trying to understand privatisation across market imperfection economics, the new institutional economics, the new political economy, rent-seeking, neo-Austrianism and so on. Whatever theoretical and empirical insights they offer, they tend to suffer from two common drawbacks – improper understandings of both ownership and the state, and the powers they bestow and deploy. In particular, the postures of the World Bank have been particularly interesting, shifting from being gung-ho, just do it, to a more tempered position – in the wake of opposition, failures, and the wish to promote the use of the state's resources to promote private finance in private provision of public services whether through privatisation or contracting out.[3] Interestingly, the World Bank comes up with an ordered shopping list of what should be privatised – with telecoms at the top and water at the bottom, with transport relatively low unlike energy. So, South Africa does not entirely conform apart from SASOL. My own take on public sector provision, forged during the MERG (1993) process (for which I took responsibility for drafting proposals

2 Zav and I symbolically, but futilely, sought to get the Afrikaner "Eskom" replaced by the English "Escom" when both were in use.

3 For all of this, see Bayliss and Fine (eds) (2008), Bayliss and Fine (2020), Bayliss et al. (2016) and Fine (2020).

on electrification, health, housing and education) was, in the South African context, to emphasise that the main constraint was the institutional capacity to deliver rather than the finance to fund delivery – and that electrification offered the opportunities to develop any number of electricity-using activities that had previously been constrained for which Eskom could play a leading role as an effective 'institution' albeit created under apartheid. Unfortunately, my strictures have only been observed in the breach.

Presentation of Main Points

Discussion and debate around privatisation is characterised by the following features:

(a) The literature is marked by its circumstantial origins – emerging in developed countries as a market-led and politically and ideologically inspired response to the collapse of the post-war boom from the mid-1970s onwards. This raises doubts about its applicability to developing economies and those in transition. The analytical framework is narrow in scope, deriving more from fashions within economic theory than the genuine problems posed by privatisation and the relations between the public and private sectors. The literature has often responded chaotically to current issues as they have emerged with the experience of privatisation itself – moving, for example, from concern over the merits of public versus private ownership to the problems of regulation. However, irrespective of the understanding of the immediate impact and problems posed by privatisation, mainstream economists' understanding of the longer-term and broader systemic significance of privatisation remains sorely inadequate.

(b) The literature is often based upon a false dichotomy between state and market, and public and private, with an undue bias in theory and evidence towards favouring the role of the market and private capital. This sets aside the important role to be played by the state and the wide range of ways in which it can interact positively with the private sector. There is a presumption that the public sector crowds out the private sector rather than crowding it in, as is suggested by much of the empirical evidence, especially in the context of developing countries.

(c) As a result of the narrow analytical terrain on which privatisation has been studied, conclusions drawn have been overgeneralised and insensitive to the range of economic and political factors involved as well as the variety of ways in which they interact with one another. Each privatisation needs to be assessed within a specific context, addressing the sectoral issues involved as well as underlying economic and political interests.

(d) There is a tendency to suffer from the panacea syndrome – the notion not only that privatisation will improve the performance of the economy under current economic and political circumstances but that these will themselves be enhanced by virtue of a privatisation programme. The merits of the alternative of developing the capacity for 'good governance' within the context of the continuing public sector, instead of devoting considerable government administrative resources to privatisation and regulation, are rarely considered adequately. Scarce public sector resources devoted to the implementation of a privatisation programme might be better employed within the public sector itself to devise and deliver substantive reform programmes.

(e) The impact of the pressure for privatisation upon the motivation and ethos of public service has been neglected. The public sector is increasingly being told that it should mimic the market relative to which it is a second-best option. Further, on the basis of limited resources, the public sector is often required to provide for those services which have been neglected by the private sector as unprofitable, setting it at a comparative disadvantage with private sector institutions and reinforcing the ideology of the inadequacy of the public sector.

(f) Privatisation has been examined within analytical and policy frameworks that have been too narrow. The implicit understanding of industrial policy has been limited in scope; there has been a neglect of the broader macroeconomic impact and context; and the history and dynamic of both the public and the private sectors have been overlooked in setting aside the issues of economic and political power that are attached to the redistribution and redefinition of property rights. Privatisation has generally led to a further consolidation of economic power, with an increased concentration of corporate ownership even where there has been the aim of spreading share ownership.[4]

(g) With privatisation of public utilities, the quality, pricing and scope of service provision will depend upon the role of explicit or implicit regulation and subsidies, especially where this is in conflict with narrowly-defined commercial criteria. Regulation is an extremely demanding task upon

4 Moving forward to the present day, privatisation also has to be seen in the context of financialisation.

government and is marked by certain drawbacks. It is open to regulatory capture in which too cosy a relationship evolves between regulator and regulated, with corporations pressing for ever-weaker regulation in favour of their commercial interests; even so, the regulator has limited powers according to a legally defined role which will allow no leverage over many decisive corporate decisions such as levels of investment, training and employment; and the regulator will only be indirectly and infrequently democratically accountable, with contested decisions tending to be settled, for example, by horse-trading with the regulator or over longer periods through the courts.

(h) The incidence of privatisation shows no systematic relation to economic and political variables although, in developing economies and those in transition, pressure from (international) donor agencies has been particularly strong. Whether privatisation occurs and how successful it is depends upon a complex range of economic and political pre-conditions. Consequently, the World Bank has become less enthusiastic about the immediate prospects for rapid privatisation and advises a more cautious approach. Whilst this remarkable shift in policy stance is in deference to the acknowledged failure of its obsessive focus upon privatisation, the analytical and policy framework being employed remains remarkably unchanged and uncritical.

(i) The more guarded approach to privatisation that now marks international agencies such as the World Bank has as its counterpart a recognition that the longer-term prospects for privatisation depend upon significant changes in economic and political conditions. Whether explicitly or not, and often presented in neutral terms, this will lead donor aid and support to pursue policies on terms that promote the interests of those who favour and stand to gain from privatisation.

Against this background of the experience and understanding of privatisation, it is possible to assess South African prospects and initiatives. There are a number of positive features.

(a) A cautious sectoral approach, with attention to sequencing of policy and with a demonstrated capacity to resist pressures for privatisation from IFIs and commercial and other economic and political interest groups.

(b) Participation of the trade union movement and other popular interests in negotiations.

(c) The tying of restructuring of state assets to sectoral, supply-side policies in which closely negotiated joint ventures are prominent rather than simply selling off of public enterprises.

However, there are a number of negative features. These include:

(a) An unwarranted belief in the role that privatisation might play in financing the RDP. However, within the context of a broader investigation of the role of the financial system, the relationship between the restructuring of state assets and the financial system needs to be assessed for its impact on government finances in general and on the levels and composition of industrial (and other) investment.

(b) An inevitable dependence of privatisation upon finance provided by South Africa's major conglomerates which are themselves more strategically focused on globalising their productive and financial operations. Foreign investors are faced with a wide choice of alternative assets around the world. These factors will place downward pressure upon privatisation revenues and will lead to an increase in what is already a highly concentrated level of corporate ownership and control.

(c) The process of privatisation is expensive in terms of costs and administration. Apart from draining resources, it tends to undermine the ethos, morale and motivation of the public sector where South African capacity is already limited. No careful consideration seems to have been given to whether resources being devoted to the privatisation programme and future regulation might not be better allocated to reforming and enhancing the present public administration and to delivering RDP programmes directly through public sector agencies.

(d) Although restructuring of state enterprises is being considered with the context of specific enterprises and sectors, it is not clear that the associated policies:

  (i) employ full social cost-benefit analysis of projected outcomes;

  (ii) incorporate an overall strategic vision for the South African economy with due attention to its strength and weaknesses and the goals of the RDP;

  (iii) are sufficiently developed in detail in depth and scope; and

  (iv) will have in place, in advance, the necessary measures for ensuring continuing commitment to, and delivery of, intended outcomes in view of commercial and other pressures for them to be undermined.

(e) There is an excessive deference to an elusive business confidence in economic policy in which privatisation is seen as an objective in its own right, thereby hastening privatisation unduly and leading to misguided policies.

1 Introduction

Privatisation has increasingly grown in prominence across the world over the last fifteen years and has now become extremely important in policy debate for developing countries. Corresponding to this wave of privatisation, there has been a wealth of theoretical and empirical research – for example, more than three thousand articles in academic journals over the past four years. The academic literature has been concerned with the motives for, and the methods and consequences of privatisation, together with the problems posed by post-privatisation regulation. Discussion other than for the developed capitalist countries has, however, typically focused either on the 'successful' privatisers in Latin America and Southeast Asia or upon the more substantive issues posed by the economies in transition from central planning, predominantly those in Eastern Europe. The situation in Africa has not been ignored but its experience of privatisation has been neglected by comparison with the attention devoted elsewhere. Privatisation has not been considered a success, even amongst those who have been its strongest advocates. Lack of recent empirical research on privatisation in comparison to the extensive coverage in the early 1980s seems to indicate that the World Bank has lessened its interest in privatisation in Sub-Saharan Africa (SSA), and informal talks with its representatives have confirmed that there is a "great deal of (concealed) disappointment on this issue" (Fontaine and Geronimi, 1995, p. 147).

Although a stated policy objective in many African countries for some years, the implementation of privatisation programmes has been sluggish. Yet the pressure to privatise continues to gather strength. International donors have called for an increase in the pace of privatisation in a number of countries. In addition, it seems that individual governments have, if anything, raised their commitment to privatisation even as the international financial institutions (IFIs) have become more pessimistic about its potential impact. This increased enthusiasm, in part, reflects the hype that surrounds privatisation as a panacea, along with other market-based liberalisation measures. It may also be a response to the need to meet loan conditionalities, for which the raising of privatisation funds is a short-run expedient to alleviate budget deficits. Privatisation can also be used to further rather than to undermine the economic interests of domestic elites, despite assertions to the contrary.

Many of these points will be taken up in more detail later. This Report consists of four main sections. The first reviews the theoretical and some of the other literature on privatisation. It is followed by an account of privatisation experience in Africa. The third section offers a critical assessment of the World Bank's own review of privatisation experience. The final section draws out implications for South Africa.

2 New Public Sector Economics for Old

First, it is worth observing, as in many other policy areas, that South Africa does not conform neatly to a simple case study, with the advantage of being able to learn readily from the experience of other countries. Rather, corresponding to its own social and economic characteristics, it has lessons to learn from the comparative privatisation experience drawn from three different contexts, from developed and developing countries, and from those economies in transition, especially in eastern Europe.[5] Despite the very different backgrounds to privatisation within and across each of these broad categories, the literature, including analytical and policy frameworks for assessing privatisation, is dominated by a "new synthesis" in economic thinking,[6] which has evolved in the specific context of privatisation in developed countries.

The new synthesis is marked by a number of general features. First, it emerged initially, and all the key elements were put in place, prior to privatisation being considered of relevance to developing countries and those in transition. As was proudly and perversely proclaimed at the time, privatisation was the UK's most successful export, a boast tempered by the corresponding continuing deindustrialisation of the most severe kind and disastrous performance in manufacturing exports. In short, privatisation theory is a response, sometimes critical, to Thatcherism and is marked by its contextual origins. Second, the privatisation literature followed in the wake of the privatisation process as it evolved. Considerations of the economics of regulation only appeared at a later date, after the terms of the debate over the merits of public and private ownership had already been settled. Third, by the same token, the literature has only just begun to be informed by the consequences of privatisation in

5 This Chapter limits its scope by not covering the literature, and issues, raised by privatisation in the economies under transition in eastern Europe and elsewhere. For evidence that the World Bank remains as committed as ever to privatisation in eastern Europe, irrespective of growing misgivings elsewhere, see World Bank (1996a). For an account of the impact of the policies associated with the Washington Consensus on the Russian economy, see Standing (1996). Note his emphasis on lack of regard to appropriate sequencing in policymaking including privatisation.

6 The term is taken from Fine (1990a and b) where the arguments in this section are developed in depth.

practice, otherwise depending upon limited experience whether sectorally, comparatively and over time. Fourth, whilst, as emphasised, a response to particular economic and political circumstances, the theory of privatisation has also been heavily influenced by particular fashionable developments that have been taking place in economic theory, even though these have nothing as such to do with privatisation, merely serving as a convenient and fashionable illustration for the theory. For a variety of reasons, economic theory has been pre-occupied with issues of asymmetric and incomplete information and the costs of transactions within a market system. Privatisation proved a natural application, even though such factors are far from being its sole nor most important determinants.

Finally, irrespective of the applicability of the new synthesis to developed countries, the application of its analytical and policy framework to the radically different circumstances to be found in developing countries and economies in transition is most questionable. Indeed, it can be argued that the more pronounced changes and policy goals in such countries would have provided a sounder footing on which to formulate a theory of privatisation, since the issues and consequences involved present themselves more clearly and cannot be overlooked Anticipating what is to follow, the significance of the definition, redistribution and use of property rights emerges particularly sharply in the context of economies in transition or transformation.

In short, the privatisation literature suffers from the limitations of its analytical and empirical origins which, in principle, ought to have restricted its scope of application. This has not been so in practice and, partly and explicitly driven by a pro-market ideology despite its humble analytical foundations and origins, the momentum behind privatisation has swept much before it. Ideally, it would be best to wipe the analytical slate clean and start again. A start is made here by a critical assessment of the key components of the new synthesis.

It can in part be seen as a reaction against the earlier tradition of 'old' public sector economics. This was itself firmly based upon the notion of market failures. These fall into two types – the supposedly 'natural' or given as opposed to the 'artificial' or those created by economic agents. The first refers to conditions in production and/or consumption which lead to inefficiency in the context of a perfectly competitive, i.e. price-taking, economy. These might include economies of scale (natural monopoly) and externalities. In addition, the private sector might be considered to be naturally unsatisfactory if it provides an inequitable distribution of income or if it encourages or discourages consumption of goods that are considered undesirable or desirable, respectively, what are termed demerit (alcohol to be taxed for example) or merit (education to be subsidised) goods. In this way, the economic theory of market imperfections provided the rationale for public sector intervention, for which public ownership was one extreme form relative to subsidies and taxes for example. In addition, having identified the role for the public sector, it was more or less presumed that the benevolent welfare state would effortlessly implement the policies necessary both to rectify inefficiency and to meet social goals. On the other hand, artificial market failure arises out of the uncompetitive behaviour of economic agents, especially firms. In this case, the idea is that prices will be unduly high and the market restricted, providing a role for the state to control prices.

The old public sector economics was very much a product of the Keynesian and welfarist ideology of the post-war boom. The new synthesis is a response to the collapse of that boom, and the issue that emerged in the late 1970s of public versus private ownership. Whilst the old tradition was particularly ill-suited to address the question of ownership, simply presuming the state would do what the market would not, the new synthesis continues to be marked by emphasis on how to deal with potential market failure. Interestingly, the ways in which it has evolved can be seen as pulling in opposite directions in terms of conclusions about the relative merits of forms of public and private ownership. On the one hand, the scope of market failure has been considerably widened. It now includes issues such as how property rights are defined and utilised, informational imperfections and asymmetries, and the effects of transaction costs. The recognition of these additional market failures might be expected to enhance the potential role of the state in sorting them out. On the other hand, however, the state itself is placed under closer scrutiny. It is no longer presumed that the solution to a market failure can be safely left to be remedied by benevolent intervention, partly because the state may not be benevolent, in so far as it reflects and incorporates the actions of officials and others with interests of their own, and partly because the state may have neither the knowledge nor the capacity more generally to implement what is required of it. In short, the new synthesis accepts, and even extends, the framework of market failure but also questions whether the state is able and willing to provide a corrective improvement. Complementing market failure is its *alter ego* in the form of regulatory failure. It cannot be presumed that the state will put right what the market gets wrong. It is a matter of a trade-off between the two.[7]

7 As Jasinski and Yarrow (1996, p. 43) conclude from their four volume collection of articles on privatisation, "Very roughly, privatization can be viewed as a means of reducing the impacts of both monitoring failures and government failures at the risk of increasing the effects of market failures." For a conventional account of privatisation theory, see also Vickers and

The New Synthesis of New Political Economy, New Institutional Economics, and Neo-Austrian Economics

The first point about the new synthesis, then, is that it supplements the old public sector economics and, in doing so, it draws upon three separate and broader types of literature (Rowthorn and Chang, 1995). One is derived from the new political economy which emphasises the role and realm of the state as revolving around rent-seeking. In this view, the state's interventions not only distort the economy away from the conditions of beneficial perfect competition, they also encourage agents to incur the wasteful, and possibly illegal, expenditure of resources to gain such an advantage. Now, in this form, the notion of rent-seeking has a precise meaning and also a precise calculus of effects under given conditions – those of perfect competition and partial equilibrium. For, it is a static theory of distortion from market-led economic efficiency, with the added wrinkle that the inefficiencies are compounded by the costs of obtaining and sustaining them. However, and this is of more general significance for other parts of the literature, the notion of rent-seeking has readily taken on a life of its own, often divorced from its origins and limited sphere of applicability. Any economic intervention by the state, in a wide variety of circumstances, has become viewed as potentially a counter-productive policy response or an invitation to rent-seeking behaviour.

The new institutional economics has also contributed to the new synthesis. Its starting point is to explain the division between market and non-market institutions, especially the internal organisation of the firm as opposed to its external market relations.[8] At its core lies the notion that market transactions are not costless and that the capacity of economic agents to uncover and incorporate all potentially relevant information is bounded. Consequently, non-market institutional forms will emerge as well as customary and collective, rather than individualistic, optimising behaviour. Moreover, these are not, as such, evidence of inefficiency. Thus, non-market institutions, such as the state itself but also the internal organisation of large corporations, are inevitably the spontaneous consequence of the inadequacies of exclusive reliance upon the market alone. As in the case of rent-seeking, the new institutional economics has produced a terminology of its own, even if more technical and less focused.

Yarrow (1988). Clarke (1993) reviews the UK experience, arguing that it is far from a blueprint for other countries to follow, pro-market dogma to the contrary.

8 For presentations and assessments of the new institutional economics in the context of development, see Harriss et al. (eds) (1995). For a critical assessment in the context of labour markets, see Fine (1998a, Chapter 4).

It is deployed widely and freely. Central is the notion of principal-agent problems (in which there are problems monitoring those with whom one contracts because they have better knowledge than you over what they are doing and with what effects). There are the also problems of the definition and nature of property rights, and how the broader legal and other institutional environments interact with the generation and receipt of information. Like the new political economy, however, even if the latter marches under its limited banner of rent-seeking, the new institutional economics is essentially a static theory, even if of allocation of activity within and between market and non-market institutions. This does not prevent it from being applied in a much wider range of circumstances as if this were a simple corollary. In this way, for example, increasingly in the most recent literature, the historical evolution of institutions is seen as a dynamic interaction between institutions that generate property relations, information and corresponding contracts, and vice-versa.

This brings the new institutional economics into common ground with the neo-Austrian school of economics which differs from the other two influences on the new synthesis in that it is primarily concerned with the dynamics of the market economy in the context of an uncertain and changing world. In this respect, there is an antipathy to the notion of equilibrium and to the formal mathematical modelling that often characterises the new political economy and the new institutional economics. Instead, emphasis is placed upon the greater potential for decentralised decision-making. Individual economic agents are better placed both to generate and deploy new resources and information themselves and to do the same with that generated by others. Within the neo-Austrian tradition, the market is taken to be the most appropriate institutional form in which to accommodate such creation and diffusion of innovation and change. More important, however, is that the issue is raised in the neo-Austrian literature of how economic agents create and respond to a dynamic world of change and uncertainty irrespective of whether the market is favoured or not.

As a first point about the new synthesis, then, it is able to draw upon three separate, new or revitalised traditions. Each of these has itself developed in peculiar ways, from relatively narrow analytical origins. Taken together, especially in informal discourse, there is considerable licence to move seamlessly between a variety of concepts as if they were rigorously and coherently founded and integrated – which they are not. Further, there tends to be a presumption that these new analytical developments have shifted the balance in favour of the market and against the state – because of rent-seeking, the spontaneous formation of appropriate institutions, and the individual economic agent best knowing and responding to change.[9] Finally, with the exception of the neo-Austrians, the focus of the old public sector economics, with its emphasis on market failure, remains central – even if supplemented by notions of regulatory failure. To a large extent, this justifies the conclusion that ownership as such does not matter as opposed to the conditions of competition and regulation governing that ownership. But, if a choice has to be made on ownership, then the new influences on the synthesis have shifted the balance in favour of the market and privatisation.

Market Failure, Competition, and Industrial Economics and Policy

A second central point to the new synthesis is that there is a core section of the economy that is best left to the market and only to be subject to the interventions of the state in order to enhance competition, especially through easing regulations, for example, that inhibit ease of entry to a particular sector. This has been termed the quantity theory of competition (Weeks, 1981) – the idea that a sector is more competitive if there are more competitors and that more of such competition is beneficial. However, this can only be shown to be true within orthodox neoclassical economics under the most highly restrictive assumptions such as absence of externalities, decreasing returns to scale and partial equilibrium.[10]

In addition, the quantity theory of competition involves a very narrow notion of market competition for product markets, as opposed to the competition in product quality and differentiation, technological progress, access to finance, etc. This leads to a third, more general point concerning the way in which the new synthesis has changed the understanding of what constitutes industrial economics. Previously, the latter incorporated a substantial component of informal and institutional analysis as admirably summarised within the notion of structure-conduct-performance, the SCP approach. This

9 In the context of industrial policy, Chang (1994) has shown decisively that this is not so.

10 As Schmalensee (1988, p. 677) observes in his centenary survey on industrial economics for the *Economic Journal*, "Recent theoretical research suggests that market conduct depends in complex ways on a host of factors, and the empirical literature offers few simple robust structural relations on which general policies can be confidently based. Moreover, formal models of imperfect competition rarely generate unambiguous conclusions. In such models, feasible policy options usually involve movements *towards* but not *to* perfect competition, so that welfare analysis involves second-best comparisons amongst distorted equilibria. In particular, there is no guarantee that making markets 'more competitive' will generally enhance welfare, particularly if non-price rivalry is intensified."

suggested that the structure of an industrial sector, such as the degree of monopolisation, would affect the way in which a corporation would conduct its business and, consequently, have an impact upon its own and more general economic performance. It allowed a whole range of factors to be brought into consideration, not least the internal organisation of firms and their capacity to innovate and diversify. Now, in deference to mathematical models within industrial economics, the descriptive framework provided by SCP has been rejected for notions of equilibrium in which the anticipated effect of one's own and one's rivals' performance affects the choice of conduct and structure so that a unilinear causal relationship between the three factors is rejected. Modelling techniques have also been expanded to include game theory.

In short, irrespective of the merits of the old industrial economics, the use of the new industrial economics by the new synthesis has narrowed the range of the explanatory factors to be taken into consideration. They are confined to those that are readily amenable to formal modelling, although these models can become extremely sophisticated in terms of strategy and counterstrategy. Here, in conjunction with the previous points, the new synthesis appears to have selected the worst of all possible worlds. For, on the one hand, formal mathematical models do not sustain the simple conclusions concerning the benefits of competition. On the other hand, they involve the exclusion of factors which are known to be crucial to industrial performance. In this light, it is not surprising that the more informal approaches to the issues of rent-seeking, institutions and neo-Austrianism should have gained in prominence more recently, especially in the context of the economies in transition where the changes associated with privatisation are so much more dramatic and wide-ranging.

Restricting the scope of industrial economics, not surprisingly, leads to the fourth point about the new synthesis – it places a particular focus on what is the scope of industrial policy. Taking a longer view on this issue, it is apparent that the definition of industrial policy is itself highly variable both over time and between countries. This is a consequence of the capacity for almost all economic policies to affect industrial performance and for one or other of these policies to be decisive at one time or set of circumstances as opposed to another. Trade, R&D, skills, finance for industry, vertical integration, small business, provision of infrastructure, etc have all from time to time been seen, rightly or wrongly at the time, as the appropriate focus for industrial policy. For the new synthesis, the focus is far narrower – confined to competition, regulation (on which see later) and ownership. It follows that, just as crucial factors are neglected, so will be the corresponding policy considerations. This is true of other economic factors, especially where dynamic considerations of change are concerned, as in technological change and the generation of productivity increase and comparative advantage.

So far, the discussion has primarily been organised around the role of competition. The other side of the coin for the new synthesis is theory and policy where competitive outcomes are not appropriate as for natural monopoly, in the presence of economies of scale and scope. Here, the idea is that there is no possibility of a competitive equilibrium output so that, as best it can, a regulatory body must set prices or limit excessive profits, as well as securing quality and spread of provision to customers. A fifth point on the new synthesis, then, is that it presumes that there is a ready distinction, both conceptually and practically, between artificial and natural monopoly for which there are corresponding industrial policies, namely enhancing competition and regulation, respectively. It is relatively easy to show, however, that the notion of natural monopoly is not sustainable in the sense that it cannot be identified independently of the economic environment in which it operates. Consider, for example, a situation in which wages are driven down. This almost certainly reduces the scope for the economies of scale associated with natural monopoly as small-scale producers become more commercially viable. It might even be argued that driving down wages is a means of promoting the case for privatisation and enhanced competition (and vice-versa)! Consequently, natural monopoly cannot be defined independently of the economic conditions in which it is presumed to operate and, moreover, policy itself may change whether an industry is interpreted as a natural monopoly or not (Fine, 1989b and 1990a).

This leads to a sixth, more general, point about the new synthesis. This is its failure to take broader social and economic conditions into account. This is evident in a number of ways. Property rights are, for example, conceived of very simply as a residual claim to income – whatever profits are left over after costs are paid either go to the state or to a private company according to ownership. Not surprisingly, this tends to lead to the conclusion that ownership as such does not matter except as a secondary issue relative to competition and regulation. But property rights in general and privatisation in particular are much more complex. For privatisation can involve a decisive shift in the way in which property rights are exercised. Putting it too sharply, the public sector is to a greater or lesser extent subject to a political process which is quite distinct from the market process attached to private property. This is true even if both public and private sectors are subject to competition and regulation. It is much harder for broad-based interests to be represented politically when it comes to the private than to the public sector although, of course, there is no guarantee that political responses and processes within the public sector are always advantageous to the majority. But they do have to be taken into account and are liable to be highly variable and complex.

Two different aspects are involved in deepening the approach to the understanding of what constitutes and what is the impact of property rights. One, the less fundamental conceptually, concerns the effect of redistributing given property rights. According to longstanding theory from the literature on transaction costs, externalities and the theory of the firm, the redistribution of property rights does not matter for efficiency as long as they are properly defined and owned. This has, however, been shown to be incorrect when there are residual property rights, those aspects of economic life over which it is difficult or too costly to determine precisely within a contract. Then, who has ownership is important, not only, for example, in the power associated with the redistribution of wealth but also for the efficiency with which that wealth is used (Grossman and Hart, 1986). This point is readily understandable in the context of South Africa. The presence or not, for example, of racial discrimination in employment practices is very hard to pin down. It would make a difference who owned the companies and how they set about ensuring that managers deal with the potential for racism and other issues that cannot be solely reduced to commercial or contractual conditions and for which there is considerable managerial discretion.

A more fundamental aspect in approaching the issue of property rights is to acknowledge that these might not only have an impact through being redistributed but that their very nature is not fixed but subject to change through how the exercise of property rights is dependent upon economic and social factors. It has been argued, for example, that the impact of privatisation is very different according to the culture and institutions through which the state operates (Prosser, 1995). In the UK, compared to France, there is a relatively weak tradition of the state acceptably and legitimately interfering to regulate private capital in the public interest. One result is that UK regulation has been perceived to be the responsibility of the regulator, to be personalised rather than a matter of participatory accountability. As one commentator put it (Prosser, 1995, p. 512):

> Powers have been conferred personally on regulators and the assumptions seems to be that if the right people are appointed this is in itself a guarantee of legitimacy.

It follows that what is being privatised depends upon a broader set of considerations than those narrowly defined by a tranche of physical property and set of regulations. What these allow for in practice is highly contingent upon society-specific factors.

A separate way of seeing this aspect of property rights, the neglect of the socioeconomic environment, is the failure of the new synthesis to take into account the specific histories of nationalised industries, their dynamic and their broader social and economic significance. In Britain, for example, the strong popular commitment to the National Health Service is almost certainly a consequence of the tradition of free and universal provision that it embodies. There has also been a more general commitment to public service, including the ethos of public provision as opposed to pursuit of self-interest, although this is being eroded with the progress of privatisation.

This is because privatisation has been heavily associated with an ideology, through anti-statism, of 'bureaucratic bashing'. This places the legitimacy of government into question as well as public service ethos and motivation. To be a state official is potentially to court the reputation for being superfluous, inefficient relative to the private sector, and rent-seeking if not corrupt. The consequences have not been purely ideological or damaging to public service morale. For the public sector has found it necessary to mimic the practices and criteria of the private sector in order to avoid or deflect such accusations and perceptions.[11] Further, irrespective of the damage done to the morale and ethos of the public sector, there is an impact on recruitment to civil service employment. Although subject to nepotism, the state has often been able to enjoy a commitment from its workforce which has allowed lower wages to be paid than in the private sector and for a benefit to accrue from the pursuit of a career as a state employee. With a shift in the ethos of public service, state employment is liable to lose such advantages, leading to inefficiencies through high turnover of staff, and the civil service merely seen as an alternative or stepping stone to

---

11 For a comprehensive discussion of these issues, see Haque (1996). He argues, p. 191, "The current ethical challenge to the public service emanates basically from an attempt of various agencies to restore their weakened legitimacy or revive their lost public confidence by adopting the values of private enterprises, although such values are relatively incompatible with mainstream public service norms. However, this incorporation of market values in the public service may lead to a further decline in its legitimacy, because there is no reason to believe that the public will have more confidence in a public service driven by market values than one based on traditional, largely democratic, values." See also Fine and Leopold (1993, Chapter 21) where it is pointed out that public provision is increasingly being treated as an alternative form of private provision, with a corresponding language of client, customer, etc. For a discussion of the sea-change in attitudes towards the relative merits of the state and market in the context of Latin America, see Baer (1996).

more remunerative employment in the private sector. Moreover, the notion of 'good governance', leaving aside relatively neutral content such as lack of corruption and efficient administration, has become increasingly oriented by international agencies towards public sector support for the market. As discussed later, this can even take precedence over the democratic legitimacy of government (Busumtwi-Sam, 1996).

These considerations are particularly relevant in the South African context. Whilst government in the form of the ANC commands extremely high popular support, the same is not so true of the administration of the state. It remains marked by both the structures and many of the personnel that were part and parcel of the apartheid regime. Unfortunately, rightly or wrongly, as part of the transitional settlement and the incorporation of the former homelands, the majority of white civil servants have retained their privileged employment and benefits, whilst black government employees have frequently faced the threat of redundancy as duplicate and paper functions have been rationalised. Moreover, the institutional capacity of government is itself being (re)constructed at many different tiers and across a range of departments, against a background of impatience for delivery of basic services for those most in need, it is imperative that the legitimacy, ethics and motivation of state employees be sustained and even advanced. The ideology and practices associated with privatisation are damaging in this respect. There is a danger of the private sector 'creaming' the most easily sourced and commercially viable services, leaving the state with the responsibility of providing a safety net for those hardest to serve. Poorly resourced and regarded, the ethos of public service is undermined.[12]

History is also important in the assessment of the performance of the public sector. In Britain, for example, most of the major nationalisations arose immediately after the second world war out of the positive experience of war-time controls in sharp contrast to the failures of the industries under private ownership during the inter-war period (Fine and O'Donnell, 1981 and 1985). In many ways, the industries' experience before privatisation can be described as a period of successful restoration to commercial viability, something that had to occur in any case before the private sector would be willing

12 As Haque (1996, p. 200) observes, "In most of the market economies, the productive, efficient, and profitable sectors are dominated by private firms, whereas the public sector is left with activities which are socially unavoidable but economically non-profit-making and unattractive, such as health care, food provision, housing, and education for the poor ... Due to this monopolization of profitable enterprises by the private sector and the imposition of economically less viable functions on the public sector, the comparison between the two becomes relatively unjust."

to purchase them. More generally, in assessing performance, there tends to be an in-built bias against the public sector for two reasons. On the one hand, there is sample-selection bias – if the private sector were not performing well, it would be eliminated and not remain to be counted. Whilst this is considered to be a virtuous property of the market mechanism, this would discount their relatively negative contribution for the time that they are in existence. It is like assessing health care provision on the basis of live patients alone. On the other hand, the relative performance of the public and private sectors tends to be assessed on the basis of the criteria laid down for the private sector, more or less direct measures of commercial achievement at the expense of the equally important social measures such as employment generation and security, contribution to skills, and universal and collective provision.

In general, popular ideology to the contrary, the balance of evidence in favour of either the public or private sector is mixed and fairly balanced.[13] It is, however, difficult to make comparisons in the context of denationalisation, partly because it is relatively recent, limiting the capacity for before and after comparisons, and partly because it is rare that public and private sector companies operate in otherwise comparable conditions. This leads to a rather different point, re-emphasising the need to address historical and socioeconomic factors; the differences between public and private sector performance within a country are liable to be small relative to the differences in performance of both relative to other countries. Thus, in the case of Britain, the problem is not so much the difference between public and private sector performance as the poor overall industrial performance relative to other countries. Put another way, if the productivity performance between the private and public sectors within countries were equalised, then this would make very little difference to the comparison of productivities between countries. This is not the same thing as saying that ownership as such does not matter, since the running of the state sector can form part of, and a platform for, industrial policies more generally which do affect the performance of both private and public sectors.

This leads to a seventh point about the new synthesis which incorporates many of the earlier points. Because it is essentially microeconomic and partial in its analytical scope, it takes no account of the macroeconomic environment. The theory is perceived to be generally applicable across a range of

13 See Rowthorn and Chang (1992) and Chang and Singh (1993) for example. See also Haque (1996, p. 197), "There is sufficient reason to suspect the claims of efficiency and competition made by the privatization advocates and there is need for more comprehensive studies and critical research to evaluate such claims." For an overall assessment of the results of the UK privatisation programme, see Parker and Martin (1995).

circumstance give or take a detail or two. This has proved disastrous in the British case where privatisation has led to the simultaneous decline or lack of integration of industries that are mutually dependent upon one another through the input-output table – coal, steel, electricity, cars, and water, for example. Further, treatment of privatisation ignores key characteristics of the British economy – its failure to provide finance for industry, its low levels of productivity and wages, its deindustrialisation and casualisation and the low pay and low skills of much of the workforce, the chronic lack of coherent industrial policy, and persistently high levels of unemployment, etc. Theory proceeds as if these were incidental or, occasionally explicitly, as if they should be corrected by other policies, independently conceived and implemented. Macroeconomics should correct unemployment, for example, and income subsidies should be used to ensure that the poor can afford public utilities rather than distorting prices by making them cheaper. As Alan Walters, a prominent economic advisor to Mrs. Thatcher, reputedly argued in response to the idea that rail fares should be subsidised, "Why do you want to favour poor people simply because they go by railway. If you regard them as poor give them money" (as quoted in Bos, 1996, p. 53). The idea is that this will allow the poor to buy what they want and also not impair allocative efficiency by distorting price signals with a subsidy.

Of course, the unemployed and the poor might feel rather differently about whether such policies will actually be implemented. Those who favour such market-led solutions are also notorious for opposing income redistribution as providing negative incentives against the rich who would pay higher taxes, as well as discouraging the supposedly work-shy unemployed from taking up work. This is of particular significance in Britain, where the programme of privatisation has been associated with a dramatic increase in income inequality. The same applies to the increasing inequality elsewhere in the world of privatisation. Whatever benefits privatisation brings, they do not appear to filter down to the poor.[14]

14 For Haque (1996, p. 198), "During the period of privatization between 1980 and 1992, the number of people in poverty in Latin America increased from 136 million to 266 million, and in Africa, the number of people in poverty has already reached 200 million ... In terms of living standards, the incidence of undernutrition increased from 22% in 1979–81 to 26% in 1983–85 in sub-Saharan Africa, and health services have become less affordable to the poor in countries such as Zaire, Swaziland, Lesotho, and Uganda ... More recently, in many of the emerging market economies in Eastern Europe and the former Soviet republics, the standards of living have deteriorated significantly. Although these examples do not prove that privatization has caused this decline in living standards in these Third World and post-socialist countries, which might be caused by other unknown

A final point about the new synthesis is its understanding of regulation. Here, for natural monopolies, the idea is that the regulator should impose conditions on prices and quality, etc, of service. Whilst this is all very well in principle, there is much detail to be determined in practice and, echoing an earlier point, how the public and private sectors relate to, and attempt to manipulate, regulation is liable to be very different as each is governed by different goals and processes. Here, however, it is worth emphasising a different aspect of regulation which follows from the other features of the new synthesis. This is that the regulator is essentially a surrogate for industrial policy but with two special features. The first is the extremely limited powers that the regulator commands – given a focus primarily on pricing and profit at the level of the enterprise, there is usually no way of directly influencing wage differentials, employment levels, R&D, skills and training of the workforce, the promotion of economies of scope, etc. The second feature is the limited accountability of the regulator over extended periods in terms of democratic representation. Whilst this might be seen as a positive aspect in terms of independence from particular interests, including those of an established government, it is more fundamentally a negation of popular participation in decisions that often crucially affect the day-to-day lives of citizens dependent upon the provision of basic utilities.

From Theory to Practice

The theoretical literature on privatisation is, then, sorely limited in its ability to address the issues with which it is concerned. This is not simply a matter of omissions which can be corrected. The whole approach is deficient for its undue generality, for being exclusively concerned with static conditions of resource allocation and efficiency as opposed to the dynamics of industrial change, and for its lack of socioeconomic, political and historical content. The reasons for this lie in part in the attempt to impose previously developed theory to a host of very different circumstances. It is like the drunk who is found looking for his door key under a lamppost and, when asked if that is where it was lost, replies not but that it is the only place where it can be seen. Not surprisingly, however, as the search proves futile, tentative attempts are made further afield. This explains the previously observed process of incorporation of supposed insights from the new political economy, the new institutional economics, and neo-Austrianism. Developing countries and the economies in

factors, they at least represent the fact that privatization does not necessarily enhance the welfare of common people."

transition have been pressed into privatisation before analytical and practical lessons have been learnt even from experience in the developed countries.

As observed already, the process of privatisation involves both a redistribution of property rights and their redefinition. In addition, as a consequence, the process of privatisation is itself a particularly profitable business for many of those concerned. The cost of arranging the sale of assets, including the commission, is usually three or four percent of their value. But this can be a huge amount of money. It is hardly surprising that financial institutions should be keen on privatisations taking place. Often there has been a close relationship between political and financial advisors. As one of these commented (Letwin, 1988, p. 61):

> So, my first advice is to take the plunge. My second advice is, don't listen too much to too many experienced professionals. Choose advisers who will take the plunge with you and get with it. You will find as I say, that it's not perfect, but it does work.

But for whom does it work, apart from those who advise to take the plunge? For, in order to obtain cooperation from workforces and, especially, management in valuing businesses and in keeping them in running order, their cooperation often has to be recompensed. In Britain, there has been a public scandal over the extent to which the managers of previously public corporations have been rewarded with share options and increases in salaries. More than fifty directors of previously publicly-owned utilities have each made more than £1 million more in salaries, share options and pension rights than they would have before privatisation.[15]

An interesting aspect of this scandal is that the UK public were outraged both by the extent of the rewards received by the management in the newly privatised enterprises and by the absolute levels of these rewards. Not surprisingly, the rather lame but, in some sense, legitimate defence on the managers' behalf has been that their remuneration was simply being raised to a level comparable to the private sector. In effect, this suggests two different conclusions: how outrageously high but unnoticed are the levels of rewards common within the private sector and only brought to attention in the context of change from public to private sector management; and how substantially and quickly can the ethos of public sector management be transformed to that of the private

15 See Conyon (1995) for a full account of directors' pay in the UK privatised industries. He finds no correlation between the extent of increases in rewards and enterprise performance.

sector. And, of course, there is nothing that a regulator nor the government can do about it.

A rather different index of the shift in property relations, broadly interpreted, concerns the way in which the privatised companies have been able to relate to the rest of the economy. Under public ownership, the companies were generally prohibited from diversifying into other sectors for fear of their competing with the private sector. In addition, the public sector was used more positively to promote the private sector by, for example, the orders that it made for equipment which often reflected broader strategic goals. Under privatisation, such restrictions on diversification no longer hold and strategic goals are different, primarily tuned to profitability. Thus, for example, the first takeover bid for a UK electricity distribution company was made by a general holding company, seeking to set the electricity company's profits against its own losses in order to reduce an overall tax liability. More generally, and hardly surprisingly, the newly privatised companies have used their considerable financial muscle to speculate in the acquisition of other companies on the basis of acquiring capital gains rather than on the basis of economies of scale and scope. Inevitably, these operations involve internationalisation of investment, whether inward foreign investment in public utilities or outward investment by the newly privatised companies. This makes industrial policymaking even more difficult. Interestingly, even as this paper was being written, British Telecom has merged with the US company, MCI, to form the second largest telecommunications company in the world. This may or may not be an advantageous strategic move but, more significant, it has been made without any apparent reference to UK industrial policy or broader objectives as defined by government policy.

Similarly, as already noted, the use of domestically produced coal within the UK electricity industry has been sacrificed for reliance upon other energy sources irrespective of the direct impact on domestic employment within the coal industry itself, quite apart from the indirect effects through the multiplier. In addition, coal-fired power stations have been set aside for gas-fired power stations, as the latter require less capital expenditure and incur lower risks for individual power suppliers if not for the system as a whole. These effects together have had a large negative impact upon the British engineering industry; major parts of its market were suddenly spirited away without the opportunity to retool and retrain for provision of the new equipment irrespective of the rationale for its being preferred.[16]

16 On a slightly different point, see Fine and Poletti (1992) for a discussion of the British steel industry and how its preparation for privatisation was based upon considerable

In discussing, however suitably, the process of privatisation, and the corresponding redefinition and redistribution of property rights, the literature has inevitably moved forward to the results of privatisation itself for this is nothing other than the exercise of those newly formed property rights. Whilst there has, in Britain for example, quite correctly been considerable emphasis on the excessive profits that were made out of the privatisation process (with selling prices often offered too low) and the excessive profits made by privatised utilities, even leading to the imposition of an extra tax (thereby undermining or revealing the weakness of regulation), this is to some extent misleading. For it involves treating the privatised utilities as if they were simply the public utilities under private ownership. But this is not the case, as will become increasingly apparent over time as they diversify their activities in sectoral and global scope (or become the victims of others doing likewise). It is far from clear that this is the best way to conduct industrial policy in Britain, let alone in economies undergoing transition, or seeking reconstruction and development.

3 Origins and Patterns of Privatisation: The African Context

Many of the points already covered can be assessed in the light of experience of privatisation in Africa. There seems to be a consensus that state-owned enterprises (SOEs) had not been performing well in the 1970s (Kikeri et al. 1994), and various reasons have been put forward for this including poor investment decisions and inappropriate pricing policies, managerial impediments such as overstaffing, political interference in day-to-day management decisions, unclear objectives, weak human resource base and incompatibility of civil service procedures with commercial operations, lack of infrastructure, excessive centralisation, and lack of capital (Ndongko, 1991; and Wessel, 1991).

Explanations for the thrust behind privatisation as a policy in Africa vary. Naturally, some see it as a response to the poor performance of SOEs.[17] Reference is also made to shifts in development theory and ideologies in the face of mounting SOE losses, the collapse of communism in Eastern Europe, and the apparent successes of early privatisers such as those in the UK. Other observers trace the origins of the policy back to the adverse economic circumstances of the 1970s (Ndongko, 1991).

---

destruction of public sector basic capacity prior to privatisation in order to guarantee profitability of the continuing private finished steels sub-sectors.

17 Kikeri et al. (1994, p. 241) attribute the rise in privatisation principally to "years of disappointing SOE performance and a history of half-hearted ineffectual attempts at reform".

One of the key driving forces behind privatisation in Africa has been the increasing role of policy-based lending – of which privatisation is often a component – from the international finance institutions, IFIs. Between June 1981 and December 1991, 182 World Bank operations supported divestiture in 67 countries, half of them in Africa. Divestiture components are to be found in 70 percent of all structural adjustment loans and 40 percent of sectoral adjustment operations. In 1992, there were also 60 technical assistance projects in support of privatisation efforts, mostly in SSA and almost all aimed at strengthening capacities to divest (Berg, 1994). A strong link has been found between privatisation policy and dependence on international agencies (Ramamurti, 1992). Thus, the ideological shift in industrialised countries has been one of the driving forces behind the increased emphasis on privatisation in developing countries, and the extent of privatisation seems to be determined more by dependence upon structural adjustment and stabilisation funding than a case-by-case assessment of the merits involved.[18] The academic literature reveals that, at best, there seems to be no systematic reason why some countries embark upon more ambitious privatisation programmes than others.[19]

Note, however, that the difficulty of finding straightforward statistical correlations between the extent of privatisation and a range of other variables does not imply that the latter are unimportant. Consider the role of the trade union movement, for example, especially within the public sector itself and the

18 As Kumssa (1996, p. 79) observes, "Although privatization in SSA is influenced by neoclassical ideology, the decision to embark upon the programme is due to some external and internal factors. For example, some SSA countries see privatization as a means of raising government revenue, and countries which have acute financial problems are quick to resort to privatization to reduce their fiscal and credit pressures ... Pressure on SSA to privatize public enterprises also comes from external sources – SSA countries must privatize their public enterprises if they are to qualify for the stabilization and structural adjustment loans provided by the World Bank and IMF. Whenever countries refuse to accept this prescription, these powerful financial institutions deny them financial assistance ... The structural adjustment loan to Guinea in 1986, for example, was made contingent upon the privatization of public enterprises. Similarly, every privatization undertaken in Togo, Ghana, Uganda, Nigeria and other SSA countries has been at least partly due to pressure from the international financial institutions."

19 See especially Hemming and Unnithan (1996) who find that the most significant (negative) influence is the strength of the labour movement in a country. Reviewing the literature, the following other potential factors are identified: pragmatism and expediency (in securing foreign assistance); growing budget deficits in part required to cover SOE losses; belief that privatisation revenues will ease deficits; the wish to reduce taxes, internal and external pressures from lenders concerning the size of the public sector; and dissatisfaction with SOE performance.

associated fear of loss of employment or worsening of wages and conditions. If the labour movement is strong, it can resist privatisation. On the other hand, anti-union governments can take privatisation as a strategy for weakening the trade union movement, as clearly illustrated by the Thatcher government's determination to privatise the British coal industry (Fine, 1990a). Moreover, in other circumstances, the strength of the trade unions in an enterprise can allow it to negotiate favourable terms from privatisation, although this is more likely to arise out of the need to obtain management cooperation in the valuation and handover of assets. Whilst, then, the strength of the trade union movement can be a decisive factor influencing the extent of privatisation, it does not have a simple effect.

Similar considerations apply to the performance of the enterprises themselves. Whilst a SOE is performing badly, making large losses for example, it may be attractive to privatise it to reduce state expenditure and the budget deficit. These, however, are precisely the circumstances in which the private sector is unlikely to wish to purchase the enterprise – poorly performing in what are likely to be more generally unfavourable domestic economic circumstances. For this reason, privatisation is often a last ditch attempt to deal with underlying problems in the performance of public enterprises which do not necessarily derive from the form of ownership as such.[20] By the same token, if a state-owned enterprise is performing extremely well, in an economy that is prospering, the pressure to privatise might be diminished but the ease of doing so is considerably greater.

Two important conclusions follow. First, programmes for, and patterns of, privatisation will not reflect a systematic and economic logic. Second, the study of privatisation and its effects needs to be very tightly focused on the configuration of economic and political circumstances of the countries, sectors and enterprises concerned. Thus, in Africa, the actual number of enterprises privatised is considerably less than the targets set in many privatisation policy announcements.[21] 80% of privatisation implementation has been concentrated in six African countries, Benin, Ghana, Mozambique, Guinea Nigeria and Senegal. In SSA, industry and services accounted for most asset sales. As a rule, privatisation of manufacturing appears to be relatively more important

20 See Grosh and Mukandala (1994, p. 250), "Many of the (privatisation) reforms being tried recently have been proposed repeatedly over the years. Why have these measures, resisted effectively for so long, finally become acceptable? The answer appears, in many cases, to be that certain organizations or states have declines so far that they have hit bottom."

21 For example, Adam et al. (1992) reporting of Kenya that to all intents and purposes there has been no privatisation to speak of.

within lower income economies, accounting for up to 40–50% of revenue. Foreign investment accounts for a higher share of privatisation in developing countries. Whilst African privatisation has been relatively insignificant in world terms, it relies to a greater extent than other developing countries on foreign investors (Cook and Kirkpatrick, eds, 1995). Direct domestic private sector participation has been concentrated in smaller scale activities associated with commerce, manufacturing services and agricultural sectors. Larger sales in utilities and infrastructure depend more on direct foreign investment and public share issues. In general, the higher the value of sales, the more likely is a higher proportion of foreign investment.[22]

Despite these general conclusions about privatisation, it has been embraced as an economic policy that serves almost as a panacea for a range of, if not for all, economic problems. In general, the rationale behind the move to privatise state enterprises is assumed to be one of welfare improvement (Galal et al. 1994). The scenario by which this is supposedly achieved runs along the following lines. Most African countries began public enterprise reform programmes primarily to ease the fiscal burden, and supply-side efficiency and other motives have usually been secondary.[23] Privatisation is expected to improve the government's macroeconomic position because state enterprises are frequently loss-making and, hence, net receivers of government funds. Loss-making SOEs can contribute to fiscal deficits, and this can generate a downward spiral as the ensuing fiscal constraints mean that the state's administrative capacity may be weakened. State expenditure is a prime target for budget cuts and, without the resources for public investment taken by loss-making state-owned

22 See Adam et al. (1992). With greater participation of foreign firms, the chances that privatisation will lead to 'popular capitalism' and a 'share-owning democracy' become even less than has been experienced in the more favourable circumstances of the developed countries. In Britain, for example, whilst the number of shareholders did increase from two to nine million in the first five years of the privatisation programme, the percentage of shares owned by individuals had declined over the decade to 1989 from 33% to 21% – as the bulk of privatised shares had been purchased by institutional investors. Similarly, the privatisation programme in Japan has witnessed a fall to 23% in the proportion of shares owned by individuals. See Haque (1996, p. 199) for a discussion. The concentration of corporate ownership of privatised utilities has meant that share ownership democracy has become a farce. This was illustrated in the UK where outrage at the high rewards paid by management to themselves led to popular votes for their removal. These were, however, swamped by the votes of financial institutions in backing incumbent management.

23 As suggested by the World Bank (1994a), and confirmed by other commentators (Adam et al. 1992).

commercial enterprises, the quality of products, infrastructure and services deteriorates further.[24]

By transferring SOEs to the private sector, it is argued that not only will the state receive an injection of funds from the sales but the resource drain from deficits will be removed. If privatisation improves the efficiency of production, the state can also expect increased income in the future through tax revenues. Foreign exchange constraints make sales to foreign investors attractive, leading to an inflow of capital. The more acute the fiscal problem, the more urgent the need for the privatisation programme. It is also expected to contribute to the wider development of the private sector. Privatisation is also perceived to contribute to the development of weak or non-existent capital markets and hence to enhance domestic savings mobilisation. By privatising a state company through equity markets, the level of market activity is expected to increase dramatically. If the capital market is starting from a weak base, it will have to improve to accommodate the transaction, thus kick-starting the market.[25]

The rosy picture presented in the previous two paragraphs has been shown to depend upon a range of specific favourable factors that are too readily overlooked. One of the principal requirements for the implementation of a privatisation programme is an adequate administrative capacity. Divestiture is a technically demanding exercise, even in advanced economies. Most of the African divestiture programmes are dependent on technical assistance or financial aid provided by external agencies. Establishing an effective machinery to manage divestiture programmes has proved difficult in Africa (Young, 1995). The administrative capacity can have a significant effect on policy outcomes. For example, long delays in sales can have a damaging impact. In addition to the mechanics of the sale, the administrative capacity is stretched further in the preparation of enterprises for divestiture. Although it has been argued that restructuring should be left to new private owners (World Bank, 1994a) to avoid wasting resources, preparations that may need to be made prior to sale include redundancies, plant closures, legal restructuring and debt write-downs.

Not surprisingly, a number of studies have shown that the *market structure* in which an enterprise operates is more important than ownership in determining economic performance (Nyong, 1994). This is more straightforward for enterprises that produce tradeables in competitive sectors, particularly if privatisation also expands market competition, as this is expected to bring about rapid economic benefits (Kikeri et al. 1994). Divestiture in itself can bring

24 See Pinheiro and Schneider (1995) for a discussion in in the context of Latin America.

25 For a presentation of this optimistic outlook, see Adam et al. (1992).

about changes in market structure. For example, mergers with existing private sector enterprises can occur which increase the degree of monopoly, or divestiture of segments of a national utility may reduce the degree of monopoly. There is evidence that monopoly power of privatised enterprises has increased in developing countries, particularly where there has been more divestiture in utilities and where market concentration is already more prevalent (Cook and Kirkpatrick, 1995).

In the absence of an appropriately competitive environment, a strong *regulatory framework* is required, as is strong capacity to implement the regulations. This is necessary to guard against abuses of monopoly power such as price fixing and collusion. There are a number of factors to be considered including the timing and clarity of regulation, as well as arbitration mechanisms for conflicts over regulatory decisions. Little exists by way of regulatory capacity in much of Africa. By 1992 only 16 developing and transitional economies had restrictive business practice legislation in place, and the only one of these from SSA was Kenya.[26] Foreign direct investors frequently meet with very tight regulation of access to the domestic economy but, once in the country, such investors found their positions rarely challenged.[27]

Access to *technology* is an important determinant of both productivity increase and market structure. High levels of minimum efficient scale of production and large-scale, capital-intensive production can present a barrier to market entry. This has some bearing on the impact of privatisation. Anticipated productivity increases would be restricted given the cost of new technology. The picture may be further clouded by the fact that SOEs prior to privatisation have faced severe restrictions on their ability to invest.[28] Technical innovation is to be expected to hinge on the access of enterprises to imported technology. It is unwise, and inefficient, to leave technological advance to the vagaries of market forces alone, and especially to the instrument of privatisation alone.

For employment, privatisation is frequently associated with staff reduction. The state sector is often characterised by strong trade unions and, as a result, the cost of shedding staff in political as well as economic terms can be so great that the continued employment of excess labour is preferred. The workforce may also take action to impede the privatisation process in the expectation that private ownership will reduce staff levels. This further politicises the

26 See Bennett (1993) cited in Cook and Kirkpatrick (1995).

27 See Adam et al. (1992). The problem of weak regulatory capacity in Africa is acknowledged by the World Bank (1994a, p. 204) which states that, as a result, "divestiture of public utility management poses special challenges".

28 As reported for Mozambique, for example, by the World Bank (1995b).

privatisation programme. It may be that state employees are not favoured by the private sector as they have been cocooned in state employment for many years. Private investors may be deterred from purchasing state enterprises as they will either inherit a public sector oriented workforce or be faced with the substantial expense of dismissing staff. The costs of this can be extensive with many staff entitled to severance pay. Alternatively, attempts can be made to increase employee productivity, for example, by making provisions for employee share ownership schemes (Galal et al. 1994).

A well-developed *financial sector* is expected to contribute to the efficiency of the privatisation process. A factor in determining the economic impact of privatisation is the ability of the capital market, in addition to mobilising savings for investment, to provide price signals to enhance resource allocation and impose market discipline in enterprise management.[29] Given that the financial sector is weak in many African countries, public flotations of shares have accounted for a very small proportion of divestitures in Africa (2.5 percent in 1989 even if on the increase). This demonstrates that the menu of options available for methods of privatisation is shaped by the underdeveloped nature of African capital markets (Young, 1995). Whilst it is not essential to have a capital market to privatise, it means that the options for privatisation are wider. Domestic financial markets are unlikely to have the resources to finance large scale privatisations and will compound the requirement for foreign capital. Nonetheless, privatisation can stimulate the financial sector, strengthening existing trading patterns in finance or promoting new forms. The merits of this cannot be taken for granted, since a greater volume of share trading might not be what is most required of a country's financial system.[30]

Privatisation is intended to have an impact on, or compensate for, low levels of *domestic savings*. From 1987 to 1991, the average level of gross domestic savings was about 8% of GDP across all African countries (World Bank, 1994a). There is a doubt about whether domestic saving will be sufficient to provide for

---

29 See Adam et al. (1992). In their nine country study – which includes Ghana and Senegal – the World Bank (1994b) concludes that the evidence is consistent with the hypothesis that the pre-existence of a well-developed financial system helps to promote successful public enterprise reform.

30 Kikeri et al. (1994) cite examples of countries where privatisation has promoted the growth of the financial system, including Nigeria, Tunisia, Chile, France, the UK, Trinidad and Tobago, Jamaica and Japan. However, they warn against neglecting the problems that this can cause, since the sorts of trading and financial markets encouraged by privatisation are not necessarily the most important in reforming the financial system in a developing economy nor will the effect on the sequencing of financial and more general adjustment be appropriate.

the purchase of privatised companies. There are four means of circumventing such capital constraints. The first is to have partial sales, where full managerial control is passed to private investors; the second is to relax constraints on inflows of capital to attract back flight capital (although the ability to achieve this will also depend on a number of other factors such as the political and economic climate); the third is to sell in instalments; and the fourth is to rely on foreign capital which effectively amounts to substituting foreign for government ownership. Even in developed countries without unduly low levels of domestic saving, privatisation has had led to the increased concentration of enterprise ownership in the hands of a domestic elite or foreign investors.

The macroeconomic and microeconomic impacts of privatisation programmes are closely interlinked. A positive fiscal impact depends crucially on privatised enterprises being more efficient than if remaining in state hands, creating more profit and hence more tax revenue for the government. Otherwise, the exercise consists of swapping a future income stream for a current asset with no net contribution to public accounts. Research on Latin America found that proceeds from privatisation had an insignificant impact in terms of reducing government deficits, and high growth in privatisation has had only a modest impact on fiscal accounts from a present value perspective (Pinheiro and Schneider, 1995).

In many African countries, the actual receipt of funds from enterprise sales is not expected to have a major fiscal impact given the capital constraints. Gains to public revenues are expected to be achieved more by putting a stop to the financial drain of transferring funds to loss-making SOEs.[31] However, African states have been advised by the World Bank to transfer their most profitable assets first.[32] This means that the revenue position of governments may suffer rather than benefit in the short term as the profitable enterprises are transferred, although this may be ameliorated in the longer term by a higher revenue base if private enterprises are more efficient and profitable.

Accelerating the pace of privatisation, in part to comply with IFI conditionality, has become a policy objective in itself. The pressure to meet targets has led on occasion to poor programme management and inadequate preparation of enterprises for sale, although donors have tended to tolerate slippage when it comes to privatisation conditionality (Adam et al. 1992). With the onset of an accelerated programme, the administrative costs and strains increase substantially. Some countries (eg Ghana) are making arrangements to contract out

31 As in Tanzania on which see Henley (1993).

32 As discussed by Berg (1994) who argues that there is universal agreement that viable winners should be the first targets for privatisation.

components of the divestiture process as the government does not have the resources to meet the targets any other way. This is also expected to contribute to indigenous private sector consultancy development but points to limited administrative capacity without necessarily rectifying it.

Privatisation is normally a component of a wider structural reform programme. It should, therefore, be judged in the context of an overall adjustment strategy or within a policy framework that incorporates the sequencing of reforms. Other policies in an adjustment programme may include currency devaluation, restructuring of tariffs, trade and payments liberalisation, reduction in public expenditure, wage restraint, removal of subsidies, removal of administrative controls in the shift towards reduced or restructured state participation in the economy. Choices have to be made concerning the order in which polices are implemented as they will have an impact on one another. As discussed above, any industrial restructuring programme will depend for its success on the macroeconomic policy framework, infrastructure, international markets and availability of skilled personnel.

The significance of policy sequencing is shown by studies that have concluded that structural adjustment often results in a decline in investment for a number of reasons. In an eight-country study, it was found that only in Ghana was privatisation associated with rising private investment (Fontaine and Geronimi, 1995). This is because public investment had actually increased in the initial stages of the adjustment programme and, as a result, private investment was crowded in. Once domestic activity had picked up then privatisation became effective, and this was enhanced by the prior state-led restoration of capacity utilisation. Hence the timing of privatisation within the overall adjustment programme can be significant. There is more widespread evidence that public investment crowds in rather than crowds out private investment (Fontaine and Geronimi, 1995). This suggests that privatisation, by reducing public investment, could reduce rather than expand private sector investment. A key consideration in this respect is the sectoral impact of privatisation, and the vertical linkages with other sectors in terms of inputs and outputs and the associated economies of scope.

Privatisation policies in SSA have been pursued in what have often been depressed international conditions. This tends to restrict the level of foreign capital available, and substantial efforts are needed to attract funds from overseas, especially as different countries engage in competition with one another for foreign investment, whether in the form of privatisation or otherwise. Furthermore, the performance of domestic industries trying to compete in the export market, following trade liberalisation measures, may further depress investment. Foreign investors in privatised companies are looking for secure domestic markets and not necessarily to serve export markets. The overall impact of privatisation on the balance of payments needs to be examined carefully.

Lack of regard for the historical and political context of privatisation may give rise to inappropriate policy prescriptions. Given that the state sector is the vehicle for a large proportion of economic activity – SOEs account for 90% of manufacturing value added in Ethiopia, 80% in Somalia, more than 50% in Zambia, and 40% in Cameroon (Nellis, 1994) – economic performance is heavily dependent on the fortunes of the state sector. During the period of poor SOE performance, most African countries faced adverse economic circumstances particularly with regard to rising debt and falling exports. With a high level of state sector activity, this means that there is a danger of falsely attributing these circumstances to state ownership alone. Many of the problems facing SOEs would also be faced by the private sector (eg poor infrastructure, low skills base, lack of capital, political interference, uncompetitive markets). The question arises of whether these problems would be removed by transferring ownership. One study of seven countries found that SOE reform (including price and tariff restructuring, production rationalisation, restructuring of management and capital, corporate planning and the introduction of arm's length monitoring schemes) contributed much more to the rationalisation of public finances than had privatisation (Adam et al. 1992).

Many studies of privatisation cite lack of 'political will' as a reason for poor progress in implementation of privatisation programmes. This lack of political will reflects a number of concerns and possibly vested interests. It may be due to donor funding softening harsh budget constraints (Berg, 1994). The political environment may even increase the pace of privatisation. For example, in Zambia, the speed of divestiture increased because of the fluid nature of the political situation which meant that government felt it had a short time to make irreversible ownership changes, lacking confidence of remaining in office (Yaffey, 1995).

Uncritical faith in the market mechanism ignores the potential for privatisation to entrench rather than eradicate patronage and 'cronyism'. Research on Tunisia, for example, shows that there is a class in the private sector who are nurtured by the state. The profitability of their private sector industrial ventures has been enhanced through government mediation, and the members of this private sector class have very close personal relations with the members of the state elite. This private sector elite then is in a position to extract economic rent giving rise to the 'rentier syndrome'. Yet this syndrome does not necessarily give rise to a drop in welfare. What is important is the politics of the state rather than the cronies themselves.[33] Research on Nigeria, on the other hand, shows that the process of structural adjustment has offered numerous outlets for rents and patronage, and the Babangida regime has sought simply to appease large segments of the political class and business community. This has obstructed the adoption of policies that could have provided inducements for productive activity and remains a continued obstacle for development (Lewis, 1994).

The review of privatisation in an African context shows that the impact is complex, situation-specific and touches upon a wide range of economic and political effects. Not surprisingly, this has led its enthusiasts to view it as a panacea in two different broad respects. Privatisation will lead the economy to a superior performance under prevailing conditions, and it will lead to positive changes in those conditions themselves. Paradoxically, this can lead to arguments against privatisation being used to support it. For if the conditions are not suitable for privatisation, carrying out the policy will make them so! In this way, the objectives of privatisation and the conditions for its success are not kept entirely separate because of the assumption, often implicit, that conditions for successful achievement of the objectives can be brought forth simply by virtue of the need for them. For example, a strong financial sector is often both an objective of, and a condition for, privatisation. The very act of privatising will supposedly strengthen a weak financial sector. Similarly, a competitive market structure is often seen both as a requirement and a result of privatisation policies.

This Panglossian view of the world has been subject to substantial critical scrutiny, even by those who favour privatisation but who wish to ensure that it is implemented when and how it is appropriate to do so. The factors covered above need to be taken into account and to be shown, on balance, to favour privatisation.[34] The framework for planning and implementing privatisation

---

33 See Bellin (1994). See also Khan (1996) who shows that the impact of corruption depends upon the economic and political circumstances in which it is exercised, in South Korea as opposed to other countries for example.

34 As Rodinelli and Iacono (1996, p. 261) conclude, "Although privatization is an essential instrument for transforming government-controlled economies into market-oriented systems and for making established market economies more efficient, it is neither a panacea for all government's ills nor sufficient to ensure economic progress. Privatization is most effective when it is part of a broader programme of economic policy reforms and institutional development. The advantages of privatization can be maximized when

is extremely demanding. The experience of privatisation in practice can be perverse relative to a market-led ideology, with little improvement, if any, in economic performance at both macroeconomic and microeconomic levels, and continuing state intervention. This suggests that other problems have to be handled prior to consideration of privatisation and, even then, privatisation may no longer be appropriate nor be of a high strategic priority.[35]

4 Addressing the World Bank

Much of the pressure for privatisation, then, comes from:
(a) an unfounded belief in the superiority of the private over the public sector, and of the amorphous market over the state.
(b) a neglect of the pre-conditions for privatisation to be successfully managed or simple faith that those conditions will be induced by virtue of embarking upon a privatisation programme.
(c) a neglect of the broader social, political and economic environment in which privatisation is located.

Such conclusions have recently received support from an entirely unexpected quarter, the World Bank, in its review, *Bureaucrats in Business*, of the experience of privatisation. It is dissatisfied with the extent to which privatisation

---

government assures a competitive environment, has adequate procedures for promoting cost reduction and service quality, strongly supports small- and medium-scale enterprise development and SOE restructuring, and performs an effective regulatory role to minimize corruption and inequity." If all such conditions could be met, it is difficult to imagine why privatisation would be necessary!

35 See Kumssa (1996, p. 85), "Since there is considerable evidence which indicates that the problem of public enterprises is due to the inefficiency of management, lower productivity and lack of autonomy, the policy reform must focus on ways and means of achieving the higher levels of efficiency, higher productivity and managerial autonomy in the operational process, with the aim of achieving substantial cost reductions. It should also seek ways to create a competitive environment and price reform that will enhance the incentive and efficiency of public enterprises. Simply prescribing privatization as a panacea for the poor economic performance of public enterprises will not bring about sustainable development in SSA. On the contrary, it will aggravate already existing social and economic problems and engulf SSA in further economic and social difficulties ... The problem of public enterprises in SSA countries should not be analyzed in isolation but rather in relation to the whole socio-economic situation of these countries." See also Grosh and Mukandala (1994, p. 247) whose study of state-owned enterprises in Africa concludes, "The debate on public enterprise should focus on how to implement positive roles for public enterprises. The time is past for simplistic ideological positions for or against public enterprises or for or against privatization."

has taken place and with the results where it has. It might be worth, first of all, however, placing this Report in context. It follows three earlier reports, *The East Asian Miracle*, *Adjustment in Africa* and *Averting the Old Age Crisis* which are seen by the World Bank as part of a series of which *Bureaucrats in Business* is the fourth, that, according to self-promotion, "bring to a broad audience the results of World Bank research on policy issues". Without commenting on the third, the first two of these previous volumes, which are centrally concerned with economic policy, have been shown to be sorely inadequate.[36] In other words, despite its pro-market stance, even the World Bank has become unenthused with privatisation as a policy measure. But its analysis remains seriously flawed for a number of reasons.

Basically, the weaknesses of the World Bank position, especially in the *Bureaucrats in Business* Report, are that:[37]

(a) it constructs its understanding in terms of a simple dichotomy, and hence conflict, between the state and the market.[38]

(b) within this framework, it takes an ideologically favourable stance towards the market, thereby overlooking or negatively reinterpreting evidence on state economic intervention.

(c) it takes a very narrow view of what constitutes industrial policy, tending to interpret it alone in terms of whether there are price distortions or not.

(d) very much in conformity with *The East Asian Miracle*, an analytical framework is constructed in which even contrary evidence is used to support the pro-market stance. Thus, for example, state intervention in this case is perceived, when successful, to have been market-conforming. In other words, the evidence will rarely if ever contradict the pre-determined analytical and policy stances.

---

36 See Amsden (ed.) (1994), Fine and Stoneman (1996), Wade (1996) and Mosley et al. (1995) for devastating critical discussion of these World Bank Reports and the thinking and methods that have informed them.

37 See Bayliss and Fine (1998) for a fuller, subsequent critique of the Report.

38 See Hoshino (1996) who shows how *nationalisation* of the banks in Mexico in the early 1980s allowed new industrial entrepreneurs to emerge in the private sector on the basis of the compensation received. See also Haque (1996, pp. 202/3), for whom, "The rationale for the privatization of the public sector makes sense only on the assumption that there is a clearly discernible state-market dichotomy and that the role of the state is hardly complementary to the functions of private enterprise ... However, in reality, such a strict state-market dichotomy and incompatibility rarely exist ... In short, the expansion of the public sector in response to different market crises, the gains of private enterprises from various state activities, and the current state initiative to privatize public assets that benefit private enterprises, indicate that the assumption of a functional state-market or public-private dichotomy is questionable."

(e) despite (d), the use of empirical evidence is selective, biased and tied to much stronger conclusions than are warranted even if the evidence itself could be considered satisfactory.

In short, this Report falls into the pattern of those that came before, although it is less researched and substantive than the *Miracle*. It is impossible to take it seriously as a piece of research, either in coming to analytical and empirical conclusion or in offering policy advice. It also occupies a peculiar position relative to the *Miracle*, which it follows by more than a year in publication. In terms of its analytical, empirical and policy posture, it represents a considerable step backwards. For, unlike the earlier report, it has once again narrowed the terrain of discussion around industrial policy towards narrow parameters. It fails to consider (dynamic) economies of scale and scope, the creation rather than the use of comparative advantage, and reference to selective finance, subsidies, etc is all from a perspective that primarily emphasises their negative consequences from a perspective of laissez-faire dogma. At least the *Miracle* recognised the positive, even the essential role, to be played by industrial policy beyond provision of infrastructure, although it tended to be interpreted as what the market would have done if it had been perfect.[39] On the other hand, this Report goes beyond the *Miracle* and most, if not all, previous Reports by the extent to which it implicitly points towards donor agencies, presumably including itself, exerting an indirect influence on countries' political outcomes.

This arises from the broad conclusions of the Report which are as follows. Privatisation is in most cases desirable and, where it is not, regulation of state-owned or private enterprises (as in contracted out services) are more desirable the closer they come to the market in the form that they assume. This raises the issue of why more privatisations have not taken place and why they have not always been successful when they have occurred – the Report is dissatisfied with the extent of privatisation, especially in low-income countries where it feels the benefits are liable to be particularly great. Of course, one obvious conclusion to investigate from this evidence is that privatisation has not occurred so much because it is undesirable and that it has often been unsuccessful because it has been forced through when it should not have been; and this is especially so for low-income countries where, at an early stage of development, state ownership might be essential.

---

39 The *Miracle* also argues that the market-conforming policies of East Asia cannot be replicated in other countries. According to Busumtwi-Sam (1996), this stance is contradicted in a confidential World Bank report on Ghana which suggests that it follow the East Asian model of economic development.

To some extent, the Report accepts that privatisation might have been unsuccessfully adopted as a policy but only if done so prematurely. It even suggests that the World Bank has itself been guilty in this respect by promoting premature privatisations, although the Report is notably short of details of this (where and when) and of self-criticism in examining how this could have come about. Nor is there any examination of what follows logically from this admission of premature privatisation – that they might be reversed or that there may be private capitals that should be taken into public ownership; better a bad privatisation or private sector than to encourage state ownership! What the Report argues in order to explain limited privatisation and less than perfect success in privatisations is that three conditions have to be met for the desired outcome.

First, in order to explain why privatisation does or does not take place and whether it is successful or not, emphasis is placed upon the criterion of its depending upon *political desirability*. In other words, there has to be government support for the policy. It is argued that this is liable to come about either through a shift in political regime (change of power bloc by whatever means) or through an economic crisis that shifts the perceived balance of costs and benefits for an existing regime. Although it is not a step that is taken in the Report, it follows logically that a shift in regime or even the engineering or threat of an economic crisis might be desirable in order to attain the longer-term goals of more and more successful privatisation.

Second, there is the need for the privatisations to be politically feasible. This implies that those who lose by the policies have to be defeated or compensated if they have the power to obstruct them. The Report hastens to observe that it does not necessarily see this as less of a problem in an authoritarian regime, especially in conjunction with desirability and credibility (on which see next), but does seem to regard favourably the link between feasibility and authoritarianism.[40]

Third, government reform has to be credible. Other agents have to have confidence that policy intentions will actually be carried out, this implying

40 Thus, World Bank (1995, p. 191), "whether a country has a more or less authoritarian form of government is therefore a strong indicator of feasibility". See Busumtwi-Sam (1996) for a discussion, in the context of Ghana, of the irrelevance of authoritarianism versus democracy as a starting point for addressing the performance of the state. For similar, more general conclusions, see Haggard and Kaufman (eds) (1992) and Haggard and Webb (1993).

the creation of a reputation for honouring commitments and the presence of domestic and international restraints on policy reversals.[41]

The triplet of political desirability, political feasibility and credibility provide for an analytical and empirical guarantee that whatever outcomes or evidence might present themselves, they will conform to the previously developed hypotheses. If privatisation does not occur or is unsuccessful, it can be readily interpreted as either having lacked desirability, feasibility or credibility. These three factors provide a descriptive framework into which success or failure almost inevitably sits comfortably. This is so even if the framework is not entirely devoid of causal content with, for example, the feasibility factor operationalised by measures of overstaffing – as an index of the problems in making redundancies in state-owned companies prior to, or in the wake of, privatisation.

But, to return to the earlier theme of this World Bank Report going beyond those earlier in the series of which it is a part, there is the obvious implication, and it is made explicit in a significantly short final chapter (two and a half pages out of a total of 260, plus 80 statistics and references), that international financial assistance should be organised around the achievement of privatisation through supporting differentially according to whether desirability, feasibility and credibility have been established, and all of these together are perceived as essential for success. In other words, support for public sector reform and for privatisation should be withheld until all three conditions have been met. Again, it is but a short step to see this as an implicit form of political conditionality, the latter being quite extensive in terms of regime or power bloc shift, appeasing those who are both powerful and liable to lose by the privatisation process, and giving high priority to both domestic and foreign interests in pre-empting policy reversals (thereby tying the hands of future governments).

In another respect, this Report goes beyond others in recognising that the market does not always work best, at least immediately, in all but a few areas characterised by market imperfections, as for (social) infrastructure for example. The message is that privatisation (and more general support for reform of state enterprises) ought to wait upon other reforms or changes in political conditions. Put another way, this is an argument for sequencing, in which privatisation needs to be delayed until other economic and political conditions have been met. This raises the issue of what should be done in the meantime. In this case, the answer is a step back into orthodoxy once again, with emphasis on policies that are conducive to the growth of, and dependence upon, market

41 The notion of credibility has its origins in part in game theory, where agents have to be assured that those with whom they bargain, including the state, will keep to their word.

forces. Until privatisation can proceed, it is essential to adopt policies that correspond to orthodox stabilisation and structural adjustment, and these are accepted uncritically despite the record of poor outcomes whatever the claims of *Adjustment in Africa* to the contrary.

To sum up so far, this Report can be seen as constructing an analytical, empirical and policy framework in which the evidence inevitably points to the desirability of as much privatisation as possible or as much reliance upon market forces as possible where state ownership is maintained. However, it does suggest that privatisation programmes need to be sequenced with other economic conditions and, especially, with political conditions. It suggests that international financial assistance should be geared to these conditions, and this is an implicit use of such assistance to support certain political as well as economic changes as opposed to others.

Central to the Report's outlook is that the private sector performs better than the public sector. It presents limited and questionable evidence in support of this view and, as is habitual in its publications in general, overlooks the literature that questions this conclusion. A number of points need to be made here, even if replicating those made earlier. First, quite apart from the difficulties in devising and making appropriate measures of performance between public and private enterprises, the criteria employed generally favour the private sector since the public sector may be subject to other conditions of operation. Second, there is a sense in which the sample is biased since those private sector enterprises that fail will be excluded from the sampling. Third, it is forgotten that privatisation often arises out of the creation of enterprises through state-inspired initiatives that would not have occurred under private enterprise and which may be abandoned by the private sector in less favourable circumstances in the future.

Even leaving these considerations aside, the evidence of significant difference between public and private enterprise performance is extremely weak. Sometimes one is superior, sometimes the other even by the criteria of the private sector itself. What is much more important is that the difference in performance between enterprises of one country as opposed to another is far more significant than the differences of ownership within countries. It is what private and public share in common within a country that needs to be examined carefully. Even if the performance of public and private enterprises were equalised within countries, this would raise economic performance very little compared to the differences of performance from one country to the next. The focus upon differences in ownership rather than common conditions of operation is a major weakness of this Report both analytically and in policy proposals, discussed further below.

To support its outlook, the Report examines five policy features around state enterprise reform – the extent of divestiture, the intensity of competition, the hardness of budgets, the extent of financial sector reform, and the institutional arrangements between government and enterprises. Essentially, the more these are market-like the more they are concluded to have been successful. However, this procedure is, once again, bound to yield the desired results. For, suppose for the sake of argument that enterprise performance is independent of these factors or policies. Suppose also that there is considerable pressure for privatisation from domestic as well as international agencies. Then, it is possible to infer that the associations of the market-led policies with successful state sector reform are causal in the opposite direction! It is easier to divest more fully if your enterprises are successful rather than vice-versa; similarly, you can bear competition in product markets, impose hard budget constraints, draw upon and sustain financial sector reform, and arrange for greater independence of enterprises from government!

Paradoxically, this alternative perspective can be used to interpret what are perverse results for the Report. It finds that public enterprise performance improves as well as privatised companies when the latter are successful and when the public sector performance had already been successful. It suggests somewhat weakly that this might be due to the enhanced competition exerted on the public by the enlarged private sector. But this is hardly plausible given the limited weight of privatisation and what is liable to be an extremely narrow overlap between the markets served by the private and the continuing public sector. A much more obvious explanation is that there are similar factors or policies that have enhanced the performance of both public and private sectors independent of privatisation as such.

Similar reservations can be made about the discussion of policy towards continuing state enterprises or services. The Report distinguishes three types of arrangements – performance contracts, management contracts and regulation. Subject to capacity to implement, it favours these in the opposite order of listing. It does so on the basis of another triplet of putative causal factors: first, informational considerations which it sees somewhat strangely as being enhanced exclusively by competition rather than, for example, by auditing even of the type that it is itself engaged upon in this Report; second, the use of rewards and penalties to provide appropriate incentives; third, commitment to ensure that contracts are properly formulated and monitored by government or independent agency. Once again, the desired analytical and empirical results can be interpreted as almost inevitably corresponding to the descriptive framework, and the causal associations could easily function in the opposite direction. The critique of performance contracts, for example, is quite detailed but more in the vein of their inadequate specification and implementation than their unsuitability per se. But should they have been or have been able to have been better specified and carried out, one suspects that they might have ended up as, or been interpreted as, management contracts or even regulated enterprises.

Without going into details or covering all points, it can be added that much of the analysis falls into this or other varieties of ad hocery that are simply designed to support pre-determined conclusions. The treatment of China, for example, is extremely superficial. Also, we are treated to the observation that there is a cross-country correlation between greater deficits on the public enterprise account and the overall fiscal deficit – leading to the conclusion that state-ownership is bad for public finance. However, such a correlation is automatic given that the one deficit is a part of the other!

It has already been observed that the Report implicitly takes an extremely narrow view of what constitutes industrial policy (of which public or private ownership and forms of competition and regulation are just a part and not necessarily the most important part). One consequence of this is that its policy proposals are generalised without sensitivity either to the specifics of the country concerned – its level of development, its position in the world economy, its internal economic and political dynamic, etc – nor to the specifics of the sectors involved. This leads to overgeneralisation both in terms of the policy framework adopted and in the empirical evidence employed.

This is evident in the policy "Decision Tree for State-Owned Enterprise Reform" which appears both as the first and, in replicate, as the last figure in the Report. Are we really to believe that this is an adequate decision tree, irrespective of the sector concerned and irrespective of the country, region or level of development? This is not a matter of detail, which is thin within the figure, but whether the same species of tree is appropriate in all circumstances. This is especially important in view of the narrow experience upon which the Report draws irrespective of how well it does so. It is itself aware that the privatisations that have occurred are primarily drawn from Latin America and the previously centrally planned economies, and upon infrastructure, petrol and minerals and agribusiness. Indeed, over the period from 1988, the value of infrastructural privatisations in developing countries is totally dominated by telecommunications (60%) and, to a lesser extent, power which accounts for a further 27%! And gas distribution takes an additional 10%. Can we extrapolate from these examples? The answer is surely in the negative because telecommunications does have unique features which do not prevail in other sectors and which do not apply at all or in the same way in other sectors of the economy – these include the (prospective) scale of the market and existing state of the network, the linkages upstream and downstream with other activity such as electronic and electrical goods manufacture and data processing, the availability of skilled labour, and the need to engage in joint ventures and negotiate with powerful transnational corporations.

Such considerations, significantly, do not figure in the decision tree nor in the Report's analysis at all. Their incidence will be different and they will interact differently from one country to the next and from one sector to the next. Accordingly, in general the Report is not suitable as a guide to policy – indeed, it is a contribution only in the negative sense of precluding the sort of policy frameworks and policies themselves that might be most apposite. For, far from starting from a dogmatic position favouring the market, in the context of reform of public sector enterprise, it is more appropriate to make a sector-specific and country-specific industrial policy. This should take into account economies of scale and scope, technological imperatives, economic linkages, macroeconomic impact, financing requirements, etc. Then, on this basis, although the sequencing between policy formulation and forms of implementation need not be so rigidly separated, decisions can be made concerning what are the most appropriate forms of state economic intervention, including ownership decisions, in order to pursue the strategy formulated.

It can even be argued that this is the way in which policy is in fact implemented even if in favour of special interests, and not always as consciously as laid out here and with as wide a scope of factors taken into account. Further, the successful late developers can be interpreted as having consciously employed such a policy process in conjunction with specific development goals. By contrast, not only is such a targeted framework eschewed by this Report in favour of a generalised reliance upon the market as far as political conditions allow, it even sets aside scope for the formulation and use of industrial policy where privatisation is recommended however appropriately. For one policy recommendation is to devote as few resources as possible to public enterprises targeted for privatisation in view of the limited extent to which such resources are liable to be well-spent and to accrue a return in the sale price. The only exceptions made are for smoothing the privatisation process itself through capital write-offs and redundancy payments to reduce overstaffing. In short, nothing could illustrate better the extent to which the Report is ideologically wedded to a general belief in the superiority of the market and the futility of the state deploying an industrial policy even where this is to function through prospective privatised enterprises.

5 Implications for South Africa

From the previous discussion, a number of conclusions can be drawn about the impact of privatisation and the literature and corresponding policy frameworks that have been used to address it. Whilst the implications for South Africa are of greater or lesser relevance, it is important that account be taken of them in the restructuring of state assets. In general, the discussion is made in the context of privatisation in the form of selling off of state assets. This is one, the most extreme form, of privatisation, and there are a variety of forms and methods. Nonetheless, the factors discussed also remain relevant to a greater or lesser extent.

(a) The literature is marked by its circumstantial origins – emerging in developed countries as a market-led and politically-inspired response to the collapse of the post-war boom. This raises doubts about its applicability to developing economies and those in transition. The analytical framework is narrow in scope, deriving more from fashions within economic theory than the genuine problems posed by privatisation and the relations between the public and private sectors. The literature has responded to issues as they have emerged with experience of privatisation itself – moving, for example, from concern over the merits of public versus private ownership to the problems of regulation. However, irrespective of the understanding of the immediate impact and problems posed by privatisation, the understanding of the longer term and broader systemic significance of privatisation remains sorely inadequate.

(b) The literature is often based upon a false dichotomy between state and market, and public and private, with an undue bias in theory and evidence towards favouring the role of the market and private capital. This sets aside the important role to be played by the state and the wide range of ways in which it can interact positively with the private sector. There is a presumption that the public sector crowds out the private sector rather than crowding it in, as is suggested by much of the empirical evidence, especially in the context of developing countries.

(c) As a result of the narrow analytical terrain on which privatisation has been studied, conclusions drawn have been overgeneralised and insensitive to the range of economic and political factors involved as well as the variety of ways in which they interact with one another. Each privatisation needs to be assessed within a specific context, addressing the sectoral issues involved as well as underlying economic and political interests.

(d) There is a tendency to suffer from the panacea syndrome – the notion not only that privatisation will improve the performance of the economy under current economic and political circumstances but that these will themselves be enhanced by virtue of a privatisation programme. The merits of the alternative of developing the capacity for 'good governance' within the context of the continuing public sector, instead of using government administrative resources for privatisation and regulation, is rarely considered adequately. Scarce public sector resources devoted to the implementation of a privatisation programme might be better employed within the public sector itself to devise and deliver programmes.

(e) The impact of the pressure for privatisation upon the motivation and ethos of public service has been neglected. The public sector is increasingly being told that it should mimic the market relative to which it is a second-best option. Further, on the basis of limited resources, the public sector is often required to provide for those services which have been neglected by the private sector as unprofitable, setting it at a comparative disadvantage with the private sector.

(f) Privatisation has been examined within a framework that has been too narrow – in its understanding of industrial policy by limiting its scope, by neglecting the broader macroeconomic impact and context, in overlooking the history and dynamic of both the public and the private sectors, and in setting aside the issues of economic and political power that are attached to the redistribution and redefinition of property rights. Privatisation has generally led to a further consolidation of economic power, with an increased concentration of corporate ownership even where there has been the aim of spreading share ownership.

(g) With privatisation of public utilities, the quality, pricing and scope of service provision will depend upon the role of regulation and subsidy, especially where this is in conflict with narrowly defined commercial criteria. Regulation is an extremely demanding task upon government and is marked by certain drawbacks. It is open to regulatory capture in which too cosy a relationship evolves between regulator and regulated, with corporations pressing for ever-weaker regulation in favour of its commercial interests; even so, the regulator has limited powers according to a legally defined role which will allow no leverage over many decisive corporate decisions such as levels of investment, training, employment, etc; and the regulator will only be indirectly and infrequently democratically accountable, with contested decisions tending to be settled, for example, by horse-trading with the regulator or over longer periods through the courts.

(h) The incidence of privatisation shows no systematic relation to economic and political variables although, in developing economies and those in transition, pressure from donor agencies as been particularly strong. Whether privatisation occurs and how successful it depends upon a complex range of economic and political pre-conditions. Consequently, the World Bank has become less enthusiastic about the immediate prospects for privatisation and advises a more cautious approach. Whilst this remarkable shift in policy stance is in deference to the acknowledged failure of its obsessive focus upon privatisation, the analytical and policy framework being employed remains remarkably unchanged and uncritical.

(i) The more guarded approach to privatisation that now marks international agencies such as the World Bank has as its counterpart a recognition that the longer-term prospects for privatisation depend upon significant economic and political changes. Whether explicitly or not, and often presented in neutral terms, this will lead donor aid and support to pursue policies and good governance on terms that promote the interests and position of those who favour and stand to gain from privatisation.

Against this background of the experience and understanding of privatisation, it is possible to assess South African prospects and initiatives. There are a number of positive features. First, there are the historical aspects to privatisation in South Africa. Huge state corporations, such as ESKOM, SASOL, TRANSNET and ISCOR have been built up in the past, partly as a strategic element in securing the apartheid regime against the threat of international sanctions, but also as a concerted attempt to provide infrastructural and other economic support to large-scale private capital and secure jobs for working class Afrikaners. In the mid-eighties, policy gradually switched towards privatisation of these and other corporations. The rationale at that time was relatively clear. The apartheid regime sought to obtain short-term funding in order to handle the economic and political crisis that it faced, especially in the wake of the international debt freeze of 1985. In addition, privatisation held out the prospect of removing the ownership and control of significant assets from the hands of a prospective democratic government.[42]

In the event, the government's strategy was primarily defeated, partly as a consequence of political opposition, especially that emanating from the trade

42 For a discussion of past and present proposals for privatisation, see Fine (1995a). See also Makgetla (1995).

union movement which could easily have been swayed by the offer of sweet deals. Current proposals for privatisation continue to recognise the influence of the trade union movement, as in the National Framework Agreement for negotiating "the restructuring of state enterprises". This last phrase is itself an encouraging sign in so far as it distances itself from the terminology of privatisation as the only or main form of dealing with public enterprise. In this respect, it will be crucial to keep under close scrutiny the substance that is given in practice to the restructuring of state assets within the context of the National Framework Agreement. Privatisation does tend to have a logic of its own, generating a momentum that veers towards the incorporation of commercial at the expense of social or other criteria, particularly during the process of negotiating the details of implementation and putting them into place. Good and honest intentions in advance tend to be sacrificed to the dictates of commercial viability – not least in response to the pressures generated by IFIs and private domestic and foreign business interests.

It must also be borne in mind that the failure of the apartheid regime's attempts at privatisation did not derive exclusively from political opposition. On any realistic assessment, particularly at a time of international sanctions, the only major source of finance for purchasing privatised assets must have been the South African conglomerates. The limited extent of privatisation that did occur reflected the unwillingness of these corporations to invest in privatised utilities for a variety of reasons, including a reluctance to commit large-scale finance in political uncertain conditions together with the comfortable relationship that was enjoyed with the state corporations in any case. To have forced South African corporations into financing privatisation would have been equivalent to a policy of proscribed assets. However, with the demise of apartheid, much of the political uncertainty surrounding the future of privatised assets will have been removed, opening the way for investment by both domestic and international interests.

However, other circumstances have also changed. The spread of privatisation around the world means that the portfolio of choice available to investors in privatised utilities is considerable. The pricing of privatised assets would have to be extremely keen. More important, the wish for South African corporations to avoid tying up their capital in privatised utilities remains. South African corporations are continuing to seek to globalise their operations. Also, as in the past, the extent to which they will fund privatisation will depend upon the alternative uses to which they can put their finances and their strategic stance towards the South African economy.

It is crucial to recognise, however, that both of these factors should not be taken as given – they are open to be influenced by government policy and strategy. In these respects, the current situation is far from positive in some respects. On the financial side, government has argued that privatisation will be a source of funding for the RDP, although such earmarking has always proved elusive, and there are already signs that privatisation funds will be set against the government deficit. In addition, the notion that privatisation will provide funds for the RDP is misleading in the sense that it suggests that the major constraint on RDP delivery is availability of finance. This is arguable given that much of the funding for RDP programmes remains unspent, and that the continuing major constraint on delivery is the institutional capacity to deliver for which the creation of public sectors skills and ethos is of paramount importance. There is no evidence nor guarantee that the finance raised through privatisations will in fact be earmarked and used for progressive policies, such as the RDP in the South African case. In fact, the funds simply become a general part of government revenue, and it can always be said that whatever is spent on the RDP came out of the privatisation fund. Further, funding the RDP out of privatisation revenues is to concede the principle that its policies are contingent upon a successful raising of revenue so that they are always a hostage to the more general fortunes of the state's finances. Moreover, those supporting privatisation as an economic policy more generally are usually conservative in economic outlook and will be prepared to sacrifice the RDP, and even to abandon it, whether privatisation is successful or not. In short, the RDP should take priority as an economic policy and not be made contingent upon a privatisation programme.

Moreover, the argument concerning privatisation as a source of potential funding is incorrect or, at least, fundamentally misguided. As is generally recognised, as far as state financing is concerned, privatisation merely substitutes one form of asset for another. In the ideal world of perfect capital markets, this should make no difference to the state's finances, although it could bear losses through the costs of privatisation itself and from selling shares in a large tranche, thereby depressing the sale price. In addition, the privatisation programme would inevitably be wasteful in transforming the state's physical assets into finance. The process of privatisation is itself expensive in terms of consultancy fees, advertising, share issues, etc and can cost up to 10% of the value of the revenue raised.[43] Experience suggests that in order to guarantee a successful privatisation, in terms of a complete and assured sale, the share

43 When Simpson McKie James Capel, a subsidiary of the Hong Kong and Shanghai Bank, was appointed as advisor on the restructuring of state assets to the South African Government in August 1996, the fee bandied about for a year's service was quoted by the *Financial Mail* as around R10 million.

price has to be set at a level below real worth, partly because most companies' shares are only sold piecemeal and not all at once. This is widely reflected in the immediate rise in a privatised company's shares following flotation, and has the effect of rewarding those who are already in the advantageous position of being able to afford to purchase shares, further consolidating inequality in wealth. Further, privatisations place unusually large demands upon financial markets and tend to crowd out the availability of finance for other investments.

In terms of switching a long-term physical asset into short-term finance, for example, it must be asked why the state is unable to raise such finance more readily and cheaply through more conventional methods of financing government expenditure such as by issuing a bond of the preferred time structure for repayment. The obvious answer is that the capital market is far from perfect. This does not imply, however, that privatisation is preferable as a means of raising finance. Doing so may worsen the market imperfections and their consequences. As has been witnessed in the case of developing countries, privatisation does not appear to improve the ability of government to raise finance, nor does it necessarily call forth or strengthen financial markets that are otherwise absent and, even if it does, the sequencing in doing so may not be ideal.

Such considerations do not apply to the South African financial system in the same way, but they are of relevance. South Africa has an extremely well-developed financial system, along the lines of developed countries, especially the UK model, in terms of the range of markets and institutions available. But it is marked by a number of features which are particularly relevant to the impact that might result from privatisation. Without going into details,[44] the South African financial system is deficient in the level and composition of investment that it generates for industry, and this is in part a consequence of its speculative and short-term orientation despite the conglomerate ownership of both industrial and financial corporations. The consequences of funding government expenditure or relieving government debt through privatising is liable to worsen this situation, since it will add nothing to real productive investment in the economy and it will add to the portfolio of assets around which there can be speculative activity.

The implications of this analysis are more far-reaching. It is to observe that government has presumed, irrespective of the merits on other grounds, that privatisation will have a positive impact upon the levels of domestic and foreign investment and on the functioning of the financial system, especially in so far as the funding of government expenditure and debt are concerned.

---

44 See the companion piece to this on industrial strategy (Fine, 1997a).

From a theoretical point of view, this can only be so if the financial markets are working imperfectly. For, if not, reorganisation of public and private finance would be best achieved through more direct methods, rather than through the indirect method of exchanging one form of asset for another. Consequently, the government's case must rest on the presence of market imperfections. No attempt, however, has been made to identify what these are and whether the financial consequences of privatisation will remedy or worsen them. The latter seems most likely given the deficiencies currently observable in the financial system as a source of investment for industry. Elsewhere, it has been argued that the financial system needs to be subject to critical public scrutiny for the role that it plays in raising finance for and monitoring and coordinating investment, in funding government expenditure, and in influencing macroeconomic policy more generally (Fine, 1997a). To these should be added the relationship between the public enterprises and the financial system. Further, all proposals for the restructuring of state assets, taken singly or as a programme, need to be fully assessed in terms of their impact upon the functioning of the financial system as a whole without presuming that advantages necessarily accrue directly or in net terms from the short-term flows of funds that result. Thus, a drawback of a privatisation programme is that it will strengthen what are already bloated institutions in South Africa dealing in the speculative buying and selling of financial assets. What is needed are financial institutions primarily geared to the raising and directing of funds into productive investment.

The role played by the financial system and the financial institutions within it, as argued, is not pre-determined but depends in part upon government policy towards it. But finance does not operate in a vacuum, merely responding to options for industrial investment according to their profitability. For the portfolio of possible options will depend upon the industrial policies adopted and the determination with which they are pursued. Here again, there are some positive features of the South African situation. Policy has not been contingent nor driven primarily by World Bank, market-led dogma. Plans for restructuring of state assets have, in principle, been sector and corporation specific and reviewed at some level of detail. In addition, such considerations have taken precedence over whether privatisation should be a preferred policy option and, if so, what form privatisation should take. The pursuit of joint ventures, to enhance technological capability, for example, and the retention of majority state ownership is a sensible way of proceeding subject to informed and hard bargaining, rather than handing over state assets in return for cash and then letting the private sector get on with it.

However, this still leaves open the substance of what is to be bargained and how it is to be bargained. This has a number of separate components (Fine,

1997a). First, there is the issue of the overall strategic vision of industrial policy of which the restructuring of state assets is a part. The priority must be the goals of the RDP, but these are increasingly being displaced by secondary or intermediate objectives, which have become primary targets of their own – most notably in the predominance of conservative macroeconomic policy. In addition, the goals of the RDP are themselves being weakened in so far as the highest priority to basic needs and redistribution is concerned. Accordingly, plans for restructuring state assets must specifically and explicitly account for the goals of the RDP, justify other intermediate criteria – such as commercial viability, export earnings, and employment creations – and ensure that outcomes are accountable in these respects.

Second, the strategic vision must itself go far beyond a set of goals and come to terms with key aspects of the economic and political realities of the South African economy. It needs to take account of the low levels of industrial investment, that its composition is skewed towards capital-intensive mega-projects, the poor level of export performance, low levels of formal skills amongst the workforce, the skewed distribution of infrastructure, and the limited capacity in intermediate and capital goods which has substantially constrained the ability to develop dynamic economies of scale and scope. On the other hand, South African conglomerates have long displayed a strategy of organising their productive and financial assets globally with an emphasis towards capital export for almost two decades. The restructuring of state assets needs to build upon the inherited strengths of the South African economy but also to address the continuing weaknesses and the causes that have created them.

To a large extent, third, this must be done through well-developed and more broadly informed but specific, case-by-case consideration for individual state enterprises in the context of a sectoral strategy. As mentioned, there are encouraging signs in so far as the DTI has proposed a supply-side policy which goes beyond privatisation alone and getting the prices right, and seeks to provide support for clusters of enterprises through a variety of mechanisms. But it is not clear that such welcome supply-side measures have gone far enough in a number of respects, nor that they are always taking precedence over more conventional market-led policies such as excessive trade liberalisation. For example, it is questionable whether sector strategy has been worked out, let alone implemented in sufficient detail – what are the plans and prospects for levels of investment, output, exports, employment, training, technological upgrading, coordination with other sectors, etc. Nor does government appear to have the capacity to undertake full social cost-benefit analysis of the impact of its plans for the restructuring of state assets with adequate weight given to RDP goals. Further, responsibility for state assets is fragmented across a number of ministries and departments so that the prospects for individual and collective strategic planning and implementation is limited. In most of the proposals for privatisation, it is notable that two crucial issues have been neglected. On the one hand, there is the issue of promoting economies of scope, i.e. horizontal and vertical integrations, as well as of economies of scale. How are the public utilities to be integrated with other sectors? On the other hand, there has been a total neglect of the extent to which privatised utilities will engage in financial speculation and internationalised acquisitions and mergers, rather than develop productive investments for the direct or indirect provision of basic needs within the domestic economy. This is especially true of Eskom, for example, given its already large-scale involvement in international financial markets.[45]

Fourth, then, whether in institutional or personnel terms, there must be doubts about the capacity of government to undertake privatisation and subsequent regulation in a way that maintains consistency with RDP goals and corresponding strategic and sectoral goals. This is, in part, simply a matter of existing administrative capacity.[46] But it has to be set against the power and resources of the corporate capital with which administration will be dealing and which will be pressing for commercial criteria alone within existing regulatory and administrative frameworks and for the transformation of those frameworks in the direction of commercial rather than social goals. Further, careful consideration must be given to whether the devotion of scarce resources to privatisation and regulation might not be better deployed in more extensive and efficient commitment to public enterprise and delivery, especially as this is generally deficient even where the public sector is not being considered for privatisation. The latter also has the effect of undermining the morale, ethos and motivation of the continuing public sector. This is of general importance but also of relevance to the pace and content of the privatisation process itself. IFIs and business interests exert a constant pressure for privatisation and can judge government economy policy accordingly. In order to meet demands for delivery of a privatisation programme, this may lead to privatisation being embarked upon before all options have been taken into account and properly

45 By way of examples, government proposals from the Ministry of Public Enterprises (1995) for the restructuring of state assets, Goldman and Sachs (1995) in its detailed promotional literature as a privatisation advisor, and Eskom's (1995) own submission on restructuring, all essentially overlook the issue of intersectoral and financial restructuring.

46 For some discussion of these points in the context of South African transport, see Roberts (1996). See also Makgetla (1995) for reservations about the institutional environment within which privatisation is being contemplated.

considered and before measures to ensure orderly and efficient restructuring have been put in place.

In short, privatisation is not itself a simple policy to implement, like buying or selling food in a supermarket. It requires that assets are fully identified and valued, that finance is raised, that the conditions under which the company will operate under private ownership should be determined, etc. These requirements mean that scarce resources and skills in management and government, etc will be commandeered to implement the privatisation programme when they could more usefully be used to implement the RDP directly. Interestingly, one of the first arguments used against renationalisation is the demands it would place upon the legislative programme of the government concerned. Exactly, the same applies to privatisation.

Finally, what is the likely impact of privatisation upon the redistribution of wealth? Evidence from around the world is that it leads to a further concentration of corporate control and even of ownership. This is despite the sweetener deals that might be used to solicit trade union and management support for the privatisation process itself. Besides, these schemes have certain drawbacks. Management tends to be disproportionately advantaged. Individual worker shareholdings and even those owned collectively by trade unions tend to come under the control of financial corporations. Such redistribution of shares is, in any case, highly skewed in so far as only those already in employment can benefit directly. This constitutes a minority and unrepresentative section of the population and workforce – those who have already benefited to a greater or lesser extent from state employment, thereby disproportionately excluding women, those in rural areas, the long-term unemployed, those employed non-commercially in the state sector, etc. Last, but by no means least, comparative evidence suggests that increases in productive efficiency do not depend as such upon employee or other participation in share-ownership but upon the greater participation of the workforce in day-to-day and strategic decision-making.[47] This participation may more easily and directly be achieved, and prosper, within public enterprise but, in any case, can and should be pursued independently of the form taken by the restructuring of state assets.

---

47 See Cable and Wilson (1989 and 1990) for example.

References

Abe, E. and R. Fitzgerald (eds) (1995) *The Origins of Japanese Industrial Power: Strategy, Institutions and the Development of Organisational Capability*, London: Frank Cass.

Adam, C., W. Cavendish, P. Mistry and J. Currey (1992) *Adjusting to Privatisation: Case Studies for Developing Countries*, London: James Curry Ltd.

Adelzadeh, A. (1996) "From the RDP to GEAR: the Gradual Embracing of Neo-Liberalism in Economic Policy", NIEP Occasional Paper Series, no 3, Johannesburg: National Institute for Economic Policy.

Adler, G. (1989) "Withdrawal Pains: General Motors and Ford Disinvest from South Africa", *South African Review*, vol 5, pp. 300–21.

Agenor, P. (1996) "The Labor Market and Economic Adjustment", *IMF Staff Papers*, vol 43, no 2, pp. 261–35.

AISI (1997) *Public Policy Statements: on behalf of Its US Producer Members*, Washington: American Iron and Steel Institute.

Aitken, M. and R. Wood (1989) "Employee Stock Ownership Plans: Issues and Evidence", *Journal of Industrial Relations*, vol 31, no 2, pp. 147–68.

Amin, A. and D. Thomas (1996) "The Negotiated Economy: State and Civic Institutions in Denmark", *Economy and Society*, vol 25, no 2, pp. 255–81.

Amsden, A. (ed.) (1994) "The World Bank's *The East Asian Miracle*: Economic Growth and Public Policy", special section, *World Development*, vol 22, no 4.

Anam, M., S.-H. Chiang and K. Shrestha (1996) "Dumping with Correlated Demand", *Southern Economic Journal*, vol 62, no 4, pp. 1072–78.

Anderson, G. and W. Block (1993) "Economic Response to a Guaranteed Annual Income: Experience from Canada and the United States: Comment", *Journal of Labor Economics*, vol 11, no 1, pp. 348–63.

Anderson, J. (1992) "Domino Dumping, I: Competitive Exporters", *American Economic Review*, vol 82, no 1, pp. 65–83.

Anderson, M. and J. Holmes (1995) "High-Skill, Low-Wage Manufacturing in North America – a Case Study from the Automotive Parts Industry", *Regional Studies*, vol 29, no 7, pp. 655–71.

Anderson, P. and P. Camiller (eds) (1994) *Mapping the West European Left*, London: Verso.

Anderson, S., N. Schmitt and J.-F. Thisse (1995) "Who Benefits from Antidumping Legislation?", *Journal of International Economics*, vol 38, no 3–4, pp. 311–37.

Andreff, W. and R. Frensch (eds) (1997) "Institutional Changes and Problems of Economic Adjustment", *Economic Systems*, vol 21, no 4, pp. 347–82.

Anon (n.d.) "Embargo Non-Implemented: 25 Years of South African Arms Procurement in the Shadow of the UN Arms Embargoes", mimeo.

Aoki, M. (1994) "Monitoring Characteristics of the Main Bank System: an Analytical and Developmental View", in Aoki and Patrick (eds) (1994), pp. 109–41.

Aoki, M. and H. Patrick (1994) "Introduction", in Aoki and Patrick (eds) (1994), pp. xxi–xxxii.

Aoki, M. and H. Patrick (eds) (1994) *The Japanese Main Bank System: Its Relevance for Developing and Transforming Economies*, Oxford: Oxford University Press.

Aoki, M., H. Patrick and P. Sheard (1994) "The Japanese Main Bank System: an Introductory Overview", in Aoki and Patrick (eds) (1994), pp. 3–50.

Arestis, P. and M. Sawyer (1994) *Handbook of Radical Political Economy*, Cheltenham: Edward Elgar.

Ashman, S., B. Fine and S. Newman (2010) "The Developmental State and Post-Liberation South Africa", in Misra-Dexter and February (eds) (2010), pp. 23–45.

Atkinson, A. (1987) "Income Maintenance and Social Insurance: a Survey", in Auerbach and Feldstein (eds) (1987), pp. 779–908.

Atkinson, A. (1995) "Capabilities, Exclusion, and the Supply of Goods", in Basu et al. (eds) (1995), pp. 17–31.

Auerbach, A. and M. Feldstein (eds) (1987) *Handbook of Public Economics*, vol II, Amsterdam: Elsevier.

Auty, R. (1993) *Sustaining Development in Mineral Economies: the Resource Curse Thesis*, London: Routledge.

Auty, R. (1994) "Industrial Policy Reform in Six Large Newly Industrialising Countries the Resource Curse Thesis", *World Development*, vol 22, no 1, pp. 11–26.

Azrak, P. and K. Wynne (1995) "Protectionism and Japanese Direct Investment in the United States", *Journal of Policy Modeling*, vol 17, no 3, pp. 293–305.

Baddon, L., L. Hunter, J. Leopold, J. Hyman and H. Ramsay (1989) *People's Capitalism: a Critical Analysis of Profit-Sharing and Employee Share Ownership*, London: Routledge.

Baer, W. (1996) "Changing Paradigms – Changing Interpretations of the Public Sector in Latin American Economies", *Public Choice*, vol 88, no 3–4, pp. 365–79.

Bailey, P., A. Parisotto and G. Renshaw (eds) (1993) *Multinationals and Employment: the Global Economy of the 1990s*, Geneva: ILO.

Baldwin, R. (1994) "The Impact of the 1986 US-Japan Semiconductor Agreement", *Japan and the World Economy*, vol 6, no 2, pp. 171–93.

Ball, N. (1989) *Security and Economy in the Third World*, London: Adamantine Press.

Barratt Brown, M. (ed.) (1989) *Conversion: Can We Really Disarm?*, Nottingham: Spokesman.

Barro, R. and X. Sala-i-Martin (1994) *Economic Growth*, New York: McGraw-Hill.

Basu, K., P. Pattanaik and K. Suzumura (eds) (1995) *Choice, Welfare, and Development: a Festschrift in Honour of Amartya K. Sen*, Oxford: Clarendon Press.

Bayliss, K. and B. Fine (1998) "Beyond *Bureaucrats in Business*: a Critical Review of the World Bank Approach to Privatisation and Public Sector Reform", *Journal of International Development*, vol 10, no 7, pp. 841–55.

Bayliss, K. and B. Fine (2020) "Financialisation and the Future for SOEs", in Bernier et al. (eds) (2020), pp. 354–71.

Bayliss, K. and B. Fine (2021) *A Guide to the Systems of Provision Approach: Who Gets What, How and Why*, Basingstoke: Palgrave MacMillan.

Bayliss, K. and B. Fine (eds) (2008) *Privatization and Alternative Public Sector Reform in Sub-Saharan Africa: Delivering on Electricity and Water*, London: Palgrave MacMillan.

Bayliss, K., B. Fine and M. Robertson (2016) "The Role of the State in Financialised Systems of Provision: Social Compacting, Social Policy, and Privatisation", FESSUD, Working Paper Series, no 154, https://fessud.org/wp-content/uploads/2015/03/Role-of-the-state-working-paper-154.pdf.

BDM (1996) "State Asset Restructuring: Development Finance Institutions", Report for submission to Naledi.

Belderbos, R. (1997) "Anti-Dumping and Tariff Jumping: Japanese Firms DFI in the European Union and the United States", *Weltwirtschaftliches Archiv*, vol 133, no 3, pp. 419–57.

Bell, T. (1993) "Should South Africa Further Liberalise Its Foreign Trade?", in Lipton and Simkins (eds) (1993), pp. 81–127.

Bell, T. (1997) "Trade Policy", in Michie and Padayachee (eds) (1997), pp. 71–90.

Bell, T. and N. Cattaneo (1997) "Foreign Trade and Employment in South African Manufacturing Industry", Employment and Training Department, Occasional Report, no 4, ILO: Geneva.

Bellin, E. (1994) "The Profits of Politics in Tunisia – the Utility of the Rentier Paradigm", *World Development*, vol 22, no 3, pp. 427–36.

Benner, A. and B. Jun (1996) "Employee Buy-Out in a Bargaining Game with Asymmetric Information", *American Economic Review*, vol 86, no 3, pp. 502–23.

Bennett, A. (1993) "Regulatory Framework for Privatised Monopolies", in *Methods and Practices of Privatisation*, UN Department for Development Support and Management Services, New York: UN.

Berg, E. (1994) *Privatisation in Sub-Saharan Africa: Results, Prospects and New Approaches*, Development Alternatives Inc, February, (World Bank).

Bernhofen, D. (1995) "Price Dumping in Intermediate Good Markets", *Journal of International Economics*, vol 39, no 1–2, pp. 159–73.

Bernier, L., M. Florio and P. Bance (eds) *Handbook on State-Owned Enterprises*, London: Routledge.

Beseler, J. and A. Williams (1986) *Anti-Dumping and Anti-Subsidy Law: the European Communities*, London: Sweet and Maxwell.

Besley, T. and S. Coate (1995) "The Design of Income Maintenance Programmes", *Review of Economic Studies*, vol 62, no 2, pp. 187–221.

Blanchflower, D. and A. Oswald (1987) "Profit-Sharing – Can It Work", *Oxford Economic Papers*, vol 39, no 1, pp. 1–19.

Blanchflower, D. and A. Oswald (1988) "Profit-Related Pay: Prose Discovered?", *Economic Journal*, vol 98, Sept, pp. 720–30.

Blinder, A. (ed.) (1990) *Paying for Productivity*, Washington: Brookings.

Blomstrom, M., A. Kokko and M. Zejan (1994) "Host Country Competition, Labor Skills, and Technology-Transfer by Multinationals", *Weltwirtschaftliches Archiv*, vol 130, no 3, pp. 521–33.

Blumberg, L. (1996) "South Africa", in Steele (ed.) (1996), pp. 213–26.

Board of Trade and Industries (1974) *Inquiry into the Collection, Marketing and Supply of Ferrous Scrap in the Republic of South Africa*, Report No 1974, Pretoria: Government Printer.

Boltuck, R. and R. Litan (1991) "America's 'Unfair' Trade Laws", in Boltuck and Litan (eds) (1991), pp. 1–22.

Boltuck, R. and R. Litan (eds) (1991) *Down in the Dumps: Administration of the US Unfair Trade Laws*, Washington: Brookings Institute.

Bond, P. et al. (1996) "A National Housing Agency and State-Centred, Market-Assisted Housing", a Report to Naledi, Cosatu, Fedsal and Nactu on the Restructuring of State Assets, NIEP.

Bond, S. and J. Jenkinson (1996) "The Assessment: Investment Performance and Policy", *Oxford Review of Economic Policy*, vol 12, no 2, pp. 1–27.

Bos, D. (1996) "Arguments on Privatization", in Yarrow and Jasinski (eds) (1996), volume 1, pp. 44–60, reproduced from *Privatization: a Theoretical Treatment*, Oxford: Clarendon Press, 1991.

Bourgeois, J. and P. Demaret (1995) "The Working of EC Policies on Competition, Industry and Trade: a Legal Analysis", in Buiges et al. (eds) (1995), pp. 65–114.

Bradley, K. and A. Gelb (1986) *Share Ownership for Employees*, Public Policy Centre: London.

Brannlund, R. and K. Lofgren (1995) "Cyclical Dumping and Correlated Business Cycles in Imperfect Markets: Empirical Applications to the Canadian Pulp and Paper Industry", *Applied Economics*, vol 27, no 11, pp. 1081–91.

Brautigam, D. (1994) "What Can Africa Learn from Taiwan – Political Economy, Industrial Policy, and Adjustment", *Journal of Modern African Studies*, vol 32, no 1, pp. 111–38.

Buckley, P. and J. Clegg (eds) (1991) *Multinational Enterprises in Less Developed Countries*, London: MacMillan.

Buiges, P., A. Jacquemin and A. Sapir (eds) (1995) *European Policies on Competition, Trade and Industry*, Aldershot: Edward Elgar.

Bureau, J. and N. Kalaitzandonakes (1995) "Measuring Effective Protection as a Superlative Index Number – an Application to European Agriculture", *American Journal of Agricultural Economics*, vol 77, no 2, pp. 279–90.

Business Bulletin (1996) "Steel Prices", Cape Chamber of Commerce and Industry, Issue no 30, 28th August.

Busumtwi-Sam, J. (1996) "Models of Economic Development in Africa: Lessons from the Experiences of Ghana, 1975–95", *Journal of Commonwealth and Comparative Politics*, vol 34, no 3, pp. 174–98.

Byerlee, D. and M. Morris (1993) "Calculating Levels of Protection Is It Always Appropriate to Use World Reference Prices Based on Current Trading Status?", *World Development*, vol 21, no 5, pp. 805–15.

Cable, J. (1985) "Capital Market Information and Industrial Performance: the Role of West German Banks", *Economic Journal*, vol 95, March, pp. 118–32.

Cable, J. (1988) "Is Profit-Sharing Participation? Evidence on Alternative Firm Types from West Germany", *International Journal of Industrial Organization*, vol 6, no 1, pp. 69–90, in Estrin et al. (eds) (1988).

Cable, J. and N. Wilson (1989) "Profit-Sharing and Productivity: an Analysis of UK Engineering Firms", *Economic Journal*, vol 99, June, pp. 366–75.

Cable, J. and N. Wilson (1990) "Profit-Sharing and Productivity: Some Further Evidence", *Economic Journal*, vol 100, June, pp. 550–55.

Callaghy, T. and J. Ravenhill (eds) (1993) *Hemmed in: Responses to Africa's Economic Decline*, New York: Columbia University Press.

Calvo, G., L. Leiderman and C. Reinhart (1994) "The Capital Inflows Problem – Concepts and Issues", *Contemporary Economic Policy*, vol 12, no 3, pp. 54–66.

Canoy, M. (1994) "Natural Monopoly and Differential Pricing", *Journal of Economics*, vol 59, no 3, pp. 287–309.

Cantwell, J. (ed.) (1992) *Multinational Investment in Modern Europe: Strategic Interaction in the Integrated Community*, Aldershot: Edward Elgar.

Capie, F. (1991) "Effective Protection and Economic Recovery in the United Kingdom during the 1930s", *Economic History Review*, vol 44, no 2, pp. 328–38.

Carim, X. (1994) "Some Trends in Foreign Direct Investment: Implications for South Africa", Southern African Perspectives Working Paper, no 34, University of Western Cape.

Caves, R. (1996) *Multinational Enterprises and Economic Analysis*, Cambridge: Cambridge University Press, second edition.

Cawthra, G. (1986) *Brutal Force: the Apartheid War Machine*, London: IDAF.

Chang, H.-J. (1994) *The Political Economy of Industrial Policy*, London: MacMillan.

Chang, H.-J. (1997) "The Economics and Political of Regulation", *Cambridge Journal of Economics*, vol 21, no 6, pp. 703–28.

Chang, H.-J. and A. Singh (1993) "Public Enterprises in Developing Countries and Economic Efficiency: a Critical Examination of Analytical, Empirical and Policy Issues", *UNCTAD Review*, no 4, pp. 45–82.

Cheng, L. and M. Kreinin (1996) "Supplier Preferences and Dumping: an Analysis of Japanese Corporate Groups", *Southern Economic Journal*, vol 63, no 1, pp. 51–59.

Cho, S. (1996) "The Power Industry in Korea: the Business Environment for the Participation of the Private Sector", *Energy Policy*, vol 24, no 5, pp. 471–76.

Church, R. (1971) "Profit-Sharing and Labour Relations in England in the Nineteenth Century", *International Review of Social History*, vol XVI, no 1, pp. 1–16.

Clark, N. (1994) *Manufacturing Apartheid: State Corporations in South Africa*, New Haven: Yale University Press.

Clarke, T. (1993) "The Political Economy of the UK Privatization Programme: a Blueprint for Other Countries?", in Clarke and Pitelis (eds) (1993), pp. 20–33.

Clarke, T. and C. Pitelis (eds) (1993) *The Political Economy of Privatization*, London: Routledge.

Cock, J. (1989) "Keeping the Fires Burning: Militarisation and the Politics of Gender in South Africa", *Review of African Political Economy*, no 45/6, pp. 50–64.

Cock, J. and L. Nathan (eds) (1989) *War and Society*, Cape Town & Johannesburg: David Philip.

Competition Board (1985) *Investigation into Collusion on Prices and Conditions, Market Sharing and Tender Practices*, Report No 15, Pretoria: Government Printer.

Competition Board (1989) *Investigation into Restrictive Practices and Monopoly Situations in the Gypsum Industry*, Report No 22, Pretoria: Government Printer.

Competition Board (1991) *Investigation into Allegations of Restrictive Practices by or Involving Pharmaceutical Wholesalers and Retail Pharmacies*, Report No 27, Pretoria: Government Printer.

Competition Board (1995) *Investigation into Restrictive Practices that Exist or May Come into Existence in the Distribution of One or More of the Following Products: Iron, Steel, Stainless Steel, Non-Ferrous Metals, Ferrous and Non-Ferrous Scrap Metals*, Report No 37, Pretoria: Government Printer.

Conway, P. and M. Bale (1988) "Approximating the Effective Protection Coefficient without Reference to Technological Data", *World Bank Economic Review*, vol 2, no 3, pp. 349–63.

Conyon, M. (1995) "Directors' Pay in the Privatized Utilities", *British Journal of Industrial Relations*, vol 33, no 2, pp. 159–71.

Cook, P. and C. Kirkpatrick (eds) (1988) *Privatisation in Less Developed Countries*, Brighton: Wheatsheaf.

Cook, P. and C. Kirkpatrick (eds) (1995) *Privatisation Policy and Performance: International Perspectives*, New York: Prentice Hall.

Corbett, J. (1987) "International Perspectives on Financing: Evidence from Japan", *Oxford Review of Economic Policy*, vol 3, no 4, pp. 30–55.

Corbett, J. and T. Jenkinson (1996) "The Financing of Industry, 1970–1989: an International Comparison", *Journal of the Japanese and International Economies*, vol 10, no 1, pp. 71–96.

Costello, N., J. Michie and S. Milne (1989) *Beyond the Casino Economy*, London: Verso.

Crandall, R. (1996) "From Competitiveness to Competition: the Threat of Minimills to Large National Steel Companies", *Resources Policy*, vol 22, nos 1/2, pp. 107–18.

Crankshaw, P. (1986) "Privatisation: No Answer for the Masses", *South African Labour Bulletin*, vol 11, no 6, pp. 35–36.

Creally, E. (1992) *Judicial Review of Anti-Dumping and Other Safeguard Measures in the European Community*, London: Butterworth.

Crompton, R. (1995) *An Industrial Strategy for the Commodity Plastics Sector*, Cape Town: UCT Press.

Currie, D. and R. Smith (eds) (1981) *Socialist Economic Review*, vol 1, London: Merlin Press.

Dale, R. (1980) *Anti-Dumping Law in a Liberal Trade Order*, London: MacMillan.

Dalgleish, K., P. Lawless and G. Vigar (1994) *Urban Innovation and Employment Generation: Environmental, Social and Economic Initiatives in European Towns and Cities*, European Foundation for the Improvement of Living and Working Conditions, Dublin, Luxembourg: Office for Official Publications of the European Community.

Damania, D. and J. Madsen (1995) "Monetary Policy and Macroeconomic Equilibrium in an Oligopolistic Economy", *Journal of Macroeconomics*, vol 17, no 4, pp. 651–65.

Damodaran, S., S. Gupta, S. Mitra and D. Sinha (eds) (2025) *Development, Transformations and the Human Condition: Volume in Honour of Professor Jayati Ghosh*, New Delhi: Routledge.

de Beer, Z. (1987) "Privatisation", in Jacobs (1987), pp. 91–107.

Deardoff, A. (1990) "Economic Perspectives on Anti-Dumping Law", in Jackson and Vermulst (eds) (1990), pp. 23–39.

Devault, J. (1996) "The Welfare Effects of US Antidumping Duties", *Open Economies Review*, vol 7, no 1, pp. 19–33.

Dhillon, U. and G. Ramirez (1994) "Employee Stock Ownership and Corporate Control – an Empirical Study", *Journal of Banking and Finance*, vol 18, no 1, pp. 9–26.

Didsbury, B. (1989) "Conversion and Jobs", in Barratt Brown (ed.) (1989), pp. 31–46.

Dornbusch, R. (1992) "The Case for Trade Liberalisation in Developing Countries", *Journal of Economic Perspectives*, vol 6, no 1, pp. 69–85.

Doucouliagos, C. (1995) "Worker Participation and Productivity in Labor-Managed and Participatory Capitalist Firms – a Meta-Analysis", *Industrial and Labor Relations Review*, vol 49, no 1, pp. 58–77.

DTI (1997) "Proposed Guidelines for Competition Policy: a Framework for Competition, Competitiveness and Development", Pretoria: Department of Trade and Industry, 27th November.

du Plessis, B. (1988) "One Step Forward", Interview with *Leadership*, vol 7, no 1, pp 12–17.

Duncan, C. (1988) "Why Profit Related Pay Will Fail", *Industrial Relations Journal*, vol 19, no 3, pp. 186–200.

Dunne, P. and R. Smith (1990) "Military Expenditure and Structural Adjustment", mimeo.

Dunning, J. (1992) "Multinational Investment in the EC: Some Policy Implications", in Cantwell (ed.) (1992), pp. 349–82.

Ebrahim, S. (2016) "Equal Pay for Work of Equal Value in Terms of the Employment Equity Act 55 of 1998: Lessons from the International Labour Organisation and the United Kingdom", *Potchefstroom Electronic Law Journal*, vol 19, PER 32, https://www.saflii.org/za/journals/PER/2016/32.html.

Edigheji, O. (ed.) (2010) *Constructing a Democratic Developmental State in South Africa: Potentials and Challenges*, Cape Town: Human Sciences Research Council Press.

Edwards, S. (1993) "Openness, Trade Liberalization, and Growth in Developing Countries", *Journal of Economic Literature*, vol XXXI, no 3, pp. 1358–93.

Eldor, R. (1984) "On the Risk-Adjusted Effective Protection Rate" *Review of Economics and Statistics*, vol 66, no 2, pp. 235–41.

Eldor, R. (1986) "The Effective Protection Rate under Uncertainty – a Note", *Economic Record*, vol 62, no 179, pp. 485–89.

EROSA (1989) "Employee Share Ownership Plans: Its Significance for South Africa", Economic Research on South Africa, mimeo. See Chapter 2.

EROSA (1990) "Employee Share Ownership: an Update", Economic Research on South Africa, mimeo. See Chapter 2.

Eskom (1995) "Restructuring of State Owned Enterprises, with Special Emphasis on the Energy Industry and on Eskom", Submission by Eskom's Management Board to the Portfolio Committee on Public Enterprises.

Estrin, S., P. Geroski and G. Stewart (eds) (1988) "Employee Share Ownership, Profit-Sharing and Participation", Special Issue of *International Journal of Industrial Organization*, vol 6, no 1, pp. 1–154.

Estrin, S. and S. Wadhwani (1986) *Will Profit-Sharing Work?*, London: Employment Institute.

Ettori, F. (1992) "Measure and Interpretation of Effective Protection in the Presence of High Capital Costs: Evidence from India", Policy Research paper, no 873, World Bank.

Falkena, H., L. Fourie and W. Kok (eds) (1995) *The South African Financial System*, Halfway House: Southern Book Publishers.

Fine, B. (1987) "Segmented Labour Market Theory: a Critical Assessment", Birkbeck Discussion Papers in Economics, no 87/12.

Fine, B. (1989a) "Privatisation of the Electricity Supply Industry: Broadening the Debate", *Energy Policy*, vol 17, no 3, pp. 24–32.

Fine, B. (1989b) "Privatisation", in Green (ed.) (1989), pp. 225–41.

Fine, B. (1990a) *The Coal Question: Political Economy and Industrial Change from the Nineteenth Century to the Present Day*, London: Routledge.

Fine, B. (1990b) "Scaling the Commanding Heights of Public Sector Economics", *Cambridge Journal of Economics*, vol 14, no 2, pp. 127–42.

Fine, B. (1990c) "Segmented Labour Market Theory: a Critical Assessment", *Thames Papers in Political Economy*.

Fine, B. (1993a) "Economic Development and Technological Change: from Linkage to Agency" in G. Liodakis (ed.) *Society, Technology and Restructuring of Production*, Athens: V. Papazissis, (in Greek), October, 1993, pp. 111–30, previously SOAS Working Paper, no 14, March 1992.

Fine, B. (1993b) "The Military-Industrial Complex: an Analytical Assessment", *Cyprus Journal of Economics*, vol 6, no 1, pp. 1–26.

Fine, B. (1993c) "Segmented Labour Market Theory and Flexible Specialisation: a Critical Assessment", *Thesis*, no 43, pp. 107–21, translated into Greek.

Fine, B. (1994a) "'Politics and Economics in ANC Economic Policy': an Alternative Assessment", *Transformation*, no 25, pp. 19–33.

Fine, B. (1994b) "Segmented Labour Market Theory", in Arestis and Sawyer (eds), pp. 346–49.

Fine, B. (1995a) "Privatisation and the RDP: a Critical Assessment", *Transformation*, no 27, pp. 1–23. See Chapter 4.

Fine, B. (1995b) "'Politics and Economics in ANC Economic Policy': an Alternative Assessment", *Transformation*, no 25, pp. 19–33.

Fine, B. (1995c) "Flexible Production and Flexible Theory: the Case of South Africa", *Geoforum*, no 26, no 2, pp. 107–19.

Fine, B. (1996a) "Some Perspectives on the Provision of Social and Economic Infrastructure", https://eprints.soas.ac.uk/32961/.

Fine, B. (1996b) "A Formal Note on New Theories of International Trade and Development", *Journal of International Development*, vol 8, no 6, pp. 805–11.

Fine, B. (1997a) "Industrial Policy and South Africa: a Strategic View", NIEP Occasional Paper Series, no 5, pp. 1–71, Johannesburg, National Institute for Economic Policy. See Chapter 6.

Fine, B. (1997b) "Vertical Relations in the South African Steel Industry", NIEP Occasional Paper Series, no 13, Johannesburg: National Institute for Economic Policy, originally a report for NUMSA Investment Company, December. See Chapter 7.

Fine, B. (1997c) "Privatisation and the Restructuring of State Assets in South Africa: a Strategic View", NIEP Occasional Paper Series, no 7, Johannesburg, National Institute for Economic Policy. See Chapter 8.

Fine, B. (1997d) "Industrial and Energy Policy", in Michie and Padayachee (eds) (1997), pp. 125–53.

Fine, B. (1997e) "Privatisation: Theory and Lessons from the UK and South Africa", *Seoul Journal of Economics*, vol 10, no 4, pp. 373–414.

Fine, B. (1998a) *Labour Market Theory: a Constructive Reassessment*, London: Routledge, listed as forthcoming in original drafts under a different title, reprinted in paperback, 2010.

Fine, B. (1998b) *The Political Economy of Diet, Health and Food Policy*, London: Routledge, reprinted as Routledge Revival, 2013.

Fine, B. (1999a) "Privatization: Theory with Lessons from the United Kingdom", in A. Vlachou (ed.) (1999), pp. 41–66.

Fine, B. (1999b) "Competition and Market Structure Reconsidered", *Metroeconomica*, vol 50, no 2, pp. 194–218.

Fine, B. (2000) "ESOP's Fable: Golden Egg or Sour Grapes?", in Toporowski (ed.) (2000), pp. 179–93.

Fine, B. (2003) "Beyond the Developmental State: towards a Political Economy of Development", in Hirakawa et al. (eds) (2003), (in Japanese), pp. 21–43, with English version in Lapavitsas and Noguchi (eds) (2005), pp. 17–33.

Fine, B. (2007) "State, Development and Inequality: the Curious Incidence of the Developmental State in the Night-Time", paper presented to Sanpad Conference, Durban, June 26–30, www.networkideas.org/ideasact/jan09/PDF/Fine.pdf.

Fine, B. (2010a) "Can South Africa Be a Developmental State?", in Edigheji (ed.) (2010), pp. 169–82.

Fine, B. (2010b) "The Developmental State?", in Maharaj et al. (eds) (2010), pp. 101–24.

Fine, B. (2011) "Locating the Developmental State and Industrial and Social Policy after the Crisis", UNCTAD, The Least Developed Countries Report 2011: *The Potential Role of South-South Cooperation for Inclusive and Sustainable Development*, Background Paper, no 3, https://eprints.soas.ac.uk/13440/3/Fine_unctadnotrack.pdf.

Fine, B. (2013a) "Beyond the Developmental State: an Introduction", in Fine et al. (eds) (2013), pp. 1–32.

Fine, B. (2013b) "Beyond the Developmental State", *African Communist*, no 186, pp. 40–54.

Fine, B. (2016a) *Microeconomics: a Critical Companion*, London: Pluto.

Fine, B. (2016b) "Across Developmental State and Social Compacting: the Peculiar Case of South Africa", ISER Working Paper, no 2016/1, Grahamstown: Institute of

Social and Economic Research, Rhodes University, https://eprints.soas.ac.uk/34148/1/iserwp.pdf.

Fine, B. (2020) "Situating PPPs", in Gideon and Unterhalter (eds) (2020), pp. 26–38.

Fine, B. (2022) "The Enigma of the Post-Apartheid Economic Transition: Insights from the Fate of MERG and a Personal Journey", mimeo, to appear in third forthcoming Volume on South Africa.

Fine, B. (2023) "Discrimination through Bargaining Structures: Gender Bias in the National Coal Board and British Coal", *Historical Studies in Industrial Relations*, vol 44, no 1, pp. 63–74.

Fine, B. (2024a) *Economics Imperialism and Interdisciplinarity: before the Watershed; Critical Reconstructions of Political Economy*, Volume 1, Leiden: Brill, and Chicago: Haymarket.

Fine, B. (2024b) *Economics Imperialism and Interdisciplinarity: the Watershed and After; Critical Reconstructions of Political Economy*, Volume 2, Leiden: Brill, and Chicago: Haymarket.

Fine, B. (2024c) *Cliometrics as Economics Imperialism: across the Watershed; Critical Reconstructions of Political Economy*, Volume 3, Leiden: Brill, and Chicago: Haymarket.

Fine, B. (2025a) *The Financialisation of Social Reproduction in the Age of Neoliberalism: from Theory to Case Studies; Critical Reconstructions of Political Economy*, Volume 4, Leiden Brill, with K. Bayliss, M. Robertson and A. Saad-Filho.

Fine, B. (2025b) *In and against Development: from New to Newest Development Economics: Critical Reconstructions of Political Economy*, Volume 5, Leiden: Brill.

Fine, B. (2025c) *In and against Development: the World Bank behind the Looking Glass: Critical Reconstructions of Political Economy*, Volume 6, Leiden: Brill.

Fine, B. (2025d) "Social Capital: the Indian Connection", in Damodaran et al. (eds) (2025), pp. 54–67.

Fine, B. and O. Dimakou (2016) *Macroeconomics: a Critical Companion*, London: Pluto.

Fine, B. and D. Hall (2012) "Terrains of Neoliberalism: Constraints and Opportunities for Alternative Models of Service Delivery", McDonald and Ruiters (eds) (2012), pp. 45–70.

Fine, B. and L. Harris (1985) *The Peculiarities of the British Economy*, London: Lawrence and Wishart.

Fine, B., M. Heasman and J. Wright (1996) *Consumption in the Age of Affluence: the World of Food*, London: Routledge.

Fine, B. and E. Leopold (1993) *The World of Consumption*, London: Routledge.

Fine, B. and S. Mohamed (2023) "Locating Industrial Policy in Developmental Transformation: Lessons from the Past, Prospects for the Future", in Mohamed et al. (eds), pp. 22–58, shortened version under same title of SOAS Department of Economics Working Paper, no 246, 2022.

Fine, B. and K. O'Donnell (1981) "The Nationalised Industries", in Currie and Smith (eds) (1981), pp. 265–86.

Fine, B. and K. O'Donnell (1985) "The Nationalised Industries", in Fine and Harris (1985), pp. 147–66.

Fine, B. and C. Poletti (1992) "Industrial Policy in the Light of Privatisation", in Michie (ed.) (1992), pp. 315–29.

Fine, B. and G. Pollen (2018) "The Developmental State Paradigm in the Age of Financialisation", in Hyland and Munck (eds) (2018) pp. 211–27.

Fine, B. and Z. Rustomjee (1996) *South Africa's Political Economy: from Minerals-Energy Complex to Industrialisation*, Johannesburg: Wits University Press.

Fine, B., J. Saraswati and D. Tavasci (eds) (2013) *Beyond the Developmental State: Industrial Policy into the 21st Century*, London: Pluto.

Fine, B. and C. Stoneman (1996) "Introduction: State and Development", *Journal of Southern African Studies*, vol 22, no 1, pp. 5–26.

Fine, B. and E. Van Waeyenberge (2013) "A Paradigm Shift that Never Was: Justin Lin's New Structural Economics", *Competition and Change*, vol 17, no 4, pp. 355–71; for longer version, "A Paradigm Shift that Never Will Be?: Justin Lin's New Structural Economics", with E. Van Waeyenberge, SOAS Department of Economics Working Paper Series, no 179, 2013, http://www.soas.ac.uk/economics/research/working papers/file81928.pdf.

Finger, J. (1991) "The Meaning of 'Unfair' in US Import Policy", Trade Policy Working Paper, No 745, World Bank.

Finger, J. (1993) (ed.) *Antidumping: How It Works and Who Gets Hurt*, Ann Arbor: University of Michigan Press.

Fontaine, J.-M. and V. Geronimi (1995) "Private Investment and Privatisation in sub-Saharan Africa", in Cook and Kirkpatrick (eds) (1995), pp. 139–61.

Fors, G. (1991) "Stainless Steel in Sweden: Antidumping Attacks Good International Citizenship", World Bank, Policy, Research, and External Affairs Working Papers, no 744, reproduced in Finger (ed.) (1993), pp. 137–62.

Frankel, P. (1984) *Pretoria's Praetorians: Civil-Military Relations in South Africa*, Cambridge: Cambridge University Press.

Galal, A., L. Jones, P. Tandon and I. Vogelsang (1992) *Welfare Consequences of Selling Public Enterprises: Case Studies from Chile, Malaysia, Mexico, and the UK*, Washington: World Bank.

Gallett, C. (1997) "Cyclical Fluctuations and Coordination in the US Steel Industry", *Applied Economics*, vol 29, no 3, pp. 279–86.

Garner, J. (1993) "Determinants of Recent Direct Investment Flows to South Africa", LSE Centre for the Study of the South African Economy and International Finance, Research Paper, no 8.

Gianaris, N. (1996) *Modern Capitalism: Privatization, Employee Ownership, and Industrial Democracy*, Westport: Connecticut.

Gideon, J. and E. Unterhalter (eds) (2020) *Critical Reflections on Public Private Partnerships*, London: Routledge.

Glais, M. (1995) "Steel Industry", in Buiges et al. (eds) (1995), pp. 219–59.

GLC (1985a) *The London Industrial Strategy*, London: Greater London Council.

GLC (1985b) "Arms Conversion", in GLC (1985a), pp. 285–312.

GLC (1986) *The London Labour Plan*, London: Greater London Council.

Goldman Sachs International (1995) "Public Sector Restructuring", March.

Green, F. (ed.) (1989) *Restructuring the British Economy*, Brighton: Harvester.

Greenaway, D. and C. Milner (1987) "Effective Protection and Intra-Industry Trade Some Positive and Normative Issues", *Journal of Economic Issues*, vol 14, no 5, pp. 38–53.

Grosh, B. and R. Mukandala (1994) "Tying It All Together: What Do We Know?", in Grosh and Mukandala (eds) (1994), pp. 245–252.

Grosh, B. and R. Mukandala (eds) (1994) *State-Owned Enterprises in Africa*, Boulder: Lynne Rienner.

Grossman, S. and O. Hart (1986) "The Costs and Benefits of Ownership: a Theory of Vertical and Lateral Integration", in Yarrow and Jasinski (eds) (1996), volume 1, pp. 61–88, reproduced from *Journal of Political Economy*, vol 94, no 4, 1986, pp. 691–719.

Grunberg, L., S. Moore and E. Greenberg (1996) "The Relationship of Employee Ownership and Participation to Workplace Safety", *Economic and Industrial Democracy*, vol 17, no 2, pp. 221–41.

Grundy, K. (1988) *The Militarization of South African Politics*, Oxford: Oxford University Press.

Gual, J. (1995) "The Three Common Policies: an Economic Analysis", in Buiges et al. (eds) (1995), pp. 3–48.

Haddad, M. and A. Harrison (1993) "Are There Positive Spillovers from Direct Foreign Investment? Evidence from Panel Data for Morocco", *Journal of Development Economics*, vol 42, no 1, pp. 51–74.

Haggard, S. and R. Kaufman (eds) (1992) *The Politics of Economic Adjustment*, Princeton: Princeton University Press.

Haggard, S. and S. Webb (1993) "What Do We Know about the Political Economy of Economic Policy Reform", *The World Bank Research Observer*, vol 8, no 2, pp. 143–68.

Haque, M. (1996) "The Public Service under Challenge in the Age of Privatization", *Governance*, vol 9, no 2, pp. 186–216.

Harris, J. (1994) "Manual Wage Differentials, Collective Bargaining and Multilocational Firms – an Analysis Using Northern Ireland NES Data", *Regional Studies*, vol 28, no 5, pp. 483–93.

Harris, L. (1994) "Financing Post Apartheid South Africa: Theoretical Aspects", SOAS Discussion Paper, no 46, University of London.

Harriss, J., J. Hunter and C. Lewis (eds) (1995) *The New Institutional Economics and Third World Development*, London: Routledge.

Hartigan, J. (1994) "Dumping and Signaling", *Journal of Economic Behavior and Organization*, vol 23, no 1, pp. 69–81.

Hartigan, J. (1996) "Perverse Consequences of the GATT: Export Subsidies and Switching Costs", *Economica*, vol 63, no 249, pp. 153–61.

Hatton, T. (1988) "Profit-sharing in British Industry, 1865–1913", *International Journal of Industrial Organization*, vol 6, no 1, pp. 69–90, in Estrin et al. (eds) (1988).

Havenga, M. (1996) "South African Trade Policy", Sandton: IDC, August, mimeo.

Helleiner, G. (ed.) (1994) *Trade Policy and Industrialization in Turbulent Times*, London: Routledge.

Helleiner, G. (ed.) (1995) *Manufacturing for Export in the Developing World: Problems and Possibilities*, London: Routledge.

Hemming, E. and N. Unnithan (1996) "Determinants of Privatization Levels in Developing Countries", *Social Science Quarterly*, vol 77, no 2, pp. 434–44.

Henley, J. (1993) "Privatisation in Africa: Prospects for Tanzania", in Clarke and Pitelis (eds) (1993), pp. 455–76.

Hirakawa, H., M. Noguchi and M. Sano (eds) (2003) *Beyond Market-Driven Development: A New Stream of Political Economy of Development*, Tokyo: Nihon Hyoron Sha, in Japanese.

HMSO (1986) *Profit Related Pay: a Consultative Document*, London, Cmnd 9835.

Hoekman, B. and P. Mavroidis (1996) "Dumping, Antidumping and Antitrust", *Journal of World Trade*, vol 30, no 1, pp. 27–52.

Hofmeyr, M. (1988) "Who Dares Wins", Interview with *Leadership*, vol 7, no 2, pp. 6–10.

Hogan, W. (1983) *World Steel in the 1980s: a Case of Survival*, Lexington: Lexington Books.

Hogan, W. (1991) *Global Steel in the 1990s: Growth or Decline*, Lexington: Lexington Books.

Hogan, W. (1994) *Steel in the 21st Century: Competition Forges a New World Order*, New York: Lexington Books.

Holden, M. (1993) "Lessons for South Africa from the New Growth and Trade Theories", *South African Journal of Economics*, vol 61, no 4, pp. 215–28.

Holden, M. et al. (1996) "Trade and Industrial Policy and Competition", AIPSA Project, Economic Policy Reform in South Africa, Economic Research Unit, University of Natal, Durban, mimeo.

Holmes, T. (1996) "Can Consumers Benefit from a Policy Limiting the Market Share of a Dominant Firm?", *International Journal of Industrial Organisation*, vol 14, no 3, pp. 365–87.

Hooker, L. (2024) "'We Did It!' Next Shop Workers Win Equal Pay Claim", BBC News, August 27th, https://www.bbc.co.uk/news/articles/cj0817jd9dqo.

Hoshino, T. (1996) "Privatization of Mexico's Public Enterprises and the Restructuring of the Private Sector", *Developing Economies*, vol 34, no 1, pp. 34–60.

Hum, D. and W. Simpson (1993) "Economic Response to a Guaranteed Annual Income: Experience from Canada and the United States", *Journal of Labor Economics*, vol 11, no 1, pp. S263–S96.

Hyland, M. and R. Munck (eds) (2018) *Handbook on Development and Social Change*, Cheltenham: Edward Elgar.

IDC (1990) *Modification of the Application of Protection Policy: Policy Document*, Sandton: Industrial Development Corporation.

IDC (1997a) "Automotive Body Pressing Mini-Cluster", Cluster Paper Series, CS1/97, Sandton: IDC.

IDC (1997b) "Structural Steel Mini-Cluster Volume I – Industry Analysis", Cluster Paper Series, CS2/97, Sandton: IDC.

IDC (1997c) "Structural Steel Mini-Cluster Volume II – Benchmarking Results", Cluster Paper Series, CS3/97, Sandton: IDC.

IDC (1997d) "Wire and Wire Products Mini-Cluster Study", Cluster Paper Series, CS4/97, Sandton: IDC.

ILO (1996) *Restructuring the Labour Market: the South African Challenge – an ILO Country Review*, Geneva: ILO, co-authored by Guy Standing, John Sender and John Weeks.

Ingham, G. (1988) "Commercial Capital and British Development a Reply", *New Left Review*, no 172, pp. 45–65.

Innes, D. (1987) "Privatisation: the Solution", *South African Review*, vol 4, pp. 551–67.

ISP (A. Joffe, D. Kaplan, R. Kaplinsky and D. Lewis) (1995) *Improving Manufacturing Performance in South Africa: Report of the Industrial Strategy Project*, Cape Town: UCT Press.

ITAC (2022) "International Trade Administration Commission of South Africa Annual Performance Plan, 2022/2023", February 2022, https://www.thedtic.gov.za/wp-content/uploads/ITAC-APP-2022-2023.pdf.

Itagaki, T. (1983) "Multinational Firms and the Theory of Effective Protection", *Oxford Economic Papers*, vol 35, no 3, pp. 447–62.

ITC (1997a) "Circular Welded Non-Alloy Steel Pipe from Romania and South Africa", Report of United States International Trade Commission, Investigations Nos 731-TA-732 and 733 (Final), Report for hearings held in Washington, 14th May.

ITC (1997b) "Cut-to-Length Carbon Steel Plate from China, Russia, South Africa, and Ukraine", Report of United States International Trade Commission, Investigations Nos 731-TA-753 (Preliminary), Report for hearings held in Washington, 26th November.

Jack, A. (1991) "ESOPs in South Africa: a Critical Assessment", mimeo.

Jackson, J. and E. Vermulst (eds) (1990) *Anti-Dumping Law and Practice*, Ann Arbor: University of Michigan.

Jackson, P., P. Russell and N. Ward (2004) "Commodity Chains and the Politics of Food", Cultures of Consumption Working Paper Series, no 18, retrieved from http://www.consume.bbk.ac.uk/publications.html.

Jacobs, G. ed (1987) *South Africa: the Road Ahead*, Jonathan Ball: Bergvlei.

Jasinski, P. and G. Yarrow (1996) "Privatization: an Overview of the Issues", in Yarrow and Jasinski (eds) (1996), volume 1, pp. 1–48.

Jenkins, R. (1995) "The Political Economy of Industrial Policy – Automobile Manufacture in the Newly Industrialising Countries", *Cambridge Journal of Economics*, vol 19, no 5, pp. 625–45.

Jones, D. and T. Kato (1993a) "The Scope, Nature, and Effects of Employee Stock Ownership Plans in Japan", *Industrial and Labor Relations Review*, vol 46, no 2, pp. 352–67.

Jones, D. and T. Kato (1993b) "Employee Stock Ownership Plans and Productivity in Japanese Manufacturing Firms", *British Journal of Industrial Relations*, vol 31, no 3, pp. 331–46.

Kap-Young, J. (1997) "A Product of Political-Business Nexus", *Korea Focus*, vol 5, no 1, pp. 117–19.

Kasrils, R. (2013) "How the ANC's Faustian Pact Sold out South Africa's Poorest", *Black Agenda Report*, 26 June, https://blackagendareport.com/content/how-ancs-faustian-pact-sold-out-south-africas-poorest.

Kaufman, R. and R. Russell (1995) "Government Support for Profit-Sharing, Gainsharing, ESOPs, and TQM", *Contemporary Economic Policy*, vol 13, no 2, pp. 38–48.

Keizer, W. (1997) "Negotiations on Harmonized Non-Preferential Rules of Origin – a Useless Task from a Trade Policy Perspective?", *Journal of World Trade*, vol 31, no 4, pp. 145–51.

Key Note (1996) *The Steel Industry: 1996 Market Report*, London: Key Note Publications.

Khan, M. (1996) "The Efficiency Implications of Corruption", *Journal of International Development*, vol 8, no 5, pp. 683–96.

Kikeri, S., J. Nellis and M. Shirley (1994) "Privatisation: Lessons from Market Economies", *World Bank Research Observer*, vol 9, no 2, pp. 241–72.

Kipping, M. (1995) "Industrial Policy and Inter-Firm Relations: the French Steel Producers and Users in Historical and Comparative Perspective", University of Reading Discussion Paper, no 312, Series A, Vol VIII (1995/96).

Kirkpatrick, C. and J. Weiss (1995) "Trade Policy Reforms and Performance in Africa in the 1980s", *Journal of Modern African Studies*, vol 33, no 2, pp. 285–98.

Kitson, M. and J. Michie (1995) "Conflict, Cooperation, and Change: the Political Economy of Trade and Trade Policy", *Review of International Political Economy*, vol 2, no 4, pp. 632–57.

Kitson, M., S. Solomou and M. Weale (1991) "Effective Protection and Economic Recovery in Britain, 1932–1937", *Economic History Review*, vol 44, no 2, pp. 339–42.

Kleu Report (1983) *Report of the Study Group on Industrial Development Strategy*, Pretoria: Government Printer.

Knutsen, S. (1997) "Post-War Strategic Capitalism in Norway: a Theoretical and Analytical Framework", *Business History*, vol 39, no 4, pp. 106–27.

Koechlin, T. (1995) "The Globalization of Investment", *Contemporary Economic Policy*, vol 13, no 1, pp. 92–100.

Kokko, A. and M. Blomstrom (1995) "Inward Technology-Transfer and Competitiveness – the Foreign Multinationals", *World Development*, vol 46, no 1, pp. 109–22.

Konopelko, E. (2023) *Factors behind the Introduction and Design of a National Minimum Wage Policy: with Application to South Africa*, unpublished Phd, SOAS University of London.

Krugman, P. and A. Smith (eds) (1994) *Empirical Studies of Strategic Trade Policy*, Chicago: Chicago University Press.

Krupp, C. (1994) "Antidumping Cases in the US Chemical Industry: a Panel Data Approach", *Journal of Industrial Economics*, vol 42, no 3, pp. 299–311.

Kruse, D. (1996) "Why Do Firms Adopt Profit-Sharing and Employee Ownership Plans", *British Journal of Industrial Relations*, vol 34, no 4, pp. 515–38.

Kumar, N. (1994) "Determinants of Export Orientation of Foreign Production by United States Multinationals – an Inter-Country Analysis", *Journal of International Business Studies*, vol 25, no 1, pp. 141–56.

Kumssa, A. (1996) "The Political Economy of Privatization in Sub-Saharan Africa", *International Review of Administrative Sciences*, vol 62, no 1, pp. 75–87.

Landgren, S. (1989) *Embargo Disimplemented: South Africa's Military Industry*, Oxford: Oxford University Press.

Lapavitsas, C. (1997) "Transition and Crisis in the Japanese Financial System: an Analytical Overview", *Capital and Class*, vol 21, no 2, pp. 21–47.

Laussel, D. and C. Montet (1995) "The Three Common Policies: an Economic Analysis, Discussion", in Buiges et al. (eds) (1995), pp. 49–64.

Leidy, M. (1994) "Trade Policy and Indirect Rent Seeking: a Synthesis of Recent Work", *Economics and Politics*, vol 6, no 2, pp. 97–118.

Leidy, M. (1997) "Macroeconomic Conditions and Pressures for Protection under Antidumping and Countervailing Duty Laws: Evidence from the United States", *IMF Staff Papers*, vol 44, no 1, pp. 132–44.

Lenway, S., R. Morck and B. Yeung (1996) "Rent-Seeking, Protectionism and Innovation in the American Steel Industry", *Economic Journal*, vol 106, no 435, pp. 410–21.

Leslie, D. and S. Reimer (1999) "Spatializing Commodity Chains", *Progress in Human Geography*, vol 23, no 3, pp. 401–20.

Letwin, O. (1988) "International Experience in the Politics of Privatisation" in Walker (ed.) (1988), pp. 49–60.

Levinsohn, J. (1994) "International Trade and the US Automobile Industry – Current Research, Issues and Questions", *Japan and the World Economy*, vol 6, no 4, pp. 335–57.

Lewis, P. (1994) "Development Strategy and State Sector Expansion in Nigeria", in Grosh and Mukandala (eds) (1994), pp. 63–82.

Lin, J. (2012) *New Structural Economics: a Framework for Rethinking Development and Policy*, Washington: World Bank, http://siteresources.worldbank.org/DEC/Resources/84797-1104785060319/598886-1104951889260/NSE-Book.pdf.

Liodakis, G. (ed.) (1993) *Society, Technology and Restructuring of Production*, Athens: V. Papazissis.

Lipton, M. and C. Simkins (eds) (1993) *State and Market in Post-Apartheid South Africa*, Johannesburg: Wits University Press.

LMC (1996) *Restructuring the South African Labour Market: Report of the Presidential Commission to Investigate Labour Market Policy*, Pretoria: Government Printer.

Mabathoana, M. (2019) "A Comparative Study on the Principles of Equal Pay for Equal Work in South Africa in the Context of Gender Discrimination", dissertation accepted in partial fulfilment of the requirements for the degree Magister Legum at the North-West University.

Madsen, J. (1995) "Inflation and Aggregate Demand Shocks", *Journal of Policy Modeling*, vol 17, no 6, pp. 659–66.

Mahadea, D. (1988) "Returning the State's Assets to the Private Sector: a Review of the Case for Privatisation", *Development Southern Africa*, vol 5, no 2, pp. 142–54.

Maharaj, B., A. Desai and P. Bond (eds) (2010) *Zuma's Own Goal: Losing South Africa's 'War on Poverty'*, Trenton, NJ: Africa World Press, Inc.

Majumdar, S. (1996) "Government Policies and Industrial Performance: an Institutional Analysis of the Indian Experience", *Journal of Institutional and Theoretical Economics*, vol 152, no 2, pp. 380–411.

Makgetla, N. (1995) "The New Privatisation Debate", Research Report, January.

Maller, J. (1987) "Employee Share-Ownership – South Africa's New Capitalists?", *South African Labour Bulletin*, vol 12, no 8, pp. 50–59.

Maller, J. (1988) *ESOP's Fables*, Johannesburg: LERC.

Maller, J. (1989a) "Worker Participation – Reply to Martin Nicol", *South African Labour Bulletin*, vol 14, no 1, pp. 97–103.

Maller, J. (1989b) "Employee Share Ownership: Co-option or Co-operation", *South African Review*, vol 5, pp. 348–56.

Marceau, G. (1994) *Anti-Dumping and Anti-Trust Issues in Free-Trade Areas*, Oxford: Clarendon Press.

Marchionatti, R. and S. Usai (1997) "Voluntary Export Restraints, Dumping and Excess Capacity", *Manchester School of Economic and Social Studies*, vol LXV, no 5, pp. 499–512.

Matiko, J. (1988) "SAMCOR – Workers Strike Against Share Ownership", *South African Labour Bulletin*, vol 13, no 6, pp. 24–38.

Matthews, D. (1989) "The British Experience of Profit-Sharing", *Economic History Review*, vol XLII, no 4, pp. 439–64.

Matthews, R. (1988) "The Development of the South African Military-Industrial Complex", *Defense Analysis*, vol 4, no 1, pp. 7–24.

Matthews, R. (1989) "The ARMSCOR Paradox", *RUSI Journal*, vol 134, no 4, pp. 40–46.

Mayer, C. (1987) "The Assessment: Financial Systems and Corporate Investment", *Oxford Review of Economic Policy*, vol 3, no 4, pp. i–xvi.

Mayer, C. (1988) "New Issues in Corporate Finance", *European Economic Review*, vol 32, no 4, pp. 1167–89.

Mazzucato, M. and S. Gasperin (2023) "Transforming the System of SoEs in South Africa: towards a Mission-Oriented State Holding Company", IIPP Policy Brief, no 27, Institute for Innovation and Public Purpose, University College, London, https://www.ucl.ac.uk/bartlett/public-purpose/publications/2023/nov/transforming-system-soes-south-africa-towards-mission-oriented-state-holding.

McChesney, F. (1997) "The Role of Economists in Modern Anti-Trust: an Overview and Summary", *Managerial and Decision Economics*, vol 17, no 2, pp. 119–26.

McDonald, D. and G. Ruiters (eds) (2012) *Alternatives to Privatization: Exploring Non-Commercial Service Delivery Options in the Global South*, London: Routledge.

McElrath, R. and R. Rowan (1992) "The American Labor Movement and Employee Ownership – Objections to and Uses of Employee Ownership Plans", *Journal of Labor Research*, vol 13, no 1, pp. 99–119.

McGregor, R. (ed.) (1987) *Privatisation in South Africa*, Juta and Co: Cape Town.

McWilliams, J. (1989) *ARMSCOR: South Africa's Arms Merchant*, London: Brassey's.

Meade, J. (1986) *Alternative Systems of Business Organisation and of Workers' Remuneration*, Allen and Unwin: London.

Meidner, R. (1993) "Why Did the Swedish Model Fail?", in Miliband and Panitch (eds) (1993), pp. 221–28.

Meijer, J., H. Falkena and E. Van der Merwe (eds) (1991) *Financial Policy in South Africa: Essays on the South African Financial Markets*, Cape Town: Southern Book Publishers.

MERG (Macroeconomic Research Group) (1993) *Making Democracy Work: a Framework for Macroeconomic Policy in South Africa*, Cape Town: CDS.

Messerlin, P. (1990) "The Antidumping Regulations of the European Community: the 'Privatisation' of Administered Protection", in Trebilcock and York (eds) (1990), pp. 107–39.

Michie, J. (1990) "Military Spending and Defence Conversion", mimeo.

Michie, J. (ed.) (1992) *The Economic Legacy, 1979–1992*, London: Academic Press.

Michie, J. and V. Padayachee (eds) (1997) *The Political Economy of South Africa's Transition – Policy Perspectives in the Late 1990s*, London: Dryden Press.

Miliband, R. and L. Panitch (eds) (1993) *Real Problems, False Solutions, Socialist Register, 1993*, London: Merlin Press.

Milner, C. (1994) "Trade Strategy and Revealed Trade Bias – an Evaluation for a Small Industrializing Economy", *World Development*, vol 22, no 4, pp. 587–99.

Ministry for Public Enterprises (1995) "Discussion Document by the Government of National Unity on the Consultative and Implementation Framework for the Restructuring of State Assets", July.

Minns, R. (1982) *Take Over the City*, Pluto Press: London.

Minns, R. (1996) "The Social Ownership of Capital", *New Left Review*, no 219, pp. 42–61.

Minor, M. (1994) "The Demise of Expropriation as an Instrument of LDC Policy, 1980–1992", *Journal of International Business Studies*, vol 25, no 1, pp. 177–88.

Misra-Dexter, N. and J. February (eds) (2010) *Testing Democracy: Which Way Is South Africa Going?*, Institute for a Democratic South Africa, Cape Town: ABC Press.

Mitchell, D. (1995) "Profit-Sharing and Employee Ownership – Policy Implications", *Contemporary Economic Policy*, vol 13, no 2, pp. 16–25.

Moll, T. (1990) *Output and Productivity Trends in South Africa: Apartheid and Economic Growth*, Phd thesis, University of Cambridge.

Moore, M. (1994) "Steel Protection in the 1980s: the Waning Influence of Big Steel", NBER Working Paper, no 4760.

Mosley, P., T. Subaset and J. Weeks (1995) "Assessing 'Adjustment in Africa'", *World Development*, vol 23, no 10, pp. 1459–73.

Mullin, J. and W. Mullin (1997) "United States Steel's Acquisition of the Great Northern Ore Properties: Vertical Foreclosure or Efficient Contractual Governance?", *Journal of Law, Economics, and Organization*, vol 13, no 1, pp. 74–100.

Munday, M., J. Morris and B. Wilkinson (1995) "Factories or Warehouses – a Welsh Perspective on Japanese Transplant Manufacturing", *Regional Studies*, vol 29, no 1, pp. 1–17.

Nattrass, N. (1995) "A Reply to Ben Fine", *Transformation*, no 26, pp. 91–92.

Ndongko, W. (1991) "Commercialisation as an Alternative to Privatisation: Prospects and Problems", *Africa Development*, vol 26, pp. 101–115.

Nellis, J. (1994) "Public Enterprises in Sub-Saharan Africa", in Grosh and Mukandala (eds) (1994), pp. 1–24.

Nembhard, J. (1996) *Capital Control, Financial Regulation, and Industrial Policy in South Korea and Brazil*, Westport: Praeger.

Nicol, M. (1989) "Promoting Participation in ESOPs?", *South African Labour Bulletin*, vol 13, no 8, pp. 94–99.

Nyong, M. (1994) "Government Interventionism, Privatisation and Economic Development: a Critical Review of the Issues", *African Review of Money, Finance and Banking*, vol 1, pp. 123–38.

O'Donnell, K. (2023) "Canteen Workers' Wages and Collective Bargaining in British Coal", *Historical Studies in Industrial Relations*, vol 44, no 1, pp. 75–89.

OECD (1996) *The Steel Market in 1995 and the Outlook for 1996 and 1997*, Paris: OECD.

Ostry, S. (1990) "Antidumping: the Tip of the Iceberg", in Trebilcock and York (eds) (1990), pp. 17–23.

Outram, Q. (1985) "Weitzman in Historical Perspective", University of Leeds, Discussion Paper Series, no 144, April.

Outram, Q. (1987) "Profit Related Pay and Asymmetric Information", University of Leeds, Discussion Paper Series, 87/6, March.

Padayachee, V. and B. Fine (2019) "The Role and Influence of the IMF on Economic Policy in South Africa's Transition to Democracy: the 1993 CCFF Revisited", *Review of African Political Economy*, vol 46, no 159, pp. 157–167.

Padayachee, V. and R. van Niekerk (2019) *Shadow of Liberation: Contestation and Compromise in the Economic and Social Policy of the African National Congress, 1943–1996*, Johannesburg: Wits University Press.

Parker, D. and S. Martin (1995) "The Impact of UK Privatisation on Labour and Total Factor Productivity", *Scottish Journal of Political Economy*, vol 42, no 2, pp. 201–20.

Parker, M. (1995) "The Impact of a Hyperinflationary Economy on the Determination of Dumping", *Journal of World Trade*, vol 29, no 4, pp. 193–205.

Patrick, H. (1994) "The Relevance of Japanese Finance and Its Main Bank System", in Aoki and Patrick (eds) (1994), pp. 353–408.

Pierre, J. and S. Park (1997) "The Dynamics of Abstract and Manifest Institutional Change: MITI and the Japanese 'Economic Miracle' Reconsidered", *Governance*, vol 10, no 4, pp. 351–76.

Pigozzi, B. and S. Bagchi-Sen (1995) "Impacts of Acquisition and New Plants on the Employment in US Affiliates of Foreign Manufacturing Firms", *Tijdschrift voor Economische en Sociale Geografie*, vol 86, no 4, pp. 328–38.

Pinheiro, A. and B. Schneider (1995) "The Fiscal Impact of Privatisation in Latin America", *Journal of Development Studies*, vol 31, no 5, pp. 751–776.

Pontusson, J. (1987) "Radicalization and Retreat in Swedish Social Democracy", *New Left Review*, no 165, Sept/Oct, pp. 5–33.

Pontusson, J. (1994) "Sweden after the Golden Age", in Anderson and Camiller (eds) (1994), pp. 23–54.

Poole, M. (1988) "Factors Affecting the Development of Employee Financial Participation in Contemporary Britain: Evidence from a National Survey", *British Journal of Industrial Relations*, vol 26, no 1, pp. 21–36.

President's Council (1984) *Measures which Restrict the Functioning of a Free Market Orientated System in South Africa*, Committee for Economic Affairs, Pretoria, PC 1/1984.

Project Free Enterprise (1989) *Wealth Creation: Strategies for Economic Freedom and Growth*, Pretoria.

Prosser, T. (1995) "The State, Constitutions, and Implementing Economic Policy – Privatization and Regulation in the UK, France and the USA", *Social and Legal Studies*, vol 4, no 4, pp. 507–15.

Pryce, V. and C. Nicholson (1988) "The Problems and Performance of Employee Ownership Firms", *Employment Gazette*, June, pp. 346–50.

Quigley, P. (1989) *Tanks and Turbines: Jobs in Coventry's Defence Industry*, Coventry: Alternative Employment Research.

Raafat, F. and M. Salehizadeh (1994) "Dumping – the Influence of Currency Movements", *Journal of World Trade*, vol 28, no 3, pp. 181–94.

Ramamurti, R. (1992) "Why Are Developing Countries Privatising?", *Journal of International Business Studies*, vol 23, no 2, pp. 225–50.

Rasiah, R. (1995) *Foreign Capital and Industrialization in Malaysia*, New York: St Martin's Press.

RDP (1994) *The Reconstruction and Development Programme: a Policy Framework*, Johannesburg: Umanyano Publications.

Renshaw, G. (1993) "Overview and Conclusions", in Bailey et al. (eds) (1993), pp. 293–325.

Riddell, R. (1993) "The Future of the Manufacturing Sector in Sub-Saharan Africa", in Callaghy and Ravenhill (eds) (1993), pp. 215–47.

Roberts, S. (1996) "State Asset Restructuring in the Transport Sector", Report Submitted to Naledi.

Roberts, S. and Z. Rustomjee (2009) "Industrial Policy under Democracy: Apartheid's Grown-up Infant Industries? Iscor and Sasol", *Transformation*, no 71, pp. 50–75.

Robertson, K. (1997) "The Pricing of Steel in South Africa", a Presentation to the Department of Trade and Industry, 23rd October.

Rodinelli, D. and M. Iacono (1996) "Strategic Management of Privatization – a Framework for Planning and Implementation", *Public Administration and Development*, vol 16, no 3, pp. 247–63.

Rodrik, D. (1992) "The Limits of Trade Policy Reform in Developing Countries", *Journal of Economic Perspectives*, vol 6, no 1, pp. 87–105.

Rousslang, D. and T. To (1993) "Domestic Trade and Transportation Costs as Barriers to International Trade", *Canadian Journal of Economics*, vol 26, no 1, pp. 208–21.

Rowthorn, R. and H.-J. Chang (1992) "The Political Economy of Privatisation", *Economic and Labour Relations Review*, vol 3, no 2, pp. 1–17.

Rowthorn, R. and H.-J. Chang (1995) "The Role of the State in Economic Change: Entrepreneurship and Conflict Management", in Rowthorn and Chang (eds) (1995), pp. 30–50.

Rowthorn, R. and H.-J. Chang (eds) (1995) *The Role of the State in Economic Change*, Oxford: Clarendon Press.

Rustomjee, C. (1993) "Private Sector Investment in the South African Economy: Comments on Investment Function Analysis", MERG Discussion Paper.

Rustomjee, Z. (1991) "Capital Flight from South Africa, 1970–1988", *Transformation*, no 15, pp. 89–103.

Sainsbury, D. (1993) "Dual Welfare and Sex Segregation of Access to Social Benefits: Income Maintenance Policies in the UK, the US, the Netherlands and Sweden", *Journal of Social Policy*, vol 22, no 1, pp. 69–98.

SALB (1996) "Union Investment: New Opportunities, New Threats", *South African Labour Bulletin*, vol 20, no 5.

SALB (1997) "An Open Letter to Johnny Copelyn and Marcel Golding", *South African Labour Bulletin*, vol 21, no 1.

Sander, A. (1996) "'From Competitiveness to Competition: the Threat of Minimills to Large National Steel Companies' – Comment", *Resources Policy*, vol 22, nos 1/2, pp. 119–21.

Schmalensee, R. (1988) "Industrial Economics: an Overview", *Economic Journal*, vol 98, September, pp. 643–81.

Schmidt, C. and F. Blackaby (eds) (1987) *Peace, Defence and Economic Analysis*, London: MacMillan.

Scholes, M. and M. Wolfson (1989) "Employee Stock Ownership Plans and Corporate Restructuring", *NBER Working Paper*, no 3094, Sept.

Schuler, D. (1996) "Corporate Political Strategy and Foreign Competition – the Case of the Steel Industry", *Academy of Management Journal*, vol 39, no 3, pp. 720–37.

Sen, A. (1987) "Comment" in Schmidt and Blackaby (eds) (1987), pp. 45–52.

Sen, A. and J. Ghosh (1993) *Trends in Rural Employment and the Poverty-Employment Linkage*, New Delhi: ILO.

Shin, J. (1996) *The Economics of Latecomers: Catching-Up, Technology Transfer and Institutions in Germany, Japan and South Korea*, London: Routledge.

Simpson, G. (1989) "The Politics and Economics of the Armaments Industry in South Africa", in Cock and Nathan (eds) (1989), pp. 217–31.

Singh, A. (1992) "The Stock Market and Economic Development: Should Developing Countries Encourage Stock Markets?", UNCTAD Discussion Paper, no 49.

Smit, S. (2024) "ESOP – Achieving BEE Ownership Through Employee Ownership", *Transcend Capital*, January 8th, https://www.transcend.co.za/learn/achieving-bee-ownership-through-employee-ownership.

Smith, G. (1986) "Profit-Sharing and Employee Share Ownership in Britain", *Employment Gazette*, Sept, pp. 380–85.

Smith, S. (1995) "Internal Cooperation and Competitive Success: the Case of the US Steel Minimill Sector", *Cambridge Journal of Economics*, vol 19, no 2, pp. 277–304.

Staiger, R. and F. Wolak (1994) "Measuring Industry-Specific Protection: Antidumping in the United States", *Brookings Papers on Economic Activity: Microeconomics*, pp. 51–118.

Standard Bank Review (1987) "Privatisation in South Africa – Not a Dead Issue", December, pp. 1–3.

Standing, G. (1988) *Unemployment and Labour Market Flexibility: Sweden*, Geneva: ILO.

Standing, G. (1996) *Russian Unemployment and Enterprise Restructuring: Reviving Dead Souls*, London: MacMillan.

Steele, K. (1996) "An Introductory Overview", in Steele (ed.) (1996), pp. 1–34.

Steele, K. (eds) (1996) *Anti-Dumping under the WTO: a Comparative Review*, London: Kluwer Law International.

Stein, H. (ed.) (1995) *Asian Industrialization and Africa: Studies in Policy Alternatives to Structural Adjustment*, New York: St Martin's Press.

Stern, J., J.-B. Kim, D. Perkins and J. Yoo (eds) (1995) *Industrialisation and the State: the Korean Heavy and Chemical Industry Drive*, Cambridge: Harvard University Press.

Stewart, J. (1996) "Solving the Riddle of Industrial Policy – a Comparative Perspective", *Australian Journal Political Science*, vol 31, no 1, pp. 25–36.

Stiglitz, J. (1985) "Credit Markets and the Control of Capital", *Journal of Money, Credit, and Banking*, vol 17, no 2, pp. 133–52.

Stiglitz, J. (1997) "Dumping on Free Trade: the U.S. Import Trade Laws", *Southern Economic Journal*, vol 64, no 2, pp. 402–24.

Sykes, A. (1990) "GATT Safeguards Reform: the Injury Test", in Trebilcock and York (eds) (1990), pp. 203-30.

Targetti, F. and A. Foti (1997) "Growth and Productivity: a Model of Cumulative Growth and Catching Up", *Cambridge Journal of Economics*, vol 21, no 1, pp. 27–43.

Taylor, I. (1988) *Fair Shares for all the Workers*, London: Adam Smith Institute.

Tharakan, P. and J. Waelbroeck (1994) "Antidumping and Countervailing Duty Decisions in the EC and in the US", *European Economic Review*, vol 38, no 1, pp. 171–93.

Thomas, C. and E. Friberg (1994) "To Market, to Market, with What? – Some Observations on Labor-Market Rationales for Industrial Policy", *Journal of Economic Perspectives*, vol 28, no 2, pp. 609–17.

To, T. (1994) "Export Subsidies and Oligopoly with Switching Costs", *Journal of International Economics*, vol 37, no 1–2, pp. 97–110.

Toporowski, J. (ed.) (2000), *Political Economy and the New Capitalism: Essays in Honour of Sam Aaronovitch*, London: Routledge.

Trebilcock, M. (1990) "Throwing Deep: Trade Remedy Laws in a First-Best World", in Trebilcock and York (eds) (1990), pp. pp. 249–50.

Trebilcock, M. and R. York (eds) (1990) *Fair Exchange: Reforming Trade Remedy Laws*, Ottawa: Howe Institute.

Tucker, J., S. Nock and D. Toscano (1989) "Employee Ownership and Perceptions of Work – the Effect of an Employee Stock Ownership Plan", *Work and Occupations*, vol 16, no 1, pp. 26–42.

UN (1995) *Foreign Direct Investment in Africa*, New York: United Nations.

UNCHS/ILO (1995) *Shelter Provision and Employment Generation*, Geneva: ILO.

Uys, D. (1995) "The System of National Financial Accounts", in Falkena et al. (eds) (1995), pp. 20-51.

Venables, A. (1996) "Trade Policy, Cumulative Causation, and Industrial Development", *Journal of Development Economics*, vol 49, no 1, pp. 179–97.

Vermulst, E. (1997) "Adopting and Implementing Anti-Dumping Laws", *Journal of World Trade*, vol 31, no 2, pp. 5–23.

Vermulst, E., J. Bourgeois and P. Waer (eds) (1994) *Rules of Origin in International Trade: a Comparative Study*, Ann Arbor: University of Michigan Press.

Vermulst, E. and N. Komuro (1997) "Anti-Dumping Disputes in the GATT/WTO – Navigating Dire Straits", *Journal of World Trade*, vol 31, no 1, pp. 5–44.

Vermulst, E. and P. Waer (1991) "The Calculation of Injury Margins and EC Anti-Dumping Proceedings", *Journal of World Trade*, vol 25, no 6, pp. 5–42.

Vickers, J. and G. Yarrow (1988) *Privatisation: an Economic Analysis*, Cambridge: The MIT Press.

Viner, J. (1923) *Dumping: a Problem in International Trade*, Chicago: University of Chicago Press.

Vlachou, A. (ed.) (1999) *Contemporary Economic Theory: Radical Critiques of Neoliberalism*, London: MacMillan.

Wade, R. (1996) "Japan, the World Bank, and the Art of Paradigm Maintenance: *the East Asian Miracle* in Political Perspective", *New Left Review*, no 217, May/June, pp. 3–37.

Wadhwani, S. and M. Wall (1990) "The Effects of Profit-Sharing on Employment, Wages, Stock Returns and Productivity: Evidence from UK Micro-Data", *Economic Journal*, vol 100, March, pp. 1–17.

Walker, M. (ed.) (1988) *Privatisation: Tactics and Techniques*, Vancouver: Fraser Institute.

Wassenaar, A. (1977) *Assault on Private Enterprise: the Freeway to Communism*, Cape Town: Tafelberg.

Webster, E., K. Joynt and A. Metcalfe (2013) *Repositioning Peak-Level Social Dialogue in South Africa: NEDLAC into the Future. External Review*, Johannesburg: National Economic Development and Labour Council.

Weeks, J. (1981) *Capital and Exploitation*, London: Edward Arnold.

Weitzman, M. (1984) *The Share Economy: Conquering Stagflation*, Harvard University Press: Cambridge.

Wessel, R. (1991) "Privatisation in Africa", *African Review of Money, Finance and Banking*, vol 2, pp. 182–94.

White Paper (1985) *Industrial Development Strategy in the Republic of South Africa*, Pretoria, WPG85.

White Paper (1987) *Privatisation and Deregulation in the Republic of South Africa*, Pretoria, August, WPG87, reproduced in McGregor (ed.) (1987).

White, H. (1996) "Review Article: Adjustment in Africa", *Development and Change*, vol 27, no 4, pp. 785–815.

White, J. (1997) "A Test of Consistency in the Administration of US Anti-Dumping Law", *Journal of World Trade*, vol 31, no 4, pp. 117–28.

Wilkins, M. (1994) "Comparative Hosts", *Business History*, vol 36, no 1, pp. 18–50.

Williams, D. (1995) "Entry Mode Decisions of Multinational Enterprises and Their Impact on the Regional Economy: a Framework for Analysis", *British Review of Economic Issues*, vol 17, no 43, pp. 27–52.

Williams, D. (1996) "Analyzing the Regional Impact of Foreign Manufacturing Firms", *Tijdschrift voor Economische en Sociale Geografie*, vol 87, no 3, pp. 259–65.

Wood, E. (1995) *Essays on Trade and Manufacturing Industry in South Africa*, PhD thesis, University of Cambridge.

World Bank (1993) *The East Asian Miracle: Economic Growth and Public Policy, a World Bank Policy Research Report*, Oxford: Oxford University Press.

World Bank (1994a) *Adjustment in Africa: Reforms, Results and the Road Ahead*, Policy Research Report, Washington DC: World Bank.

World Bank (1994b) "The Financial System and Public Enterprise Reform: Concepts and Cases", Policy Research Working Paper no 1319. Finance and Private Sector Development Division.

World Bank (1995a) *Bureaucrats in Business: the Economics and Politics of Government Ownership*, Oxford: Oxford University Press.

World Bank (1995b) *Mozambique: Impediments to Industrial Sector Recovery*, Report no 13752-MOZ, Washington DC: World Bank.

World Bank (1996a) *From Plan to Market, World Development Report*, Washington DC: World Bank.

World Bank (1996b) *Global Economic Prospects and the Developing Countries*, Washington DC: World Bank.

Yaffey, M. (1995) "Privatisation Policy: the Lessons of Nationalisation in East Africa", in Cook and Kirkpatrick (eds) (1995), pp. 198–212.

Yano, M. (1989) "Voluntary Export Restraints and Exportations: an Analysis of Export Quotas in Oligopolistic Markets", *International Economic Review*, vol 30, no 4, pp. 707–24.

Yarrow, G. and P. Jasinski (eds) (1996) *Privatization: Critical Perspectives on the World Economy*, four volumes, London: Routledge.

Young, R. (1995) "Privatisation: African Perspectives", in Cook and Kirkpatrick (eds) (1995), pp. 162–75.

Young, S., N. Hood and E. Peters (1994) "Multinational Enterprises and Regional Economic Development", *Regional Studies*, vol 28, no 7, pp. 657–77.

Zalk, N. (2017) *The Things We Lost in the Fire: the Political Economy of Post-Apartheid Restructuring of the South African Steel and* Engineering Sectors, SOAS University of London, PhD thesis, http://eprints.soas.ac.uk/26166.

Zysman, J. (1983) *Governments, Markets, and Growth*, Oxford: Martin Robertson.

Index

www.ingramcontent.com/pod-product-compliance
Lightning Source LLC
LaVergne TN
LVHW021548230526
839611LV00034B/436

9798888907986